Readings from the
First-Century World

Readings from the First-Century World

Primary Sources
for New Testament Study

Edited by

Walter A. Elwell

and Robert W. Yarbrough

Baker Books
A Division of Baker Book House Co
Grand Rapids, Michigan 49516

Published by Baker Books
a division of Baker Book House Company
P.O Box 6287, Grand Rapids, MI 49516-6287

Printed in the United States of America

Library of Congress Cataloging-in-Publication Data

Readings from the first-century world : Primary sources for New Testament study / edited by Walter A. Elwell and Robert W. Yarbrough.
    p. cm. — (Encountering biblical studies)
    Includes bibliographical references and indexes.
    ISBN 0-8010-2157-X (paper)
    1. Church history—Primitive and early church, ca. 30–600—Sources. 2. Bible—Quotations. I. Elwell, Walter A. II. Yarbrough, Robert W. III. Series.
BR167.R43   1998
225.9′5—dc21
                                 98-27716

For information about academic books, resources for Christian leaders, and all new releases available from Baker Book House, visit our web site:
http://www.bakerbooks.com

The publisher and editors would like to thank the following for granting permission to reprint material from their work.

Carcanet
Graves, Robert, trans. *Suetonius: The Twelve Caesars.*
Doubleday
Charlesworth, James H., ed. *The Old Testament Pseudepigrapha.*
E. J. Brill
García Martínez, Florentino, trans. *The Dead Sea Scrolls Translated: The Qumran Texts in English.*
Fortress
Feldman, Louis H., and Meyer Reinhold, eds. *Jewish Life and Thought among Greeks and Romans: Primary Readings.*
Lohse, Eduard. *Colossians and Philemon.*
Harvard University Press and the Loeb Classical Library
Green, William M., et al., trans. *Saint Augustine: The City of God against the Pagans.*
Harmon, A. M., K. Kilburn, and

H. D. Macleod, trans. *Lucian.*
Marcus, Ralph, trans. *Philo, Supplement 1: Questions and Answers on Genesis.*
Rackham, Harris, W. H. S. Jones, and D. E. Eichholz trans. *Pliny: Natural History.*
Hendrickson
Yonge, C. D., trans. *The Works of Philo.*
Hodder & Stoughton
Bruce, F. F. *Jesus and Christian Origins outside the New Testament.*
Indiana University Press
Humphries, Rolfe, trans. *The Satires of Juvenal.*
National Council of the Churches of Christ in the USA
Revised Standard Version
Oxford University Press
Bettenson, Henry, ed. *Documents of the Christian Church.*
Danby, Herbert, trans. *The Mishnah.*
Gaster, Moses. *The Samaritans: Their History, Doctrines, and Literature.*

Oxford University Press/Cambridge University Press
New English Bible
Penguin
Sélincourt, Aubrey de, trans. *Herodotus: The Histories. Rev. ed.*
Vermes, Geza. *The Dead Sea Scrolls in English. 4th ed.*
Warner, Rex, trans. *Plutarch: Fall of the Roman Republic.*
Princeton University Press
Finegan, Jack. *The Archaeology of the New Testament: The Life of Jesus and the Beginning of the Early Church.*
Random House
Church, Alfred John, and William Jackson Brodribb, trans. *The Complete Works of Tacitus.*
Schocken
Pomeroy, Sarah B. *Goddesses, Whores, Wives, and Slaves: Women in Classical Antiquity.*
T. & T. Clark
Schürer, Emil. *The History of the Jewish People in the Age of Jesus*

Christ (175 b.c.–a.d. 135).
University of Chicago Press
Betz, Hans Dieter, ed. *The Greek Magical Papyri in Translation.*
Vandenhoeck & Ruprecht
Berger, Klaus, and Carsten Colpe, eds. *Religionsgeschichtliches Textbuch zum Neuen Testament.*
Zondervan
New International Version

Every effort has been made to contact owners or the owner's agents of copyrighted material for permission to use their material. If copyrighted material has been included without the correct copyright notice or without permission, due to error or failure to locate owners/agents or otherwise, we apologize for the error or omission and ask that the owner or owner's agent contact Baker Books and supply appropriate information. Correct information will be included in any reprinting.

Contents in Brief

Contents

Contents

Series Preface

The strength of the church and the vitality of the individual Christian's life are directly related to the role Scripture plays in them. Early believers knew the importance of this and spent their time in fellowship, prayer, and the study of God's Word. The passing of two thousand years has not changed the need, but it has changed the accessibility of many of the Bible's ideas. Time has distanced us from those days, and we often need guidance back into the world of the Old and New Testaments.

To that end Baker Book House is producing two separate but related series of biblical textbooks. The design of these new series is to put us back into the world of the biblical text, so that we may understand it as those early believers did and at the same time see it from and for our own day, thus facilitating the application of its truths to our contemporary situation.

Encountering Biblical Studies consists of undergraduate-level texts, and two surveys treating the Old and New Testaments provide the foundation for this series. Accompanying these survey texts are two collateral volumes of readings, which illuminate the world surrounding the biblical text. Built on these basic survey texts are upper-level college texts covering the books of the Bible that are most frequently offered in the curriculum of Christian colleges.

A related series, titled Engaging Biblical Studies, provides graduate-level treatments for introduction and theology courses.

Complementing both levels of textbooks is a set of standard reference books that may be consulted for answers to specific questions or more in-depth study of biblical ideas. These reference books include *Baker Commentary on the Bible, Baker Topical Guide to the Bible, Baker Encyclopedia of the Bible,* and *Baker Theological Dictionary of the Bible.*

Encountering and Engaging Biblical Studies series are written from an evangelical point of view, in the firm conviction that the Scripture is absolutely true and never misleads us. It is the sure foundation on which our faith and life may be built because it unerringly leads willing readers to Jesus Christ.

Walter A. Elwell
General Editor

Introduction

Why Another Book of Readings?

This book is needed because nothing comparable exists to serve the needs of younger college students taking basic New Testament survey, history, or backgrounds classes.

Polls suggest that Western nations, despite their largely Christian heritage, are rapidly becoming illiterate with respect to the Bible. Such lack of basic knowledge is even more acute when it comes to the various literary corpora of late classical antiquity. Even the well-informed layperson or college student is unlikely to have read any of Josephus, Philo, Tacitus, Suetonius, Plutarch, the Old Testament Apocrypha, the Mishnah, or related literatures. For an increasing number of students the Old Testament is unfamiliar ground. Yet these writings shed important light on the New Testament's text and times. To interpret the New Testament (or the Old) without at least basic understanding of prominent features of its historical setting as revealed in extant literary remains is to risk serious wresting of its contents.

The present volume, a companion to Walter A. Elwell and Robert W. Yarbrough's *Encountering the New Testament: A Historical and Theological Survey* (Grand Rapids: Baker, 1998), is an attempt to draw together a collection of readings that will help move a reader *from* little or no knowledge of ancient literature related to the New Testament *to* a basic understanding of some major authors and texts that enhance understanding of what the New Testament says. Both compilers of this book have taught New Testament survey many times to students ranging from college freshmen to master's level. We have kept in mind primarily the needs of the former

group. But the latter group as well may find much of value here if their previous studies have been lacking in explicit attention to extrabiblical writings.

Other books of this general type admittedly already exist. But none fits the needs of today's college freshman or sophomore as effectively as it might. C. K. Barrett's well-known *The New Testament Background* contains too much material that is peripheral and that reflects settings much later than New Testament times. The impressive volume *Hellenistic Commentary to the New Testament* edited by M. Eugene Boring, Klaus Berger, and Carsten Colpe is out of many students' reach financially and is in some ways more of a reference volume than a survey class companion, at least at the undergraduate level. Craig S. Keener's popular *The Bible Background Commentary: New Testament* is likewise a reference volume, unsuited for cover-to-cover reading in a survey class. And the first edition, at least, lacks references to primary sources, thus forcing students to rely on hearsay (however well-informed) rather than to dig into the primary sources for themselves. Everett Ferguson's noteworthy *Backgrounds of Early Christianity* is suitable for upper-level undergraduate or graduate courses on New Testament backgrounds, not undergraduate classes at the survey level. It mostly catalogues and describes the sources rather than quoting them for the reader's own perusal.

Albert A. Bell's *A Guide to the New Testament World* is a gold mine of wise, topically oriented commentary and references to secondary sources. But it contains no extended primary source readings at all. It is precisely the primary sources to which the present volume seeks to expose students.

Possible False Impressions and Parallelomania

The most important background sources for understanding New Testament documents are (1) the other New Testament writings and (2) the Old Testament. This collection of readings in no way seeks to minimize the importance of interbiblical connections and redemptive history for understanding the canonical text. No amount of "backgrounds" can replace intimate familiarity with the Christian Scriptures—in their entirety—and the drama they herald. A class in New Testament survey should survey primarily the New Testament itself, not nonbiblical writings related to it.

Yet at the same time canonical documents are in certain respects of a piece with other writings from similar cultural settings. They should not be reduced to *no more than* noncanonical writings—the Bible is more than "just another book"—but they should not be read in isolation from them. What Josephus says can be invaluable for interpretation of the Gospels. Suetonius alerts us to the mood and many particulars of first-century Roman and Hellenistic society; his accounts and insights can transform our grasp of New Testament issues and claims. The Old Testament apocryphal books and the Dead Sea Scrolls offer many valuable insights into the history and belief of various peoples, especially the Jews, in the half millennium between Old and New Testament periods. Documents or inscriptions uncovered by archaeological research can likewise prove suggestive or even definitively important. All of this suggests that basic familiarity with extra–New Testament literature and related findings can open up previously unimagined vistas for understanding the New Testament itself.

A word is in order about the inclusion of a number of Old Testament texts. The New Testament itself contains over three hundred explicit quotations and many hundred more additional allusions.[1] We have generally avoided direct reference to these. But the time is past when it could be assumed that college students studying religion or Bible formally for the first time would already have a command of at least the basics of Old Testament content as it relates to and undergirds the New Testament. It has become necessary to point directly to what previous anthologies may have been able tacitly to assume. For that reason an admittedly sparse range of Old Testament citations is woven in along with the more numerous references to extrabiblical material. This should have two advantages. First, it avoids creating the impression that the primary literary background of the New Testament is pagan or sectarian writings, or even writings like the Old Testament apocrypha, which the New Testament writers seldom if ever cite, much less base doctrines on. Second, and positively, it encourages students to embrace the same respect for and familiarity with Old Testament Scripture that the New Testament writers themselves reflect. Even if students do not share the New Testament writers' faith in those writings, they can at least begin to appreciate their primary written knowledge base for such issues as God, humankind, sin, and redemption. The result of reading primary sources shedding light on the New Testament should be enhanced knowledge of and curiosity about the Old Testament, not ignorance or amnesia regarding the documents that New Testament writers (in part likely due to Jesus' influence) regarded as divinely given and necessary for the knowledge that leads to eternal life.

Limitations and Value

This anthology makes no pretense of being comprehensive. A recent exhaustive collection of New Testament parallels runs to 1,750 pages—and fills two volumes, covers only Romans–Revelation, deals only with Hellenistic material (not Jewish), and costs more than $300![2]

---

[1] Quotations are collected in, e.g., Robert G. Bratcher, ed., *Old Testament Quotations in the New Testament*, 3rd ed. (New York: United Bible Societies, 1987); Glea-son L. Archer and Gregory Chirichigno, *Old Testament Quotations in the New Testament* (Chicago: Moody, 1983).

[2] Georg Strecker and U. Schnelle with G. Seelig, *Texte zum Neuen Testament aus Griechentum und Hellenismus*, Vol. 2 [in two single volumes]: *Texte zur Briefliteratur und zur Johannesapokalypse* (Berlin/New York: de Gruyter, 1995).

The present work seeks to be no more than a companion volume for a freshman or sophomore level college text. This means that both breadth and scope of coverage will frustrate the specialist.

This limitation is offset by certain strengths. It should prove affordable, even as an ancillary text. It gathers into a central location a mass of material that students would find difficult to access in most libraries. While it is allusive rather than comprehensive, doubtless *some* primary source knowledge, even if it is rather random and impressionistic, is better than little or no knowledge at all. It contains a range of Jewish, Roman, and Hellenistic readings, as well as selected key Old Testament passages, thus bearing witness to the major cultural syntheses relevant to New Testament documents. A number of the readings will convey not only information but also impetus, stirring up good students to further study. Many will serve as springboards for class instruction. Creative teachers will find numerous ways of exploiting the light these texts shed on New Testament history, thought, belief, and practice.

Advanced critical issues have been left to the side for the most part. We have not entered into debates about authorship or dates of various New Testament books or hypothetical sources lying behind them. Occasionally dates or provenance of sources is provided where important for assessing the reading's relation to canonical material.

Organization

A most difficult question has been how to deal with the Gospels, on the one hand, and the rest of the New Testament, on the other. To run through all four of the former, one after the other, would have been repetitious, or would have involved a Byzantine cross-referencing system. It was decided instead to cover the Gospel literature and history in topical fashion. Students can check for individual passages using the indexes. Otherwise, the Gospel parallels can be read, as a whole or in assigned sections, in conjunction with simultaneous readings of the Gospels themselves. The cumulative effect of the mass of information assembled is sure to illuminate any thoughtful person's apprehension of the life and ministry of Jesus Christ.

This anthology does not, then, seek to relate sources specifically to the respective Gospel communities that discrete pericopes in Matthew, Mark, Luke, and John are commonly supposed to address. Strong support for this more general, wholistic approach to Gospel backgrounds comes from recent research.[3] Richard Bauckham and others argue convincingly that the Gospels are intended more to reflect the actual life setting of Jesus than the concerns and convictions of the late-first-century ecclesiastical settings in which they were allegedly written. While this viewpoint is not likely to find acceptance by all New Testament scholars, it can hardly fail to be more convincing than the unsubstantiated consensus it challenges. But if the Gospels are meant to witness to Jesus' life and times, then the Palestinian background as we know it from Josephus and other Jewish and Roman sources will be more important than other primary backgrounds sometimes proposed (Apollonius of Tyana; Cynic philosophers; Q community; Thomasine church), for which evidence of demonstrable connection with Jesus' life and actual historical setting may be thin. It seems well advised for students at the beginning stage to assimilate a broad selection of texts most likely related to Jesus' life setting overall. We have attempted to provide a good sample of such passages.

Acts, the Epistles, and Revelation are covered by a collection of readings designed above all to give students a feel for the world surrounding, assumed, or even addressed by each respective document. It will be obvious to the specialist that the selections are lamentably few. But the book's purpose must be recalled once more: to introduce students being exposed to formal New Testament study for the first time to a literary and ideological world, and societal realities, very probably foreign to them. If in a survey course students read carefully, say, the Book of Acts, then read a chapter or two of a textbook and hear two or three classroom lectures on that same New Testament book, there will hardly be

---

[3]Richard Bauckham, ed., *The Gospels for All Christians: Rethinking the Gospel Audiences* (Grand Rapids/Cambridge: Eerdmans, 1998).

Table 1: Dates of Most Frequently Cited Non-Biblical Sources

Aristeas, Letter of	285–247 B.C.
Augustine	A.D. 354–430
Babylonian Talmud	A.D. c. 600
Cicero	106–43 B.C.
Dead Sea Scrolls: 4QAramaic Apocalypse	pre-A.D. 70
Dead Sea Scrolls: 4QGenesis Pesher	pre-A.D. 70
Dead Sea Scrolls: 4QFlorilegium	pre-A.D. 70
Dead Sea Scrolls: 4Q War Scroll	pre-A.D. 70
Dead Sea Scrolls: Damascus Document	pre-A.D. 70
Dead Sea Scrolls: Messianic Rule	pre-A.D. 70
Dead Sea Scrolls: Rule of the Community	pre-A.D. 70
Dio Cassius	A.D. 150–235
Eusebius	A.D. 260–340
Herodotus	480–425 B.C.
Horace	65–8 B.C.
Josephus	A.D. 37–100 (?)
Josephus (Arabic version)	A.D. 10th cent.
Justin Martyr	A.D. 100–165 (?)
Juvenal	c. A.D. 5th cent.
Livy	59 B.C.–A.D. 17
Lucian	A.D. 115–200
Mishnah	c. A.D. 200
Origen	A.D. 185–254
Philo	25 B.C.–A.D. 45
Pliny (the Elder; *Natural History*)	A.D. 23–79
Pliny the Younger	A.D. 61 or 62–131
Plutarch	A.D. 46–120
Pseudo-Phocylides	c. 1st cent. B.C.–1st cent. A.D.
Seneca	4 B.C.–A.D. 65
Suetonius	55 B.C. (?)–A.D. 37
Tacitus	A.D. 55–120
Trajan	A.D. 98–117

additional time for working through much more than the couple of dozen readings illustrating Acts provided here. The same holds true for the various Epistles. While it would have been possible to multiply readings almost endlessly, we have tried to stick to the modest and strategic aims that the book seeks to meet. The idea has been to give the flavor and whet the appetite, not to furnish every course of a feast.

Walter A. Elwell
Robert W. Yarbrough
September 1998

Part

1

The Gospels
and Jesus

1 The Land of Palestine

The physical land of Palestine has always had a profound place in the thinking of both Jews and Christians. For the Jews, it was part of the original covenant made with Abraham (Gn 17:8); and for Christians, it is the land where the incarnate Son of God ministered, died, and rose again, and where the church began.

In the past century extensive research has been done on the land of Palestine—climate, geological history, topography, historical geography. For those interested in detailed studies of these things, the following provide an excellent introduction: Denis Baly, *The Geography of the Bible*; Yohanan Aharoni, *The Land of the Bible*; George Adam Smith, *The Historical Geography of the Holy Land*; Alastair I. Mackay, *Farming and Gardening in the Bible*; George A. Turner, *Historical Geography of the Holy Land*; A. S. van der Woude (ed.), *The World of the Bible*; Martin Noth, *The Old Testament World*; Michael Avi-Yonah, *Gazeteer of Roman Palestine*; Denis Baly, *Geographical Companion to the Bible*; Gustaf Dalman, *Sacred Sites and Ways: Studies in the Topography of the Gospels*; George Adam Smith, *Jerusalem: The Topography, Economics and History from the Earliest Times to A.D. 70* (2 vols.); Nelson Glueck, *The Other Side of the Jordan*; Nelson Glueck, *The River Jordan*; Walter Brueggemann, *The Land*. Most of these books have excellent bibliographies that can also be consulted.

The Physical Features of the Land

(#1) The Roman historian Tacitus provides us with a general description of Palestine, focusing on the Dead Sea and its environs.

#1: A Roman Description of Palestine
(Tacitus, *Histories* 5.6–7)

[6]Eastward the country is bounded by Arabia; to the south lies Egypt; on the west are Phoenicia and the Mediterranean. Northward it commands an extensive prospect over Syria. The inhabitants are healthy and able to bear fatigue. Rain is uncommon, but the soil is fertile. Its products resemble our own. They have, besides, the balsam-tree and the palm. The palm-groves are tall and graceful. The balsam is a shrub; each branch, as it fills with sap, may be pierced with a fragment of stone or pottery. If steel is employed, the veins shrink up. The sap is used by physicians. Libanus is the principal mountain, and has, strange to say, amidst these burning heats, a summit shaded with trees and never deserted by its snows. The same range supplies and sends forth the stream of Jordan. This river does not discharge itself into the sea, but flows entire through two lakes, and is lost in the third. This is a lake of vast circumference; it resembles the sea, but is more nauseous in taste; it breeds pestilence among those who live near by its noisesome odor; it cannot be moved by the wind, and it affords no home either to fish or water-birds. These strange waters support what is thrown upon them, as on a solid surface, and all persons, whether they can swim or no, are equally buoyed up by the waves. At a certain season of the year the lake throws up bitumen, and the method of collecting it has been taught by that experience which teaches all other arts. It is naturally a fluid of dark color; when vinegar is sprinkled upon it, it coagulates and floats upon the surface. Those whose business it is take it with the hand, and draw it on to the deck of the boat; it then continues of itself to

flow in and lade the vessel till the stream is cut off. . . . Such is the account of old authors; but those who know the country say that the bitumen moves in heaving masses on the water, that it is drawn by hand to the shore, and that there, when dried by the evaporation of the earth and the power of the sun, it is cut into pieces with axes and wedges just as timber or stone would be.

[7]Not far from this lake lies a plain, once fertile, they say, and the site of great cities, but afterwards struck by lightning and consumed. Of this event, they declare, traces still remain, for the soil, which is scorched in appearance, has lost its productive power. Everything that grows spontaneously, as well as what is planted by hand, either when the leaf or flower have been developed, or after maturing in the usual form, become black and rotten, and crumbles into a kind of dust. I am ready to allow, on one hand, that cities, once famous, may have been consumed by fire from heaven, while, on the other, I imagine that the earth is infected by the exhalations of the lake, that the surrounding air is tainted, and that thus the growth of harvest and the fruits of autumn decay under the equally noxious influences of soil and climate. The river Belus also flows into the Jewish sea. About its mouth is a kind of sand which is collected, mixed with nitre, and fused into glass. This shore is of limited extent, but furnishes an inexhaustible supply to the exporter.

Galilee and Perea

(#2) Herod Antipas administered Galilee and Perea from 4 B.C. to A.D. 39. Much of Jesus' ministry was in these districts, and it was at Machaerus in Perea that John the Baptist was executed (Mk 6:17–29; Josephus, *Ant.* 18.5.2).

#2: Josephus's Description of Galilee and Perea

(Josephus, *Jewish War* 3.3.1–3 §§35, 37, 41–47)

1. [35]Now Phoenicia and Syria encompass about the Galilees, which are two, and called the Upper Galilee and the Lower. They are bounded towards the sun-setting, with the borders of the territory belonging to Ptolemais, and by Carmel. . . . [37]They are bounded on the south with Samaria and Scythopolis, as far as the river Jordan; on the east with Hippene and Gadaris, and also with Gaulanitis, and the borders of the kingdom of Agrippa; its northern parts are bounded by Tyre, and the country of the Tyrians. . . .

2. [41]These two Galilees, of so great largeness, and encompassed with so many nations of foreigners, have always been able to make a strong resistance on all occasions of war; [42]for the Galileans are inured to war from their infancy, and have been always very numerous; nor has the country been ever destitute of men of courage, or wanted a numerous set of them; for their soil is universally rich and fruitful, and full of the plantations of trees of all sorts, insomuch that it invites the most slothful to take pains in its cultivation, by its fruitfulness: [43]accordingly, it is all cultivated by its inhabitants, and no part of it lies idle. Moreover, the cities lie here very thick; and the very many villages there are here, are everywhere so full of people, by the richness of their soil, that the very least of them contain above fifteen thousand inhabitants.

3. [44]In short, if any one will suppose that Galilee is inferior to Perea in magnitude, he will be obliged to prefer it before it in its strength: for this is all capable of cultivation, and is everywhere fruitful; but for Perea, which is indeed much larger in extent, the greater part of it is a desert, and rough, and much less disposed for the production of the milder kinds of fruits; [45]yet it has a moist soil [in other parts,] and produces all kinds of fruits, and its plains are planted with trees of all sorts, while yet the olive-tree, the vine, and the palm-tree, are chiefly cultivated there. It is also sufficiently watered with torrents, which issue out of the mountains, and with springs that never fail to run, even when the torrents fail them, as they do in the dog-days. [46]Now the length of Perea is from Machaerus to Pella, and its breadth from Philadelphia to Jordan: [47]its northern parts are bounded by Pella, as we have already said, as well as its western with Jordan; the land of Moab, is its southern border, and its eastern limits reach

to Arabia, and Sibonitis, and besides to Philadelphene and Gerasa.

The Sea of Galilee, Tiberius, and the Plain of Gennesaret

(#3) Herod Antipas established his capital at Tiberius, and Jesus made his headquarters at Capernaum (#4), both of which were on the Sea of Galilee (Mt 4:13; Josephus, *Ant.* 18. 2.3). Peter, Andrew, James, and John all fished the sea (Mt 4:18–22), and Jesus crossed it on several occasions (Lk 8:22; Mk 8:13), as well as teaching from it while in a boat (Lk 5:3) and near its shoreline. (#5) Jesus also knew the marvelous Plain of Gennesaret, which provided so much produce for the whole nation (Mt 14:34; Mk 6:53).

#3: Herod Antipas Builds Tiberias
(Josephus, *Ant.* 18.2.3 §§36–38)

3. [36]And now Herod the tetrarch, who was in great favor with Tiberius, built a city of the same name with him, and called it Tiberias. He built it in the best part of Galilee, at the lake of Gennesaret. There are warm baths at a little distance from it, in a village named Emmaus. [37]Strangers came and inhabited this city; a great number of the inhabitants were Galileans also; and many were forced by Herod to come thither out of the country belonging to him, and were by force compelled to be its inhabitants; some of them were persons of eminence. He also admitted poor people, such as those that were collected from all parts, to dwell in it. Nay, some of them were not quite freemen; [38]and these he was a benefactor to, and made them free in great numbers; but obliged them not to forsake the city, by building them very good houses at his own expenses, and by giving them land also; for he was aware, that to make this place a habitation was to transgress the Jewish ancient laws, because many sepulchres were to be here taken away, in order to make room for the city Tiberias.

#4: Description of the Sea of Galilee
(Josephus, *Jewish War* 3.10.7 §§506–9, 512–13, 515)

7. [506]Now this lake of Gennesaret is so called from the country adjoining to it. Its breadth is forty furlongs [i.e., 5 miles; actually it is about 8 miles], and its length one hundred and forty [i.e., 17 1/2 miles; actually it is about 12 miles]; its waters are sweet, and very agreeable for drinking, [507]for they are finer than the thick waters of other fens; the lake is also pure, and on every side ends directly at the shores and at the sand; it is also of a temperate nature when you draw it up, and of a more gentle nature than river or fountain water, and yet always cooler than one

The northern portion of the Sea of Galilee looking toward Capernaum over the plains of Gennesaret.

could expect in so diffuse a place as this is. [508]Now, when this water is kept in the open air, it is as cold as the snow which the country people are accustomed to make by night in summer. There are several kinds of fish in it, different both to the taste and the sight from those elsewhere: [509]it is divided into two parts by the river Jordan. [512]. . . The origin of [the river] Jordan was formerly not known, but it was discovered when Philip was tetrarch of Trachonitis; [513]for he had chaff thrown into Phiala, and it was found at Panium [Caesarea Philippi], where the ancients thought the fountain-head of the river was, whither it had been therefore carried [by the waters]. . . . [515]Now Jordan's visible stream arises from this cavern, and divides the marshes and fens of the lake Semechonitis: when it has run another hundred and twenty furlongs [about 15 miles], it first passes by the city Julias [Bethsaida], and then passes through the middle of the lake Gennesaret; after which it runs a long way over a desert, and then makes its exit into the lake Asphaltitis [the Dead Sea].

#5: The Fertile Plain of Gennesaret

(Josephus, *Jewish War* 3.10.8 §§516–19, 521)

8. [516]The country also that lies over against this lake has the same name of Gennesaret; its nature is wonderful as well as its beauty; its soil is so fruitful that all sorts of trees can grow upon it, and the inhabitants accordingly plant all sorts of trees there; for the temper of the air is so well mixed, that it agrees very well with those several sorts, [517]particularly walnuts, which require the coldest air, flourish there in vast plenty; there are palm-trees also, which grow best in hot air; fig-trees also and olives grow near them, which yet require an air that is more temperate. [518]One may call this place the ambition of nature, where it forces those plants that are naturally enemies to one another to agree together: it is a happy contention of the seasons, as if every one of them laid claim to this country; for it not only nourishes different sorts of autumnal fruit beyond men's expectation, but preserves them a great while; [519]it supplies men with the principal fruits, with grapes and figs continually, during ten months in the year, and the rest of the fruits as they become ripe together, through the whole year; for besides the good temperature of the air, it is also watered from a most fertile fountain. The people of the country call it Capernaum. . . . [521]The length of this country extends itself along the banks of this lake that bears the same name, for thirty furlongs [about 4 miles], and is in breadth twenty [about 2 1/2 miles].

Samaria and Judea

(#6) Jesus, contrary to normal Jewish custom, traveled through Samaria, even speaking to a woman who was at a well. Many Samaritans believed in him (Jn 4:4–42). The gospel spread very early to Samaria at Jesus' command and as the result of persecutions (Acts 1:8; 8:1, 4–25). Near the end of Jesus' life he undertook a rather extensive ministry that took him throughout Judea, Samaria, and Perea. (#7) A brief description of Jericho, the home of Zacchaeus (Lk 19:1–10) and Bartimaeus (Mk 10:46–52), is given by Josephus.

#6: Samaria and Judea

(Josephus, *Jewish War* 3.3.4–5 §§48–54)

4. [48]Now, as to the country of Samaria, it lies between Judea and Galilee . . . and is entirely of the same nature with Judea; [49]for both countries are made up of hills and valleys, and are moist for agriculture, and are very fruitful. They have abundance of trees, and are full of autumnal fruit, both that which grows wild, and that which is the effect of cultivation. They are not naturally watered with many rivers, but derive their chief moisture from rainwater, of which they have no want; [50]and for those rivers which they have, all their waters are exceeding sweet: by reason also of the excellent grass they have, their cattle yield more milk than do those in other places; and, what is the greatest sign of excellency and abundance, they each of them are very full of people.

5. [51]In the limits of Samaria and Judea lies the village Anuath, which is also named Borceos. This is the northern boundary of Judea. The southern parts of Judea, if they be

measured lengthways, are bounded by a village adjoining to the confines of Arabia; the Jews that dwell there call it Jordan. However, its breadth is extended from the river Jordan to Joppa. [52]The city Jerusalem is situated in the very middle; on which account some have, with sagacity enough, called that city the navel of the country. [53]Nor indeed is Judea destitute of such delights as come from the sea, since its maritime places extend as far as Ptolemais; [54]it was parted into eleven portions, of which the royal city Jerusalem was the supreme, and presided over all the neighboring country, as the head does over the body.

#7: The Fruitful Region of Jericho
(Josephus, *Jewish War* 1.6.6 §138)

[138]Now here [in Jericho] is the most fruitful country about Judea, which bears a vast number of palm-trees, besides the balsam-tree, whose sprouts they cut with sharp stones, and at the incisions they gather the juice, which drops down like tears.

Jerusalem

Jerusalem was the most important city of biblical times. It was here that the great temple of God was to be found and that Jesus died and rose again. The city became a symbol even of heaven, which is called the "new Jerusalem" (Rv 21:1–4). (#8) Josephus provides us with a description of how it looked in New Testament times. The Roman general Titus left standing the three towers Josephus mentions (Hippicus, Phasaelus, and Mariamme) as a monument to Rome's military might; parts of Hippicus remain to this day in the citadel area near the Jaffa Gate.

#8: The City of Jerusalem
(Josephus, *Jewish War* 5.4.1–3 §§136–42, 144, 146–52, 155–56, 159, 161–71)

1. [136]The city of Jerusalem was fortified with three walls, on such parts as were not surrounded by unpassable valleys; for in such places it had but one wall. The city was built upon two hills which are opposite to one an-

other, and have a valley to divide them asunder; at which valley the corresponding rows of houses on both hills end. [137]Of these hills, that which contains the upper city is much higher, and in length more direct . . . called the "Upper Marketplace." But the other hill, which was called "Acra," and sustains the lower city, is of the shape of a moon when she is horned; [138]over-against this was a third hill, but naturally lower than Acra, and parted formerly from the other by a broad valley. [139]However, in those times when the Hasmoneans reigned, they filled up that valley with earth, and had a mind to join the city to the temple. They then took off part of the height of Acra, and reduced it to be of less elevation than it was before, that the temple might be superior to it. [140]Now the Valley of the Cheesemongers [Tyropoeon], as it was called, distinguished the hill of the upper city from that of the lower, extended as far as Siloam; for that is the name of a fountain which has sweet waters in it, and this in great plenty also. [141]But on the outsides, these hills are surrounded by deep valleys, and by reason of the precipices to them belonging on both sides, they are everywhere unpassable.

2. [142]Now, of these three walls, the old one was hard to be taken, both by reason of the valleys, and of that hill on which it was built, and which was above them. . . . [144][The first] wall began on the north, at the tower called "Hippicus," and extended as far as the "Xistus," a place so called, and then joining at the council-house, ended at the west cloister of the temple. . . . [146]The second wall took its beginning from that gate which they called "Gennath," which belonged to the first wall; it only encompassed the northern quarter of the city, and reached as far as the tower Antonia. [147]The beginning of the third wall was at the tower Hippicus, whence it reached as far as the north quarter of the city, and the tower Psephinus, and then was so far extended till it came over against the monuments of Helena, which Helena was queen of Adiabene, the daughter of Izates; it then extended further to a great length, and passed by the sepulchral caverns of the kings, and bent again at the tower of the corner, at the monument which is called the "Monument

of the Fuller," and joined to the old wall at the valley called the Kidron Valley. [148]It was Agrippa who encompassed the parts added to the old city with this wall, which had been all naked before; for as the city grew more populous, it gradually crept beyond its old limits, [149]and those parts of it that stood northward of the temple, and joined that hill to the city, made it considerably larger, and occasioned that hill, which is in number the fourth, and is called "Bezetha," to be inhabited also. It lies over against the tower Antonia, but is divided from it by a deep valley, [150]which was dug on purpose, and that in order to hinder the foundations of the tower of Antonia from joining to this hill, and thereby affording an opportunity for getting to it with ease, and hindering the security that arose from its superior elevation; [151]for which reason also that depth of the ditch made the elevation of the towers more remarkable. This new-built part of the city was called "Bezetha," in our language, which, if interpreted in the Grecian language, may be called the "New City." [152]Since, therefore, its inhabitants stood in need of a covering, the father of the present king, and of the same name with him, Agrippa, began that wall we spoke of; but he left off building it when he had only laid the foundation, out of the fear he was in of Claudius Caesar, lest he should suspect that so strong a wall was built in order to make some innovation in public affairs. . . . [155]After this it was erected with great diligence by the Jews, as high as twenty cubits [30 ft.], above which it had battlements of two cubits [3 ft.], and turrets of three cubits [4 1/2 ft.] altitude, insomuch that the entire altitude extended as far as twenty-five cubits [37 1/2 ft.].

3. [156]Now the towers that were upon it were twenty cubits [30 ft.] in breadth and twenty cubits in height; they were square and solid, as was the wall itself, wherein the niceness of the joints and the beauty of the stones were no way inferior to those of the holy house itself . . . ; [159]but in the middle wall were forty towers, and the old wall was parted into sixty, while the whole compass of the city was thirty-three furlongs [about 4 miles]. . . . [161][King Herod had built three towers that] were for largeness, beauty, and strength, be-

yond all that were in the habitable earth: [162]for besides the magnanimity of his nature, and his munificence towards the city on other occasions, he built these after such an extraordinary manner, to gratify his own private affections, and dedicated these towers to the memory of those three persons who had been the dearest to him, and from whom he named them. They were his brother, his friend, and his wife. This wife he had slain out of his love [and jealousy,], . . . the other two he lost in war, as they were courageously fighting. [163]Hippicus, so named from his friend, was square; its length and breadth each twenty-five cubits [37 1/2 ft.], and its height thirty [45 ft.], and it was solid throughout. [164]Over this solid building, which was composed of great stones united together, there was a reservoir twenty cubits deep, [165]over which there was a house of two stories, whose height was twenty-five cubits [37 1/2 ft.], and divided into several parts; over which were battlements of two cubits [3 ft.], and turrets all round of three cubits [4 1/2 ft.] high, insomuch that the entire height added together amounted to fourscore cubits [120 ft.]. [166]The second tower which he named from his brother Phasaelus, had its breadth and its height equal, each of them forty cubits [60 ft.]; [167]over which a cloister went round about, whose height was ten cubits [15 ft.], and it was covered from enemies by breast-works and bulwarks. [168]There was also built over that cloister another tower, parted into magnificent rooms and a place for bathing; so that this tower wanted nothing that might make it appear to be a royal palace. It was also adorned with battlements and turrets, more than was the foregoing, [169]and the entire altitude was about ninety cubits [135 ft.]. . . . [170]The third tower was Mariamme, for that was his queen's name; it was solid as high as twenty cubits [30 ft.]; its breadth and its length were twenty cubits, and were equal to each other; [171]its upper buildings were more magnificent, and had greater variety than the other towers had; for the king thought it most proper for him to adorn that which was denominated from his wife, better than those denominated from men, as those were built stronger than

Tower of Hippicus that still stands today, the bottom portion of which was built by Herod the Great

this that bore his wife's name. The entire height of this tower was fifty cubits [75 ft.].

The Holiness of Israel

(#9) In the Mishnah one can sense something of the deep feeling and commitment the Jews had for their land. For them the land of Israel was the holiest land in all the earth. Everything within it is holy, but there are grades of holiness even there. Walled cities are holy but Jerusalem is the holiest city of all. The temple within it is holier, but the Holy of Holies surpasses everything because there God is to be met. It is in Israel alone that this Holy of Holies exists and where God may be known to the highest degree. (#10) In the Psalms of Solomon, it is also to the land of Israel that God's holy people will return and find their ultimate place. No other place on earth will do for them.

#9: The Land of Israel: Holy unto the Lord
(Mishnah, Tractate *Kelim* 1.6–9)

[6]There are ten degrees of holiness. The Land of Israel is holier than any other land. Wherein lies its holiness? In that from it they may bring the *Omer*, the Firstfruits, and the Two Loaves, which they may not bring from any other land.
[7]The Walled cities [of the Land of Israel] are still more holy, in that they must send forth the lepers from their midst; moreover they may carry around a corpse therein whereso-

ever they will, but once it is gone forth [from the city] they may not bring it back.

[8]Within the wall [of Jerusalem] is still more holy, for there [only] they may eat the Lesser Holy Things and the Second Tithe. The Temple Mount is still more holy, for no man or woman that has a flux, no menstruant, and no woman after childbirth may enter therein. The Rampart is still more holy, for no gentiles and none that have contracted uncleanness from a corpse may enter therein. The Court of the Women is still more holy, for none that had immersed himself the selfsame day [because of uncleanness] may enter therein, yet none would thereby become liable to a Sin-offering. The Court of the Israelites is still more holy, for none whose atonement is yet incomplete may enter therein, and they would thereby become liable to a Sin-offering. The Court of the Priests is still more holy, for Israelites may not enter therein save only when they must perform the laying on of hands, slaughtering, and waving.

[9]Between the Porch and the Altar is still more holy, for none that has a blemish or whose hair is unloosed may enter there. The Sanctuary is still more holy, for none may enter therein with hands and feet unwashed. The Holy of Holies is still more holy, for none may enter therein save only the High Priest on the Day of Atonement at the time of the [Temple-] service.

#10: The Future Glory of the Land
(Psalms of Solomon 17.26–29)

[26]He will gather a holy people
  whom he will lead in righteousness,
and he will judge the tribes of the people
    that have been made holy by the Lord
    their God.
[27]He will not tolerate unrighteousness
    (even) to pause among them,
  and any person who knows wickedness
    shall not live with them.
For he shall know them
  that they are all children of their God.
[28]He will distribute them upon the land
    according to their tribes;
the alien and the foreigner will no longer
    live near them.
[29]He will judge peoples and nations in the
    wisdom of his righteousness.

23

2 The History of the Jews

Judaism and Christianity are historical religions. That is, they include within their fundamental understanding of reality the idea that God created the universe, intervenes in world affairs, directs history, elected Israel for his own redemptive purposes, and will bring history to a conclusion when his purposes have been fulfilled. Christians, of course, add the decisive intervention of the incarnation, death, and resurrection of the Son of God in history.

Because of this emphasis on history, a large portion of both the Old Testament and the New Testament is given over to historical narrative, often just a recitation of events, from the mundane—the digging of a well—to the magnificent—the building of Solomon's temple. And most of biblical theology is a reflection on what God has done, is doing, and is going to do in history. God is not an abstract principle or an impersonal force, but a personal God who acts redemptively (or in judgment) in the lives of his people. He is the God of Abraham, Isaac, and Jacob, and the Father of our Lord Jesus Christ.

Because there is such an emphasis on history in the Bible, it is important for us to pick up this historical thread as a necessary part of understanding New Testament believers. Our readings will pick up at that decisive moment when the Jews began to reassert themselves as the result of Antiochus's outrage in the second century B.C.

If you want to pursue this history in more depth after you have gone through these readings, there are numerous books you can choose from. The following are only a selection to get you started and provide a comprehensive overview: Michael Avi-Yonah (ed.), *The Herodian Period;* Abraham Schalit (ed.), *The Hellenistic Age;* Michael Avi-Yonah, *The Holy Land from the Persian to the Arab Conquests (536 B.C. to A.D. 640);* Emil Schürer, *The History of the Jewish People in the Age of Jesus Christ (175 B.C.–A.D. 135)* (New English Edition, 3 vols.); William D. Davies and Louis Finkelstein (eds.), *The Cambridge History of Judaism: The Hellenistic Age;* S. Safrai and Menahem Stern (eds.), *The Jewish People in the First Century* (2 vols.); Lester L. Grabbe, *Judaism from Cyrus to Hadrian;* Werner Foerster, *Palestinian Judaism in NT Times;* Peter Richardson, *Herod;* Stewart Perowne, *The Later Herods;* Stewart Perowne, *The Life and Times of Herod the Great;* Harold Hoehner, *Herod Antipas.*

Antiochus Epiphanes to Pompey (175–63 B.C.)

Antiochus Hellenizes Palestine

After Alexander the Great died in 323 B.C. following his subjugation of the Middle East, his territory was divided up among his generals, with two families finally emerging as dominant, the Seleucids in Syria and the Ptolemies in Egypt. The Ptolemies were the first to rule over Palestine (for about one hundred years). The Seleucids then gained control and in 175 B.C., Antiochus, who called himself Epiphanes ([God] Manifest), became the ruler. (#11) In 2 Maccabees we read of how he began to Hellenize the land with the connivance of a corrupt priesthood. It was this sort of thing that ultimately led to the Maccabean revolt.

#11: Hellenization Reaches Palestine (2 Maccabees 4.7–15)

[7]When Seleucus died and Antiochus who was called Epiphanes succeeded to the kingdom, Jason the brother of Onias obtained the high priesthood by corruption, [8]promising the king at an interview three hundred and sixty talents of silver and, from another source of

revenue, eighty talents. [9]In addition to this he promised to pay one hundred and fifty more if permission were given to establish by his authority a gymnasium and a body of youth for it, and to enroll the men of Jerusalem as citizens of Antioch. [10]When the king assented and Jason came to office, he at once shifted his countrymen over to the Greek way of life. [11]He set aside the existing royal concessions to the Jews, secured through John the father of Eupolemus, who went on the mission to establish friendship and alliance with the Romans; and he destroyed the lawful ways of living and introduced new customs contrary to the law. [12]For with alacrity he founded a gymnasium right under the citadel, and he induced the noblest of the young men to wear the Greek hat. [13]There was such an extreme of Hellenization and increase in the adoption of foreign ways because of the surpassing wickedness of Jason, who was ungodly and no high priest, [14]that the priests were no longer intent upon their service at the altar. Despising the sanctuary and neglecting the sacrifices, they hastened to take part in the unlawful proceedings in the wrestling arena after the call to the discus, [15]disdaining the honors prized by their fathers and putting the highest value upon Greek forms of prestige.

Antiochus Destroys Jerusalem and Desecrates the Temple

(#12) Following more outrages and a murderous attack on Jerusalem in 169 B.C., Antiochus pushed his program of Hellenization to the limit by desecrating the temple and setting up statues to Olympian Zeus, both in the temple and throughout the land (167 B.C.). This was in partial fulfillment of the "Abomination of Desolation" prophesied by Daniel (Dn 9:27; 11:31; 12:11) and later referred to by Jesus as he looked to the end of the age (Mt 24:15). Josephus graphically describes those awful days (cf. also 1 Macc. 1:29–64 and Josephus's summary in *War* 1.1.1, 2).

#12: The Destruction of Jerusalem and the Desecration of the Temple
(Josephus, *Ant.* 12.5.4 §§248–56)

4. [248]Now it came to pass, after two years, in the hundred and forty-fifth year (167 B.C.), on the twenty-fifth day of that month which is by us called Kislev (December), . . . that the king [Antiochus] came up to Jerusalem, and, pretending peace, he got possession of the city by treachery: [249]at which time he did not spare even those who admitted him into it, on account of the riches that lay in the temple; but, led by his covetous inclination (for he saw there was in it a great deal of gold, and many ornaments that had been dedicated to it of very great value), and in order to plunder its wealth, he ventured to break the agreement he had made. [250]So he left the temple bare, and took away the golden candlesticks, and the golden altar [of incense], and table [of shewbread], and the altar [of burnt-offering]; and did not abstain from even the veils, which were made of fine linen and scarlet. He also emptied it of its secret treasures, and left nothing at all remaining; and by this means cast the Jews into great lamentation, [251]for he forbade them to offer those daily sacrifices which they used to offer to God, according to the law. And when he had pillaged the whole city, some of the inhabitants he killed, and some he carried captive, together with their wives and children, so that the multitude of those captives that were taken alive amounted to about ten thousand. [252]He also burnt down the finest buildings; and when he had overthrown the city walls, he built a citadel in the lower part of the city, for the place was high, and overlooked the temple on which account he fortified it with high walls and towers, and put into it a garrison of Macedonians. However, in that citadel dwelt the impious and wicked part of the [Jewish] multitude, from whom it proved that the citizens suffered many heavy calamities. [253]And when the king had built an idol altar upon God's altar, he slew swine upon it, and so offered a sacrifice neither according to the law, nor the Jewish religious worship in that country. [254]He also compelled them to forsake the worship which they paid their own God, and to adore those whom he took to be gods; and made them build temples, and raise idol altars, in every city and village, and offer swine upon them every day. He also commanded them not to circumcise their sons, and threatened to pun-

ish any that should be found to have transgressed his injunction.

He also appointed overseers, who should compel them to do what he commanded. [255]And indeed there were many Jews who complied with the king's commands, either voluntarily, or out of fear of the penalty that was announced: but the best men, and those of the noblest souls, did not regard him, but paid a greater respect to the customs of their country than concern as to the punishment which he threatened to the disobedient; on which account they every day underwent great miseries and bitter torments; [256]for they were whipped with rods, and their bodies were torn to pieces, and were crucified while they were still alive and breathed: they also strangled those women and their sons whom they had circumcised, as the king had appointed, hanging their sons about their necks as they were upon the crosses. And if there were any sacred book of the law found, it was destroyed; and those with whom they were found, miserably perished also.

The Maccabean Revolt Begins (167 B.C.)

(#13) Shortly after Antiochus desecrated the temple in Jerusalem, Mattathias and his five sons led a revolt against the Syrians in the Maccabean rebellion, so named after a son named Judas, whose nickname was Maccabeus ("the Hammerer"), as recounted in 1 Maccabees.

#13: The Revolt Breaks Out
(1 Maccabees 2.1–28)

[1]In those days Mattathias the son of John, son of Simeon, a priest of the sons of Joarib, moved from Jerusalem and settled in Modein. [2]He had five sons, John surnamed Gaddi, [3]Simon called Thassi, [4]Judas called Maccabeus, [5]Eleazar called Avaran, and Jonathan called Apphus. [6]He saw the blasphemies being committed in Judah and Jerusalem, [7]and said,

"Alas! Why was I born to see this,
the ruin of my people, the ruin of the holy city,
and to dwell there when it was given over to the enemy,

the sanctuary given over to aliens?
[8]Her temple has become like a man without honor;
[9]her glorious vessels have been carried into captivity.
Her babes have been killed in her streets,
her youths by the sword of the foe.
[10]What nation has not inherited her palaces and has not seized her spoils?
[11]All her adornment has been taken away;
no longer free, she has become a slave.
[12]And behold, our holy place, our beauty, and our glory have been laid waste;
the Gentiles have profaned it.
[13]Why should we live any longer?"

[14]And Mattathias and his sons rent their clothes, put on sackcloth, and mourned greatly. [15]Then the king's officers who were enforcing the apostasy came to the city of Modein to make them offer sacrifice. [16]Many from Israel came to them; and Mattathias and his sons were assembled. [17]Then the king's officers spoke to Mattathias as follows. "You are a leader, honored and great in this city, and supported by sons and brothers. [18]Now be the first to come and do what the king commands, as all the Gentiles and the men of Judah and those that are left in Jerusalem have done. Then you and your sons will be numbered among the friends of the king, and you and your sons will be honored with silver and gold and many gifts."

[19]But Mattathias answered and said in a loud voice: "Even if all the nations that live under the rule of the king obey him, and have chosen to do his commandments, departing each one from the religion of his fathers, [20]yet I and my sons and my brothers will live by the covenant of our fathers. [21]Far be it from us to desert the law and the ordinances. [22]We will not obey the king's words by turning aside from our religion to the right hand or to the left."

[23]When he had finished speaking these words, a Jew came forward in the sight of all to offer sacrifice upon the altar in Modein, according to the king's command. [24]When Mattathias saw it, he burned with zeal and his heart was stirred. He gave vent to righteous

anger; he ran and killed him upon the altar. [25]At the same time he killed the king's officer who was forcing them to sacrifice, and he tore down the altar. [26]Thus he burned with zeal for the law, as Phinehas did against Zimri the son of Salu.

[27]Then Mattathias cried out in the city with a loud voice, saying: "Let every one who is zealous for the law and supports the covenant come out with me!" [28]And he and his sons fled to the hills and left all that they had in the city.

The Rededication of the Temple (164 B.C.)

(#14) The Maccabean revolt succeeded and independence was finally won. On Kislev 25, 164 B.C., exactly three years after the sacrilege, the altar in Jerusalem was rededicated, inaugurating an eight-day ceremony that has become known as Hanukkah, or the Feast of Lights, because the lamps were relit in the temple. That glorious event is described in 1 Maccabees.

#14: The Rededication of the Temple
(1 Maccabees 4.36–59)

[36]Then said Judas and his brothers, "Behold, our enemies are crushed; let us go up to cleanse the sanctuary and dedicate it." [37]So all the army assembled and they went up to Mount Zion. [38]And they saw the sanctuary desolate, the altar profaned, and the gates burned. In the courts they saw bushes sprung up as in a thicket, or as on one of the mountains. They saw also the chambers of the priests in ruins. [39]Then they rent their clothes, and mourned with great lamentation, and sprinkled themselves with ashes. [40]They fell face down on the ground, and sounded the signal on the trumpets, and cried out to Heaven. [41]Then Judas detailed men to fight against those in the citadel until he had cleansed the sanctuary.

[42]He chose blameless priests devoted to the law, [43]and they cleansed the sanctuary and removed the defiled stones to an unclean place. [44]They deliberated what to do about the altar of burnt offering, which had been profaned. [45]And they thought it best to tear it down, lest it bring reproach upon them, for

the Gentiles had defiled it. So they tore down the altar, [46]and stored the stones in a convenient place on the temple hill until there should come a prophet to tell what to do with them. [47]Then they took unhewn stones, as the law directs, and built a new altar like the former one. [48]They also rebuilt the sanctuary and the interior of the temple, and consecrated the courts. [49]They made new holy vessels, and brought the lampstand, the altar of incense, and the table into the temple. [50]Then they burned incense on the altar and lighted the lamps on the lampstand, and these gave light in the temple. [51]They placed the bread on the table and hung up the curtains. Thus they finished all the work they had undertaken.

[52]Early in the morning on the twenty-fifth day of the ninth month, which is the month of Chislev (December), in the one hundred and forty-eighth year (164 B.C.), [53]they rose and offered sacrifice, as the law directs, on the new altar of burnt offering which they had built. [54]At the very season and on the very day that the Gentiles had profaned it, it was dedicated with songs and harps and lutes and cymbals. [55]All the people fell on their faces and worshiped and blessed Heaven, who had prospered them. [56]So they celebrated the dedication of the altar for eight days, and offered burnt offerings with gladness; they offered a sacrifice of deliverance and praise. [57]They decorated the front of the temple with golden crowns and small shields; they restored the gates and the chambers for the priests, and furnished them with doors. [58]There was very great gladness among the people, and the reproach of the Gentiles was removed.

[59]Then Judas and his brothers and all the assembly of Israel determined that every year at that season the days of the dedication of the altar should be observed with gladness and joy for eight days, beginning with the twenty-fifth day of the month of Chislev.

Pompey Takes Jerusalem and Establishes Roman Rule (63 B.C.)

(#15) After a hundred rocky years of independence, a disastrous conflict between two of the Hasmonean (descendants of the Maccabees) claimants to the right to rule, Aristobulus II and

John Hyrcanus, brought the Roman general Pompey into Jerusalem to subjugate it in 63 B.C. and (#16) ultimately to establish Roman rule in the land. Thus began direct Roman involvement in Palestine's affairs.

#15: Pompey Conquers Jerusalem
(Josephus, *Jewish War* 1.7.1–6 §§141–53)

1. [141]Pompey was very angry, and took Aristobulus into custody; and when he was come to the city he looked about where he might make his attack; for he saw the walls were so firm that it would be hard to overcome them, and that the valley before the walls was terrible; and that the temple, which was within that valley, was itself encompassed with a very strong wall, insomuch that if the city were taken, the temple would be a second place of refuge for the enemy to retire to.

2. [142]Now, as he was long in deliberating about this matter, a sedition arose among the people within the city; Aristobulus's party being willing to fight, and to set their king at liberty, while the party of Hyrcanus were for opening the gates to Pompey; and the dread people were in, occasioned these last to be a very numerous party, when they looked upon the excellent order the Roman soldiers were in. [143]So Aristobulus's party was worsted, and retired into the temple, and cut off the communication between the temple and the city, by breaking down the bridge that joined them together, and prepared to make an opposition to the utmost; but as the others had received the Romans into the city, and had delivered up the palace to him, Pompey sent Piso, one of his great officers, into that palace with an army, [144]who distributed a garrison about the city, because he could not persuade any one of those that had fled to the temple to come to terms of accommodation; he then disposed all things that were round about them so as might favor their attacks, as having Hyrcanus's party very ready to afford them both counsel and assistance.

3. [145]But Pompey himself filled up the ditch that was on the north side of the temple, and the entire valley also, the army itself being obliged to carry the materials for that purpose. And indeed it was a hard thing to fill up that valley, by reason of its immense depth, especially as the Jews used all the means possible to repel them from their superior station; [146]nor had the Romans succeeded in their endeavors, had not Pompey taken notice of the seventh days, on which the Jews abstain from all sorts of work on a religious account, and raised his bank, but restrained his soldiers from fighting on those days; for the Jews only acted defensively on Sabbath-days. [147]But as soon as Pompey had filled up the valley, he erected high towers upon the bank, and brought those engines which they had fetched from Tyre near to the wall, and tried to batter it down; and the slingers of stones beat off those that stood above them, and drove them away: but the towers on this side of the city made very great resistance, and were indeed extraordinary both for largeness and magnificence.

4. [148]Now, here it was that, upon the many hardships which the Romans underwent, Pompey could not but admire not only at the other instances of the Jews' fortitude, but especially that they did not at all interrupt their religious services, even when they were encompassed with arrows on all sides; for, as if the city were in full peace, their daily sacrifices and purifications, and every branch of their religious worship, were still performed to God with the utmost exactness. Nor, indeed, when the temple was actually taken, and they were every day slain about the altar, did they leave off the instances of their divine worship that were appointed by their law; [149]for it was in the third month of the siege before the Romans could even with great difficulty overthrow one of the towers, and get into the temple. . . .

5. [150]And now did many of the priests, even when they saw their enemies assailing them with swords in their hands, without any disturbance, go on with their divine worship, and were slain while they were offering their drink-offerings and burning their incense, as preferring the duties about their worship to God before their own preservation. The greatest part of them were slain by their own countrymen of the adverse faction, and an innumerable multitude threw themselves down precipices; nay, some there were who were so

distracted among the insuperable difficulties they were under, that they set fire to the buildings that were near to the wall, and were burnt together with them. [151]Now of the Jews were slain twelve thousand; but of the Romans very few were slain, but a greater number was wounded.

6. [152]But there was nothing that affected the nation so much, in the calamities they were then under, as that their holy place, which had been hitherto seen by none, should be laid open to strangers; for Pompey, and those that were about him, went into the temple itself, whither it was not lawful for any to enter but the high priest, and saw what was reposited therein, the candlestick with its lamps, and the table, and the pouring vessels, and the censers, all made entirely of gold, as also a great quantity of spices heaped together, with two thousand talents of sacred money. [153]Yet he did not touch the money, nor anything else that was there reposited; but he commanded the ministers about the temple, the very next day after he had taken it, to cleanse it, and to perform their accustomed sacrifices. . . . by which means he acted the part of a good general, and reconciled the people to him more by benevolence than by terror. . . . and [Pompey] laid a tribute upon the country, and upon Jerusalem itself.

#16: Roman Rule Begins in Palestine
(Josephus, *Jewish War* 1.7.7 §§155–57)

7. [155]Pompey also took away from the nation all those cities they had formerly taken, and that belonged to Coelesyria, and made them subject to him that was at that time appointed to be the Roman president there, and reduced Judea within its proper bounds. He also rebuilt Gadara, that had been demolished by the Jews. . . . [156]He also made other cities free from their dominion, that lay in the midst of the country—such, I mean, as they had not demolished before that time; Hippos and Scythopolis, as also Pella, and Samaria, and Marissa: and besides these, Ashdod, and Jamnia, and Arethusa; and in like manner dealt he with the maritime cities, Gaza, and Joppa, and Dora, and that which was anciently called Strato's Tower, but was afterwards rebuilt

with the most magnificent edifices, and had its name changed to Caesarea by king Herod. [157]All which he restored to their own citizens and put them under the province of Syria; which province, together with Judea, and the countries as far as Egypt, and Euphrates, he committed to Scaurus as their governor, and gave him two legions to support him.

The Rule of Herod the Great (37–4 B.C.)

Herod's Rebuilding of the Temple

(#17) After being confirmed as king by Julius Caesar in 37 B.C., Herod ruled for thirty-four years, dying in 4 B.C. Among the many important things he did the most significant was to rebuild the temple in Jerusalem; some of the remains (the "western wall") exist until this day. The temple was magnificent beyond words and the center of Jewish life. Here Jesus taught, Paul preached, and Peter healed. Jesus foretold its coming destruction (Mt 24:1–3) because in God's plan worship would be of the heart and not tied to locality. In A.D. 70 Titus's Roman army demolished Jerusalem and the temple that Herod had built. Josephus provides an elaborate description of the temple as he knew it. Examples of the warning inscriptions that he mentions have been found by archaeologists.

#17: Herod Rebuilds the Temple
(Josephus, *Ant.* 15.11.1–5 §§380, 390–403, 409–19)

1. [380]And now Herod, in the eighteenth year of his reign, . . . undertook a very great work, that is, to build of himself the temple of God. . . .

2. . . . [390]so he got ready a thousand wagons, that were to bring stones for the building, and chose out ten thousand of the most skillful workmen, and bought a thousand sacerdotal garments for the priests, and had some of them taught the arts of stonecutters, and others of carpenters, and then began to build; but this not till everything was well prepared for the work.

A modern replica of the temple as it existed in Jesus' day.

3. [391]So Herod took away the old foundations, and laid others, and erected the temple upon them, being in length a hundred cubits [150 ft.], and in height twenty additional cubits [30 ft.]. . . . [392]Now the temple was built of stones that were white and strong, and each of their length was twenty-five cubits [37.5 ft.], their height was eight [12 ft.], and their breadth about twelve [18 ft.]; [393]and the whole structure, as also the structure of the royal cloister, was on each side much lower, but the middle was much higher, till they were visible to those that dwelt in the country for a great many miles, but chiefly to such as lived over against them, and those that approached to them. [394]The temple had doors also at the entrance, and lintels over them, of the same height with the temple itself. They were adorned with embroidered veils, with their flowers of purple, and pillars interwoven: [395]and over these, but under the crown-work, was spread out a golden vine, with its branches hanging down from a great height, the largeness and fine workmanship of which

was a surprising sight to the spectators, to see what vast materials there were, and with what great skill the workmanship was done. [396]He also encompassed the entire temple with very large cloisters, contriving them to be in a due proportion thereto; and he laid out larger sums of money upon them than had been done before him, till it seemed that no one else had so greatly adorned the temple as he had done. There was a large wall to both the cloisters; which wall was itself the most prodigious work that was ever heard of by man. [397]The hill was a rocky ascent, that declined by degrees towards the east parts of the city, till it came to an elevated level. [398]This hill it was which Solomon, who was the first of our kings, by divine revelation, encompassed with a wall; it was of excellent workmanship upwards, and round the top of it. He also built a wall below, beginning at the bottom, which was encompassed by a deep valley; and at the south side he laid rocks together, and bound them one to another with lead, and included some of the inner parts, till it proceeded to a great height, [399]and till both the largeness of the square edifice and its altitude were immense, and till the vastness of the stones in the front were plainly visible on the outside, yet so that the inward parts were fastened with iron, and preserved the joints immovable for all future times. [400]When this work [for the foundation] was done in this manner, and joined together as a part of the hill itself to the very top of it, he wrought it all into one outward surface, and filled up the hollow places which were about the wall, and made it a level on the external upper surface, and a smooth level also. This hill was walled all round, and in compass four furlongs [$^1/_2$ mile], [the distance of] each angle containing in length a furlong [$^1/_8$ mile]: [401]but within this wall, and on the very top of all, there ran another wall of stone also, having, on the east quarter, a double cloister, of the same length with the wall; in the midst of which was the temple itself. This cloister looked to the gates of the temple; and it had been adorned by many kings in former times; [402]and round about the entire temple were fixed the spoils taken from barbarous nations; all these had been dedicated to the temple by Herod, with the addition of those he had taken from the Arabians.

4. [403]Now on the north side [of the temple] was built a citadel, whose walls were square and strong, and of extraordinary firmness. This citadel was built by the kings of the Hasmonean race, who were also high priests before Herod, and they called it the Tower, in which were reposited the vestments of the high priest, which the high priest only put on at the time when he was to offer sacrifice.

[409]. . . but for the tower itself, when Herod the king of the Jews had fortified it more firmly than before, in order to secure and guard the temple, he gratified Antonius, who was his friend, and the Roman ruler, and then gave it the name of the Tower of Antonia.

5. [410]Now, in the western quarter of the enclosures of the temple there were four gates; the first led to the king's palace, and went to a passage over the intermediate valley; two more led to the suburbs of the city; and the last led to the other city, where the road descended down into the valley by a great number of steps, and thence up again by the ascent; for the city lay over against the temple in the manner of a theater, and was encompassed with a deep valley along the entire south quarter; [411]but the fourth front of the temple, which was southward, had indeed itself gates in its middle, as also it had the royal cloisters, with three walks, which reached in length from the east valley unto that on the west, for it was impossible it should reach any further: [412]and this cloister deserves to be mentioned better than any other under the sun; for while the valley was very deep, and its bottom could not be seen, if you looked from above into the depth, this further vastly high elevation of the cloister stood upon that height, insomuch that if anyone looked down from the top of the battlements, or down both these altitudes, he would be giddy, while his sight could not reach to such an immense depth. [413]This cloister had pillars that stood in four rows one over against the other all along, for the fourth row was interwoven into the wall, which [also was built of stone;] and the thickness of each pillar was such, that three men might, with their arms extended, fathom it round, and join their hands again, while its length was twenty-seven feet, with a double spiral at its basis; [414]and the number of all the pillars [in that court] was a hundred and sixty-two. Their capitals were made with sculptures after the Corinthian order, and caused an amazement [to the spectators,] by reason of the grandeur of the whole. [415]These four rows of pillars included three intervals for walking in the middle of this cloister; two of which walks were made parallel to each other, and were contrived after the same manner; the breadth of each of them was thirty feet, the length was a furlong, and the height fifty feet: but the breadth of the middle part of the cloister was one and a half of the other, and the height was double, for it was much higher than those on each side; [416]but the roofs were adorned with deep sculptures in wood, representing many sorts of figures: the middle was much higher than the rest, and the wall of the front was adorned with beams, resting upon pillars, that were interwoven into it, and that front was all of polished stone, insomuch that its fineness, to such as had not seen it,

was incredible, and to such as had seen it, was greatly amazing. [417]Thus was the first enclosure. In the midst of which, and not far from it, was the second, to be gone up to by a few steps: this was encompassed by a stone wall for a partition, with an inscription, which forbade any foreigner to go in under pain of death. [418]Now this inner enclosure had on its southern and northern quarters three gates [equally] distant from one another; but on the east quarter, towards the sun-rising, there was one large gate through which such as were pure came in, together with their wives; but the temple further inward in that gate was not allowed to the women; [419]but still more inward was there a third [court of the] temple, where into it was not lawful for any but the priests alone to enter. The temple itself was within this; and before that temple was the altar, upon which we offer our sacrifices and burnt offerings to God.

The Rule of Herod Described

Herod's complex personality caused him to seek approval from foreign powers, in whose territories he spent vast sums on extravagant building projects. He did this at the expense of his own people, who were often brutally treated, although on occasion he could show a more benevolent side. Nor did he neglect his own comforts, building fabulous palaces at Jericho, Herodion, Masada, and Jerusalem, much of which remains to this day. Three readings provide (#18) a partial description of Herod's actions, with an assessment by Josephus, (#19) a description of the police state Herod established in order to accomplish his purposes, and (#20) a brief description of his palace in Jerusalem. It was to this palace, in all probability, that Jesus was taken to be interrogated by Pilate (Jn 18:28).

#18: Herod's Extravagance and Personality
(Josephus, *Ant.* 16.5.1, 3–4 §§136–40, 146–59)

1. [136]About this time it was that Cesarea Sebaste, which he had built, was finished. The entire building being accomplished in the tenth year, the solemnity of it fell into the twenty-eighth year of Herod's reign, and into the hundred and ninety-second olympiad; [137]there was accordingly a great festival, and most sumptuous preparations made presently, in order to its dedication; for he had appointed a contest in music, and games to be performed naked; he had also gotten ready a great number of those that fight single combats, and of beasts for the like purpose; horse races also, and the most chargeable of such sports and shows as used to be exhibited at Rome and in other places. [138]He consecrated this combat to Caesar, and ordered it to be celebrated every fifth year. He also sent all sorts of ornaments for it out of his own furniture, that it might want nothing to make it decent; [139]nay, Julia, Caesar's wife, sent a great part of her most valuable furniture [from Rome,] insomuch that he had no want of anything; the sum of them all was estimated at five hundred talents. [140]Now when a great multitude was come to that city to see the shows, as well as the ambassadors whom other people sent, on account of the benefits they had received [from Herod,] he entertained them all in the public inns, and at public tables, and with perpetual feasts; this solemnity having in the day-time the diversions of fights, and in the night-time such merry meetings as cost vast sums of money. . . .

3. [146]But as for his other benefits, it is impossible to reckon them up, those which he bestowed on cities, both in Syria and in Greece, and in all the places he came to in his voyages; for he seems to have conferred, and that after a most plentiful manner, what would minister to many necessities, and the building of public works, and gave them the money that was necessary to such works as wanted it, to support them upon the failure of their other revenues; [147]but what was the greatest and most illustrious of all his works, he erected Apollo's temple at Rhodes, at his own expense, and gave them a great number of talents of silver for the repair of their fleet. He also built the greatest part of the public buildings for the inhabitants of Nicopolis, at Actium; [148]and for the Antiochians, the inhabitants of the principal city of Syria, where a broad street cuts through the place lengthways, he built cloisters along it on both sides, and laid the open road with polished stone,

which was of very great advantage to the inhabitants; [149]and as to the olympic games, which were in a very low condition, by reason of the failure of their revenues, he recovered their reputation, and appointed revenues for their maintenance, and made that solemn meeting more venerable, as to the sacrifices and other ornaments; and by reason of this vast liberality, he was generally declared in their inscriptions to be one of the perpetual managers of those games.

4. [150]Now some there are who stand amazed at the diversity of Herod's nature and purposes; for when we have respect to his magnificence, and the benefits which he bestowed on all mankind, there is no possibility for even those that had the least respect for him to deny, or not openly to confess, that he had a nature vastly beneficent; [151]but when any one looks upon the punishments he inflicted, and the injuries he did, not only to his subjects, but to his nearest relations, and takes notice of his severe and unrelenting disposition there, he will be forced to allow that he was brutish, and a stranger to all humanity; [152]insomuch that these men suppose his nature to be different, and sometimes at contradiction with itself; but I am myself of another opinion, and imagine that the occasion of both these sorts of actions was one and the same; [153]for being a man ambitious of honor, and quite overcome by that passion, he was induced to be magnificent wherever there appeared any hopes of future memorial, or of reputation at present; [154]and as his expenses were beyond his abilities, he was forced to be harsh with his subjects; for the persons on whom he expended his money were so many, that they made him a very bad procurer of it; [155]and because he was conscious that he was hated by those under him, for the injuries he did them, he thought it not an easy thing to amend his offenses, for that was inconvenient for his revenue; he therefore strove on the other side to make their ill-will an occasion of his gains. [156]As to his own court, therefore, if anyone was not very obsequious to him in his language, and would not confess himself to be his slave, or but seeming to think of any innovation in his government, he was not able to contain himself, but prosecuted his very

kindred and friends, and punished them as if they were enemies; and this wickedness he undertook out of a desire that he might be himself alone honored. [157]Now for this my assertion about that passion of his, we have the greatest evidence, by what he did to honor Caesar and Agrippa, and his other friends; for with what honors he paid his respects to them who were his superiors, the same did he desire to be paid to himself; and what he thought the most excellent present he could make another, he discovered an inclination to have the like presented to himself; [158]but now the Jewish nation is by their law a stranger to all such things, and accustomed to prefer righteousness to glory; for which reason that nation was not agreeable to him, because it was out of their power to flatter the king's ambition with statues or temples, or any other such performances; [159]and this seems to me to have been at once the occasion of Herod's crimes as to his own courtiers and counselors, and of his benefactions as to foreigners and those that had no relation to him.

#19: Herod's Police State
(Josephus, *Ant.* 15.10.4 §§365–69)

4. [365]So Herod returned to his subjects a third of their taxes, under pretence indeed of relieving them after the dearth they had had; but the main reason was, to recover their good-will, which he now wanted; for they were uneasy at him, because of the innovations he had introduced in their practices of the dissolution of their religion, and of the disuse of their own customs, and the people everywhere talked against him, like those that were still more provoked and disturbed at his procedure; [366]against which discontents he greatly guarded himself, and took away the opportunities they might have to disturb him, and enjoined them to be always at work; nor did he permit the citizens either to meet together, or to walk, or eat together, but watched everything they did, and when any were caught, they were severely punished; and many there were who were brought to the citadel Hyrcania, both openly and secretly, and were there put to death; and there were

spies set everywhere, both in the city and in the roads, who watched those that met together; [367]nay, it is reported that he did not himself neglect this part of caution, but that he would oftentimes himself dress like a private man, and mix among the multitude in the night-time, and make trial what opinion they had of his government; [368]and as for those that could be no way reduced to acquiesce under his scheme of government, he persecuted them all manner of ways; but for the rest of the multitude, he required that they should be obliged to take an oath of fidelity to him, and at the same time compelled them to swear that they would bear him good-will and continue certainly so to do, in his management of the government; [369]and indeed a great part of them, either to please him, or out of fear of him, yielded to what he required of them.

#20: Herod's Sumptuous Palace
(Josephus, *Jewish War* 5.4.4 §§176–82)

[176]Now as these towers [Hippicus, Phasaelus, and Mariamme] were themselves on the north side of the wall, the king had a palace inwardly thereto adjoined, which exceeds all my ability to describe it; [177]for it was so extraordinary as to lack no cost or skill in its construction, but was entirely walled about to the height of thirty cubits [45 ft.], and was adorned with towers at equal distances, and with large bed-chambers that would contain beds for a hundred guests a-piece, [178]in which the variety of the stones is not to be expressed; for a large quantity of those that were rare of that kind was collected together. Their roofs were also wonderful, both for the length of the beams and the splendor of their ornaments. [179]The number of the rooms was also very great, and the variety of the figures that were about them was prodigious; their furniture was complete, and the greatest part of the vessels that were put in them was of silver and gold. [180]There were besides many porticoes, one beyond another, round about, and in each of those porticoes gorgeous pillars; yet were all the courts that were exposed to the air everywhere green. [181]There were moreover several groves of trees and long walks through them, with deep canals, and cisterns, that in several parts were filled with bronze statues, through which the water ran out. There were also many dove-cotes of tame pigeons about the canals; [182]but, indeed, it is not possible to give a complete description of these palaces.

The Death of Herod the Great (4 B.C.)

(#21) Herod died in agony in 4 B.C., leaving orders to massacre the nation's leading citizens (an order not carried out) so there would be mourning in the land. He rightly understood that he was despised by his people and would otherwise die unmourned. Josephus describes at some length the death and funeral of Herod to highlight the justice of God in dealing with the man.

#21: Herod's Last Days and Death
(Josephus, *Ant.* 17.6.5 §§168–71, 173–75, 178)

5. [168]But now Herod's illness greatly increased upon him after a severe manner, and this by God's judgment upon him for his sins: for a fire glowed in him slowly, which did not so much appear to the touch outwardly, as it augmented his pains inwardly; [169]for it brought upon him a vehement appetite to eating, which he could not avoid to supply with one sort of food or other. His entrails were also ulcerated, and the chief violence of his pain lay on his colon; an aqueous and transparent fluid also had settled itself about his feet, and a like matter afflicted him at the bottom of his belly. Nay, further, his genitals were putrefied, and produced worms; and when he sat upright he had a difficulty of breathing, which was very loathsome, on account of the stench of his breath and the quickness of his panting; he had also convulsions in all parts of his body, which increased his strength to an insufferable degree. [170]It was said by those who pretended to divine, and who were endued with wisdom to foretell such things, that God inflicted this punishment on the king on account of his great impiety; [171]yet was he still in hopes of recovering, though his afflic-

tions seemed greater than anyone could bear. . . .

[173]He grew so choleric, that it brought him to do all things like a madman; and though he were near his death, he contrived the following wicked designs. [174]He commanded that all the principal men of the entire Jewish nation, wheresoever they lived, should be called to him. Accordingly, there were a great number that came, because the whole nation was called, and all men heard of this call, and death was the penalty of such as should ignore the letters that were sent to call them. And now the king was in a wild rage against them all, the innocent as well as those that had afforded him ground for accusations; and when they were come, [175]he ordered them all to be shut up in the hippodrome, and sent for his sister Salome, and her husband Alexas, and spake thus to them: "I shall die in a little time, so great are my pains; which death ought to be cheerfully borne, and to be welcomed by all men; but what principally troubles me is this, that I shall die without being lamented, and without such mourning as men usually expect at a king's death." . . .

[178]He desired therefore that as soon as they see he had died, they shall place soldiers round the hippodrome, while they do not know that he is dead; and that they shall not declare his death to the multitude till this is done, but that they shall give orders to have those that are in custody shot with their arrows; and that this slaughter of them all will cause that he shall not miss to rejoice on a double account; that as he is dying, they will make him secure that his will shall be executed in what he charges them to do; that he shall have the honor of a memorable mourning at his funeral.

(Josephus, *Ant.* 17.8.1–2 §§ 191, 193–94)

1. [191]And so Herod died, the fifth day after he had caused Antipater to be slain; having reigned, since he had procured Antigonus to be slain, thirty-four years; but since he had been declared king by the Romans, thirty-seven.—A man he was of great barbarity towards all men equally, and a slave to his pas-

sions; and above any consideration of what was right. . . .

2. [193]Now Salome and Alexas, before the king's death was made known, dismissed those that were shut up in the hippodrome, and told them that the king ordered them to go away to their own lands, and take care of their own affairs, which was esteemed by the nation a great benefit; [194]and now the king's death was made public.

An Evaluation of Herod's Reign

(#22) A delegation of fifty Jewish ambassadors begged Rome that Palestine be made part of Syria in order to free them from Herod's family rule. In their petition they summarized their opinion of Herod's rule. (#23) The pseudepigraphal "Assumption of Moses," written before A.D. 70, also provides a description, in cryptic language, of Herod's reign.

#22: The Jewish Hatred of Herod
(Josephus, *Jewish War* 2.6.2 §§84–86)

2. [84]And now, upon the permission that was given the delegates to speak, they, in the first place, went over Herod's breaches of their law, and said that he was not a king, but the most barbarous of all tyrants, and that they had found him to be such by the sufferings they underwent from him: that when a very great number had been slain by him, those that were left had endured such miseries, that they called those that were dead happy men; [85]that he had not only tortured the bodies of his subjects, but entire cities, and had done much harm to the cities of his own country, while he adorned those that belonged to foreigners; and he shed the blood of Jews in order to do kindness to those people who were out of their bounds: [86]that he had filled the nation full of poverty, and of the greatest iniquity, instead of that happiness and those laws which they had anciently enjoyed; that, in short, the Jews had borne more calamities from Herod, in a few years, than had their forefathers during all that interval of time that had passed since they had come out of Babylon, and returned home in the reign of Xerxes.

#23: Herod, the Insolent King
(Assumption of Moses 6.1–9)

[1]Then there shall be raised up unto them kings bearing rule, and they shall call themselves priests of the Most High God: they shall assuredly work iniquity in the holy of holies. [2]And an insolent king shall succeed them, who will not be of the race of the priests, a man bold and shameless, and he shall judge them as they shall deserve. [3]And he shall cut off their chief men with the sword, and shall destroy *them* in secret places, so that no one may know where their bodies are. [4]He shall slay the old and the young, and he shall not spare. [5]Then the fear of him shall be bitter unto them in their land. [6]And he shall execute judgments on them as the Egyptians executed upon them, during thirty and four years, and he shall punish them. [7]And he shall beget children (who) succeeding him shall rule for shorter periods. [8]Into their parts cohorts and a powerful king of the west shall come, who shall conquer them: [9]and he shall take them captive, and burn a part of their temple with fire, (and) shall crucify some around their colony.

The Rule of Herod's Sons and Grandson, Agrippa I (4 B.C.–A.D. 44)

The Division of the Land by Augustus Caesar

(#24) A delegation went to Rome, where Augustus Caesar divided the land among three of Herod's sons: Archelaus, Antipas, and Philip. Some cities were allowed their freedom and some of them became part of what was the "Decapolis" mentioned in the Gospels (Mt 4:25; Mk 5:20; 7:31).

#24: Augustus Divides the Land
(Josephus, *Jewish War* 2.6.3 §§93–97)

3. [93]So Caesar, after he had heard both sides, dissolved the assembly for that time; but a few days afterward, he gave the one half of Herod's kingdom to Archelaus, by the name of Ethnarch, and promised to make him king also afterward, if he rendered himself worthy of that dignity; [94]but as to the other half, he divided it into two tetrarchies, and gave them to two other sons of Herod, the one of them to Philip, and the other to that Antipas who contested the kingdom with Archelaus. [95]Under this last was Perea and Galilee, with a revenue of two hundred talents: but Batanea and Trachonitis, and Auranitis, and certain parts of Zeno's house about Jamnia, with a revenue of a hundred talents, were made subject to Philip; [96]while Idumea, and all Judea, and Samaria, were parts of the ethnarchy of Archelaus, although Samaria was eased of one quarter of its taxes, out of regard to their not having revolted with the rest of the nation. [97]He also made subject to him the following cities, viz. Strato's Tower, and Sebaste, and Joppa, and Jerusalem; but as to the Grecian cities Gaza and Gadara, and Hippos, he cut them off from the kingdom and added them to Syria. Now the revenue of the country that was given to Archelaus was four hundred talents.

Archelaus's Rule (4 B.C.–A.D. 6)

(#25) Archelaus's bloody entrance into office is described by a delegation to Rome who went requesting relief. (#26) After ten brutal years of rule, Archelaus was banished by Caesar to Gaul. When still in Egypt, Joseph and Mary heard that Archelaus was ruling over Judea, so they returned to Nazareth rather than to Bethlehem, in order to escape living under his jurisdiction (Mt 2:19–23).

#25: Archelaus's Slaughter of His People
(Josephus, *Jewish War* 2.6.2 §§89–91)

[89]Archelaus, . . . [they declared], began his reign with the murder of three thousand citizens; as if he had a mind to offer so many bloody sacrifices to God for his government, and to fill the temple with the like number of dead bodies at that festival: [90]that, however, those that were left after so many miseries, had just reason to consider now at last the calamities they had undergone, and to op-

pose themselves, like soldiers in war, to receive those stripes upon their faces [but not upon their backs as hitherto]. Whereupon they prayed that the Romans would have compassion upon the [poor] remains of Judea, and not expose what was left of them to such as barbarously tore them to pieces, [91]and that they would join their country to Syria and administer the government by their own commanders.

#26: The Banishment of Archelaus
(Josephus, *Ant.* 17.13.2, 5 §§342–44, 355)

2. [342]But in the tenth year [A.D. 6] of Archelaus's government, both his brethren and the principal men of Judea and Samaria, not being able to bear his barbarous and tyrannical usage of them, accused him before Caesar, and that especially because they knew he had broken the commands of Caesar, which obliged him to behave himself with moderation among them. [343]Whereupon Caesar, when he heard it, was very angry, and called for Archelaus's steward, who took care of his affairs at Rome, and whose name was Archelaus also; and thinking it beneath him to write to Archelaus, he bade him sail away as soon as possible and bring him to Rome; [344]so the man made haste in his voyage, and when he came into Judea he found Archelaus feasting his friends; so he told him what Caesar had sent him about, and hastened him away. And when he was come [to Rome] to Caesar, upon hearing what certain accusers of his had to say, and what reply he could make, both banished him and appointed Vienna, a city of Gaul, to be the place of his habitation, and took his money away from him. . . .

5. [355]So Archelaus's country was laid to the province of Syria; and Cyrenius, one that had been consul, was sent by Caesar to take account of people's effects in Syria and to sell the house of Archelaus.

Herod Antipas, "That Fox"
(4 B.C.–A.D. 39)

Antipas ruled for forty-three years and was in some respects a good ruler, being concerned about the sensibilities of his people. (#27) In typical Herodian fashion, he engaged in elaborate building projects. (#28) He violated Jewish law by marrying his brother's wife, (#29) which eventuated in the death of John the Baptist (Mk 6:14–29). (#30) Overreaching pride brought about his downfall and banishment when goaded by his wife to seek a title equal to his nephew's.

#27: Antipas the Builder
(Josephus, *Ant.* 18.2.1 §27)

[27]So Herod [Antipas] and Philip had each of them received their own tetrarchy, and settled the affairs thereof. Herod also built a wall about Sepphoris (which is the security of all Galilee), and made it the metropolis of the country. He also built a wall round Betharamphtha, which was itself a city also, and called it Julias, from the name of the emperor's wife. . . .

(Josephus, *Ant.* 18.2.3 §36)

3. [36]He also built a city of the same name with the emperor and called it Tiberias. He built it in the best part of Galilee; at the lake of Gennesaret.

#28: Antipas's Marriage to Herodias
(Josephus, *Ant.* 18.5.1 §§109–10, 112–14)

1. [109]About this time Aretas (the king of Arabia Petrea) and Herod [Antipas] had a quarrel, on the account following: Herod the tetrarch had married the daughter of Aretas, and had lived with her a great while; but when he was once at Rome, he lodged with Herod [Philip], who was his brother indeed, but not by the same mother; for this Herod was the son of the high priest Simon's daughter. [110]However, he fell in love with Herodias, this last Herod's wife, who was the daughter of Aristobulus their brother, and the sister of Agrippa the Great. This man ventured to talk to her about a marriage between them; which when she accepted, an agreement was made for her to change her habitation and come to him as soon as he should return from Rome: one article of this marriage also was this, that he should divorce Aretas's daughter. . . . [112]Accordingly Herod sent his wife away, as thinking she had not perceived anything; now she had sent a good while before to Machaerus,

which was subject to her father, and so all things necessary for her journey were made ready for her by the general of Aretas's army, and by that means she soon came to Arabia, under the conduct of the several generals, who carried her from one to another successively; and she soon came to her father, and told him of Herod's intentions. [113]So Aretas made this the first occasion of his enmity between him and Herod, who had also some quarrel with him about their limits at the country of Gamalitis. So they raised armies on both sides, and prepared for war, and sent their generals to fight instead of themselves; [114]and, when they had joined battle, all Herod's army was destroyed by the treachery of some fugitives, though they were of the tetrarchy of Philip, joined with Aretas's army.

#29: The Murder of John the Baptist
(Josephus, *Ant.* 18.5.2 §§116–19)

2. [116]Now, some of the Jews thought that the destruction of Herod's army came from God, and that very justly, as a punishment of what he did against John, that was called the *Baptist;* [117]for Herod slew him, who was a good man, and commanded the Jews to exercise virtue, both as to righteousness towards one another, and piety towards God, and so to come to baptism; for that the washing [with water] would be acceptable to him, if they made use of it, not in order to the putting away [or the remission] of some sins [only], but for the purification of the body: supposing still that the soul was thoroughly purified beforehand by righteousness. [118]Now, when [many] others came to crowd about him, for they were greatly moved [or pleased] by hearing his words, Herod, who feared lest the great influence John had over the people might put it into his power and inclination to raise a rebellion (for they seemed ready to do anything he should advise), thought it best, by putting him to death, to prevent any mischief he might cause, and not bring himself into difficulties, by sparing a man who might make him repent of it when it should be too late. [119]Accordingly he was sent a prisoner, out of Herod's suspicious temper, to Machaerus . . . and was there put to death.

#30: The Banishment of Antipas
(Josephus, *Ant.* 18.7.1–2 §§240–44, 246, 251–52)

1. [240]Herodias, Agrippa's sister, who now lived as wife to Herod, who was tetrarch of Galilee and Perea, took this authority of her brother in an envious manner, particularly when she saw that he had a greater dignity bestowed on him than her husband had; since, when he ran away, he was not able to pay his debts; and now he was come back, it was because he was in a way of dignity and of great fortune. [241]She was therefore grieved and much displeased at so great a change of his affairs; and chiefly when she saw him marching among the multitude with the usual ensigns of royal authority, she was not able to conceal how miserable she was, by reason of the envy she had towards him; but she excited her husband and desired him that he would sail to Rome, to court honors equal to his; [242]for she said, that she could not bear to live any longer, while Agrippa, the son of that Aristobulus, who was condemned to die by his father, one that came to her husband in such extreme poverty, that the necessities of life were forced to be entirely supplied him day by day; and when he fled away from his creditors by sea, he now returned a king: while he was himself the son of a king, and while the near relation he bare to royal authority called upon him to gain the like dignity, he sat still, and was contented with a private life. [243]"But then, Herod, although you were formerly not concerned to be in a lower condition than your father, from whom you were derived, had been, yet you should now seek after the dignity which your kinsman has attained to; and do not you bear this contempt, that a man who admired your riches should be in greater honor than yourself; nor suffer his poverty to show itself able to purchase greater things than our abundance; and do not esteem it other than a shameful thing to be inferior to one who, the other day, lived upon your charity. [244]But let us go to Rome, and let us spare no pains nor expenses, either of silver or gold, since they cannot be kept for any better use than for the obtaining of a kingdom." . . .

2. [246]So he got all things ready, after as sumptuous a manner as he was able, and spared for nothing, and went up to Rome, and took Herodias along with him. . . .

[251]In the meantime word had reached Gaius [Caligula] that Herod had armor sufficient for seventy thousand men ready in his armory. Gaius [Caligula] was moved at this information, and asked Herod, whether what was said about the armor was true; [252]and when he confessed there was such armor there, for he could not deny the same, the truth of it being too notorious, Gaius [Caligula] took that to be a sufficient proof of the accusation, that he intended to revolt. So he took away from him his tetrarchy, and gave it by way of addition to Agrippa's kingdom; he also gave Herod's money to Agrippa, and, by way of punishment, awarded him a perpetual banishment, and appointed Lyons, a city of Gaul, to be his place of habitation.

Herod Philip (4 B.C.–A.D. 34)

Philip ruled for thirty-seven years and was universally appreciated by his people. (#31) He undertook some building projects, but nothing like his father or even his brother, Antipas. Caesarea Philippi (Mk 8:27) and Bethsaida (Mk 8:22) were both rebuilt by Philip. (#32) Josephus praises the reign of Philip as being one of moderation and peace.

#31: Philip's Building Projects
(Josephus, *Ant.* 18.2.1 §28)

1. [28]When Philip, also, had built Paneas, a city, at the fountains of Jordan, he named it Caesarea [Philippi]. He also advanced the village Bethsaida, situated at the lake of Gennesaret, unto the dignity of a city, both by the number of inhabitants it contained, and its other grandeur, and called it by the name of Julias, the name of Caesar's daughter.

#32: The Just and Moderate Rule of Philip
(Josephus, *Ant.* 18.4.6 §§106–8)

6. [106]About this time it was that Philip, Herod's brother, departed this life, in the twentieth year of the reign of Tiberius [A.D. 37], after he had been tetrarch of Trachonitis, and Gaulonitis, and of the nation of the Bataneans also, thirty-seven years. He had shown himself a person of moderation and quietness in the conduct of his life and government; [107]he constantly lived in that country which was subject to him; he used to make his progress with a few chosen friends; his tribunal also, on which he sat in judgment, followed him in his progress; and when any one met him who wanted his assistance, he made no delay, but had his tribunal set down immediately, wheresoever he happened to be, and sat down upon it, and heard his complaint: he there ordered the guilty that were convicted to be punished, and absolved those that had been accused unjustly. [108]He died at Julias; and when he was carried to that monument which he had already erected for himself beforehand, he was buried with great pomp.

Herod Agrippa I (A.D. 41–44)

In A.D. 37 Agrippa, who was Herod the Great's grandson, was given the former territories of Philip and that of Lysanias, as well as the title of king. In A.D. 40 Herod Antipas's territory was added and in A.D. 41 the territories of Judea and Samaria. For the next three years, Agrippa ruled over a territory equal to that of his grandfather. (#33) Agrippa was basically a mild-mannered and generous person. (#34) Unfortunately he allowed the praises of the crowd to go to his head, and he died a painful death in Caesarea (Acts 12:19–23). (#35) He was remembered favorably by the Jewish sages.

#33: The Character of Herod Agrippa I
(Josephus, *Ant.* 19.7.3 §§328–31)

3. [328]Now, this king was by nature very beneficent and liberal in his gifts, and very concerned to oblige people with such large donations; and he made himself very illustrious by the many expensive presents he made them. He took delight in giving, and rejoiced in living with good reputation. He was not at all like that Herod who reigned before him; [329]for that Herod was ill-natured, and severe in his punishments, and had no mercy on them that he hated; and every one perceived that he was more friendly to the

Greeks than to the Jews; for he adorned foreign cities with large presents in money; with building them baths and theaters besides; nay, in some of those places, he erected temples, and porticoes in others; but he did not condescend to raise one of the least edifices in any Jewish city, or make them any donation that was worth mentioning. [330]But Agrippa's temperament was mild and equally liberal to all men. He was humane to foreigners, and made them aware of his liberality. He was in like manner rather of a gentle and compassionate temper. [331]Accordingly, he loved to live continually at Jerusalem, and was exceedingly precise in the observance of the laws of his country. He therefore kept himself entirely pure: nor did any day pass over his head without its appointed sacrifice.

#34: The Death of Herod Agrippa I
(Josephus, *Ant.* 19.8.2 §§343–50)

2. [343]Now, when Agrippa had reigned three years over all Judea, he came to the city Caesarea, and there he exhibited shows in honor of Caesar, upon his being informed that there was a certain festival celebrated to make vows for his safety. At which festival, a great multitude was gotten together of the principal persons, and such as were of dignity through his province. [344]On the second day of which shows he put on a garment made wholly of silver, and of a texture truly wonderful, and came into the theater early in the morning; at which time the silver of his garment being illuminated by the fresh reflection of the sun's rays upon it, blazed forth in a surprising manner, and was so resplendent as to spread a horror over those that looked intently upon him: [345]and presently his flatterers cried out, one from one place, and another from another (though not for his good), that he was a god: and they added,—"Be thou merciful to us; for although we have hitherto reverenced thee only as a man, yet shall we henceforth own thee as superior to mortal nature." [346]Upon this the king did neither rebuke them nor re-

Caesarea—the seat of Roman authority in New Testament times, where the procurators lived and Agrippa I died. Its aqueduct is shown here.

ject their impious flattery. But, as he presently afterwards looked up, he saw an owl sitting on a certain rope over his head, and immediately understood that this bird was the messenger of ill tidings, as it had once been the messenger of good tidings to him; and fell into the deepest sorrow. A severe pain also arose in his belly, and began in a most violent manner. [347]He therefore looked upon his friends, and said,—"I, whom you call a god, am commanded presently to depart this life; while Providence thus reproves the lying words you just now said to me; and I, who was by you called immortal, am immediately to be hurried away by death. But I am bound to accept of what Providence allots, as it pleases God; for we have by no means lived ill, but in a splendid and happy manner." [348]When he had said this, his pain was become violent. Accordingly he was carried into the palace; and the rumor went abroad everywhere, that he would certainly die in a little time. [349]But the multitude presently sat in sackcloth, with their wives and children, after the law of their country, and besought God for the king's recovery. All places were also full of mourning and lamentation. Now the king rested in a high chamber and as he saw them below lying prostrate on the ground, he could not himself keep from weeping. [350]And when he had been quite worn out by the pain in his belly for five days, he departed this life, being in the fifty-fourth year of his age and the seventh year of his reign.

#35: Jewish Praise of Herod Agrippa I
(Mishnah, Tractate *Sotah* 7.8)

[8]After what manner was the paragraph of the king? After the close of the first Festival-day of the Feast [of Tabernacles], in the eighth year, after the going forth of the Seventh Year, they used to prepare for him in the Temple Court a wooden platform on which he sat, for it is written, *At the end of every seven years in the set time. . . .* The minister of the synagogue used to take a scroll of the Law and give it to the chief of the synagogue, and the chief of the synagogue gave it to the Prefect, and the Prefect gave it to the High Priest, and the High Priest gave it to the king, and the king received

it standing and read it sitting. King Agrippa received it standing and read it standing, and for this the Sages praised him. And when he reached *Thou mayest not put a foreigner over thee which is not thy brother*, his eyes flowed with tears; but they called to him, "Our brother art thou! Our brother art thou! Our brother art thou!"

The Rule of the Procurators in Judea

The Early Procurators in Judea

After the removal of Archelaus in A.D. 6, Rome appointed a series of procurators, who were directly answerable to the emperor. They are as follows: Coponius (A.D. 6–9), Marcus Ambibulus (A.D. 9–12), Annius Rufus (A.D. 12–15), Valerius Gratus (A.D. 15–26), Pontius Pilate (A.D. 26–36), Marcellus (A.D. 36–37), and Marullus (A.D. 37–41). We know very little about the rule of these procurators, with the exception of Pontius Pilate. The rest receive only a summary account in Josephus (*Ant.* 18.2.2.). (#36) Significantly, the procurators were given the power to enforce the death penalty.

#36: The Procurator's Possession of the Death Penalty
(Josephus, *Jewish War* 2.8.1 §117)

1. [117]And now Archelaus's part of Judea was reduced into a province, and Coponius, one of the equestrian order among the Romans, was sent as a procurator, having the power of [life and] death put into his hands by Caesar.

The Rule of Pontius Pilate (A.D. 26–36)

The procurator of most interest to New Testament students is, of course, Pontius Pilate. He despised the Jews and openly provoked them on more than one occasion. (#37) A very negative account is given of him by Philo, and while this might be exaggerated two additional episodes (##38, 39) related by Josephus do show him in a very unfavorable light. His brutal treatment of the

Samaritans brought about his recall to Rome, but he never went to trial, because of the emperor Tiberius's death. Of his later years we know nothing certain, but Eusebius, (#40) referring to an earlier Greek source, says he committed suicide.

#37: The Character of Pilate
(Philo, *On the Embassy to Gaius* 38 §§299–305)

38. [299]Pilate was one of the emperor's [Tiberius's] lieutenants, having been appointed governor of Judea. He, not more with the object of doing honor to Tiberius than with that of vexing the multitude, dedicated some gilt shields in the palace of Herod, in the holy city. . . . [300]But when the multitude heard what had been done . . . then the people put forward the four sons of the king . . . who entreated him to alter and to rectify the innovation which he had committed in respect of the shields; and not to make any alteration in their national customs, which had hitherto been preserved without any interruption, without being in the least degree changed by any king or emperor. [301]"But when he steadfastly refused this petition (for he was a man of a very inflexible disposition and very merciless as well as very obstinate), they cried out: "Do not cause a sedition; do not make war upon us; do not destroy the peace which exists. The honor of the emperor is not identical with dishonor to the ancient laws; let it not be to you a pretence for heaping insult on our nation. Tiberius is not desirous that any of our laws or customs shall be destroyed. And if you yourself say that he is, show us either some command from him, or some letter, or something of the kind, that we, who have been sent to you as ambassadors, may cease to trouble you, and may address our supplications to your master." [302]"But this last sentence exasperated him in the greatest possible degree, as he feared lest they might in reality go on an embassy to the emperor, and might impeach him with respect to other particulars of his government, in respect of his corruption, and his acts of insolence, and his rapine, and his habit of insulting people, and his cruelty, and his continual

murders of people untried and uncondemned, and his never ending, and gratuitous, and most grievous inhumanity. [303]Therefore, being exceedingly angry, and being at all times a man of most ferocious passions, he was in great perplexity, neither venturing to take down what he had once set up, nor wishing to do any thing which could be acceptable to his subjects, and at the same time being sufficiently acquainted with the firmness of Tiberius on these points. And those who were in power in our nation, seeing this, and perceiving that he was inclined to change his mind as to what he had done, but that he was not willing to be thought to do so, wrote a most supplicatory letter to Tiberius. [304]And he, when he had read it, what did he say of Pilate, and what threats did he utter against him! . . .

[305]The next day, Tiberius wrote a letter, reproaching and reviling him in the most bitter manner for his act of unprecedented audacity and wickedness and commanding him immediately to take down the shields and to convey them away from the metropolis of Judea to Caesarea.

#38: Pilate Violates the Temple and Beats the Jews
(Josephus, *Jewish War* 2.9.4 §§175–77)

4. [175]After this he raised another disturbance, by expending that sacred treasure which is called Corban upon aqueducts, whereby he brought water from the distance of four hundred furlongs [50 miles]. At this the multitude had great indignation; and when Pilate was come to Jerusalem, they came about his tribunal and made a clamor at it. [176]Now when he was apprised beforehand of this disturbance, he mixed his own soldiers in their armor with the multitude, and ordered them to conceal themselves under the habits of private men, and not indeed to use their swords, but with staves to beat those that made the clamor. He then gave the signal from his tribunal [to do as he had bidden them]. [177]Now the Jews were so badly beaten, that many of them perished by the blows they received, and many of them perished as trodden to death, by which means the multitude

was astonished at the calamity of those that were slain, and held their peace.

#39: Pilate's Slaughter of the Samaritans
(Josephus, *Ant.* 18.4.1–2 §§85–89)

1. [85]But the nation of the Samaritans did not escape without tumults. The man who excited them to it, was one who thought lying a thing of little consequence, and who contrived everything so that the multitude might be pleased; so he bade them get together upon Mount Gerizzim, which is by them looked upon as the most holy of all mountains, and assured them that, when they were come thither, he would show them those sacred vessels which were laid under that place, because Moses put them there. [86]So they came thither armed, and thought the discourse of the man probable; and as they abode at a certain village, which was called Tirathaba, they got the rest together to them, and desired to go up the mountain in a great multitude together. [87]But Pilate prevented their going up, by seizing upon the roads with a great band of horsemen and footmen, who fell upon those that were gotten together in the village; and when they came to an action, some of them they slew, and others of them they put to flight, and took a great many alive, the principal of whom, and also the most powerful of those that fled away, Pilate ordered to be slain.

2. [88]But when this tumult was appeased, the Samaritan senate sent an embassy to Vitellius, a man that had been consul, and who was now president of Syria, and accused Pilate of the murder of those that were killed; for that they did not go to Tirathaba in order to revolt from the Romans, but to escape the violence of Pilate. [89]So Vitellius sent Marcellus, a friend of his, to take care of the affairs of Judea, and ordered Pilate to go to Rome, to answer before the emperor to the accusation of the Jews. So Pilate, when he had tarried ten years in Judea, made haste to Rome, and this in obedience to the orders of Vitellius, which he dared not contradict; but before he could get to Rome, Tiberius was dead.

#40: The Suicide of Pilate
(Eusebius, *Ecclesiastical History* 2.7.1)

[1]It is proper also, to observe, how it is asserted that this same Pilate, who was governor at our Savior's crucifixion, in the reign of Caius [Caligula], whose times we are recording, fell into such calamities that he was forced to become his own murderer, and the avenger of his own wickedness. Divine justice, it seems, did not long protract his punishment. This is stated by those Greek historians, who have recorded the Olympiads in order, together with the transactions of the times.

The Procurator Fadus to the Outbreak of War (A.D. 44–66)

After the death of Agrippa I in A.D. 44, a series of seven procurators ruled Judea until the outbreak of the war in A.D. 66. They were: Fadus (A.D. 44–46), Tiberius Alexander (A.D. 46–48), Ventidius Cumanus (A.D. 48–52), Felix (A.D. 52–60?), Porcius Festus (A.D. 60?–62), Albinus (A.D. 62–64), and Gessius Florus (A.D. 64–66).

Two of these are mentioned in the New Testament: Felix (Acts 24:1–26) and Festus (Acts 24:27–25:12). Agrippa I's son, Agrippa II, who was ultimately given some partial rule over Palestine during these final fateful years, is also mentioned in the New Testament as one of Paul's interrogators (Acts 25:13–26:32).

The Rule of Albinus and Florus Described

(#41) The rule (misrule) of these last two procurators was so offensive that nothing could stop the war from breaking out. Josephus summarizes their disastrous reigns.

#41: The Misrule of Albinus and Gessius Florus
(Josephus, *Jewish War* 2.14.1–2 §§274–79)

1. [274]At this time it was that the enterprises of the seditious at Jerusalem were very formidable; the principal men among them bribed Albinus to let them go on with their seditious practices; while that part of the people who delighted in disturbances joined themselves to such as had fellowship with Albinus: [275]and

every one of these wicked wretches were included in his band of robbers, while he himself, like an arch-robber, or a tyrant, made a figure among his company, and abused his authority over those about him, in order to plunder those that lived quietly. [276]The effect of which was this, that those who lost their goods were forced to hold their peace, when they had reason to show great indignation at what they had suffered; but those who had escaped were forced to flatter him that deserved to be punished, out of the fear they were in of suffering equally with the others. Upon the whole, nobody dared to speak their minds, for tyranny was generally tolerated; and at this time were those seeds sown which brought the city [Jerusalem] to destruction.

2. [277]And although such was the character of Albinus, yet did Gessius Florus, who succeeded him, demonstrate him to have been a most excellent person, upon the comparison: for the former did the greatest part of his rogueries in private, and with a sort of dissimulation; but Gessius did his unjust actions to the harm of the nation after a pompous manner; and as though he had been sent as an executioner to punish condemned malefactors, he omitted no sort of rapine, or of vexation: [278]where the case was really pitiable, he was most barbarous; and in things of the greatest depravity, he was most outrageous; nor could any one outdo him in disguising the truth; nor could any one contrive more subtle ways of deceit than he did. He indeed thought it but a petty offense to extract money out of single individuals; so he spoiled whole cities, and ruined entire bodies of men at once, and did almost publicly proclaim it all over the country, that they had liberty given them to turn robbers, upon this condition, that he might go shares with them in the spoils. [279]Accordingly, this his greediness of gain was the occasion that entire toparchies were brought to desolation; and a great many of the people left their own country and fled into foreign provinces.

The Outrage of Florus in Jerusalem

(#42) After deliberate provocation at a synagogue in Caesarea by some Gentiles, rather than quiet

the unrest Florus marched on Jerusalem acting "as if he had been hired to fan the war into flame" (Josephus, *Jewish War* 2.14.6) and turned his soldiers loose on the people.

#42: Florus's Brutal Behavior in Jerusalem
(Josephus, *Jewish War* 2.14.9 §§305–8)

9. [305]Florus called out aloud to the soldiers to plunder that which was called the Upper Market Place, and to slay such as they met with. So the soldiers, taking this exhortation of their commander in a sense agreeable to their desire of gain, did not only plunder the place they were sent to, but forcing themselves into every house, they slew its inhabitants; [306]so the citizens fled along the narrow lanes, and the soldiers slew those that they caught, and no method of plunder was omitted; they also caught many of the quiet people, and brought them before Florus, whom he first had publicly whipped, and then crucified. [307]Accordingly, the whole number of those that were destroyed that day, with their wives and children (for they did not spare the infants themselves), was about three thousand six hundred; and what made this calamity the heavier, was this new method of Roman barbarity; [308]for Florus ventured then to do what no one had done before, that is, to have men of the equestrian order whipped, and nailed to the cross before his tribunal; who, although they were by birth Jews, yet were they of Roman dignity notwithstanding.

The Jewish War (A.D. 66-73)

The Outbreak of the War in A.D. 66

Agrippa II sought to intervene to prevent civil war and revolt against Rome but to no avail. (#43) The insurgents attacked Masada, and the sacrifice offered in honor of Caesar was suspended; Josephus counts this as the true beginning of the war. (#44) The public records containing all debts were burned and the Tower of Antonia was attacked, driving out the Roman soldiers. Thus began the Jewish War that lasted from 66 to 73.

#43: The Outbreak of the War

(Josephus, *Jewish War* 2.17.2 §§408–10)

2. [408]And at this time it was that some of those that principally excited the people to go to war, made an assault upon a certain fortress called Masada. They took it by treachery, and slew the Romans that were there, and put others of their own party to keep it. [409]At the same time Eleazar, the son of Ananias the high priest, a very bold youth, who was at that time governor of the temple, persuaded those that officiated in the divine service to receive no gift or sacrifice for any foreigner. And this was the true beginning of our war with the Romans: for they rejected the sacrifice of Caesar on this account: [410]and when many of the high priests and principal men besought them not to omit the sacrifice, which it was customary for them to offer for their princes, they would not be prevailed upon. These relied much upon their multitude, for the most flourishing part of the innovators assisted them; but they had the chief regard to Eleazar, the governor of the temple.

#44: The Public Records Are Burned and the Romans Driven Out

(Josephus, *Jewish War* 2.17.6–7 §§425–32)

6. [425]Now it was the festival of Xylophory; upon which the custom was for every one to bring wood for the altar. . . . Upon that day they excluded the opposite party from the observation of this part of religion. And when they had joined to themselves many of the Sicarii, who crowded in among the weaker people (that was the name of such robbers as had under their robes swords called Sicae), they grew bolder, and carried their undertakings further, [426]insomuch that the king's soldiers were overpowered by their multitude and boldness; and so they gave way, and were driven out of the upper city by force. The others then set fire to the house of Ananias the high priest, and to the palaces of Agrippa and Bernice; [427]after which they carried the fire to the place where the archives were reposited and made haste to burn the contracts belonging to their creditors, and thereby dissolve their obligations for paying their debts; and this was done, in order to gain the multitude of those who had been debtors, and that they might persuade the poorer sort to join in their insurrection with safety against the more wealthy; so the keepers of the records fled away, and the rest set fire to them. [428]And when they had thus burnt down the nerves of the city, they fell upon their enemies; at which time some of the men of power, and of the high priests, went into the vaults under ground and concealed themselves, [429]while others fled with the king's soldiers to the upper palace, and shut the gates immediately: among whom were Ananias the high priest, and the ambassadors that had been sent to Agrippa. And now the seditious were contented with the victory they had gotten, and the buildings they had burnt down, and proceeded no further.

7. [430]But on the next day . . . they made an assault upon Antonia, and besieged the garrison which was in it two days, and then took the garrison, and slew them, and set the citadel on fire; [431]after which they marched to the palace, whither the king's soldiers were fled, and parted themselves into four bodies, and made an attack upon the walls. As for those that were within it, no one had the courage to sally out, because those that assaulted them were so numerous; but they distributed themselves into breastworks and turrets, and shot at the besiegers, whereby many of the robbers fell under the walls; [432]nor did they cease to fight one with another either by night or by day.

The Destruction of the Temple and the City in A.D. 70

Civil war in Rome (A.D. 68–69) took the military leader Vespasian away from the Jewish War back to Italy, where he eventually became emperor. He left his son Titus in charge of the campaign, and it was he who destroyed Jerusalem. (#45) Tacitus provides an overview of the war from a Roman point of view, and (#46) Josephus gives a detailed account of the fall of the temple and (#47) of the city itself.

#45: A Roman View of the War
(Tacitus, *Histories* 5.10–13)

[10]The endurance of the Jews lasted till Gessius Florus was procurator. In his time the war broke out. Cestius Gallus, legate of Syria, who attempted to crush it, had to fight several battles, generally with ill-success. When Cestius died . . . Vespasian was sent by Nero, and by help of his good fortune, his high reputation, and his excellent subordinates, succeeded within the space of two summers in occupying with his victorious army the whole of the level country and all the cities, except Jerusalem. The following year had been wholly taken up with civil strife, and had passed, as far as the Jews were concerned, in inaction. Peace having been established in Italy, foreign affairs were once more remembered. Our indignation was heightened by the circumstance that the Jews alone had not submitted. At the same time it was held to be more expedient, in reference to the possible results and contingencies of the new reign, that Titus should remain with the army.

Accordingly he pitched his camp before the walls of Jerusalem and displayed his legions in order of battle.

[11]The Jews formed their line close under their walls, whence, if successful, they might venture to advance and where, if repulsed, they had a refuge at hand. The cavalry with some light infantry was sent to attack them, and fought without any decisive result. Shortly afterwards the enemy retreated. During the following days they fought a series of engagements in front of the gates, till they were driven within the walls by continual defeats. The Romans then began to prepare for an assault. It seemed beneath them to await the result of famine. The army demanded the more perilous alternative, some prompted by courage, many by sheer ferocity and greed of gain. Titus himself had Rome with all its wealth and pleasures before his eyes. Jerusalem must fall at once, or it would delay his enjoyment of them. But the commanding situation of the city had been strengthened by enormous works which would have been a thorough defense even for level ground. Two hills of great height were fenced in by walls which had been skillfully obliqued or bent inwards, in such a manner that the flank of an assailant was exposed to missiles. The rock terminated in a precipice; the towers were raised to a height of sixty feet, where the hill lent its aid to the fortifications, where the ground fell, to a height of one hundred and twenty. They had a marvelous appearance and to a distant spectator seemed to be of uniform elevation. Within were other walls surrounding the palace, and, rising to a conspicuous height, the tower Antonia, so called by Herod, in honor of Marcus Antonius.

[12]The temple resembled a citadel, and had its own walls, which were more laboriously constructed than the others. Even the colonnades with which it was surrounded formed an admirable outwork. It contained an inexhaustible spring; there were subterranean excavations in the hill, and tanks and cisterns for holding rain water. The founders of the state had foreseen that frequent wars would result from the singularity of its customs, and so had made every provision against the most protracted siege. After the capture of their city by Pompey [63 B.C.], experience and apprehension taught them much. Availing themselves of the sordid policy of the Claudian era to purchase the right of fortification, they raised in time of peace such walls as were suited for war. Their numbers were increased by a vast rabble collected from the overthrow of the other cities. All the most obstinate rebels had escaped into the place, and perpetual seditions were the consequence. There were three generals, and as many armies. Simon held the outer and larger circuit of walls. John, also called Bargioras, occupied the middle city. Eleazar had fortified the temple. John and Simon were strong in numbers and equipment, Eleazar in position. There were continual skirmishes, surprises, and incendiary fires, and a vast quantity of corn was burned.... [13]I have heard that the total number of the besieged, of every age and both sexes, amounted to six hundred thousand. All who were able bore arms, and a number, more than proportionate to the population, had the courage to do so. Men and women showed equal resolution, and life seemed more terrible than

death, if they were to be forced to leave their country. Such was this city and nation.

#46: The Destruction of the Temple
(Josephus, *Jewish War* 6.2.7 §§149–52)

7. [149]The Roman army had, in seven days' time, overthrown [some] foundations of the tower of Antonia, and had made a ready and broad way to the temple. [150]Then did the legions come near the first court, and began to raise their banks.... [151]However, these works were thus far advanced by the Romans, not without great pains and difficulty, and particularly by being obliged to bring their materials from the distance of over 12 miles. [152]They had further difficulties also upon them; sometimes, by the great security measures they had to take to avoid the Jewish traps laid for them, and by that boldness of the Jews which their despair of escaping had inspired in them.

(Josephus, *Jewish War* 6.4.5–7 §§249–53, 257–66)

5. [249]At length, Titus retired into the tower of Antonia, and resolved to storm the temple the next day, early in the morning, with his whole army, and to encamp round about the holy house; [250]but, as for that house, God had for certain long ago doomed it to the fire; and now that fatal day was come, according to the revolution of ages: it was the tenth day of the month Lous [Ab], upon which it was formerly burnt by the king of Babylon; [251]although these flames took their rise from the Jews themselves and were occasioned by them; for upon Titus's retiring, the seditious lay still for a little while, and then attacked the Romans again, when those that guarded the holy house fought with those that quenched the fire that was burning in the inner [court of the] temple; but these Romans put the Jews to flight, and proceeded as far as the holy house itself. [252]At which time one of the soldiers, without staying for any orders, and without any concern or dread upon him at so great an undertaking, and being hurried on by a certain divine fury, snatched something out of the materials that were on fire, and being lifted up by another soldier, he set

Arch commemorating Titus's destruction of Jerusalem and its temple.

fire to a golden window, through which there was a passage to the rooms that were round about the holy house, on the north side of it. [253]As the flames went upward the Jews made a great cry, such as so mighty an affliction required, and ran together to prevent it; and now they spared not their lives any longer, nor suffered anything to restrain their force, since that holy house was perishing, for whose sake it was that they kept such a guard about it.

6. [257]And as the Roman soldiers were crowding into the temple together, many of them were trampled on by one another, while a great number fell among the ruins of the cloisters, which were still hot and smoking, and were destroyed in the same miserable way with those whom they had conquered: [258]and when they were come near the holy house, they made as if they did not so much as hear Caesar's orders to the contrary; but they encouraged those that

Inside of Titus's Arch showing the sacred lampstands being removed from the temple.

were before them to set it on fire. [259]As for the seditious they were in too great distress already to afford their assistance [toward quenching the fire;]they were everywhere slain, and everywhere beaten; and as for a great part of the people, they were weak and without arms, and had their throats cut wherever they were caught. Now, round about the altar lay dead bodies heaped one upon another; as at the steps going up to it ran a great quantity of their blood, whither also the dead bodies that were slain above [on the altar] fell down.

7. [260]And now, since Titus was in no way able to restrain the enthusiastic fury of the soldiers, and the fire proceeded on more and more, he went into the holy place of the temple, with his commanders, and saw it; . . . [261]but as the flame had not as yet reached to its inward parts, but was still consuming the rooms that were about the holy house, and Titus supposing what the fact was, that the house itself might yet be saved, [262]he came in haste and endeavored to persuade the sol-diers to quench the fire. . . . [263]Yet the passions of the soldiers was greater than the regard they had for Caesar; and . . . their hatred of the Jews, and a certain vehement inclination to fight them, too hard for them also. [264]More-over, the hope of plunder induced many to go on, as having this opinion, that all the places within were full of money, and as see-ing that all round about it was made of gold; [265]and besides, one of those that went into the place prevented Caesar, when he ran so hastily out to restrain the soldiers, and threw the fire upon the hinges of the gate, in the dark; [266]whereby the flame burst out from within the holy house itself immediately, when the commanders retired, and Caesar with them; . . . and thus was the holy house burnt down, without Caesar's approbation.

#47: The Fall of Jerusalem
(Josephus, *Jewish War* 6.5.2 §§281–84)

2. [281]And now the Romans, judging that it was in vain to spare what was round about

the holy house, burnt all those places, as also the remains of the cloisters and the gates, two excepted; the one on the east side, and the other on the south; both which, however, they burnt afterward. [282]They also burnt down the treasury-chambers, in which was an immense quantity of money, and an immense number of garments, and other precious goods, there reposited; and, to speak all in a few words, there it was that the entire riches of the Jews were heaped up together, while the rich people had there built themselves chambers [to contain such furniture]. [283]The soldiers also came to the rest of the cloisters that were in the outer [court of the] temple, whither the women and children and a great mixed multitude of the people fled, in number about six thousand. [284]But before Caesar had determined anything about these people, or given the commanders any orders relating to them, the soldiers were in such a rage, that they set the cloister on fire; by which means it came to pass that some of these were destroyed by throwing themselves down headlong, and some were burnt in the cloisters themselves. Nor did any one of these escape with his life.

(Josephus, *Jewish War* 6.8.5 §§401–8)

5. [401]So the defenders now left these towers [of the walls] of themselves, or rather they were ejected out of them by God himself, and fled immediately to that valley which was under Siloam, where they again recovered themselves out of the dread they were in for a while, and ran violently against that part of the Roman wall which lay on that side; [402]but as their courage was too much depressed to make their attacks with sufficient force, and their power was now broken with fear and affliction, they were repulsed by the guards, and dispersing themselves at distances from each other, went down into the subterranean caverns. [403]So the Romans being now become masters of the walls, they both placed their ensigns upon the towers, and made joyful acclamations for the victory they had gained, as having found the end of this war much lighter than its beginning; for when they had gotten upon the last wall without any bloodshed, they could hardly believe what they found to be true. . . . [404]But when they went in numbers into the lanes of the city with their swords drawn, they slew those whom they overtook without mercy, and set fire to the houses whither the Jews were fled, and burnt every soul in them, and laid waste a great many of the rest; [405]and when they were come to the houses to plunder them, they found in them entire families of dead men, and the upper rooms full of dead corpses, that is of such as died by the famine; they then stood in a horror at this sight, and went out without touching any thing. [406]But although they had this commiseration for such as were destroyed in that manner, yet had they not the same for those that were still alive, but they ran every one through whom they met with, and obstructed the very lanes with their dead bodies, and made the whole city run down with blood, to such a degree indeed that the fire of many of the houses was quenched with these men's blood. [407]And truly so it happened, that though the slayers left off at the evening, yet did the fire greatly prevail in the night; and as all was burning, came that eighth day of the month Gorpieus [Elul] upon Jerusalem; [408]a city that had been liable to so many miseries during this siege. . . .

(Josephus, *Jewish War* 6.9.2 §§414–19)

2. [414]And now, since his soldiers were already quite tired with killing men, and yet there appeared to be a vast multitude still remaining alive, Caesar gave orders that they should kill none but those that were in arms, and opposed them, but should take the rest alive. [415]But, together with those whom they had orders to slay, they slew the aged and the infirm; but for those that were in their flourishing age, and who might be useful to them, they drove them together into the temple, and shut them up within the walls of the court of the women; [416]over which Caesar set one of his freedmen, as also Fronto, one of his own friends; which last was to determine every one's fate, according to his merits. [417]So this Fronto slew all those that had been seditious and robbers, who were impeached one by another; but of the young men, he chose out the tallest and most beautiful, and reserved them

for the triumph; [418]and as for the rest of the multitude that were above seventeen years old, he put them into chains and sent them to the Egyptian mines. Titus also sent a great number into the provinces, as a present to them, that they might be destroyed upon their theaters, by the sword and by the wild beasts; but those that were under seventeen years of age were sold for slaves. [419]Now, during the days wherein Fronto was distinguishing these men there perished, for want of food, eleven thousand; some of whom did not taste any food, through the hatred their guards bore to them; and others would not take in any when it was given them. The multitude also was so very great, that they were in want even of corn for their sustenance.

(Josephus, *Jewish War* 7.1.1 §§1–4)

1. [1]Now, as soon as the army had no more people to slay or to plunder, because there remained none to be the objects of their fury (for they would not have spared any, had there remained any other such work to be done), Caesar gave orders that they should now demolish the entire city and temple, but should leave as many of the towers standing as were of the greatest eminency; that is, Phasaelus, and Hippicus, and Mariamme, and so much of the wall as enclosed the city on the west side. [2]This wall was spared, in order to afford a camp for such as were to lie in garrison; as were the towers also spared, in order to demonstrate to posterity what kind of city it was, and how well fortified, which the Roman valor had subdued; [3]but for all the rest of the wall, it was so thoroughly laid even with the ground by those that dug it up to the foundation that there was left nothing to make those that came thither believe it had ever been inhabited. [4]This was the end which Jerusalem came to by the madness of those that were for innovations; a city otherwise of great magnificence, and of mighty fame among all mankind.

(Josephus, *Jewish War* 6.9.3 §420)

3. [420]Now the number of those that were carried captive during this whole war was collected to be ninety-seven thousand; as was the number of those that perished during the whole siege, one million, one hundred thousand.

The Christians Flee the City before the War

(#48) According to the church historian Eusebius, the believers in Jerusalem were warned by God to escape from the city before its destruction. He interprets the fall of the city as the judgment of God on those who crucified Christ and persecuted the believers.

#48: Christians Escape the Destruction of Jerusalem by Revelation
(Eusebius, *Ecclesiastical History* 3.5.2–3)

[2]For after the ascension of our Savior, the Jews, in addition to their wickedness against him, were now incessantly plotting mischief against his apostles. First, they slew Stephen by stoning him, next James the son of Zebedee, and the brother of John, by beheading, and finally James, who first obtained the episcopal seat at Jerusalem, after the ascension of our Savior, and was slain in the manner before related. But the rest of the apostles who were harassed in innumerable ways, with a view to destroy them, and driven from the land of Judea, had gone forth to preach the gospel to all nations, relying upon the aid of Christ, when he said, "Go ye, teach all nations in my name." [3]The whole body, however, of the church at Jerusalem, having been commanded by a divine revelation, given to men of approved piety there before the war, removed from the city, and dwelt at a certain town beyond the Jordan, called Pella. Here, those that believed in Christ, having removed from Jerusalem, as if holy men had entirely abandoned the royal city itself, and the whole land of Judea; the divine justice, for their crimes against Christ and his apostles, finally overtook them, totally destroying the whole generation of these evildoers from the earth.

A Christian Interpretation of the Destruction of the Temple

(#49) The Epistle of Barnabas, written sometime after the destruction of the temple, sees in its fall the fulfillment of prophecy. He also sees in the

Christian church the new temple that God intended all along to build, echoing the words of the apostle Paul, who calls the believer's body "a temple of the Holy Spirit" (1 Cor 6:19).

#49: The True Temple According to Barnabas
(Epistle of Barnabas 16.1–2, 6–10)

[1]Finally, I will also speak to you about the temple, and how those wretched men went astray and set their hope on the building, as though it were God's house, and not on their God who created them. [2]For they, almost like the heathen, consecrated him by means of the temple. But what does the Lord say in abolishing it? Learn! "Who measured heaven with the span of his hand, or the earth with his palm? Was it not I, says the Lord? Heaven is my throne, and the earth is a footstool for my feet. What kind of house will you build for me, or what place for me to rest?" You now know that their hope was in vain. . . .

[6]But let us inquire whether there is in fact a temple of God. There is—where he himself says he is building and completing it! For it is written: "And it will come to pass that when the week comes to an end God's temple will be built gloriously in the name of the Lord." [7]I discover, therefore, that there is in fact a temple. How, then, will it be built in the name of the Lord? Learn! Before we believed in God, our heart's dwelling-place was corrupt and weak, truly a temple built by human hands, because it was full of idolatry and was the home of demons, for we did whatever was contrary to God. [8]"But it will be built in the name of the Lord." So pay attention, in order that the Lord's temple may be built gloriously. How? Learn! By receiving the forgiveness of sins and setting our hope on the Name, we became new, created again from the beginning. Consequently God truly dwells in our dwelling-place—that is, in us. [9]How? The word of his faith, the call of his promise, the wisdom of his righteous decrees, the commandments of his teaching, he himself prophesying in us, he himself dwelling in us; opening to us who had been in bondage to death the door of the temple, which is the mouth, and granting to us repentance, he leads us into the incorruptible temple. [10]For the one

who longs to be saved looks not to the man but to the One who dwells and speaks in him, and is amazed by the fact that he had never before heard such words from the mouth of the speaker nor for his part ever desired to hear them. This is the spiritual temple that is being built for the Lord.

A Jewish Response to the Destruction of the Temple

(#50) According to the Mishnah, the day on which the temple was destroyed was to be remembered by some commemorative act of mourning.

#50: The Jews Commemorate the Temple's Destruction by Mourning
(Mishnah, Tractate *Taanith* 4.6–7)

[6]Five things befell our fathers on the 17th of Tammuz and five on the 9th of Ab. On the 17th of Tammuz the Tables [of the Ten Commandments] were broken, and the Daily Whole-offering ceased, and the City was breached, and Apostomus burnt the [Scrolls of the] Law, and an idol was set up in the Sanctuary. On the 9th of Ab it was decreed against our fathers that they should not enter into the Land [of Israel], and the Temple was destroyed the first and the second time, and Beth-Tor was captured and the City was ploughed up. When Ab comes in, gladness must be diminished.

[7]In the week wherein falls the 9th of Ab it is forbidden to cut the hair or wash the clothes; but it is permitted on the Thursday because of the honor due to the Sabbath. On the eve of the 9th of Ab let none eat of two cooked dishes, let none eat flesh and let none drink wine. Rabban Simeon b. Gamaliel says: A man need but make some difference. R. Judah says: A man must turn up his couch (i.e., sleep on the ground). But the Sages did not agree with him.

The Fall of Masada in A.D. 73

The remnants of the insurgents found themselves in Herod's fortress by the Dead Sea, Masada. There was no possibility of victory, so they chose death rather than surrender. (#51) Eleazer's speech, in the end, convinced them and 960 men, women, and children died in the execution-suicide compact. (#52) The awful deed was done and only seven (two women and five children) escaped to describe it to the Romans when they entered the citadel. Thus ended the Jewish War. The total number who died, if Josephus's calculations are used, amounted to 1,337,490.

#51: Eleazer's Final Speech
(Josephus, *Jewish War* 7.8.6 §§323–36)

6. [323]"Since we, long ago, my generous friends, resolved never to be servants to the Romans, nor to any other than to God himself, who alone is the true and just Lord of mankind, the time is now come that obliges us to make that resolution true in practice. [324]And let us not at this time bring a reproach upon ourselves for self-contradiction, while we formerly would not undergo slavery, though it were then without danger, but must now, together with slavery, choose such punishments also as are intolerable; I mean this, upon the supposition that the Romans once reduce us under their power while we are alive. We were the very first that revolted from them, and we are the last that fight against them; [325]and I cannot but esteem it as a favor that God has granted us, that it is still in our power to die bravely, and in a state of freedom, which has not been the case with others who were conquered unexpectedly. [326]It is very plain that we shall be taken within a day's time; but it is still an eligible thing to die after a glorious manner, together with our dearest friends. This is what our enemies themselves cannot by any means hinder, although they be very desirous to take us alive. Nor can we propose to ourselves any more to fight them and beat them. [327]It had been proper indeed for us to have conjectured at the purpose of God much sooner, and at the very first, when we were so desirous of defending our liberty, and when we received such sore treatment from one another, and worse treatment from our enemies, and to have been sensible that the same God, who had of old taken the Jewish nation into his favor, had now condemned them to destruction; [328]for had he either continued favorable, or been but in a lesser degree displeased with us, he had not overlooked the destruction of so many men, or delivered his most holy city to

The fortress of Masada where the Jews held out to the very end of the great war of 66–73.

be burnt and demolished by our enemies. [329]To be sure, we weakly hoped to have preserved ourselves, and ourselves alone, still in a state of freedom, as we had been guilty of no sins ourselves against God, nor been partners with those of others; we also taught other men to preserve their liberty. [330]Wherefore, consider how God has convinced us that our hopes were in vain, by bringing such distress upon us in the desperate state we are now in, and which is beyond all our expectations; [331]for the nature of this fortress, which was in itself unconquerable, has not proved a means of our deliverance; and even while we have still great abundance of food, and a great quantity of arms and other necessities more than we want, we are openly deprived by God himself of all hope of deliverance; [332]for that fire which was driven upon our enemies did not, of its own accord, turn back upon the wall which we had built: this was the effect of God's anger against us for our manifold sins, which we have been guilty of in a most insolent and extravagant manner with regard to our own countrymen; [333]the punishments of which let us not receive from the Romans, but from God himself, as executed by our own hands, for these will be more moderate than the other. [334]Let our wives die before they are abused, and our children before they have tasted of slavery; and after we have slain them, let us bestow that glorious benefit upon one another mutually, and preserve ourselves in freedom, as an excellent funeral monument for us. [335]But first let us destroy our money and the fortress by fire; for I am well assured that this will be a great grief to the Romans, that they shall not be able to seize upon our bodies, and shall fail of our wealth also: and let us spare nothing but our provisions; [336]for they will be a testimonial when we are dead that we were not subdued for want of necessities; but that, according to our original resolution, we have preferred death before slavery."

#52: The Tragic End of Masada's Defenders

(Josephus, *Jewish War* 7.9.1–2
§§394–400, 402–6)

1. [394]Everyone of them dispatched his dearest relatives. . . . So they not being able to bear the grief they were under for what they had done, any longer, and esteeming it an injury to those they had slain, to live even the shortest space of time after them—they presently laid all they had in a heap, and set fire to it. [395]They then chose ten men by lot out of them, to slay all the rest; every one of whom laid himself down by his wife and children on the ground, and threw his arms about them, and they offered their necks to the stroke of those who by lot executed that melancholy office; [396]and when these ten had, without fear, slain them all, they made the same rule for casting lots for themselves, that he whose lot it was should first kill the other nine, and after all should kill himself. Accordingly, all those had courage sufficient to be no way behind one another, in doing or suffering; [397]so, for a conclusion, the nine offered their necks to the executioner, and he who was the last of all, took a view of all the other bodies, lest perchance some or other among so many that were slain should want his assistance to be quite dispatched; and when he perceived that they were all slain, he set fire to the palace, and with the great force of his hand ran his sword entirely through himself, and fell down dead near to his own relations. [398]So these people died with this intention, that they would not have so much as one soul among them all alive to be subject to the Romans. [399]Yet was there an ancient woman, and another who was of kin to Eleazar, and superior to most women in prudence and learning, with five children, who had concealed themselves in caverns under ground, and had carried water thither for their drink, and were hidden there when the rest were intent upon the slaughter of one another. [400]These others were nine hundred and sixty in number, the women and children being withal included in that computation. . . .

2. [402]Now for the Romans, they expected that they should be fought in the morning, when accordingly they put on their armor, and laid bridges of planks upon their ladders from their banks, to make an assault upon the fortress, which they did; [403]but saw nobody as an enemy, but a terrible solitude on every side, with a fire within the place, as well as a perfect silence. So they were at a

loss to guess at what had happened. At length they made a shout, as if it had been at a blow given by a battering-ram, to try whether they could bring any one out that was within; [404]the women heard this noise and came out of their underground cavern, and informed the Romans what had been done, as it was done; and the second of them clearly described all both what was said and what was done, and the manner of it; [405]yet did they not easily give their attention to such a desperate undertaking, and did not believe it could be as they said; they also attempted to put the fire out, and quickly cutting themselves a way through it, they came within the palace, [406]and so met with the multitude of the slain, but could take no pleasure in the fact, though it were done to their enemies. Nor could they do other than wonder at the courage of their resolution, and at the immovable contempt of death which so great a number of them had shown, when they went through with such an action as that was.

3 Groups of People

The New Testament mentions various groups of people, among the better known being the Pharisees and the Sadducees, but we do not have enough contemporary material to define exactly who all these people were. The Jerusalem Talmud (*Sanhedrin* 10.6.29c), for example, says there were twenty-four sects at the time of the destruction of the temple (A.D. 70), but we do not know even the names of most of them. However, we do possess some very informative material that gives us a good idea of at least who some of these people were and how they were perceived by others.

For a more extensive study of the groups mentioned here, you could consult the following works: Marcel Simon, *Jewish Sects at the Time of Jesus;* Günter Stermberger, *Jewish Contemporaries of Jesus;* Louis Finkelstein, *The Pharisees* (2 vols.); Martin Hengel, *The Zealots;* R. Travers Herford, *The Pharisees;* James C. Vanderkam, *The Dead Sea Scrolls Today;* D. S. Russell, *The Method and Message of Jewish Apocalyptic;* Lawrence H. Schiffman, *Reclaiming the Dead Sea Scrolls;* John Macdonald, *The Theology of the Samaritans;* Richard A. Horsley, *Bandits, Prophets, and Messiahs;* Leonard Swidler, *Biblical Affirmations of Woman;* Florentino García Martínez, *The Dead Sea Scrolls Translated;* Frederick J. Murphy, *The Religious World of Jesus.*

Jewish Religious Groups

The Pharisees

(##53, 54) The Pharisees were a relatively small but highly significant group of strict, religious Jews. Their name probably derives from an Aramaic word meaning "separated" and they regarded themselves as separated from the common people and non-Pharisaic Jews. The exact origin of the group is obscure, but it probably arose alongside the Maccabean rebellion in the second century B.C. The Pharisees accepted oral tradition as equally authoritative with the Old Testament Scriptures and placed a heavy emphasis on legal and ritual purity. After the destruction of Jerusalem in A.D. 70, they played the leading role in reconstituting Judaism at Jamnia in A.D. 90 and after, thus transforming Second Temple Judaism into rabbinic Judaism.

#53: A General View of the Pharisees
(Josephus, *Ant.* 18.1.2–3 §§11–15)

2. [11]The Jews had for a great while three sects of philosophy peculiar to themselves; the sect of the Essenes, and the sect of the Sadducees, and the third sort of opinions was that of those called Pharisees. . . .

3. [12]Now, for the Pharisees, they live simply, and despise delicacies in diet; and they follow the conduct of reason; and what that prescribes to them as good for them, they do; and they think they ought earnestly to strive to observe reason's dictates for practice. They also pay a respect to such as are in years; nor are they so bold as to contradict them in anything which they have introduced; [13]and, when they determine that all things are done by fate, they do not take away the freedom from men of acting as they think fit; since their notion is, that it hath pleased God to make a temperament, whereby what he wills is done, but so that the will of men can act virtuously or viciously. [14]They also believe that souls have an immortal vigor in them, and that under the earth there will be rewards or punishments, according as they have lived virtuously or viciously in this life; and the latter are to be detained in an everlasting prison, but that the former shall have power to revive and live again; [15]on account of which

doctrines, they are able greatly to persuade the body of the people; and whatsoever they do about divine worship, prayers, and sacrifices, they perform them according to their direction; insomuch that the cities gave great attestations to them on account of their entire virtuous conduct, both in the actions of their lives and their discourses also.

#54: Pharisaic Skill in the Law

(Josephus, *Jewish War* 2.8.14 §§162–63, 166)

14. [162]The Pharisees are those who are esteemed most skillful in the exact explication of their laws. . . . These ascribe all to fate [or providence], and to God, [163]and yet allow, that to act what is right, or the contrary, is principally in the power of men, although fate does co-operate in every action. They say that all souls are incorruptible; but that the souls of good men are only removed into other bodies [i.e., are resurrected],—but that the souls of bad men are subject to eternal punishment. . . . [166]Moreover, the Pharisees are friendly to one another, and are for the exercise of concord and regard for the public.

(#55) During Jesus' day the two leading schools of Pharisaic thought were those of Shammai and Hillel. This reading from the Mishnah illustrates some of the differences of the two schools, as well as what was important enough for them to disagree on.

#55: The Schools of Shammai and Hillel

(Mishnah, Tractate *Berakoth* 8.1–8)

[1]These are the things wherein the School of Shammai and the School of Hillel differ in what concerns a meal. The School of Shammai say: [On a Sabbath or a Festival-day] they say the Benediction first over the day and then over the wine. And the School of Hillel say: They say the Benediction first over the wine and then over the day.

[2]The School of Shammai say: They wash the hands and then mix the cup. And the School of Hillel say: They mix the cup and then wash the hands.

[3]The School of Shammai say: A man wipes his hands with a napkin and lays it on the table. And the School of Hillel say: [He lays it] on the cushion.

[4]The School of Shammai say: They sweep up the room and then wash the hands. And the School of Hillel say: They wash the hands and then sweep up the room.

[5]The School of Shammai say: [The order of saying the Benedictions at the outgoing of the Sabbath is] the lamp, the food, the spices and the *Habdalah* [i.e., the ceremony that marks the end of a Sabbath or Festival-day). And the School of Hillel say: The lamp, the spices, the food and the *Habdalah*. The School of Shammai say: [The Benediction over the lamp is, "Blessed art thou] who didst create the light of fire." And the School of Hillel say: ". . . who createst the lights of fire."

[6]No Benediction may be said over the lamp or the spices of gentiles, or over a lamp or spices used for the dead, or over a lamp or spices used for idolatry. No Benediction may be said over a lamp until one can enjoy its light.

[7]If a man ate and forgot to say the Benediction, the School of Shammai say: He must return to his place and say it. And the School of Hillel say: He may say it in the place where he remembers [his error]. Until what time may he say the Benediction? Until the food in his bowels is digested.

[8]If wine is brought after the food and there is but that one cup, the School of Shammai say: The Benediction is said over the wine and then over the food. And the School of Hillel say: The Benediction is said over the food and then over the wine. They may answer "Amen" after an Israelite who says a Benediction, but not after a Samaritan until they have heard the whole Benediction.

The Sadducees

Scholars today are uncertain about both the origin and the very name of "Sadducee." Some suggest that it derives from "Zadok," the high priest during Solomon's reign (1 Kgs 2:35), others that it comes from the Greek title *syndikoi* ("fiscal officials"), yet others, from an unattested Hebrew word *saddûq* ("just"). Most agree that they were a priestly aristocracy, focused upon the temple. Herod the Great distrusted them, but between A.D. 6 and 66 they fared well under Roman rule, becoming a major power in the Sanhedrin. After the destruction of the temple in A.D. 70 they faded into oblivion. (##56–59) Josephus and the Mishnah provide us with some descriptive material.

#56: A General View of the Sadducees
(Josephus, *Ant.* 18.1.4 §§16–17)

4. [16] But the doctrine of the Sadducees is this: That souls die with the bodies; nor do they regard the observation of anything besides what the law enjoins them; for they think it an instance of virtue to dispute with those teachers of philosophy whom they frequent; [17]but this doctrine is received but by a few, yet by those still of the greatest dignity; but they are able to do almost nothing of themselves; for when they become magistrates, as they are unwillingly and by force sometimes obliged to be, they addict themselves to the notions of the Pharisees, because the multitude would not otherwise bear them.

#57: Sadducean Emphasis on Free Will
(Josephus, *Jewish War* 2.8.14 §§164–66)

[164]The Sadducees deny . . . fate entirely, and suppose that God is not concerned in our doing or not doing what is evil; [165]and they say, that to act what is good, or what is evil, is at men's own choice, and that the one or the other belongs so to every one, that they may act as they please. They also take away the belief of the immortal duration of the soul, and the punishments and rewards in Hades. . . .

[166]But the behavior of the Sadducees one towards another is in some degrees wild; and their conversation with those that are of their own party is as barbarous as if they were strangers to them.

#58: Sadducees and Pharisees on Clean Hands
(Mishnah, Tractate *Yadaim* 4.6)

[6]The Sadducees say, We cry out against you, O ye Pharisees, for ye say, "The Holy Scriptures render the hands unclean," [and] "The

writings of Hamiram (Homer? Heretics?) do not render the hands unclean." Rabban Johanan b. Zakkai said, Have we naught against the Pharisees save this!—for lo, they say, "The bones of an ass are clean, and the bones of Johanan the High Priest are unclean." They said to him, As is our love for them so is their uncleanness—that no man make spoons of the bones of his father or mother. He said to them, Even so the Holy Scriptures: as is our love for them so is their uncleanness; [whereas] the writings of Hamiram which are held in no account do not render the hands unclean.

#59: Sadducees and Pharisees on Clean Water and Guilt
(Mishnah, Tractate *Yadaim* 4.7)

[7]The Sadducees say, We cry out against you, O ye Pharisees, for ye declare clean an unbroken stream of liquid. The Pharisees say, We cry out against you, O ye Sadducees, for ye declare clean a channel of water that flows from a burial ground. The Sadducees say, We cry out against you, O ye Pharisees, for ye say, "If my ox or my ass have done an injury they are culpable, but if my bondman or my bondwoman have done an injury they are not culpable"—if, in the case of my ox or my ass (about which no commandments are laid upon me) I am responsible for the injury that they do, how much more in the case of my bondman or my bondwoman (about whom certain commandments are laid upon me) must I be responsible for the injury that they do! They said to them, No!—as ye argue concerning my ox or my ass (which have no understanding) would ye likewise argue concerning my bondman or my bondwoman which have understanding?—for if I provoke him to anger he may go and set fire to another's stack of corn, and it is I that must make restitution!

The Essenes

The Essenes were a strict, ascetic sect of pious Jews that arose sometime after the Maccabean rebellion. Philo speculated that the name derived from the Greek word *hosios* ("holy"), but modern scholars suggest an Aramaic origin meaning either "healer" or "the pious." They were to be

The Scriptorium of the Qumran community near the Dead Sea where many of the scrolls were probably written.

found in cities as well as at the famous Qumran community by the Dead Sea, near where the Dead Sea Scrolls were found. The Essenes attracted the attention of even Roman writers and were respected for their consistent, rigorous approach to life. They fit within pre-A.D. 70 Judaism as an apocalyptic, ascetic sect; their relation to the early church is still much debated by scholars. The readings that follow are taken from Pliny the Elder (#60) and Josephus (#61). Philo also has a lengthy description of them (*Hypothetica,* 11:1–18).

#60: Pliny the Elder on the Essenes
(Pliny, *Natural History* 5.15 §73)

On the west side of the Dead Sea, but out of range of the noxious exhalations of the coast, is the solitary tribe of the Essenes, which is remarkable beyond all the other tribes in the whole world, as it has no women and has renounced all sexual desire, has no money, and has only palm-trees for company. Day by day the throng of refugees is recruited to an equal number by numerous accessions of

persons tired of life and driven thither by the waves of fortune to adopt their manners. Thus through thousands of ages (incredible to relate) a race in which no one is born lives on for ever: so prolific for their advantage is other men's weariness of life!

#61: A General Description of the Essenes
(Josephus, *Jewish War* 2.8.2–13 §§119–47, 150–61)

2. [119]The Essenes are Jews by birth, and seem to have a greater affection for one another than the other sects have. [120]These Essenes reject pleasures as an evil, but esteem continence, and the conquest over our passions, to be virtue. They neglect wedlock, but choose out other persons' children, while they are pliable, and fit for learning; and esteem them to be of their kindred, and form them according to their own manners. [121]They do not absolutely deny the fitness of marriage, and the succession of mankind thereby con-

tinued; but they guard against the lascivious behavior of women, and are persuaded that none of them preserve their fidelity to one man.

3. [122]These men are despisers of riches, and so very generous as raises our admiration. Nor is there any one to be found among them who has more than another; for it is a law among them, that those who come to them must let what they have be common to the whole order,—insomuch, that among them all there is no appearance of poverty or excess of riches, but everyone's possessions are intermingled with every other's possessions; and so there is, as it were, one patrimony among all the brethren. [123]They think that oil is a defilement; and if one of them be anointed without his own approbation, it is wiped off his body; for they think to be sweaty is a good thing, as they do also to be clothed in white garments. They also have stewards appointed to take care of their common affairs, who every one of them have no separate business for any, but what is for the use of them all.

4. [124]They have no particular city, but many of them dwell in every city; and if any of their sect come from other places, what they have lies open for them, just as if it were their own; and they go into such as they never knew before, as if they had been ever so long acquainted with them. [125]For which reason they carry nothing with them when they travel into remote parts, though still they take their weapons with them, for fear of thieves. Accordingly there is, in every city where they live, one appointed particularly to take care of strangers, and provide garments and other necessities for them. [126]But the habit and management of their bodies are such as children use who are in fear of their masters. Nor do they allow of the change of garments, or of shoes, till they be first entirely torn to pieces, or worn out by time. [127]Nor do they either buy or sell anything to one another; but every one of them gives what he has to him that needs it, and receives from him again in lieu of it what may be convenient for himself; and although there be no requital made, they are fully allowed to take what they need of whomsoever they please.

5. [128]And as for their piety towards God, it is very extraordinary; for before sunrise they speak not a word about profane matters, but put up certain prayers which they have received from their forefathers, as if they made a supplication for the sun's rising. [129]After this every one of them is sent away by their directors, to exercise some of those arts wherein they are skilled, in which they labor with great diligence till the fifth hour. After which they assemble themselves together again into one place; and when they have clothed themselves in white veils, they then bathe their bodies in cold water. And after this purification is over, they every one meet together in an apartment of their own, into which it is not permitted to any of another sect to enter; [130]while they go, after a pure manner, into the dining-room, as into a certain holy temple, and quietly set themselves down; upon which the baker lays them loaves in order; the cook also brings a single plate of one sort of food, and sets it before every one of them; [131]but a priest says grace before meat; and it is unlawful for any one to taste of the food before grace be said. The same priest when he has dined, says grace again after meat; and when they begin, and when they end, they praise God, as he that bestows their food upon them; after which they lay aside their [white] garments, and betake themselves to their labors again till the evening; [132]then they return home to supper, after the same manner; and if there be any strangers there, they sit down with them. Nor is there ever any clamor or disturbance to pollute their house, but they give every one leave to speak in their turn; [133]which silence thus kept in their house appears to foreigners like some tremendous mystery; the cause of which is that perpetual sobriety they exercise, and some settled measure of meat and drink that is allotted to them, and that such as is abundantly sufficient for them.

6. [134]And truly, as for other things, they do nothing but according to the injunctions of their leaders; only these two things are done among them at every one's own free will, which are, to assist those that want it, and to show mercy; for they are permitted to their own accord to afford succor to such as deserve it, when they stand in need of it, and to

bestow food on those that are in distress; but they cannot give anything to their kindred without the leader's consent. [135]They dispense their anger after a just manner, and restrain their passion. They are eminent for fidelity, and are the ministers of peace; whatsoever they say also is firmer than an oath; but swearing is avoided by them, and they esteem it worse than perjury; for they say, that he who cannot be believed without [swearing by] God, is already condemned. [136]They also take great pains in studying the writings of the ancients, and choose out of them what is most for the advantage of their soul and body; and they inquire after such roots and medicinal powders as may cure their illnesses.

7. [137]But now, if any one has a mind to come over to their sect, he is not immediately admitted, but he is prescribed the same method of living which they use, for a year, while he continues excluded; and they give him a small hatchet, and the forementioned girdle, and the white garment. [138]And when he has given evidence, during that time, that he can observe their continence, he approaches nearer to their way of living, and is made a partaker of the waters of purification; yet is he not even now admitted to live with them; for after this demonstration of his fortitude, his temper is tried two more years, and if he appear to be worthy, they then admit him into their society. [139]And before he is allowed to touch their common food, he is obliged to take tremendous oaths; that, in the first place, he will exercise piety towards God; and then, that he will observe justice towards all men; and that he will do no harm to any one, either of his own accord, or by the command of others; that he will always hate the wicked, and be assistant to the righteous; [140]that he will ever show fidelity to all men, and especially to those in authority, he will at no time whatever abuse his authority, nor endeavor to outshine his subjects, either in his garments, or any other finery; [141]that he will be perpetually a lover of truth, and propose to himself to reprove those that tell lies; that he will keep his hands clear from theft, and his soul from unlawful gains; and that he will neither conceal anything from those of his own sect, nor discover any of their doctrines to others, no,

not though any one should compel him so to do at the hazard of his life. [142]Moreover, he swears to communicate their doctrines to no one any otherwise than as he received them himself; that he will abstain from robbery, and will equally preserve the books belonging to their sect, and the names of the angels [or messengers]. These are the oaths by which they secure their proselytes to themselves.

8. [143]But for those that are caught in any heinous sins, they cast them out of their society; and he who is thus separated from them, does often die after a miserable manner; for as he is bound by the oath he has taken, and by the customs he has been engaged in, he is not at liberty to partake of that food that he meets with elsewhere, but is forced to eat grass, and to famish his body with hunger till he perish; [144]for which reason they receive many of them again when they are at their last gasp, out of compassion to them, as thinking the miseries they have endured till they come to the very brink of death to be a sufficient punishment for the sins they had been guilty of.

9. [145]But in the judgments they exercise they are most accurate and just; nor do they pass sentence by the votes of a court that is fewer than a hundred. And as to what is once determined by that number, it is unalterable. What they most of all honor, after God himself, is the name of their legislator [Moses]; whom, if any one blaspheme, he is punished capitally. [146]They also think it a good thing to obey their elders, and the major opinion. Accordingly, if ten of them be sitting together, no one of them will speak while the other nine are against it. [147]They also avoid spitting in the midst of them, or on the right side. Moreover, they are stricter than any other of the Jews in resting from their labors on the seventh day; for they not only get their food ready the day before, that they may not be obliged to kindle a fire on that day, but they will not remove any vessel out of its place, nor go to stool thereon. . . .

10. [150]Now after the time of their preparatory trial is over, they are parted into four classes; and so far are the juniors inferior to the seniors, that if the seniors should be touched by the juniors, they must wash themselves, as if they had intermixed themselves with the company of a foreigner. [151]They are long-lived

also; insomuch that many of them live above a hundred years, by means of the simplicity of their diet; nay, as I think, by means of the regular course of life they observe also. They treat with contempt the miseries of life, and are above pain, by the generosity of their mind. And as for death, if it will be for their glory, they esteem it better than living always; [152]and indeed our war with the Romans gave abundant evidences what great souls they had in their trials, wherein, although they were tortured and distorted, burnt and torn to pieces, and went through all kinds of instruments of torment, that they might be forced either to blaspheme their legislator or to eat what was forbidden them, yet could they not be made to do either of them, no, nor once to flatter their tormentors, nor to shed a tear; [153]but they smiled in their very pains, and laughed those to scorn who inflicted the torments upon them, and resigned up their souls with great alacrity, as expecting to receive them again.

11. [154]For their doctrine is this:—"That bodies are corruptible, and that the matter they are made of is not permanent; but that the souls are immortal, and continue for ever; and that they come out of the most subtle air, and are united to their bodies as in prisons, into which they are drawn by a certain natural enticement; [155]but that when they are set free from the bonds of the flesh, they then, as released from a long bondage, rejoice and mount upward. And this is like the opinion of the Greeks, that good souls have their habitations beyond the ocean, in a region that is neither oppressed with storms of rain or snow, nor with intense heat, but that this place is such as is refreshed by the gentle breathing of a west wind, that is perpetually blowing from the ocean; while they allot to bad souls a dark and tempestuous den, full of never-ceasing punishments. [156]And indeed the Greeks seem to me to have followed the same notion, when they allot the islands of the blessed to their brave men, whom they call heroes and demigods; and to the souls of the wicked, the region of the ungodly, in Hades, where their fables relate that certain persons, such as Sisyphus, and Tantalus, and Ixion, and Tityus, are punished; which is built first on this supposition, that souls are immortal;

and thence are those exhortations to virtue, and dehortations from wickedness collected; [157]whereby good men are improved in the conduct of their life, by the hope they have of reward after their death, and whereby the vehement inclinations of bad men to vice are restrained, by the fear and expectation they are in, that although they should lie concealed in this life, they should suffer immortal punishment after death. [158]These are the divine doctrines of the Essenes about the soul, which lay an unavoidable bait for such as have once had a taste for their philosophy.

12. [159]There are also among them those who undertake to foretell things to come, by reading the holy books, and using several sorts of purifications, and being perpetually conversant in the discourses of the prophets; and it is but seldom that they miss in their predictions.

13. [160]Moreover, there is another order of Essenes, who agree with the rest as to their way of living, and customs, and laws, but differ from them in the point of marriage, as thinking that by not marrying they cut off the principal part of human life, which is the prospect of succession; nay rather, that if all men should be of the same opinion, the whole race of mankind would fail. [161]However, they try their spouses for three years; and if they find that they have their natural purgations thrice, as trials that they are likely to be fruitful, they then actually marry them. But they refrain from contact with their wives when they are with child, as a demonstration that they do not marry out of regard to pleasure, but for the sake of posterity. Now the women go into the baths with some of their garments on, as the men do with somewhat girded about them. And these are the customs of this order of Essenes.

The Zealots

(#62) During New Testament times there existed a group of determined, radical Pharisees who were committed to struggle against the Romans. (#63) Josephus traces this movement to Judas the Galilean, mentioned also by Luke in Acts 5:37, beginning around A.D. 6, although the roots of it lie earlier. It continued until the destruction of the nation in A.D. 66–73, and they were leading players in that catastrophe. (#64) The exact relationship between the various factions, which probably includes the Sicarii, is debated by scholars, but they all fall broadly within the category of those committed to armed struggle to achieve their religious (and sometimes, personal) goals. One of Jesus' twelve apostles, Simon, was a former Zealot (Mt 10:4).

#62: The Zealots
(Josephus, *Ant.* 18.1.6 §§23–25)

6. [23]But of the fourth sect of Jewish philosophy, Judas the Galilean was the author. These men agree in all other things with the Pharisaic notions; but they have an inviolable attachment to liberty; and they say that God is to be their only Ruler and Lord. They are not afraid of dying any kind of death, nor indeed do they heed the deaths of their relations and friends, nor can any such fear make them call any man Lord; [24]and since this immovable resolution of theirs is well known to a great many, I shall speak no further about that matter; nor am I afraid that anything I have said of them should be disbelieved, but rather fear, that what I have said is beneath the resolution they show when they undergo pain; [25]and it was in Gessius Florus's time that the nation began to grow mad with this distemper, who was our procurator, and who occasioned the Jews to go wild with it by the abuse of his authority, and to make them revolt from the Romans.

#63: The History of the Zealot Movement
(Josephus, *Ant.* 18.1.1 §§4–9)

[4]There was one Judas, a Gaulonite, of a city whose name was Gamala, who taking with him Sadduc, a Pharisee, became zealous to draw them to a revolt, who said that this taxation was no better than an introduction to slavery, and exhorted the nation to assert their liberty; [5]as if they could procure them happiness and security for what they possessed, and an assured enjoyment of a still greater good, which was that of the honor and glory they would thereby acquire for magnanimity. They also said that God would not otherwise be assisting to them, than upon their joining with one another in such counsels as might be successful, and for their own advantage; and this especially, if they would set about great ex-

ploits, and not grow weary in executing the same; [6]so men received what they said with pleasure, and this bold attempt proceeded to a great height. All sorts of misfortunes also sprang from these men, and the nation was infected with this doctrine to an incredible degree; [7]one violent war came upon us after another, and we lost our friends, who used to alleviate our pain; there were also very great robberies and murders of our principal men. This was done in pretense indeed for the public welfare, but in reality for the hopes of gain to themselves; [8]whence arose seditions, and from them murders of men, which sometimes fell on those of their own people (by the madness of these men towards one another, while their desire was that none of the adverse party might be left), and sometimes on their enemies; a famine also coming upon us, reduced us to the last degree of despair, as did also the taking and demolishing of cities; nay, the sedition at last increased so high, that the very temple of God was burnt down by their enemy's fire. [9]Such were the consequences of this, that the customs of our fathers were altered, and such a change was made, as added a mighty weight toward bringing all to destruction, which these men occasioned by thus conspiring together; for Judas and Sadduc, who excited a fourth philosophic sect among us, and had a great many followers therein, filled our civil government with tumults at present, and laid the foundation of our future miseries.

#64: Josephus's Account of the Sicarii
(Josephus, *Jewish War* 20.8.10 §§185–88)

10. [185]Upon Festus's coming into Judea, it happened that Judea was afflicted by the robbers, while all the villages were set on fire, and plundered by them. [186]And then it was that the *sicarii*, as they were called, who were robbers, grew numerous. They made use of small swords, not much different in length from the Persian *acinacae*, but somewhat crooked, and like the Roman *sicae* [or sickles], as they were called; and from these weapons these robbers got their name; and with these weapons they slew a great many; [187]for they mingled themselves among the multitude at their festivals, when they were come up in crowds from all

parts to the city to worship God, as we said before, and easily slew those that they had a mind to slay. They also came frequently upon the villages belonging to their enemies, with their weapons, and plundered them, and set them on fire. [188]So Festus sent forces, both horsemen and footmen, to fall upon those that had been seduced by a certain impostor, who promised them deliverance and freedom from the miseries they were under, if they would but follow him as far as the wilderness. Accordingly those forces that were sent destroyed both him that had deluded them and those that were his followers also.

Other Groups

The *Am-Ha-Aretz*

The *Am-ha-aretz* ("people of the land") were the common people, who were members of no religious party, but simply lived their lives under God as best they could. Their views were closest to those of the Pharisees, but they were disdained by them as being ignorant of the law and ritually unclean. Jesus' ministry was primarily to these people (Mk 6:34) and the "common people heard him gladly" (Mk 12:37). These readings (##65–69) from the Mishnah, although some is later than the New Testament, probably reflect the attitude of many Pharisees to the common people.

#65: The *Am-ha-Aretz* Cannot Be Righteous
(Mishnah, Tractate *Aboth* 2.6)

[6]He used to say: A brutish man dreads not sin, and an ignorant man [*Am-ha-aretz*] cannot be saintly, and the shamefast man cannot learn, and the impatient man cannot teach, and he that engages overmuch in trade cannot become wise; and where there are no men strive to be a man.

#66: The Sinfulness of the *Am-ha-Aretz*
(Mishnah, Tractate *Shebiith* 5.9)

[9]A woman may lend a sifter, sieve, handmill or oven to her neighbor that is suspected of transgressing the Seventh Year law, but she may not winnow or grind corn with her. The wife of an Associate may lend a sifter or sieve to the wife of an *Am-haaretz* and may winnow, grind or sift corn with her; but when she pours water over the flour she may not draw near to her, since help may not be given to them that commit transgression.

#67: Even the Clothes of the *Am-ha-Aretz* Pollute
(Mishnah, Tractate *Hagigah* 2.7)

[7]For Pharisees the clothes of an *Am-haaretz* count as suffering *midras*-uncleanness.

#68: Pharisaic Fear of the *Am-ha-Aretz*'s Uncleanness
(Mishnah, Tractate *Eduyoth* 1.14)

[14]An earthenware vessel can protect aught [that is within it from contracting uncleanness from a corpse that is under the same roof]. So the School of Hillel. And the School of Shammai say: It can protect only foodstuffs and liquids and [other] earthenware vessels. The School of Hillel said: Why? The school of Shammai said: Because with an *Am-haaretz* it is susceptible to uncleanness, and a vessel that is susceptible to uncleanness cannot interpose [to protect from uncleanness]. The School of Hillel answered: But have ye not pronounced the foodstuffs and liquids therein clean? The School of Shammai said to them: When we pronounced the foodstuffs and liquids therein clean, we pronounced them clean for himself [alone]; but when thou declarest the vessel clean thou declarest it so for thyself as well as for him. The School of Hillel changed their opinion and taught according to the opinion of the School of Shammai.

#69: Various Judgments from Mishnah Tohoroth about the Uncleanness of the *Am-ha-Aretz*
(Mishnah, Tractate *Tohoroth* 7.1–2, 4–5; 8.1–3)

[7.1]If a seller of pots set down his pots [in the public domain] and went down to drink, the innermost pots remain clean but the outer ones become unclean. R. Jose said: This applies only if they were not tied together; but if they were tied together, all remain clean. If a man gave his key into the keeping of an *Amhaaretz*, his house still remains clean, since he only gave him the charge of guarding the key.

²If a man left an *Am-haaretz* within his house awake and found him awake, or asleep and found him asleep, or awake and found him asleep, the house remains clean; but if he left him asleep and found him awake, the house is unclean. So R. Meir. But the Sages say: Only that part is unclean which he could touch by stretching out his hand. . . .

⁴If the wife of an Associate left the wife of an *Am-haaretz* grinding flour within her house and she ceased from the grinding, the house becomes unclean; if she did not cease from the grinding, only that part of the house is unclean which she could touch by stretching out her hand. If there were two of them the house becomes unclean in either case, since the one can go about and touch while the other grinds. So R. Meir. But the Sages say: Only that part of the house becomes unclean which they could touch by stretching out their hands.

⁵If a man left an *Am-haaretz* within his house to guard it, such time as he can see them that go in and out, [only] footstuffs and liquids and open earthenware vessels become unclean, but couches and seats and earthenware vessels having a tightly stopped-up cover remain clean; if he could not see them that go in and out, even though the *Am-haaretz* could not move himself or was tied up, all becomes unclean.

8.1 If a man dwelt in the same courtyard with an *Am-haaretz*, and he forgot vessels and left them in the courtyard, even if they were jars having a tightly stopped-up cover, or an oven having a tightly stopped-up cover, they become unclean. . . .

²If a man deposited vessels with an *Amhaaretz*, they become unclean with corpse-uncleanness and *midras*-uncleanness. If the *Am-haaretz* knew him to be one that ate of Heave-offering [i.e., a priest], they do not become unclean with corpse-uncleanness, but they still become unclean with *midras*-uncleanness. . . .

³If a man lost aught and found it the same day, it remains clean. If he lost it during the day and found it during the night, or lost it during the night and found it the next day, or lost it on one day and found it on the next, it becomes unclean. This is the general rule: If a night or part of a night has passed over it, it becomes unclean. If a man spread out garments to dry in the public domain, they remain clean; but if in a private domain they become unclean; though if he guarded them they remain clean. If they fell down and he went to fetch them in, they become unclean. If his bucket fell into the cistern of an *Amhaaretz*, and he went to fetch something to draw it up, it becomes unclean, since it was left for a time in the domain of an *Am-haaretz*.

The Samaritans

The people who lived in the region of Samaria just north of Judea became a very mixed population after their resettlement following deportation in 722 B.C.; (#70) 2 Kings describes their resettlement and false worship. (#71) After Judah's return from Babylon in 539 B.C., following the destruction of Jerusalem in 586 B.C., the Jews of Judea forbade their involvement in the rebuilding of the temple. The early bad feelings described by Ezra persisted until the destruction of Jerusalem in A.D. 70. This is reflected in John's Gospel when he says "The Jews do not associate with Samaritans" (Jn 4:9). (#72) Josephus gives a general description of the Samaritans, followed by two incidents that illustrate how deeply these bad feelings went. (#73) The first incident took place in A.D. 6. (#74) The second occurred around A.D. 51, when virtual civil war broke out and is illustrative of how desperate and brutal the times were. (#75) Sirach gives a typical Jewish evaluation of the Samaritans and a series of readings from the Mishnah amplifies Jewish sentiments. (##76–79) In actual fact, the Samaritans believed much in common with the Jews. (#80) The Samaritans, on their part, rewrote the Ten Commandments in their version of the Pentateuch in order to add a new tenth commandment that justified their existence.

#70: The Apostasy of the Samaritans
(2 Kings 17:24–34)

²⁴The king of Assyria brought people from Babylon, Cuthah, Avva, Hamath and Sephar-

vaim and settled them in the towns of Samaria to replace the Israelites. They took over Samaria and lived in its towns. [25]When they first lived there, they did not worship the LORD; so he sent lions among them and they killed some of the people. [26]It was reported to the king of Assyria: "The people you deported and resettled in the towns of Samaria do not know what the god of that country requires. He has sent lions among them, which are killing them off, because the people do not know what he requires."

[27]Then the king of Assyria gave this order: "Have one of the priests you took captive from Samaria go back to live there and teach the people what the god of the land requires." [28]So one of the priests who had been exiled from Samaria came to live in Bethel and taught them how to worship the LORD.

[29]Nevertheless, each national group made its own gods in the several towns where they settled, and set them up in the shrines the people of Samaria had made at the high places. [30]The men from Babylon made Succoth Benoth, the men from Cuthah made Nergal, and the men from Hamath made Ashima; [31]the Avvites made Nibhaz and Tartak, and the Sepharvites burned their children in the fire as sacrifices to Adrammelech and Anammelech, the gods of Sepharvaim. [32]They worshiped the LORD, but they also appointed all sorts of their own people to officiate for them as priests in the shrines at the high places. [33]They worshiped the LORD, but they also served their own gods in accordance with the customs of the nations from which they had been brought.

[34]To this day they persist in their former practices. They neither worship the LORD nor adhere to the decrees and ordinances, the laws and commands that the LORD gave the descendants of Jacob, whom he named Israel.

#71: The Enemies' [Samaritans'] Offer of Help Refused
(Ezra 4:1–5)

[1]When the enemies of Judah and Benjamin heard that the exiles were building a temple for the LORD, the God of Israel, [2]they came to Zerubbabel and to the heads of the families and said, "Let us help you build because, like you, we seek your God and have been sacrificing to him since the time of Esarhaddon king of Assyria, who brought us here."

[3]But Zerubbabel, Jeshua and the rest of the heads of the families of Israel answered, "You have no part with us in building a temple to our God. We alone will build it for the LORD, the God of Israel, as King Cyrus, the king of Persia, commanded us."

[4]Then the peoples around them set out to discourage the people of Judah and make them afraid to go on building. [5]They hired counselors to work against them and frustrate their plans during the entire reign of Cyrus king of Persia and down to the reign of Darius king of Persia.

#72: Josephus's Description of the Samaritans
(Josephus, *Ant.* 9.14.3 §§288–91)

3. [288]But now the Cutheans, who removed into Samaria (for that is the name they have been called by to this time, because they were brought out of the country called Cuthah, which is a country of Persia, and there is a river of the same name in it), each of them, according to their nations, which were in number five, brought their own gods into Samaria, and by worshiping them, as was the custom of their own countries, they provoked Almighty God to be angry and displeased at them, [289]for a plague seized upon them, by which they were destroyed; and when they found no cure for their miseries, they learned by the oracle that they ought to worship Almighty God, as the method for their deliverance. So they sent ambassadors to the king of Assyria, and desired him to send them some of those priests of the Israelites whom he had taken captive. [290]And when he thereupon sent them, and the people were by them taught the laws, and the holy worship of God, they worshiped him in a respectful manner, and the plague ceased immediately; and indeed they continue to make use of the very same customs to this very time, and are called in the Hebrew tongue *Cutheans*; but in the Greek *Samaritans*. [291]And when they see the Jews in prosperity, they pretend that they are

changed, and allied to them, and call them kinsmen, as though they were derived from Joseph, and had by that means an original alliance with them: but when they see them falling into a low condition, they say they are no way related to them, and that the Jews have no right to expect any kindness or marks of kindred from them, but they declare that they are sojourners that come from other countries.

#73: The Sacrilege of the Samaritans
(Josephus, *Ant.* 18.2.2 §§29–30)

[29]As Coponius, who we told you was sent along with Cyrenius, was exercising his office of procurator, and governing Judea, the following accidents happened. As the Jews were celebrating the feast of unleavened bread, which we call the Passover, it was customary for the priests to open the temple-gates just after midnight. [30]When, therefore, those gates were first opened, some of the Samaritans came privately into Jerusalem, and threw about dead men's bodies in the cloisters; on which account the Jews afterwards excluded them out of the temple, which they had not used to do at such festivals; and on other accounts also they watched the temple more carefully than they had formerly done.

#74: The Bitter Hostility between Jews and Samaritans
(Josephus, *Ant.* 20.6.1–3 §§118–22, 124–27, 129–32, 134–36)

1. [118]Now there arose a quarrel between the Samaritans and the Jews on the occasion following:—It was the custom of the Galileans, when they came to the holy city at the festivals, to take their journeys through the country of the Samaritans; and at this time there lay, in the road they took, a village that was called Ginea, which was situated in the limits of Samaria and the great plain, where certain persons thereto belonging, fought with the Galileans, and killed a great many of them; [119]but, when the leaders of the Galileans were informed of what had been done, they came to Cumanus, and desired him to avenge the murder of those that were killed; but he was induced by the Samaritans, with money, to do nothing in the matter; [120]upon which the Galileans were much displeased, and persuaded the multitude of the Jews to betake themselves to arms, and to regain their liberty, saying, that slavery was in itself a bitter thing, but that, when it was joined with direct injuries, it was perfectly intolerable. [121]And when their principal men endeavored to pacify them, and promised to endeavor to persuade Cumanus to avenge those that were killed, they would not hearken to them, but took their weapons, and entreated the assistance of Eleazar, the son of Dineus, a robber, who had many years made his abode in the mountains, with which assistance they plundered many villages of the Samaritans. [122]When Cumanus heard of this action of theirs, he took the band of Sebaste, with four regiments of footmen, and armed the Samaritans, and marched out against the Jews, and caught them, and slew many of them, and took a great number of them alive. . . .

[124]So the people dispersed themselves, and the robbers went away again to their places of strength; and after this time all Judea was overrun with robberies.

2. [125]But the leader of the Samaritans went to Ummidius Quadratus, the governor of Syria, who at that time was at Tyre, and accused the Jews of setting their villages on fire, and plundering them; and said withal, that they were not so much displeased at what they had suffered, as they were at the contempt thereby shown to the Romans; [126]while, if they had received any injury, they ought to have made them the judges of what had been done, and not presently to make such devastations as if they had not the Romans for their governors; [127]on which account they came to him in order to obtain that vengeance they wanted. This was the accusation which the Samaritans brought against the Jews. But the Jews affirmed that the Samaritans were the authors of this tumult and fighting, and that, in the first place, Cumanus had been corrupted by their gifts, and passed over the murder of those that were slain in silence. . . .

[129]Yet was it not long before Quadratus came to Samaria; where, upon hearing the cause, he supposed that the Samaritans were the authors of that disturbance. But when he was informed that certain of the Jews were making political

changes, he ordered those to be crucified whom Cumanus had taken captive. [130]From whence he came to a certain village called Lydda . . . and there heard the Samaritan cause a second time before his tribunal, and there learned from a certain Samaritan, that one of the chief of the Jews, whose name was Dortus, and some other agitators with him, four in number, persuaded the multitude to a revolt from the Romans; [131]whom Quadratus ordered to be put to death: but still he sent away Ananias the high priest, and Ananus the commander of [the temple], in bonds to Rome, to give an account of what they had done to Claudius Caesar. [132]He also ordered the leading men, both of the Samaritans and Jews, as also Cumanus the procurator, and Celer the tribune, to go to Italy to the emperor, that he might hear their cause, and determine their differences one with another. . . .

3. [134]Now Cumanus and the principal of the Samaritans, who were sent to Rome, had a day appointed them by the emperor, whereupon they were to have pleaded their cause about the quarrels they had one with another. [135]But now Caesar's freed-men and his friends were very zealous on the behalf of Cumanus and the Samaritans; and they would have prevailed over the Jews, except that Agrippa, junior, who was then at Rome, had seen the leader of the Jews in deep trouble, and had earnestly entreated Agrippina, the emperor's wife, to persuade her husband to hear the cause, so as was agreeable to his justice, and to condemn those to be punished who were really the authors of this revolt from the Roman government:— [136]whereupon Claudius was so well disposed beforehand, that when he had heard the cause, and found that the Samaritans had been the ringleaders in those mischievous doings, he gave order that those who came up to him should be slain, and that Cumanus should be banished. He also gave order that Celer the tribune should be carried back to Jerusalem, and should be drawn through the city in the sight of all the people, and then should be slain.

#75: God's Displeasure with Samaria
(Sirach 50.25–26)

[25]With two nations my soul is vexed,
and the third is no nation:

[26]Those who live on Mount Seir,
and the Philistines,
and the foolish people that dwell in Shechem.

#76: Jewish Contempt for the Samaritans
(Mishnah, Tractate *Shebiith* 8.10)

[10]Moreover they declared before him that R. Eliezer used to say: He that eats the bread of the Samaritans is like to one that eats the flesh of swine.

#77: Samaritan Money Refused
(Mishnah, Tractate *Shekalim* 1.5)

[5]Although they have said, "They do not exact pledges from women, slaves, or minors," if they have paid the Shekel it is accepted of them; but if a gentile or a Samaritan paid the Shekel it is not accepted of them.

#78: The Word of a Samaritan Is Virtually Worthless
(Mishnah, Tractate *Gittin* 1.5)

[5]No writ is valid which has a Samaritan as witness excepting a writ of divorce or a writ of emancipation.

#79: Don't Trust a Samaritan's Benediction until You've Heard It All
(Mishnah, Tractate *Berakoth* 8.8)

[8]If wine is brought after the food and there is but that one cup, the School of Shammai say: The Benediction is said over the wine and then over the food. And the School of Hillel say: The Benediction is said over the food and then over the wine. They may answer "Amen" after an Israelite who says a Benediction, but not after a Samaritan until they have heard the whole Benediction.

#80: The New Samaritan Tenth Commandment

"And it shall come to pass when the Lord thy God will bring thee into the land of the Canaanites whither thou goest to take possession of it, thou shalt erect unto thee large stones, and thou shalt cover them with lime, and thou shalt write upon the stones all the words of this Law, and it shall come to pass when ye cross the Jordan, ye shall erect these stones which I command thee upon Mount Garizim, and thou shalt build there an altar unto the Lord thy God, an altar of stones, and thou shalt not lift up upon them iron; of perfect stones shalt thou build thine altar, and thou shalt bring up upon it burnt offerings to the Lord thy God, and thou shalt sacrifice peace offerings, and thou shalt eat there and rejoice before the Lord thy God. That mountain is on the other side of the Jordan and at the end of the road towards the going down of the sun in the land of the Canaanites who dwell in the Arabah facing Gilgal close by Elon Moreh facing Sichem."

The Gentiles

By the time of Jesus the attitude of the average Jew toward the Gentiles was almost exclusively negative. This was brought about by centuries of wars with them, persecution, invasion, and occupation by foreign armies. The general hostility of the Gentiles toward the Jews aroused a corresponding antipathy that fueled the bad feelings. And the more the Jews emphasized their own election the deeper the hatred of the Gentiles toward them. The Old Testament reflects some of this, but another side as well. God chose Abraham so that all the nations would be blessed through him (Gn 18:18; 22:18). God guides the nations of the earth (Ps 67:3, 4), he accepts their worship (Ps 86:9), and all the nations are God's inheritance (Ps 82:8). God's Servant will be a light to the Gentiles (Is 42:6) and the Gentiles will be included in eschatological salvation (Is 25:6–8; Jer 16:19; Mi 4:1–3). However, in New Testament times, as this collection of readings shows (##81–93), the attitude of the Jews was overwhelmingly negative. This makes all the more remarkable Paul's deep commitment to the Gentiles (Rom 11:13) and his assertion that neither circumcision nor uncircumcision counts for anything (Gal 5:6) but all are one in Christ (Gal 3:28).

#81: Gentiles Are "Children of Destruction"
(Jubilees 15.26)

[26]And every one that is born, the flesh of whose foreskin is not circumcised on the eighth day, belongs not to the children of the covenant which the Lord made with Abraham, but to the children of destruction; nor is there, moreover, any sign on him that he is the Lord's, but (he is destined) to be destroyed and slain from the earth, and to be rooted out of the earth, for he has broken the covenant of the Lord our God.

#82: Marrying a Gentile Is a Capital Offense
(Jubilees 30.7)

[7]And if there is any man who wishes in Israel to give his daughter or his sister to any man who is of the seed of the Gentiles he shall surely die, and they shall stone him with stones; for he hath wrought shame in Israel; and they shall burn the woman with fire, because she has dishonored the name of the house of her father, and she shall be rooted out of Israel.

#83: Killing Gentiles Counts for Righteousness
(Jubilees 30.14–17)

[14]And Israel will not be free from this uncleanness if it has a wife of the daughters of the Gentiles, or has given any of its daughters to a man who is of any of the Gentiles. [15]For there will be plague upon plague, and curse upon curse, and every judgment and plague and curse will come (upon him): if he do this thing, or hide his eyes from those who commit uncleanness, or those who defile the sanctuary of the Lord, or those who profane His holy name, (then) will the whole nation together be judged for all the uncleanness and profanation of this man. [16]And there will be no respect of persons [and no consideration of persons], and no receiving at his hands of fruits and offerings and burnt-offerings and fat, nor the fragrance of sweet savor, so as to accept it: and so fare every man or woman in Israel who defiles the sanctuary. [17]For this reason I have commanded thee, saying: "Testify this testimony to Israel: see how the Shechemites fared and their sons: how they were delivered into the hands of two sons of Jacob, and they slew them under tortures, and it was (reckoned) unto them for righteousness, and it is written down to them for righteousness."

#84: Do Not Sell to the Gentiles
(Damascus Document 12.6–11)

[6]He is not to stretch out his hand to shed the blood of one of the gentiles [7]for the sake of riches and gain. *Blank*. Neither should he take any of his riches, so that they do not [8]blaspheme, except on the advice of the company of Israel. *Blank*. No one should sell an animal, [9]or a clean bird, to the gentiles lest they sacrifice them. *Blank*. [10]And he should not sell them anything from his granary or his press, at any price. And his servant and his maidservant: he should not sell them, [11]for they entered the covenant of Abraham with him.

#85: Gentiles Have No Share in the World to Come
(Mishnah, Tractate *Sanhedrin* 10.1)

[1]All Israelites have a share in the world to come, for it is written, *Thy people also shall be all righteous, they shall inherit the land for ever; the branch of my planting, the work of my hands that I may be glorified*. And these are they that have no share in the world to come: he that says that there is no resurrection of the dead prescribed in the Law, and [he that says] that the Law is not from Heaven, and an Epicurean [i.e., a Gentile or a Jew who opposes Pharisaic teaching].

#86: Gentiles or Women Pollute Everything
(Mishnah, Tractate *Tohoroth* 7.6)

[6]If thieves entered a house, only that part is unclean that was trodden by the feet of the thieves. What do they render unclean? Foodstuffs and liquids and open earthenware vessels; but couches and seats and earthenware vessels having a tightly stopped-up cover remain clean. If a gentile or a woman was with them all becomes unclean.

#87: Utensils Bought from Gentiles Are Unclean
(Mishnah, Tractate *Abodah Zarah* 5.12)

[12]If a man bought utensils from a gentile, those which it is the custom to immerse he must immerse, those which it is the custom to scald he must scald; those which it is the custom to make white-hot in the fire he must make white-hot in the fire. A spit or gridiron must be made white-hot in the fire; but a knife needs but to be polished and it is then clean.

#88: Gentiles Are Lewd, Depraved Idolators
(Mishnah, Tractate *Abodah Zarah* 2.1)

[1]Cattle may not be left in the inns of the gentiles since they are suspected of bestiality; nor may a woman remain alone with them since they are suspected of lewdness; nor may a man remain alone with them since they are suspected of shedding blood. The daughter of an Israelite may not assist a gentile woman in childbirth since she would be assisting to bring to birth a child for idolatry, but a gentile woman may assist the daughter of an Israelite. The daughter of an Israelite may not suckle the child of a gentile woman, but a gentile woman may suckle the child of the daughter of an Israelite in this one's domain.

#89: In Israel No One May Sell or Rent Land to a Gentile
(Mishnah, Tractate *Abodah Zarah* 1.8)

[8]None may make ornaments for an idol: necklaces or ear-rings or finger-rings. R. Eliezer says: If for payment it is permitted. None may sell them what is attached to the soil but it may be sold after it has been severed. R. Judah says: One may sell it to a gentile on condition that it is severed. None may hire houses to them in the Land of Israel or, needless to say, fields; in Syria houses may be hired to them but not fields; while outside the Land houses may be sold and fields hired to them. So R. Meir. R. Jose says: In the Land of Israel houses may be hired to them but not fields; and in Syria houses may be sold and fields hired to them; while outside the Land either may be sold to them.

#90: No One May Bless a Gentile's Light or Food
(Mishnah, Tractate *Berakoth* 8.6)

[6]No Benediction may be said over the lamp or the spices of gentiles, or over a lamp or spices used for the dead, or over a lamp or

spices used for idolatry. No Benediction may be said over a lamp until one can enjoy its light.

#91: What Gentiles Slaughter Is Considered Carrion
(Mishnah, Tractate *Hullin* 1.1)

[1]All may slaughter and what they slaughter is valid, save only a deaf-mute, an imbecile, and a minor, lest they impair what they slaughter; but if any among these slaughtered while others beheld them, what they slaughter is valid. What is slaughtered by a gentile is deemed carrion, and it conveys uncleanness by carrying.

#92: Imbeciles, Gentiles, and Samaritans Are in the Same Category
(Mishnah, Tractate *Tohoroth* 5.8)

[8]If there was in the town a woman that was an imbecile or a woman that was a gentile or a Samaritan, all spittle found in the town is unclean. If a woman pressed against a man's garments or sat with him in a boat, if she perceived that he was one that ate Heave-offering his garments remain clean; if not, he must inquire of her.

#93: All Gentiles Are Consciously or Unconsciously Idolators
(Mishnah, Tractate *Hullin* 2.7)

[7]If a man slaughtered for a gentile, what he slaughters is valid, but R. Eliezer declares it invalid. R. Eliezer said: Even if he slaughtered it [with the intention] that the gentile should eat but the midriff, it is invalid, since an unexpressed intention in a gentile is directed to idolatry.

Tax Collectors

Jesus shocked the legalists of his day by eating and drinking with tax collectors (Lk 5:29, 30), befriending them (Mt 11:19), calling Matthew (a tax collector) to become a disciple (Lk 5:27, 28), and saying that they (and prostitutes) would enter the kingdom of God sooner than the merely "righteous" (Mt 21:31, 32). Jesus' attitude contrasts sharply with that of other Jews, who bitterly resented the tax collectors. (##94, 95) They

were classed with murderers and robbers and could be lied to with impunity, and (#96) money could not be taken from them, even for charity. (#97) When a tax collector enters a house, all that was within it becomes unclean.

#94: Tax Collectors May Be Lied to with Impunity
(Mishnah, Tractate *Nedarim* 3.4)

[4]Men may vow to murderers, robbers, or tax-gatherers that what they have is Heave-offering even though it is not Heave-offering; or that they belong to the king's household even though they do not belong to the king's household. The School of Shammai say: They may so vow in any form of words save in the form of an oath. And the School of Hillel say: Even in the form of an oath.

#95: Tax Collectors Are on a Par with Robbers
(Mishnah, Tractate *Baba Kamma* 10.2)

[2]If tax-gatherers took a man's ass and gave him another, or if robbers robbed a man of his coat and gave him another, they become his own, since the owner cherishes no hope of recovering them.

#96: Not Even Alms-Money Is Allowed from Tax Collectors
(Mishnah, Tractate *Baba Kamma* 10.1)

[1]None may take change for money from the counter of excisemen or from the wallet of tax-gatherers, or take any alms from them; but it may be taken from them at their own house or in the market.

#97: Tax Collectors, Thieves, Gentiles, and Women Convey Uncleanness
(Mishnah, Tractate *Tohoroth* 7.6)

[6]If tax gatherers entered a house [all that is within it] becomes unclean; even if a gentile was with them they may be believed if they say ("We did not enter"; but they may not be believed if they say) "We entered but we touched naught." If thieves entered a house, only that part is unclean that was trodden by the feet of the thieves. What do they render unclean? Foodstuffs and liquids and

open earthenware vessels; but couches and seats and earthenware vessels having a tightly stopped-up cover remain clean. If a gentile or a woman was with them all becomes unclean.

Women

The place women were allowed to play in the ministry of Jesus (Lk 8:1–3) and in the early church, where Paul speaks of Euodia and Syntyche as those "who have contended at my side in the cause of the gospel" and calls them "fellow workers" (Col 4:3) contrasts rather sharply with the place women played in Judaism at that time. (#98) In the Old Testament, women such as Deborah (Jgs 4:4–10) and Esther played significant roles in Israel's history, and the righteous woman is highly praised, (#99) a sentiment that could also be echoed in later times but a more negative note usually predominates. A series of readings (##100–107) from the pseudepigrapha, Josephus, Philo, and the Mishnah gives a general picture of the situation in New Testament times.

This stylish woman displays only one aspect of human beauty—the Scripture values inner beauty even more.

#98: The Wife of Noble Character
(Proverbs 31:10–31)

10A wife of noble character who can find?
    She is worth far more than rubies.
11Her husband has full confidence in her
    and lacks nothing of value.
12She brings him good, not harm,
    all the days of her life.
13She selects wool and flax
    and works with eager hands.
14She is like the merchant ships,
    bringing her food from afar.
15She gets up while it is still dark;
    she provides food for her family
    and portions for her servant girls.
16She considers a field and buys it;
    out of her earnings she plants a vineyard.
17She sets about her work vigorously;
    her arms are strong for her tasks.
18She sees that her trading is profitable,
    and her lamp does not go out at night.
19In her hand she holds the distaff
    and grasps the spindle with her fingers.
20She opens her arms to the poor
    and extends her hands to the needy.

21When it snows, she has no fear for her household;
    for all of them are clothed in scarlet.
22She makes coverings for her bed;
    she is clothed in fine linen and purple.
23Her husband is respected at the city gate,
    where he takes his seat among the elders of the land.
24She makes linen garments and sells them,
    and supplies the merchants with sashes.
25She is clothed with strength and dignity;
    she can laugh at the days to come.
26She speaks with wisdom,
    and faithful instruction is on her tongue.
27She watches over the affairs of her household
    and does not eat the bread of idleness.
28Her children arise and call her blessed;
    her husband also, and he praises her:
29"Many women do noble things,
    but you surpass them all."
30Charm is deceptive, and beauty is fleeting;
    but a woman who fears the LORD is to be praised.
31Give her the reward she has earned,

and let her works bring her praise at the
city gate.

#99: A Good Wife Means a Good Life
(Sirach 26.1–4)

[1]A good wife makes a happy husband;
   she doubles the length of his life.
[2]A staunch wife is her husband's joy;
   he will live out his days in peace.
[3]A good wife means a good life;
   she is one of the Lord's gifts to those
   who fear him.
[4]Rich or poor, they are light-hearted,
   and always have a smile on their faces.

#100: Man's Evil Is Better Than Woman's Good
(Sirach 42.9–14)

[9]A daughter is a secret anxiety to her father,
and the worry of her keeps him awake at
   night;
when she is young, for fear she may grow
   too old to marry,
and when she is married, for fear she may
   lose her husband's love;
[10]when she is a virgin, for fear she may be
   seduced
and become pregnant in her father's house,
when she has a husband, for fear she may
   misbehave,
and after marriage, for fear she may be
   barren.
[11]Keep close watch over a headstrong
   daughter,
or she may give your enemies cause to
   gloat,
making you the talk of the town and a by-
   word among the people,
and shaming you in the eyes of the world.
[12]Do not let her display her beauty to any
   man,
or gossip in the women's quarters.
[13]For out of clothes comes the moth,
and out of woman comes woman's
   wickedness.
[14]Better a man's wickedness than a
   woman's goodness;
it is woman who brings shame and
   disgrace.

#101: Women Are Evil
(Testament of Reuben 5.1–6)

[1]"For women are evil, my children, and by reason of their lacking authority or power over man, they scheme treacherously how they might entice him to themselves by means of their looks. [2]And whomever they cannot enchant by their appearance they conquer by a stratagem. [3]Indeed, the angel of the Lord told me and instructed me that women are more easily overcome by the spirit of promiscuity than are men. They contrive in their hearts against men, then by decking themselves out they lead men's minds astray, by a look they implant their poison, and finally in the act itself they take them captive. [4]For a woman is not able to coerce a man overtly, but by a harlot's manner she accomplishes her villainy. [5]Accordingly, my children, flee from sexual promiscuity, and order your wives and your daughters not to adorn their heads and their appearances so as to deceive men's sound minds. For every woman who schemes in these ways is destined for eternal punishment.

#102: Woman's Word Cannot Be Trusted
(Josephus, *Ant.* 4.8.15 §219)

[219]But let not a single witness be credited; but three, or two at the least, and those such whose testimony is confirmed by their good lives. But let not the testimony of women be admitted, on account of the levity and boldness of their sex.

#103: Women Are Irrational
(Philo, *Questions and Answers on Genesis* 4.15)

15. (Gen. xviii. 11) What is the meaning of the words, "There ceased to be to Sarah the ways of women"? The literal meaning is clear. For (Scripture) by a euphemism calls the monthly purification of women "the ways of women." But as for the deeper meaning, it is to be allegorized as follows. The soul has, as it were, a dwelling, partly men's quarters, partly women's quarters. Now for the men there is a place where properly dwell the mas-

culine thoughts (that are) wise, sound, just, prudent, pious, filled with freedom and boldness, and kin to wisdom. And the women's quarters are a place where womanly opinions go about and dwell, being followers of the female sex. And the female sex is irrational and akin to bestial passions, fear, sorrow, pleasure and desire, from which ensue incurable weaknesses and indescribable diseases. He who is conquered by these is unhappy, while he who controls them is happy. And longing for and desiring this happiness, and seizing a certain time to be able to escape from terrible and unbearable sorrow, which is (what is meant by) "there ceased to be the ways of women"—this clearly belongs to minds full of Law, which resemble the male sex and overcome passions and rise above all sense-pleasure and desire and are without sorrow and fear and, if one must speak the truth, without passion, not zealously practicing apathy, for this would be ungrateful and shameless and akin to arrogance and reckless boldness, but that which is consistent with the argument given, (namely) cutting the mind off from disturbing and confusing passions.

#104: Women's Evil Curiosity Renders Unclean
(Mishnah, Tractate *Tohoroth* 7.9)

[9]If a woman went in to bring out bread to a poor man and she came out and found him standing besides loaves of Heave-offering (so, too, if a woman went out and found her neighbor raking out coals under a cooking-pot in which was Heave-offering), R. Akiba declares it unclean, but the Sages declare it clean. R. Eleazar b. Pila said: But why did R. Akiba declare it unclean and the Sages clean?—because women are gluttonous; for a woman is suspected of uncovering her neighbor's cooking-pot to know what she is cooking.

#105: Women Wear Out the World
(Mishnah, Tractate *Sotah* 3.4)

[4]Hence Ben Azzai says: A man ought to give his daughter a knowledge of the Law so that if she must drink [the bitter water] she may know that the merit [that she had acquired] will hold her punishment in suspense. R. Eliezer says: If any man gives his daughter a knowledge of the Law it is as though he taught her lechery. R. Joshua says: A woman has more pleasure in one *kab* [a unit of measure] with lechery than in nine *kabs* with modesty. He used to say: A foolish saint and a cunning knave and a woman that is a hypocrite and the wounds of the Pharisees, these wear out the world.

#106: Women Bring Evil and Damnation
(Mishnah, Tractate *Aboth* 1.5)

[5]Jose b. Johanan of Jerusalem said: Let thy house be opened wide and let the needy be members of thy household; and talk not much with womankind. They said this of a man's own wife: how much more of his fellow's wife! Hence the Sages have said: He that talks much with womankind brings evil upon himself and neglects the study of the Law and at the last will inherit Gehenna.

#107: Women, Slaves, and Minors Do Not Count as Persons
(Mishnah, Tractate *Berakoth* 7.2)

[2]Women or slaves or minors may not be included [to make up the number needed] for the Common Grace. How much [should one eat] to be included [to make up the number needed] for the Common Grace? An olive's bulk. R. Judah says: An egg's bulk.

4 The Religious Life of the Jews

The Jewish people of the intertestamental period and the time of Jesus and the early church were respected and admired by the world at large, yet also despised and hated at one and the same time, and often for the same reasons. They were a people hard for the average Gentile to understand. Their sense of national and social identity was, in reality, a religious phenomenon. This was true whether they were scattered abroad (the so-called diaspora) or whether they were in their own land of Palestine. They were convinced that God had chosen them and given them a special revelation of himself and that they were all one people and would ultimately survive.

The Jewish sense of unity and destiny (providence, if you will) was expressed in their common beliefs, where a good bit of variation existed, but primarily in their common way of life. This way of life was expressed in their religious institutions, some of which stand out as of utmost significance, epitomizing their very essence.

In this section we will look at some of those institutions that profoundly bound the Jews together, in spite of the many differences that also existed among them. There will, of necessity, be an overlapping of these religious institutions with their theological beliefs, but it was thought best to separate the two for purposes of study. The theological beliefs will be looked at in the next section.

Extensive bibliography exists for those interested in further study of section 4, "The Religious Life of the Jews," and section 5, "Key Religious Ideas in Judaism." Many of the books mentioned earlier also treat these issues, but the following would be particularly helpful: J. Bonsirven, *Palestinian Judaism in the Time of Jesus Christ*; George Foot Moore, *Judaism* (3 vols.); George W. E. Nickelsburg and Michael E. Stone (eds.), *Faith and Piety in Early Judaism: Texts and Documents*; E. P. Sanders, *Judaism: Practice and Belief, 63 B.C.E.–66 C.E.*; C. G. Montefiore, *Greeks, Romans, Jews*; E. P. Sanders, *Jewish Law from Jesus to the Mishnah*; J. Julius Scott, *Customs and Controversies*; Jacob Neusner, *The Mishnah: A New Translation*; Jacob Neusner, *Introduction to Rabbinic Literature*; Jacob Neusner, *Judaism: The Evidence of the Mishnah*; Michael E. Stone (ed.), *Jewish Writings of the Second Temple Period*; James H. Charlesworth (ed.), *The Old Testament Pseudepigrapha* (2 vols.); John J. Collins, *The Scepter and the Star*; James H. Charlesworth (ed.), *The Messiah*.

A Pagan Look at Jewish Religion

(#108) In order to appreciate the distinctiveness of Jewish thought and life in the ancient world, it is helpful to look at a thoughtful pagan's description of them. It embodies that combination of fascination, respect, and disgust that so characterized the average Gentile.

#108: Tacitus's Description of Jewish Religion
(Tacitus, *Histories* 5.4–5)

[4]Moyses, wishing to secure for the future his authority over the nation, gave them a novel form of worship, opposed to all that is practiced by other men. Things sacred with us, with them have no sanctity, while they allow what with us is forbidden. In their holy place they have consecrated an image of the animal by whose guidance they found deliverance from their long and thirsty wanderings. They slay the ram, seemingly in derision of Hammon, and they sacrifice the ox,

because the Egyptians worship it as Apis. They abstain from swine's flesh, in consideration of what they suffered when they were infected by the leprosy to which this animal is liable. By their frequent fasts they still bear witness to the long hunger of former days, and the Jewish bread, made without leaven, is retained as a memorial of their hurried seizure of corn. We are told that the rest of the seventh day was adopted, because this day brought with it a termination of their toils; after a while the charm of indolence beguiled them into giving up the seventh year also to inaction. But others say that it is an observance in honor of Saturn, either from the primitive elements of their faith having been transmitted from the Idaei, who are said to have shared the flight of that god, and to have founded the race, or from the circumstance that of the seven stars which rule the destinies of men Saturn moves in the highest orbit and with the mightiest power, and that many of the heavenly bodies complete their revolutions and courses in multiples of seven.

[5]This worship, however introduced, is upheld by its antiquity; all their other customs, which are at once perverse and disgusting, owe their strength to their very badness. The most degraded out of other races, scorning their national beliefs, brought to them their contributions and presents. This augmented the wealth of the Jews, as also did the fact, that among themselves they are inflexibly honest and ever ready to show compassion, though they regard the rest of mankind with all the hatred of enemies. They sit apart at meals, they sleep apart, and though, as a nation, they are singularly prone to lust, they abstain from intercourse with foreign women; among themselves nothing is unlawful. Circumcision was adopted by them as a mark of difference from other men. Those who come over to their religion adopt the practice, and have this lesson first instilled into them, to despise all gods, to disown their country, and set at naught parents, children, and brethren. Still they provide for the increase of their numbers. It is a crime among them to kill any newly-born infant. They hold that the souls of all who perish in battle or by the hands of the executioner are immortal. Hence a passion for propagating their race and a contempt for death. They are wont to bury rather than to burn their dead, following in this the Egyptian custom; they bestow the same care on the dead, and they hold the same belief about the lower world. Quite different is their faith about things divine. The Egyptians worship many animals and images of monstrous form; the Jews have purely mental conceptions of Deity, as one in essence. They call those profane who make representations of God in human shape out of perishable materials. They believe that Being to be supreme and eternal, neither capable of representation, nor of decay. They therefore do not allow any images to stand in their cities, much less in their temples. This flattery is not paid to their kings, nor this honor to our Emperors. From the fact, however, that their priests used to chant to the music of flutes and cymbals, and to wear garlands of ivy, and that a golden vine was found in the temple, some have thought that they worshiped Father Liber, the conqueror of the East, though their institutions do not by any means harmonize with the theory; for Liber established a festive and cheerful worship, while the Jewish religion is tasteless and mean.

The Unifying Confession and Prayer of the Jews

1. The *Shema* (#109). The Shema, consisting of three passages from the Torah (Dt 6:4–9; 11:13–21; Nm 15:37–41), was a prayer-like confession of faith that was to be uttered twice a day, morning and evening, by all male Israelites. It is so important that the Mishnah allows it to be uttered in any language, not just Hebrew (M Sot 7:1). (##110–112) The Mishnah also contains other regulations regarding the recitation of the Shema, some going back to the schools of Hillel and Shammai. (#113) Josephus mentions the recitation of the Shema in his discussion of the distinctives of Jews and (#114) the respect Gamaliel, the apostle Paul's teacher, had for the Shema was remembered.

#109: The Shema^c: Israel's Confession of Faith
(Deuteronomy 6:4–9)

⁴Hear, O Israel: The LORD our God, the LORD is one. ⁵Love the LORD your God with all your heart and with all your soul and with all your strength. ⁶These commandments that I give you today are to be upon your hearts. ⁷Impress them on your children. Talk about them when you sit at home and when you walk along the road, when you lie down and when you get up. ⁸Tie them as symbols on your hands and bind them on your foreheads. ⁹Write them on the doorframes of your houses and on your gates.

(Deuteronomy 11:13–21)

¹³So if you faithfully obey the commands I am giving you today—to love the LORD your God and to serve him with all your heart and with all your soul—¹⁴then I will send rain on your land in its season, both autumn and spring rains, so that you may gather in your grain, new wine and oil. ¹⁵I will provide grass in the fields for your cattle, and you will eat and be satisfied.

¹⁶Be careful, or you will be enticed to turn away and worship other gods and bow down to them. ¹⁷Then the LORD's anger will burn against you, and he will shut the heavens so that it will not rain and the ground will yield no produce, and you will soon perish from the good land the LORD is giving you. ¹⁸Fix these words of mine in your hearts and minds; tie them as symbols on your hands and bind them on your foreheads. ¹⁹Teach them to your children, talking about them when you sit at home and when you walk along the road, when you lie down and when you get up. ²⁰Write them on the doorframes of your houses and on your gates, ²¹so that your days and the days of your children may be many in the land that the LORD swore to give your forefathers, as many as the days that the heavens are above the earth.

(Numbers 15:37–41)

³⁷The LORD said to Moses, ³⁸"Speak to the Israelites and say to them: 'Throughout the generations to come you are to make tassels on the corners of your garments, with a blue cord on each tassel. ³⁹You will have these tassels to look at and so you will remember all the commands of the LORD, that you may obey them and not prostitute yourselves by going after the lusts of your own hearts and eyes. ⁴⁰Then you will remember to obey all my commands and will be consecrated to your God. ⁴¹I am the LORD your God, who brought you out of Egypt to be your God. I am the LORD your God.'"

#110: The Evening Recitation of the Shema^c
(Mishnah, Tractate *Berakoth* 1.1)

¹From what time in the evening may the *Shema*^c be recited? From the time when the priests enter [the Temple] to eat of their Heave-offering until the end of the first watch. So R. Eliezer. But the Sages say: Until midnight. Rabban Gamaliel says: Until the rise of dawn. His sons once returned [after midnight] from a wedding feast. They said to him, "We have not recited the *Shema*^c." He said to them, "If the dawn has not risen ye are [still] bound to recite it. Moreover, wheresoever the Sages prescribe 'Until midnight' the duty of fulfillment lasts until the rise of dawn." The duty of burning the fat pieces and the members [of the animal offerings] lasts until the rise of dawn; and for all [offerings] that must be consumed "the same day," the duty lasts until the rise of dawn. Why then have the Sages said: Until midnight? To keep a man far from transgression.

#111: The Morning Recitation of the Shema^c
(Mishnah, Tractate *Berakoth* 1.2)

²From what time in the morning may the *Shema*^c be recited? So soon as one can distinguish between blue and white. R. Eliezer says: Between blue and green. And it should be finished before sunrise. R. Joshua says: Before the third hour: for so is it the way of kings, to rise up at the third hour. He that recites it from that time onward suffers no loss and is like to one that reads in the Law.

#112: Posture on Reciting the Shema^c
(Mishnah, Tractate *Berakoth* 1.3)

[3]The School of Shammai say: In the evening all should recline when they recite [the *Shema*^c] but in the morning they should stand up, for it is written, *And when thou liest down and when thou risest up.* But the School of Hillel say: They may recite it every one in his own way, for it is written, *And when thou walkest by the way.* Why then is it written, *And when thou liest down and when thou risest up?* [It means] the time when men usually lie down and the time when men usually rise up. R. Tarfon said: I was once on a journey and I reclined to recite [the *Shema*^c] in accordance with the words of the School of Shammai, and so put myself in jeopardy by reason of robbers. They said to him: Thou hadst deserved aught that befell thee in that thou didst transgress the words of the School of Hillel.

#113: The Exodus and the Shema^c
(Josephus, *Ant.* 4.8.13 §§212–13)

[212]Let every one commemorate before God the benefits which he bestowed upon them at their deliverance out of the land of Egypt, and this twice every day, both when the day begins and when the hour of sleep comes on, gratitude being in its own nature a just thing, and serving not only by way of return for past, but also by way of invitation of future favors. [213]They are also to inscribe the principal blessings they have received from God upon their doors, and show the same remembrance of them upon their arms; as also they are to bear on their forehead and their arm those wonders which declare the power of God, and his good-will towards them, that God's readiness to bless them may appear everywhere conspicuous about them.

#114: Nothing Takes Precedence over the Shema^c
(Mishnah, Tractate *Berakoth* 2.5)

[5]A bridegroom is exempt from reciting the *Shema*^c on the first night, or until the close of the [next] Sabbath if he has not consummated the marriage. Once when Rabban Gamaliel married he recited the *Shema*^c on the first night.

His disciples said to him, "Master, didst thou not teach us that a bridegroom is exempt from reciting the *Shema*^c on the first night?" He said to them, "I will not hearken to you to cast off from myself the yoke of the kingdom of heaven even for a moment."

2. *The Shemoneh ʿEsreh* (#115). The Shemoneh ʿEsreh, or "Eighteen Benedictions," in their present form are later than New Testament times, but much of it goes back to that time. They are so fundamental, as to be called "The Prayer" (Tefillah), and were to be recited by every Israelite, including slaves, women, and children, three times a day (*M. Berakoth* 3:3)—morning, at the time of the afternoon Minḥah offering, and evening. There are two major versions, the Babylonian (which has nineteen Benedictions) and the Palestinian, the one given here. Benediction #12, apparently directed against Christians, arose at Jamnia (A.D. 90) according to tradition (b. Ber 28b).

"Simeon the cotton merchant arranged the eighteen benedictions according to their order in the time of Rabban Gamaliel at Yavneh (Jamnia). Rabban Gamaliel said to the sages: Is there anyone among you who can formulate the *berakhah* against heretics? Samuel the Small then rose and formulated it."

#115: The Eighteen Benedictions

1. Blessed art thou, Lord, God of our fathers, God of Abraham, God of Isaac and God of Jacob, great, mighty and fearful God, most high God who createst heaven and earth, our shield and the shield of our fathers, our trust in every generation. *Blessed art thou, Lord, shield of Abraham.*

2. Thou art mighty, humbling the proud; strong, and judging the violent; thou livest for ever and raisest the dead; thou blowest the wind and bringest down the dew; thou providest for the living and makest the dead alive; in an instant thou causest our salvation to spring forth. *Blessed art thou, Lord, who makest the dead alive.*

3. Thou art holy and thy Name is awesome, and beside thee there is no God. *Blessed art thou Lord, the holy God.*

4. Grant us, our Father, the knowledge (which comes) from thee, and understanding

and discernment (which come) from thy Torah. *Blessed art thou Lord, who grantest knowledge.*

5. Lead us back, Lord, to thee and we shall repent. Renew our days as of old. *Blessed art thou who delightest in repentance.*

6. Forgive us, our Father, for we have sinned against thee. Wipe out and remove our evil deeds from before thine eyes. For thy mercies are many. *Blessed art thou, Lord, rich in forgiveness.*

7. Look on our affliction and plead our cause and redeem us for thy Name's sake. *Blessed art thou, Lord, redeemer of Israel.*

8. Heal us, Lord our God, of the pain of our heart; remove from us sorrow and grief and raise up healing for our wounds. *Blessed art thou who healest the sick of thy people Israel.*

9. Bless this year for us, Lord our God, and cause all its produce to prosper. Bring quickly the year of our final redemption; and give dew and rain to the land; and satisfy the world from the treasuries of thy goodness; and bless the work of our hands. *Blessed art thou, Lord, who blessest the years.*

10. Proclaim our liberation with the great trumpet and raise a banner to gather together our dispersed. *Blessed art thou, Lord, who gatherest the banished of thy people Israel.*

11. Restore our judges as in former times and our counselors as in the beginning, and reign over us, thou alone. *Blessed art thou, Lord, who lovest judgment.*

12. And for apostates let there be no hope; and may the insolent kingdom be quickly uprooted, in our days. And may the Nazarenes and the heretics perish quickly; and may they be erased from the Book of Life; and may they not be inscribed with the righteous. *Blessed art thou, Lord, who humblest the insolent.*

13. May thy mercies be showered over righteous proselytes; and give us a rich reward, together with those who do thy pleasure. *Blessed art thou, Lord, trust of the righteous.*

14. Be merciful, Lord our God, with thy great mercies, to Israel thy people and to Jerusalem thy city; and to Zion, the dwelling-place of the glory; and to thy Temple and thy habitation; and to the kingship of the house of David, thy righteous Messiah. *Blessed art thou, Lord, God of David, who buildest Jerusalem.*

15. Hear, Lord our God, the voice of our prayer, and be merciful to us; for thou art a gracious and merciful God. *Blessed art thou, Lord, who hearest prayer.*

16. Be pleased, Lord our God, and dwell in Zion; and may thy servants serve thee in Jerusalem. *Blessed art thou, Lord, whom we worship in awe.*

17. We praise thee, Lord, our God, and the God of our fathers, on account of all the goodness and grace and mercies which thou hast granted to us, and hast done to us and to our fathers before us. And if we say our feet are slipping, thy grace, O Lord, succours us. *Blessed art thou, Lord, the All-Good, thou art to be praised.*

18. Bring thy peace over Israel, thy people, and over thy city and over thine inheritance; and bless all of us together. *Blessed art thou, Lord who makest peace.*

(#116) The Mishnah directs that the Eighteen Benedictions (and all prayer) must be said with respect, reasonably, and from the heart.

#116: Prayer Must Be from the Heart
(Mishnah, *Berakoth* 4.3–5)

[3]Rabban Gamaliel says: A man should pray the Eighteen [Benedictions] every day. R. Joshua says: The substance of the Eighteen. R. Akiba says: If his prayer is fluent in his mouth he should pray the Eighteen, but if not, the substance of the Eighteen.

[4]R. Eliezer says: He that makes his prayer a fixed task, his prayer is no supplication. R. Joshua says: He that journeys in a place of danger should pray a short prayer, saying, 'Save, O Lord, the remnant of Israel; at their every cross-road let their needs come before thee. Blessed art thou, O Lord, that hearest prayer!'

[5]If he was riding on an ass he should dismount [to say the *Tefillah*]. If he cannot dismount he should turn his face [toward Jerusalem]; and if he cannot turn his face, he should direct his heart toward the Holy of Holies.

The Temple at Jerusalem

The Temple

From the time of Solomon to its destruction in A.D. 70 the temple at Jerusalem served as the center of Jewish religion. All Jews throughout the world were tied directly to it by way of the annual temple-tax that even Jesus respected (Mt 17:24–27). Jesus also predicted its time was coming to an end (Mt 24:1–3) and that in his person One greater than the temple had arrived (Mt 12:5, 6). (#117) In its day the temple was a magnificent structure, as Jesus' awe-struck disciples observed (Mk 13:1). We have already seen Josephus's description of the construction of the temple (#17). Josephus provides another elaborate description of the appearance of the building that so dazzled everyone at that time (##117, 118), from which two extracts are taken, which include the mystical sentiments aroused by a building of such unearthly beauty. An equally elaborate description of the Temple is also provided by the Mishnah (M. Midd 1:1–5:14). (#119) Many contemporaries who saw the temple could talk of little else. But it was singularly a place of solemn worship. (#120) Death awaited the Gentile who transgressed its borders as warning signs judiciously placed indicated. (#121) Death also awaited any ceremonially unclean person who violated it, even if it were a Jewish priest.

#117: The Temple's Splendor
(Josephus, *Jewish War* 5.5.6 §§ 222–23)

6. [222]Now the outward face of the temple in its front wanted nothing that was likely to surprise either men's minds or their eyes: for it was covered all over with plates of gold of great weight, and, at the first rising of the sun, reflected back a very fiery splendor, and made those who forced themselves to look upon it to turn their eyes away, just as they would have done at the sun's own rays. [223]But this temple appeared to strangers, when they were at a distance, like a mountain covered with snow; for, as to those parts of it that were not gilt, they were exceeding white.

#118: The Temple as Symbol of the Universe
(Josephus, *Jewish War* 5.5.4 §§207–14)

4. [207]As to the holy house itself, which was placed in the midst [of the inmost court] that most sacred part of the temple, it was ascended to by twelve steps; and in front its height and its breadth were equal, and each a hundred cubits, though it was behind thirty cubits narrower; for on its front it had what may be styled shoulders on each side, that passed twenty cubits farther. [208]Its first gate was seventy cubits high, and twenty-five cubits broad; but this gate had no doors; for it represented the universal visibility of heaven, and that it cannot be excluded from any place. Its front was covered with gold all over, and through it the first part of the house, that was more inward did all of it appear; which, as it was very large, so did all the parts about the more inward gate appear to shine to those that saw them; [209]but then, as the entire house was divided into two parts within, it was only the first part of it that was open to our view. Its height extended all along to ninety cubits in height, and its length was fifty cubits, and its breadth twenty; [210]but that gate which was at this end of the first part of the house was, as we have already observed, all over covered with gold, as was its whole wall about it; [211]it had also golden vines above it, from which clusters of grapes hung as tall as a man's height; but then this house, as it was divided into two parts, the inner part was lower than the appearance of the outer, and had golden doors of twenty-five cubits altitude, and sixteen in breadth; [212]but before these doors there was a veil of equal largeness with the doors. It was a Babylonian curtain, embroidered with blue and fine linen, and scarlet, and purple, and of a contexture that was truly wonderful. Nor was this mixture of colors without its mystical interpretation, but was a kind of image of the universe; [213]for by the scarlet, there seemed to be enigmatically signified fire, by the fine flax the earth, by the blue the air, and by the purple the sea; two of them having their colors this foundation of this resemblance; but the fine flax

and the purple have their own origin for that foundation, the earth producing the one, and the sea the other. [214]This curtain had also embroidered upon it all that was mystical in the heavens, excepting that of the [twelve] signs, representing living creatures.

#119: The Temple's Glory Described to the Emperor Caligula
(Philo, *On the Embassy to Gaius* 37 §§294–96, 298)

37. [294]"But why need I invoke the assistance of foreign witnesses when I have plenty with whom I can furnish you from among your own countrymen and friends? Marcus Agrippa, your own grandfather on the mother's side, the moment that he arrived in Judea, when Herod, my grandfather, was king of the country, thought fit to go up from the sea-coast to the metropolis, which was inland. [295]And when he had beheld the temple, and the decorations of the priests, and the piety and holiness of the people of the country, he marveled, looking upon the whole matter as one of great solemnity and entitled to great respect, and thinking that he had beheld what was too magnificent to be described. And he could talk of nothing else to his companions but the magnificence of the temple and everything connected with it.

[296]"Therefore, every day that he remained in the city, by reason of his friendship for Herod, he went to that sacred place, being delighted with the spectacle of the building, and of the sacrifices, and all the ceremonies connected with the worship of God, and the regularity which was observed, and the dignity and honor paid to the high priest, and his grandeur when arrayed in his sacred vestments and when about to begin the sacrifices.

[298]"What again did your other grandfather, Tiberius Caesar, do? Does not he appear to have adopted an exactly similar line of conduct? At all events, during the three and twenty years that he was emperor, he preserved the form of worship in the temple as it had been handed down from the earliest times, without abrogating or altering the slightest particular of it.

Gentiles are warned to keep out of the Jewish temple, if they value their lives. (For an English translation of this Greek text, see #120.)

#120: Temple Sign Warning Gentiles Not to Enter on Pain of Death
"Foreigners must not enter inside the balustrade or into the forecourt around the sanctuary. Whoever is caught will have himself to blame for his ensuing death."

#121: Priests Liable to Death by Uncleanness
(Mishnah, Tractate *Sanhedrin* 9.6)

[6]If a man stole a sacred vessel or cursed by Kosem or made an Aramean woman his paramor, the zealots may fall upon him. If a priest served [at the Altar] in a state of uncleanness his brethren the priests did not bring him to the court, but the young men among the priests took him outside the Temple Court and split open his brain with clubs. If one that was not a priest served in the Temple, R. Akiba says: [He must be put to death] by strangling. But the Sages say: [He shall suffer death] at the hands of Heaven.

Temple Ritual

(#122) The glorious description of Simon the high priest ministering in the temple, as provided by Ecclesiasticus, gives us something of the emotional impact of temple worship, as well as a look at the ritual. There was a constant flurry of activity going on in the temple to maintain it as a place of ritual purity and contact with God. (#123) The essence of its worship was the sacrificial system, a general description of which is provided by Josephus. The Mishnah provides an elaborate account of the many details that surrounded the offering of sacrifice, the whole fifth division (Ko-dashim: "Hallowed Things") being devoted to the subject. (#124) Amid all of the regulations governing these complex rituals the Mishnah also reminds us that the sacrifice must be made with forethought, not just as a matter of duty.

#122: Description of Simon the High Priest Ministering in the Temple (2nd century B.C.)

(Sirach 50.11–21)

[11]When he put on his glorious robe
  and clothed himself with superb perfection
and went up to the holy altar,
  he made the court of the sanctuary glorious.
[12]And when he received the portions from the hands of the priests,
  as he stood by the hearth of the altar
with a garland of brethren around him,
  he was like a young cedar on Lebanon;
and they surrounded him like the trunks of palm trees,
[13] all the sons of Aaron in their splendor
with the Lord's offering in their hands,
  before the whole congregation of Israel.
[14]Finishing the service at the altars,
  and arranging the offering to the Most High, the Almighty,
[15]he reached out his hand to the cup
  and poured a libation of the blood of the grape;
he poured it out at the foot of the altar,
  a pleasing odor to the Most High, the King of all.
[16]Then the sons of Aaron shouted,
  they sounded the trumpets of hammered work,
they made a great noise to be heard
  for remembrance before the Most High.
[17]Then all the people together made haste
  and fell to the ground upon their faces
to worship their Lord,
  the Almighty, God Most High.
[18]And the singers praised him with their voices
  in sweet and full-toned melody.
[19]And the people besought the Lord Most High

in prayer before him who is merciful,
  till the order of worship of the Lord was ended;
so they completed his service.
[20]Then Simon came down, and lifted up his hands
  over the whole congregation of the sons of Israel,
to pronounce the blessing of the Lord with his lips,
  and to glory in his name;
[21]and they bowed down in worship a second time,
  to receive the blessing from the Most High.

#123: Josephus's Account of the Offering of Sacrifice

(Josephus, *Ant.* 3.9.1–4 §§224–36)

1. [224]Sacrifices were of two sorts; of those sorts one was offered for private persons, and the other for the people in general; and they are done in two different ways: [225]in the one case, what is slain is burnt, as a whole burnt-offering, whence that name is given to it; but the other is a thank-offering, and is designed for feasting those that sacrifice. [226]I will speak of the former. Suppose a private man offer a burnt-offering, he must slay either a bull, a lamb, or a kid of the goats, and the two latter of the first year, though of bulls he is permitted to sacrifice those of a greater age; but all burnt-offerings are to be of males. When they are slain, the priests sprinkle the blood round about the altar: [227]they then cleanse the bodies, and divide them into parts, and salt them with salt, and lay them upon the altar, while the pieces of wood are piled one upon another, and the fire is burning; they next cleanse the feet of the sacrifices and the entrails in an accurate manner, and so lay them to the rest to be purged by the fire, while the priests receive the hides. This is the way of offering a burnt-offering.

2. [228]But those that offer thank-offerings do indeed sacrifice the same creatures, but such as are unblemished, and above a year old; however, they may take either males or females. They also sprinkle the altar with their blood: but they lay upon the altar the kidneys and the caul, and all the fat, and the lobe of

the liver, together with the rump of the lamb; [229]then, giving the breast and the right shoulder to the priests, the offerers feast upon the remainder of the flesh for two days; and what remains they burn.

3. [230]The sacrifices for sins are offered in the same manner as is the thank-offering. But those who are unable to purchase complete sacrifices, offer two pigeons, or turtle-doves; the one of which is made a burnt-offering to God, the other they give as food to the priests. . . . [231]But if a person fall into sin by ignorance, he offers a ewe lamb, or a female kid of the goats, of the same age; and the priests sprinkle the blood at the altar, not after the former manner, but at the corners of it. They also bring the kidneys and the rest of the fat, together with the lobe of the liver, to the altar, while the priests bear away the hides and the flesh, and dispose of it in the holy place, on the same day; for the law does not permit them to leave any of it until the morning. [232]But if any one sin, and is conscious of it himself, but has nobody that can prove it upon him, he offers a ram, the law enjoining him so to do; the flesh of which the priests eat, as before, in the holy place, on the same day. And if the rulers offer sacrifices for their sins, they bring the same oblations that private men do; only they so far differ, that they are to bring for sacrifices a bull or a kid of the goats, both males.

4. [233]Now the law requires, both in private and public sacrifices, that the finest flour be also brought; for a lamb the measure of one-tenth deal,—for a ram two,—and for a bull three. This they consecrate upon the altar, when it is mingled with oil; [234]for oil is also brought by those that sacrifice; for a bull the half of a hin, and for a ram the third part of the same measure, and one quarter of it for a lamb. . . . They bring the same quantity of oil which they do of wine, and they pour the wine about the altar; [235]but if any one does not offer a complete sacrifice of animals, but brings fine flour only for a vow, he throws a handful upon the altar as its first fruits, while the priests take the rest for their food, either boiled or mingled with oil, but made into cakes of bread. But whatsoever it be that a priest himself offers, it must of necessity be all burnt. [236]Now the law forbids us to sacrifice any animal at

The sacrificial system was in many ways the heart of ancient Israelite worship. Sacrifices were offered on altars such as this.

the same time with its dam: and, in other cases, not till the eighth day after its birth. Other sacrifices there are also appointed for escaping distempers, or for other occasions, in which meal-offerings are consumed, together with the animals that are sacrificed; of which it is not lawful to leave any part till the next day, only the priests are to take their own share.

#124: Sacrifices Must Be Offered with Understanding
(Mishnah, Tractate *Zebahim* 4.6)

[6]An offering must be slaughtered while mindful of six things: of the offerings, of the offerer, of God, of the altar-fires, of the odor, and of the sweet savor; and, if it is a Sin-offering or a Guilt-offering, also of the sin. R. Jose said: Even if a man was not mindful in his heart of one of these things, the offering is valid; for it is a condition enjoined by the court that the intention [which invalidates an offering] is dependent on him alone that performs the act.

The Synagogue

The synagogue played an important place in Judaism, particularly after the destruction of the temple in A.D. 70. But synagogues existed long before that, arising sometime after the destruction of Jerusalem in 586 B.C., as places of prayer, study, worship, and fellowship. (#125) Philo traces their origin to Moses and (#126) in a letter to the emperor Caligula (A.D. 37–41) reminds him of Caesar Augustus's positive attitude toward Jewish worship in the synagogue. (#127) He also provides an illuminating description of the synagogue service, although not all the details are given.

One of the main functions of the synagogue was study of the law, an activity of highest importance in Judaism, as a series of readings from the Mishnah shows (##128–130). Notice the connection among God, the law, ethical living, and eternal life.

Synagogues were very widespread. The Jerusalem Talmud says 480 existed in Jerusalem at the time of its destruction in A.D. 70 (J. T. Megillah 3:1), but very little is known of them archaeologically. (#131) An inscription dedicating a synagogue during Herod's reign (37–4 B.C.), found on Mount Ophel in Jerusalem in 1914, is very illuminating.

Jesus spoke frequently in synagogues (Mt 4:23; Lk 13:10), as did the apostle Paul (Acts 9:20; 13:5; 17:10; 19:8).

#125: Philo Traces the Synagogue System Back to Moses
(Philo, *Hypothetica* 7.12–13)

[12]What then did he (Moses) do on this sabbath day? he commanded all the people to assemble together in the same place, and sitting down with one another, to listen to the laws with order and reverence, in order that no one should be ignorant of anything that is contained in them; [13]and, in fact, they (the Jews) do constantly assemble together, and they do sit down one with another, the multitude in general in silence, except when it is customary to say any words of good omen, by way of assent to what is being read. And then some priest who is present, or some one of the elders, reads the sacred laws to them, and interprets each of them separately till eventide; and then when separate they depart, having gained some skill in the sacred laws, and having made great advancers towards piety.

#126: Philo's Advise to Caligula Regarding Synagogue Worship
(Philo, *On the Embassy to Gaius* 40 §§311–13)

40. [311]"And though I might be able to establish this fact, and demonstrate to you the feelings of Augustus, your great grandfather, by an abundance of proofs, I will be content

with two; for, in the first place, he sent commandments to all the governors of the different provinces throughout Asia, because he heard that the sacred first fruits were neglected, enjoining them to permit the Jews alone to assemble together in the synagogues, [312]for that these assemblies were not revels, which from drunkenness and intoxication proceeded to violence, so as to disturb the peaceful condition of the country, but were rather schools of temperance and justice, as the men who met in them were studiers of virtue, and contributed the first fruits every year, sending commissioners to convey the holy things to the temple in Jerusalem.

[313]"And, in the next place, he commanded that no one should hinder the Jews, either on their way to the synagogues, or when bringing their contributions, or when proceeding in obedience to their national laws to Jerusalem, for these things were expressly enjoined, if not in so many words, at all events in effect.

#127: Philo's Description of a Synagogue Service
(Philo, *Every Good Man Is Free* 12 §§81–83)

12. [81]Now these laws they are taught at other times, indeed, but most especially on the seventh day, for the seventh day is accounted sacred, on which they abstain from all other employments, and frequent the sacred places which are called synagogues, and there they sit according to their age in classes, the younger sitting under the elder, and listening with eager attention in becoming order. [82]Then one, indeed, takes up the holy volume and reads it, and another of the men of the greatest experience comes forward and explains what is not very intelligible, for a great many precepts are delivered in enigmatical modes of expression, and allegorically, as the old fashion was; [83]and thus the people are taught piety, and holiness, and justice, and economy, and the science of regulating the state, and the knowledge of such things as are naturally good, or bad, or indifferent, and to choose what is right and to avoid what is wrong, using a threefold variety of defini-

tions, and rules, and criteria, namely, the love of God, and the love of virtue, and the love of mankind.

#128: The Divine Presence Attends Study of the Law
(Mishnah, Tractate *Aboth* 3.6)

[6]R. Halafta b. Dosa of Kefar Hanania said: If ten men sit together and occupy themselves in the Law, the Divine Presence rests among them, for it is written, *God standeth in the congregation of God.* And whence [do we learn this] even of five? Because it is written, *And hath founded his group upon the earth.* And whence even of three? Because it is written, *He judgeth among the judges.* And whence even of two? Because it is written, *Then they that feared the Lord spake one with another: and the Lord hearkened, and heard.* And whence even of one? Because it is written, *In every place where I record my name I will come unto thee and I will bless thee.*

#129: Study of the Law Outweighs All Else
(Mishnah, Tractate *Peah* 1.1)

[1]These are things for which no measure is prescribed: *Peah* [a section of the harvest-field left for the poor], Firstfruits, the Festal Offering, deeds of loving-kindness and the study of the Law. These are things whose fruits a man enjoys in this world while the capital is laid up for him in the world to come: honoring father and mother, deeds of loving-kindness, making peace between a man and his fellow; and the study of the Law is equal to them all.

#130: To Gain the Law Is to Gain Eternal Life
(Mishnah, Tractate *Aboth* 2.7)

[7]The more study of the Law the more life; the more schooling the more wisdom; the more counsel the more understanding; the more righteousness the more peace. If a man has gained a good name he has gained [somewhat] for himself; if he has gained for himself words of the Law he has gained for himself life in the world to come.

#131: The Dedication of a Synagogue in Jerusalem
(Theodotus Synagogue Inscription)

"Theodotus Vettanos [or son of Vettanos], priest and synagogue leader, son of a synagogue leader, and grandson of a synagogue leader, built [restored?] this synagogue for the purpose of the reading of the Law and for the instruction of the commandments of the Law, the hostel and guest rooms, and the baths [ritual baths?] for foreigners who need them. This synagogue was established by his forefathers, the elders and Simonides."

The Sabbath

The Sabbath was a day of absolutely inviolable holiness in the Jewish mind, inscribed by the very finger of God as one of the ten commandments (Dt 5:22). (##132–134) Three passages from the Torah form the basis for Israel's reverence of the day.

#132: The Sabbath Commemorates Creation
(Exodus 20:8–11)

[8]"Remember the Sabbath day by keeping it holy. [9]Six days you shall labor and do all your work, [10]but the seventh day is a Sabbath to the LORD your God. On it you shall not do any work, neither you, nor your son or daughter, nor your manservant or maidservant, nor your animals, nor the alien within your gates. [11]For in six days the LORD made the heavens and the earth, the sea, and all that is in them, but he rested on the seventh day. Therefore the LORD blessed the Sabbath day and made it holy.

#133: You Must Not Work on the Sabbath
(Leviticus 23:3)

[3]"There are six days when you may work, but the seventh day is a Sabbath of rest, a day of sacred assembly. You are not to do any work; wherever you live, it is a Sabbath to the LORD.

#134: The Sabbath Commemorates the Exodus from Egypt
(Deuteronomy 5:12–15)

[12]"Observe the Sabbath day by keeping it holy, as the LORD your God has commanded you. [13]Six days you shall labor and do all your work, [14]but the seventh day is a Sabbath to the LORD your God. On it you shall not do any work, neither you, nor your son or daughter, nor your manservant or maidservant, nor your ox, your donkey or any of your animals, nor the alien within your gates, so that your manservant and maidservant may rest, as you do. [15]Remember that you were slaves in Egypt and that the LORD your God brought you out of there with a mighty hand and an outstretched arm. Therefore the LORD your God has commanded you to observe the Sabbath day.

The Meaning of the Day

For the Jews, the essence of the day was rest in honor of God (##135, 136), but to the average pagan that attitude appeared to be lazy self-indulgence (##137, 138).

#135: Josephus Explains the Meaning of Sabbath
(Josephus, *Ant.* 1.1.1 §§32–33)

1. [32]On the sixth day God created the four-footed beasts, and made them male and female: on the same day he also formed man. [33]Accordingly Moses says that in just six days the world and all that is therein was made; and that the seventh day was a rest, and a release from the labor of such operations;— whence it is that we celebrate a rest from our labors on that day, and call it the Sabbath; which word denotes *rest* in the Hebrew tongue.

#136: "Sabbath" Means Rest
(Philo, *On the Cherubim* 26 §87)

26. [87]And on this account too Moses calls the sabbath, which name being interpreted means "rest," "the sabbath of God."

#137: Seneca Condemns the Sabbath
(Augustine, *City of God* 6.11)

[11]Along with other superstitions of the civil theology Seneca also condemns the sacred institutions of the Jews, especially the sabbath. He declares that their practice is unprofitable, because by introducing one day of rest in every seven they lose in idleness almost a seventh of their life, and by failing to act in times of urgency they often suffer loss.

#138: Juvenal Sees the Sabbath as Sheer Laziness
(Juvenal, *Satire* 14.105–6)

[105]Remember the Sabbath Day, to keep it lazy. The father, [106]setting this day apart for life, is the cause and the culprit.

The Literal Meaning of "Rest"

The requirement to cease from labor was taken very seriously throughout Israel's history. (#139) Sometimes there were disastrous consequences, as during the Maccabean revolt or the siege of Jerusalem by Pompey in 63 B.C., concerning which the Roman historian Dio Cassius says (#140) the Jews could have won, except for their fanatical adherence to the law.

#139: Death Is Preferred to Violation of the Sabbath
(1 Maccabees 2.29–38)

[29]Then many [of the Jews] who were seeking righteousness and justice went down to the wilderness to dwell there, [30]they, their sons, their wives, and their cattle, because evils pressed heavily upon them. [31]And it was reported to the king's officers, and to the troops in Jerusalem the city of David, that men who had rejected the king's command had gone down to the hiding places in the wilderness. [32]Many pursued them, and overtook them; they encamped opposite them and prepared for battle against them on the sabbath day. [33]And they said to them, "Enough of this! Come out and do what the king commands, and you will live." [34]But they said, "We will not come out, nor will we do what the king commands and so profane the sabbath day."

³⁵Then the enemy hastened to attack them. ³⁶But they did not answer them or hurl a stone at them or block up their hiding places, ³⁷for they said, "Let us all die in our innocence; heaven and earth testify for us that you are killing us unjustly." ³⁸So they attacked them on the sabbath, and they died, with their wives and children and cattle, to the number of a thousand persons.

#140: Jerusalem Fell Through Inaction on the Sabbath
(Dio Cassius, *History of Rome* 37.16.2–4)

²If they [the Jews] had continued defending it [the Temple] on all days alike, he [Pompey] could not have got possession of it. As it was, they made an exception of what are called the days of Saturn, and by doing no work at all on those days afforded the Romans an opportunity in this interval to batter down the wall. ³The latter, on learning of this superstitious awe of theirs, made no serious attempts the rest of the time, but on those days, when they came round in succession, assaulted most vigorously. ⁴Thus the defenders were captured on the day of Saturn, without making any defense, and all the wealth was plundered.

Regulations Concerning the Sabbath

As the centuries passed complex regulations arose governing life on the Sabbath, covering every conceivable thing. (#141) The Book of Jubilees provides a general statement observing that the Sabbath is even kept in heaven by the angels. (#142) Philo gives a more philosophical and speculative interpretation of the Sabbath, in keeping with his attempt to make Jewish thought reasonable to thinking Gentiles. (#143) The Damascus Rule from Qumran is more detailed and statute-like, but it is the Mishnah that goes into the minutiae of the law, devoting a whole section to Sabbath regulations ("Shabbath"). (##144, 145) Two examples are given, one from the Schools of Hillel and Shammai and the other concerning what constitutes work.

#141: Israel and the Angels in Heaven Keep the Sabbath
(Jubilees 2.16–21, 29–31)

¹⁶And He finished all His work on the sixth day—all that is in the heavens and on the earth, and in the seas and in the abysses, and in the light and in the darkness, and in everything. ¹⁷And He gave us a great sign, the Sabbath day, that we should work six days, but keep Sabbath on the seventh day from all work. ¹⁸And all the angels of the presence, and all the angels of sanctification, these two great classes—He hath bidden us to keep the Sabbath with Him in heaven and on earth. ¹⁹And He said unto us: "Behold, I will separate unto Myself a people from among all the peoples, and these shall keep the Sabbath day, and I will sanctify them unto Myself as My people, and will bless them; as I have sanctified the Sabbath day and do sanctify (it) unto Myself, even so will I bless them, and they shall be My people and I will be their God. ²⁰And I have chosen the seed of Jacob from amongst all that I have seen, and have written him down as My first-born son, and have sanctified him unto Myself for ever and ever; and I will teach them the Sabbath day, that they may keep Sabbath thereon from all work." ²¹And thus He created therein a sign in accordance with which they should keep Sabbath with us on the seventh day, to eat and to drink, and to bless Him who has created all things as He has blessed and sanctified unto Himself a peculiar people above all peoples, and that they should keep Sabbath together with us. . . . ²⁹Declare and say to the children of Israel the law of this day both that they should keep Sabbath thereon, and that they should not forsake it in the error of their hearts; (and) that it is not lawful to do any work thereon which is unseemly, to do thereon their own pleasure, and that they should not prepare thereon anything to be eaten or drunk, and (that is not lawful) to draw water, or bring in or take out thereon through their gates any burden, which they had not prepared for themselves on the sixth day in their dwellings. ³⁰And they shall not bring in nor take out from house to house on that day; for that day is more holy

and blessed than any jubilee day of the jubilees; on this we kept Sabbath in the heavens before it was made known to any flesh to keep Sabbath thereon on the earth. [31]And the Creator of all things blessed it, but he did not sanctify all peoples and nations to keep Sabbath thereon, but Israel alone: them alone he permitted to eat and drink and to keep Sabbath thereon on the earth.

#142: Philo's Lofty Speculations on the Sabbath

(Philo, *Special Laws, 2* 15–16 §§59, 65–70)

15. [59][The Sabbath] may properly be called the birthday of the world, as the day in which the work of the Father, being exhibited as perfect with all its parts perfect, was commanded to rest and abstain from all works. . . .

16. [65]It is forbidden on this day to kindle a fire, as being the beginning and seed of all the business of life; since without fire it is not possible to make any of the things which are indispensably necessary for life, so that men in the absence of one single element, the highest and most ancient of all, are cut off from all works and employments of arts, especially from all handicraft trades, and also from all particular services. [66]But it seems likely that it was on account of those who were less obedient, and who were the least inclined to attend to what was done, that Moses gave additional laws, besides, thinking it right, not only that those who were free should abstain from all works on the seventh day, but also that their servants and handmaids should have respite from their tasks, proclaiming a day of freedom to them also after every space of six days, in order to teach both classes this most admirable lesson; [67]so that the masters should be accustomed to do some things with their own hands, not waiting for the services and ministrations of their servants, in order that if any unforeseen necessities came upon them, according to the changes which take place in human affairs, they might not, from being wholly unaccustomed to do anything for themselves, faint at what they had to do; but, finding the different parts of the body active and handy, might work with ease and cheerfulness; and teaching the servants not

to despair of better prospects, but having a relaxation every six days as a kind of spark and kindling of freedom, to look forward to a complete relaxation hereafter, if they continued faithful and attached to their masters.

[68]And from the occurrence of the free men at times submitting to the tasks of servants, and of the servants enjoying a respite and holiday, it will arise that the life of mankind advances in improvement towards perfect virtue, from their being thus reminded of the principles of equality, and repaying each other with necessary services, both those of high and those of obscure rank.

[69]But the law has given a relaxation, not to servants only on the seventh day, but also to the cattle. And yet by nature the servants are born free; for no man is by nature a slave. But other animals are expressly made for the use and service of man, and are therefore ranked as slaves; but, nevertheless, those that ought to bear burdens, and to endure toil and labor on behalf of their owners, do all find a respite on the seventh day. [70]And why need I mention other particulars? The ox, the animal who is born for the most important and most useful of all the purposes of life, namely, for the plough, when the earth is already prepared for seed; and again, when the sheaves are brought into the barn, for threshing in order to the purification of the crop, is on this day unharnessed, keeping as a festival that day which is the birthday of the year. And thus its holiness pervades every thing and affects every creature.

#143: Sabbath Regulations as Found at Qumran

(Damascus Document 10.14–11.18)

10. [14]. . . No man shall work on the [15]sixth day from the moment when the sun's orb is [16]distant by its own fulness from the gate (wherein it sinks); for this is what He said, *Observe* [17]*the Sabbath day to keep it holy* (Deut. v, 12). No man shall speak any [18]vain or idle word on the Sabbath day. He shall make no loan to his companion. He shall make no decision in matters of money and gain. [19]He shall say nothing about work or labor to be done on the morrow.

[20]No man shall walk abroad to do business [21]on the Sabbath. He shall not walk more than one thousand cubits beyond his town.

[22]No man shall eat on the Sabbath day except that which is already prepared. [23]He shall eat nothing lying in the fields. He shall not drink except in the camp. 11. [1]If he is on a journey and goes down to bathe, he shall drink where he stands, but he shall not draw water [2]into a vessel. He shall send out no stranger on his business on the Sabbath day.

[3]No man shall wear soiled garments, or garments brought to the store, unless [4]they have been washed with water or rubbed with incense.

No man shall willingly mingle (with others) [5]on the Sabbath.

No man shall walk more than two thousand cubits after a beast to pasture it outside his town. [6]He shall not raise his hand to strike it with his fist. If [7]it is stubborn he shall not take it out of his house.

No man shall take anything [8]out of the house or bring anything in. And if he is in a booth, let him neither take anything out [9]nor bring anything in. He shall not open a sealed vessel on the Sabbath.

No man shall carry [10]perfumes on himself whilst going and coming on the Sabbath. He shall lift neither [11]sand nor dust in his dwelling. No man minding a child shall carry it whilst going and coming on the Sabbath.

[12]No man shall chide his manservant or maidservant or laborer on the Sabbath.

[13]No man shall assist a beast to give birth on the Sabbath day. And if it should fall into a cistern [14]or pit, he shall not lift it out on the Sabbath [compare Jesus' words in Mt 12:11–13].

No man shall spend the Sabbath in a place near to [15]Gentiles on the Sabbath.

No man shall profane the Sabbath for the sake of riches or gain on the Sabbath day. [16]But should any man fall into water or fire, [17]let him be pulled out with the aid of a ladder or rope or (some such) utensil.

No man on the Sabbath shall offer anything on the altar [18]except the Sabbath burnt-offering; for it is written thus: *Except your Sabbath offerings* (Lev. xxiii, 38).

#144: Rules from Shammai and Hillel on the Sabbath
(Mishnah, Tractate *Shabbath* 1.4–10)

[4]These are among the rulings which the Sages enjoined while in the upper room of Hananiah b. Hezekiah b. Gorion. When they went up to visit him they voted, and they of the School of Shammai outnumbered them of the School of Hillel; and eighteen things did they decree on that day.

[5]The School of Shammai say: Ink, dyestuffs, or vetches may not be soaked [on a Friday] unless there is time for them to be [wholly] soaked the same day. And the School of Hillel permit it.

[6]The School of Shammai say: Bundles of flax may not be put in an oven unless there is time for them to steam off the same day; nor may wool be put into a [dyer's] cauldron unless there is time for it to absorb the color the same day. And the School of Hillel permit it. The School of Shammai say: Nets may not be spread for wild animals, birds, or fishes unless there is time for them to be caught the same day. And the School of Hillel permit it.

[7]The School of Shammai say: They may not sell aught to a gentile or help him to load his beast or raise [a burden] on his shoulders unless there is time for him to reach a place near by [the same day]. And the School of Hillel permit it.

[8]The School of Shammai say: Hides may not be given to a [gentile] tanner nor clothes to a gentile washerman unless there is time for the work to be done the same day. And all these the School of Hillel permit such time as the sun is up.

[9]Rabban Simeon b. Gamaliel said: In my father's house they used to give white clothes to a gentile washerman three days before Sabbath. Both [the School of Shammai and the School of Hillel] agree that men may lay down the olive-press beams or the winepress rollers.

[10]Flesh and onions and eggs may not be roasted unless there is time for them to be roasted the same day; nor may bread be put into the oven when darkness is falling, nor may cakes be put upon the coals unless there is time for their top surface to form into crust.

R. Eliezer says: Time for their bottom surface [only] to form into crust.

#145: The Thirty-Nine Main Classes of Work Forbidden on the Sabbath
(Mishnah, Tractate *Shabbath* 7.1–2)

[1]A great general rule have they laid down concerning the Sabbath: whosoever, forgetful of the principle of the Sabbath, committed many acts of work on many Sabbaths, is liable only to one Sin-offering; but if, mindful of the principle of the Sabbath, he yet committed many acts of work on many Sabbaths, he is liable for every Sabbath [which he profaned]. If he knew that it was the Sabbath and he yet committed many acts of work on many Sabbaths, he is liable for every main class of work [which he performed]; if he committed many acts of work of one main class, he is liable only to one Sin-offering.

[2]The main classes of work are forty save one: sowing, ploughing, reaping, binding sheaves, threshing, winnowing, cleansing crops, grinding, sifting, kneading, baking, shearing wool, washing or beating or dyeing it, spinning, weaving, making two loops, weaving two threads, separating two threads, tying [a knot], loosening [a knot], sewing two stitches, tearing in order to sew two stitches, hunting a gazelle, slaughtering or flaying or salting it or curing its skin, scraping it or cutting it up, writing two letters, erasing in order to write two letters, building, pulling down, putting out a fire, lighting a fire, striking with a hammer and taking out aught from one domain into another. These are the main classes of work: forty save one.

Circumcision

(#146) The Roman historian Tacitus understands circumcision to be simply a practical matter developed by the Jews to differentiate themselves from others, but he greatly misunderstands its meaning. (#147) Circumcision went back to the covenant made by God with Abraham and the Book of Jubilees (#148) sees it as essential to salvation; even Jews will be lost if they neglect it, and (#149) it is so important that even the an-

gels are circumcised. The apostle Paul understood circumcision to be a matter of the heart and not of the flesh (Rom 2:25–29) and the early church rejected the idea that circumcision was necessary for salvation at the Council of Jerusalem, around A.D. 49 (Acts 15:1–21)

#146: A Roman View of Circumcision
(Tacitus, *Histories* 5.5)

[5]Circumcision was adopted by them [the Jews] as a mark of difference from other men. Those who come over to their religion adopt the practice.

#147: Circumcision as the Sign the Covenant with Abraham
(Genesis 17:9–14)

[9]Then God said to Abraham, "As for you, you must keep my covenant, you and your descendants after you for the generations to come. [10]This is my covenant with you and your descendants after you, the covenant you are to keep: Every male among you shall be circumcised. [11]You are to undergo circumcision, and it will be the sign of the covenant between me and you. [12]For the generations to come every male among you who is eight days old must be circumcised, including those born in your household or bought with money from a foreigner—those who are not your offspring. [13]Whether born in your household or bought with your money, they must be circumcised. My covenant in your flesh is to be an everlasting covenant. [14]Any uncircumcised male, who has not been circumcised in the flesh, will be cut off from his people; he has broken my covenant."

#148: Neglect of Circumcision Is an Unforgivable, Eternal Error
(Jubilees 15.33–34)

[33]And now I shall announce to you that the sons of Israel will deny this ordinance and they will not circumcise their sons according to all of this law because some of the flesh of their circumcision they will leave in the circumcision of their sons. And all of the sons of Beliar will leave their sons without circumcising just as they were born. [34]And great

wrath from the LORD will be upon the sons of Israel because they have left his covenant and have turned aside from his words. And they have provoked and blasphemed inasmuch as they have not done the ordinance of this law because they have made themselves like the gentiles to be removed and be uprooted from the land. And there is therefore for them no forgiveness or pardon so that they might be pardoned and forgiven from all of the sins of this eternal error.

#149: Circumcision Is Required of Angels and of Men
(Jubilees 15.25–27)

25This law is for all the eternal generations and there is no circumcising of days and there is no passing a single day beyond eight days because it is an eternal ordinance ordained and written in the heavenly tablets. 26And anyone who is born whose own flesh is not circumcised on the eighth day is not from the sons of the covenant which the LORD made for Abraham since (he is) from the children of destruction. And there is therefore no sign upon him so that he might belong to the LORD because (he is destined) to be destroyed and annihilated from the earth and to be uprooted from the earth because he has broken the covenant of the LORD our God. 27Because the nature of all of the angels of the presence and all of the angels of sanctification was thus from the day of their creation. And in the presence of the angels of the presence and the angels of sanctification he sanctified Israel so that they might be with him and with his holy angels.

Festivals

There were numerous festivals and holy days in Israel, three of which were designated as "pilgrim festivals" because every male in Israel was theoretically to appear in Jerusalem for their observance (Dt 16:16). Of these three, Passover/Unleavened Bread, Pentecost, and Tabernacles (Dt 16:1–5), Passover had become the most emotionally charged by New Testament times, commemorating as it did Israel's deliverance from Egypt. The Romans were on special alert as hun-

dreds of thousands of Jews appeared in Jerusalem for its celebration. Many of these pilgrims were earnestly praying for (and expecting) the Messiah to appear and overthrow their hated conquerors. The Passover is especially significant for Christians because Jesus died at Passover time as "the Lamb of God, who takes away the sin of the world" (Jn 1:29) and Paul would later say "Christ our Passover Lamb has been sacrificed. Therefore let us keep the festival, not with the old yeast, the yeast of malice and wickedness, but with bread without yeast, the bread of sincerity and truth" (1 Cor 5:7, 8). It was also at the Passover meal that Jesus instituted what was to become "the Lord's Supper" (Lk 22:7–20; 1 Cor 11:23–26). The two readings that follow deal with (#150) the Passover Festival itself and (#151) from the Mishnah, the Passover meal. Josephus said that in his day 256,500 lambs were sacrificed at one of the festivals (*Jewish War* 6.9.3), which, even if exaggerated, gives us some idea of the magnitude of the celebration.

#150: Josephus's Description of the Passover Feast
(Josephus, *Ant.* 3.10.5 §§248–51)

5. 248In the month of . . . *Nisan*, which is the beginning of our year, on the fourteenth day of the lunar month, when the sun is in Aries (for in this month it was that we were delivered from bondage under the Egyptians), the law ordained that we should every year slay that sacrifice which I before told you we slew when we came out of Egypt, and which was called the *Passover*; and so do we celebrate this passover in companies, leaving nothing of what we sacrifice till the day following. 249The feast of unleavened bread succeeds that of the passover, and falls on the fifteenth day of the month, and continues seven days, wherein they feed on unleavened bread; on every one of which days two bulls are killed, and one ram, and seven lambs. Now these lambs are entirely burnt, beside the kid of the goats which is added to all the rest, for sins; for it is intended as a feast for the priest on every one of those days. 250But on the second day of unleavened bread, which is the sixteenth day of the month, they first partake of the fruits of the earth, for before that day they do not touch

them. And while they suppose it proper to honor God, from whom they obtain this plentiful provision, in the first place, they offer the first-fruits of their barley, and that in the manner following: [251]They take a handful of the ears, and dry them, then beat them small, and purge the barley from the bran; they then bring one tenth deal to the altar, to God: and, casting one handful of it upon the fire, they leave the rest for the use of the priest; and after this it is that they may publicly or privately reap their harvest. They also at this participation of the first-fruits of the earth, sacrifice a lamb, as a burnt-offering to God.

#151: The Celebration of the Passover Meal
(Mishnah, Tractate *Pesahim* 10.1–8)

[1]On the eve of Passover, from about the time of the Evening Offering, a man must eat naught until nightfall. Even the poorest in Israel must not eat unless he sits down to table, and they must not give them less than four cups of wine to drink, even if it is from the [Paupers'] Dish.

[2]After they have mixed him his first cup, the School of Shammai say: He says the Benediction first over the day and then the Benediction over the wine. And the School of Hillel say: He says the Benediction first over the wine and then the Benediction over the day.

[3]When [food] is brought before him he eats it seasoned with lettuce, until he is come to the breaking of bread; they bring before him unleavened bread and lettuce and the *haroseth* [a mixture of nuts, fruit, and vinegar], although *haroseth* is not a religious obligation. R. Eliezer b. R. Zadok says: It is a religious obligation. And in the Holy City they used to bring before him the body of the Passover-offering.

[4]They then mix him the second cup. And here the son asks his father (and if the son has not enough understanding his father instructs him [how to ask]), "Why is this night different from other nights? For on other nights we eat seasoned food once, but this night twice; on other nights we eat leavened or unleavened bread, but this night all is unleavened; on other nights we eat flesh roast, stewed, or cooked, but this night all is roast." And ac-

cording to the understanding of the son his father instructs him. He begins with the disgrace and ends with the glory; and he expounds from *A wandering Aramean was my father* . . . . until he finishes the whole section (Dt 26:5-11).

[5]Rabban Gamaliel used to say: Whosoever has not said [the verses concerning] these three things at Passover has not fulfilled his obligation. And these are they: Passover, unleavened bread, and bitter herbs: "Passover"—because God passed over the houses of our fathers in Egypt; "unleavened bread"—because our father were redeemed from Egypt; "bitter herbs"—because the Egyptians embittered the lives of our fathers in Egypt. In every generation a man must so regard himself as if he came forth himself out of Egypt, for it is written, *And thou shalt tell thy son in that day saying, It is because of that which the Lord did for me when I came forth out of Egypt.* Therefore are we bound to give thanks, to praise, to glorify, to honor, to exalt, to extol, and to bless him who wrought all these wonders for our fathers and for us. He brought us out from bondage to freedom, from sorrow to gladness, and from mourning to a Festival-day, and from darkness to great light, and from servitude to redemption; so let us say before him the *Hallelujah*.

[6]How far do they recite [the *Hallel*, i.e., Pss. 113–118]? The School of Shammai say: To *A joyful mother of children* [end of Ps. 113]. And the School of Hillel say: To *A flintstone into a springing well* [end of Ps. 114]. And this is concluded with the *Ge'ullah* [a benediction]. R. Tarfon says: "He that redeemed us and redeemed our fathers from Egypt and brought us to this night to eat therein unleavened bread and bitter herbs." But there is no concluding Benediction. R. Akiba adds: "Therefore, O Lord our God and the God of our fathers, bring us in peace to the other set feasts and festivals which are coming to meet us, while we rejoice in the building-up of thy city and are joyful in thy worship; and may we eat there of the sacrifices and of the Passover-offerings whose blood has reached with acceptance the wall of thy Altar, and let us praise thee for our redemption and for the ransoming of our soul. Blessed art thou, O Lord, who hast redeemed Israel!"

[7]After they have mixed for him the third cup he says the Benediction over his meal. [Over] a fourth [cup] he completes the *Hallel* and says after it the Benediction over song. If he is minded to drink [more] between these cups he may drink; only between the third and the fourth cups he may not drink.

[8]After the Passover meal they should not disperse to join in revelry.

5 Religious Ideas in Judaism

Israel's religious thought was developed over many centuries, drawn from its own complex experiences; reflections on its own history; interactions with other peoples; proddings and encouragements by prophets, priests, and sages; and input from numerous, varied other sources. The hand of the Lord was behind all this, guiding Israel's thinkers as they drew from this mass of information that over the years was pulled together to become the Hebrew Bible—the Christian Old Testament. Alongside the Bible, there grew up a massive collection of ideas, embodied in written documents as well as in oral sayings later written down, that constituted Israel's "traditions of the Fathers," mentioned by Paul as part of his upbringing (Gal 1:14). From these two sources, the religious ideas of intertestamental Judaism were derived.

Because Jewish religious thought centered on living rather than on theological ideas, there is no single set of doctrines to be found that was held by everyone. Rather, there was a range of ideas on a given subject that were allowed as within acceptable limits. Limitations of space do not allow us to cover every topic that is of interest as background to New Testament thought, but some of four key areas will be looked at: God and the Election of Israel; the Supremacy of the Law; the concept of the Messiah; and Eschatology.

God and the Election of Israel

The Doctrine of God

For the Jews of Jesus' day, as for Jesus and the early Christians, only one God existed, the God of Israel. This reflected Deuteronomy 4:39, "the

LORD is God in heaven above and on earth below. There is no other." The gods of the nations are nonexistent (or worse, perhaps demons) and for this reason idolatry is forbidden. God was believed to be eternal, transcendent and immanent, holy, just, truthful, loving, compassionate, forgiving, the creator and ruler of world, and active in human history. It isn't necessary to illustrate all of these basic theological ideas from the literally hundreds of references that exist. Let four representative samples suffice. (##152, 153) The first two are visions of God by Enoch that emphasize God's transcendence and glory. (#154) The third is from Qumran and illustrates God's wisdom and control of the universe. (#155) The fourth, from a somewhat later period than the New Testament, typically illustrates God as the only God.

#152: The Excellence of the Glorious God
(1 Enoch 14.17–22)

[17]As for its [heaven's] floor, it was of fire and above it was lightning and the path of the stars; and as for the ceiling, it was flaming fire, [18]And I observed and saw inside it a lofty throne—its appearance was like crystal and its wheels like the shining sun; and (I heard?) the voice of the cherubim; [19]and from beneath the throne were issuing streams of flaming fire. It was difficult to look at it. [20]And the Great Glory was sitting upon it—as for his gown, which was shining more brightly than the sun, it was whiter than any snow. [21]None of the angels was able to come in and see the face of the Excellent and the Glorious One, and no one of the flesh can see him—[22]the flaming fire was round about him, and a great fire stood before him. No one could come near unto him from among those that surrounded the tens of millions (that stood) before him.

#153: The Lord of Potentates, Whose Name Is Holy

(1 Enoch 9.4–5)

[4]And they said to the Lord of the potentates, "For he is the Lord of lords, and the God of gods, and the King of kings, and the seat of his glory (stands) throughout all the generations of the world. Your name is holy, and blessed, and glorious throughout the whole world. [5]You have made everything and with you is the authority for everything. Everything is naked and open before your sight, and you see everything; and there is nothing which can hide itself from you.

#154: The Wisdom of the God Who Rules

(Rule of the Community 11.17–20)

[17]For beyond you there is no perfect path and without your will, nothing comes to be.
You have taught all knowledge
[18]and all that exists is so by your will.
Beyond you there is no-one
to oppose your counsel,
to understand one of your holy thoughts,
[19]to gaze into the abyss of your mysteries,
to fathom all your marvels
or the strength of your might.
[20]Who can tolerate your glory?

#155: There Is No God but God

(*Midrash Exodus*, Chapter *Yitra* 29.9)

When God gave the Law, no bird sang or flew, no ox bellowed, the angels did not fly, the Seraphim ceased from saying, "Holy, holy," the sea was calm, no creature spoke; the world was silent and still, and the divine voice said: "I am the Lord thy God. . . ." If you wonder at this, think of Elijah: when he came to Mount Carmel, and summoned all the priests of Baal, and said to them, "Cry aloud, for he is a god," God caused all the world to be still, and those above and those below were silent, and the world was, as it were, empty and void, as if no creature existed, as it says, "There was no voice nor any answer" (I Kings 18:27, 29). For if anyone had spoken, the priests would have said: "Baal has answered us." So, at Sinai, God made the whole world silent, so that all the creatures should know

that there is no god beside Him, and so He spoke: "I am the Lord, thy God," and so too, in the days to come, He will say, "I, and I alone, am He that comforts you" (Isa. 51:12).

The Election of Israel

At the very heart of Israel's understanding of itself was the unshakable certainty that God had chosen them out of all the peoples of the earth to be his own special people. "You only have I chosen of all the peoples of the earth" (Am 3:2) is how the prophet spoke God's Word. (##156; 157) It was God's call of Abraham that established him and his descendants as special people; God made an everlasting covenant with him that they would be his people and he would be their God. (#158) The Book of Jubilees recalls that event and has God sending special protective angels to preserve Israel, but sending deceiving angels to the other nations to lead them astray. (#159) So special is Israel that the eternal destinies of all the other nations depends on how they knew and treated the chosen people. (#160) Josephus has Balaam expanding on Israel's privilege and election in glowingly generous terms, with the whole world designed for their habitation, not just the little land of Palestine. God will give to them all good things in times of peace and victory in times of war. (#161) The fact that Israel's exalted status did not square with its present circumstances caused some theoretical problems, but it did not change the fundamental conviction.

#156: God's Election of Abraham and His Descendants

(Genesis 17:1–8)

When Abram was ninety-nine years old, the LORD appeared to him and said, "I am God Almighty; walk before me and be blameless. [2]I will confirm my covenant between me and you and will greatly increase your numbers."
[3]Abram fell facedown, and God said to him, [4]"As for me, this is my covenant with you: You will be the father of many nations. [5]No longer will you be called Abram; your name will be Abraham, for I have made you a father of many nations. [6]I will make you very fruitful; I will make nations of you, and kings will come from you. [7]I will establish my covenant as an everlasting covenant between

me and you and your descendants after you for the generations to come, to be your God and the God of your descendants after you. [8]The whole land of Canaan, where you are now an alien, I will give as an everlasting possession to you and your descendants after you; and I will be their God."

#157: Israel's Election Is to Last Forever
(Psalms of Solomon 9.8–11)

[8]And now, you are God and we are the
  people whom you have loved;
  look and be compassionate, O God of Israel, for we are yours,
  and do not take away your mercy from
  us, lest they set upon us.
[9]For you chose the descendants of Abraham
  above all the nations,
  and you put your name upon us, Lord,
  and it will not cease forever.
[10]You made a covenant with our ancestors
  concerning us,
  and we hope in you when we turn our
  souls toward you.
[11]May the mercy of the Lord be upon the
  house of Israel forevermore.

#158: God's Election and Protection of Israel
(Jubilees 15.28–32)

[28]And you command the sons of Israel and let them keep this sign of the covenant for their generations for an eternal ordinance. And they will not be uprooted from the land [29]because the commandment was ordained for the covenant so that they might keep it forever for all of the children of Israel. [30]For the LORD did not draw Ishmael and his sons and his brothers and Esau near to himself, and he did not elect them because they are the sons of Abraham, for he knew them. But he chose Israel that they might be a people for himself. [31]And he sanctified them and gathered them from all of the sons of man because (there are) many nations and many people, and they all belong to him, but over all of them he caused spirits to rule so that they might lead them astray from following him. [32]But over Israel he did not cause any angel or spirit to rule because he alone is their ruler and he

will protect them and he will seek for them at the hand of his angels and at the hand of his spirits and at the hand of all of his authorities so that he might guard them and bless them and they might be his and he might be theirs henceforth and forever.

#159: The Destiny of the Nations Depends on Israel
(2 Baruch 72.1–6)

[1]Now, hear also about the bright waters which come at the end after these black ones. This is the word. [2]After the signs have come of which I have spoken to you before, when the nations are moved and the time of my Anointed One comes, he will call all nations, and some of them he will spare, and others he will kill. [3]These things will befall the nations which will be spared by him. [4]Every nation which has not known Israel and which has not trodden down the seed of Jacob will live. [5]And this is because some from all the nations have been subjected to your people. [6]All those, now, who have ruled over you or have known you, will be delivered up to the sword.

#160: The Glorious Place of Israel the Chosen
(Josephus, *Ant.* 4.6.4 §§114–17)

[114]Then said he [Balaam], "Happy is this people, on whom God bestows the possession of innumerable good things, and grants them his own providence to be their assistant and their guide; so that there is not any nation among mankind but you will be esteemed superior to them in virtue, and in the earnest prosecution of the best rules of life, and of such as are pure from wickedness, and will leave those rules to your excellent children, and this out of the regard that God bears to you, and the provision of such things for you as may render you happier than any other people under the sun. [115]You shall retain that land to which he hath sent you, and it shall ever be under the command of your children; and both all the earth, as well as the sea, shall be filled with your glory: and you shall be sufficiently numerous to supply the world in general, and every region of it in particular, with inhabitants out of your stock. [116]However, O blessed army! wonder that

you are become so many from one father: and truly, the land of Canaan can now hold you, as being yet comparatively few; but know ye that the whole world is proposed to be your place of habitation for ever. The multitude of your posterity also shall live as well in the islands as on the continent, and that more in number than are the stars of heaven. And when you are become so many, God will not relinquish the care of you, but will afford you an abundance of all good things in times of peace, with victory and dominion in times of war. [117]May the children of your enemies have an inclination to fight against you, and may they be so hardy as to come to arms, and to assault you in battle, for they will not return with victory, nor will their return be agreeable to their children and wives. To so great a degree of valor will you be raised by the providence of God, who is able to diminish the affluence of some, and to supply the wants of others."

#161: Israel Is God's; the Nations Are Nothing
(4 Ezra 6.55–59)

[55]"All this I have spoken before you, O Lord, because you have said that it was for us that you created this world. [56]As for the other nations which have descended from Adam, you have said that they are nothing, and that they are like spittle, and you have compared their abundance to a drop from a bucket. [57]And now, O Lord, behold, these nations, which are reputed as nothing, domineer over us and devour us. [58]But we your people, whom you have called your first-born, only begotten, zealous for you, and most dear, have been given into their hands. [59]If the world has indeed been created for us, why do we not possess our world as an inheritance? How long will this be so?

The Law

The law was foundational to Israel's understanding of itself. A fundamental aspect of their being chosen by God was that he revealed himself to them, giving them his commandments to live by. By the time of Jesus all of the material drawn together as Scripture—the law, the prophets, and the writings—were scrutinized, dissected, amplified, and made use of in formulating a way of life. It was revered as precious beyond any human treasure on earth and the Jews would rather die than violate any of its precepts, or in some instances, any of the innumerable regulations that were considered logical implications of God's precepts. (#162) Psalm 19:7–11 beautifully epitomizes something of the reverent devotion and awe that was felt toward the law of God. (#163) A verse in Deuteronomy (33:2) speaks of God's right hand giving Israel the law, so it was deduced that because God is eternal, the law itself is also eternal. (#164) Israel has a special place in the world's economy because it has the law and it was by the law (called "the precious instrument") that the world was created. (##165, 166) Not only that, but this world and the world to come were created for the sake of the law and by means of the law entrance into life in the world to come is to be gained. The reason for this is that all human beings were created for the sake of the law. (#167) Because the law comes from God and is the very essence of the universe and of human life, "everything is in it." The rabbis took this literally; they believed that all human knowledge is contained in the law, whether obviously or mystically. (#168) The law also contains practical knowledge about how to live and can be likened to a medicine that heals, giving us power over the evil impulse (yetzer) within us. (#169) The words of the law bring the presence of God down to earth, but (#170) Philo reminds us that human beings must be obedient to the law. Those who are stubborn and disobedient to the law will be destroyed.

#162: The Perfection of the Law
(Psalm 19:7–11)

[7]The law of the LORD is perfect,
    reviving the soul.
The statutes of the LORD are trustworthy,
    making wise the simple.
[8]The precepts of the LORD are right,
    giving joy to the heart.
The commands of the LORD are radiant,
    giving light to the eyes.
[9]The fear of the LORD is pure,
    enduring forever.
The ordinances of the LORD are sure
    and altogether righteous.
[10]They are more precious than gold,

than much pure gold;
they are sweeter than honey,
    than honey from the comb.
[11]By them is your servant warned;
    in keeping them there is great reward.

#163: The Eternality of the Law

(*Sifre Deuteronomy*, Chapter *Berakah* §343)

"From His right hand went a fiery law for them" (Deut. 33:2). The words of the Torah are compared to fire, for both were given from heaven, both are eternal. If a man draws near the fire, he is burned; if he keeps afar, he is frozen, so with the words of the Torah, if a man toils in them, they are life to him, if he separates from them, they kill him; fire is made use of both in this world and the next, and so too with the Torah. Fire leaves its mark on him who makes use of it, so does the Torah. As those who work with fire are recognized, so are they who toil in the Torah. For students of the Law are recognized in the street by their walk, their speech, and their dress.

#164: The World Was Created by the Law

(Mishnah, Tractate *Aboth* 3.15)

[15]Beloved are Israel, for to them was given the precious instrument [i.e., the law]; still greater was the love, in that it was made known to them that to them was given the precious instrument by which the world was created, as it is written, *For I give you good doctrine; forsake ye not my Law.*

#165: This World and the World to Come Were Created for the Sake of the Law

(*Sifre Deuteronomy*, Chapter *Eqeb* §48)

Learn Torah: the honor will come at the end of itself. R. Eliezer b. Zadok said: Do the words of the Law for the doing's sake; speak of them for their own sake. If Belshazar, because he made use of the vessels of the Temple, was deprived of this world and the world to come, how much more will this be the case with him who makes use of [i.e., uses as a means to another end] that for which both this world and the world to come were created.

#166: The Law Brings Eternal Life for Humanity

(Mishnah, Tractate *Aboth* 2.7–8)

[7]If a man has gained a good name he has gained [somewhat] for himself; if he has gained for himself words of the Law he has gained for himself life in the world to come.

[8]Rabban Johanan b. Zakkai received [the Law] from Hillel and from Shammai. He used to say: If thou hast wrought much in the Law claim not merit for thyself, for to this end wast thou created.

#167: All Knowledge Is to Be Found in the Law

(Mishnah, Tractate *Aboth* 5.22)

[22]Ben Bag-Bag said: Turn it and turn it again for everything is in it; and contemplate it and grow grey and old over it and stir not from it for than it thou canst have no better rule.

#168: The Law Is the Medicine of Life

(*Sifre Deuteronomy*, Chapter *Eqeb* §45)

The words of the Law are likened to a medicine of life. Like a king, who inflicted a big wound upon his son, and he put a plaster upon his wound. He said, "My son, so long as this plaster is on your wound, eat and drink what you like, and wash in cold or warm water, and you will suffer no harm. But if you remove it, you will get a bad boil." So God says to the Israelites, "I created within you the evil *yetzer* [impulse], but I created the Law as a medicine. As long as you occupy yourselves with the Law, the *yetzer* will not rule over you. But if you do not occupy yourselves with the Torah, then you will be delivered into the power of the *yetzer*, and all its activity will be against you."

#169: With the Law Comes the Presence of God

(Mishnah, Tractate *Aboth* 3.2–3)

[2]R. Hananiah b. Teradion said: If two sit together and no words of the Law [are spoken] between them, there is the seat of the scornful, as it is written, *Nor sitteth in the seat of the scornful.* But if two sit together and words of the Law [are spoken] between them, the Di-

vine Presence rests between them, as it is written, *Then they that feared the Lord spake one with another: and the Lord hearkened, and heard, and a book of remembrance was written before him, for them that feared the Lord, and that thought upon his name.* Scripture speaks here of "two"; whence [do we learn] that if even one sits and occupies himself in the Law, the Holy One, blessed is he, appoints him a reward? Because it is written, *Let him sit alone and keep silence, because he hath laid it upon him.*

[3]R. Simeon said: If three have eaten at one table and have not spoken over it words of the Law, it is as though they had eaten of the sacrifices of the dead, for it is written, *For all tables are full of vomit and filthiness without God.* But if three have eaten at one table and have spoken over it words of the Law, it is as if they had eaten from the table of God, for it is written, *And he said unto me, This is the table that is before the Lord.*

#170: The Law Must Be Obeyed to Benefit
(Philo, *Decalogue* 11 §§48–49)

11. [48]It is, therefore, with great beauty, and also with a proper sense of what is consistent with the dignity of God, that the voice is said to have come forth out of the fire; for the oracles of God are accurately understood and tested like gold by the fire. [49]And God also intimates to us something of this kind by a figure. Since the property of fire is partly to give light, and partly to burn, those who think fit to show themselves obedient to the sacred commands shall live for ever and ever as in a light which is never darkened, having his laws themselves as stars giving light in their soul. But all those who are stubborn and disobedient are for ever inflamed, and burnt, and consumed by their internal appetites, which, like flame, will destroy all the life of those who possess them.

The Messiah

The messianic expectation that existed in New Testament times is a complex phenomenon. There was not a single, unified expectation, but many, and in some instances no expectation of a Messiah at all. That is, God would work directly without messianic mediation. In order to simplify this somewhat, we will look at various aspects of it separately: first, general messianic expectations; second, messianic fervor and pretenders; and third, the messianic ideas current in Jesus' day.

(1) Messianic expectation was rife in Jesus' day. The later Church Father Epiphanius even makes the curious statement that Herod was considered by the Herodians to be the Messiah (Panarion 20:1). (#171) Josephus blames the Jewish War on the Jews applying an oracle to themselves that in his opinion prophesied the Roman Vespasian. (##172, 173) The Roman historians Suetonius and Tacitus refer supernatural portents and prophecies to both Vespasian and his son Titus. All of this points to a climate of expectation in which messianic speculation flourished.

#171: The Jews Apply Messianic Prophecy to Themselves
(Josephus, *Jewish War* 6.5.4. §§312–13, 315)

[312]But now, what did most elevate them [the Jews] in undertaking this war was an ambiguous oracle that was also found in their sacred writings, how "about that time, one from their country should become governor of the habitable earth." [313]The Jews took this prediction to belong to themselves in particular; and many of the wise men were thereby deceived in their determination. Now, this oracle certainly denoted the government of Vespasian, who was appointed emperor in Judea. . . . [315]But these men interpreted some of these signals according to their own pleasure . . . until their madness was demonstrated, both by the taking of their city and their own destruction.

#172: Out of Judea the World Rulers Will Come
(Suetonius, *Twelve Caesars, Vespasian* 4.5)

[5]An ancient superstition was current in the East, that out of Judea would come the rulers of the world. This prediction, as it later proved, referred to two Roman Emperors,

Vespasian and his son Titus; but the rebellious Jews, who read it as referring to themselves, murdered their Procurator, routed the Governor-general of Syria when he came down to restore order, and captured an Eagle. To crush this uprising the Romans needed a strong army under an energetic commander, who could be trusted not to abuse his plenary powers. The choice fell on Vespasian.

#173: The Prophesied Rulers Are Vespasian and Titus
(Tacitus, *Histories* 5.13)

[13]Prodigies had occurred, which this nation [the Jews], prone to superstition, but hating all religious rites, did not deem it lawful to expiate by offering and sacrifice. There had been seen hosts joining battle in the skies, the fiery gleam of arms, the temple illuminated by a sudden radiance from the clouds. The doors of the inner shrine were suddenly thrown open, and a voice of more than mortal tone was heard to cry that the Gods were departing. At the same instant there was a mighty stir as of departure. Some few put a fearful meaning on these events, but in most there was a firm persuasion, that in the ancient records of their priests was contained a prediction of how at this very time the East was to grow powerful, and rulers, coming from Judea, were to acquire universal empire. These mysterious prophecies had pointed to Vespasian and Titus, but the common people, with the usual blindness of ambition, had interpreted these mighty destinies of themselves, and could not be brought even by disasters to believe the truth.

---

(2) The messianic ferment that was in the air caused some people to claim messiahship for themselves, even royalty. Josephus gives details about three such royal pretenders—Judas (*Ant.* 17.10.5), Simon (*Ant.* 17.10.6), and (#174) Athronges, who can serve as an example. They were, in reality, criminals taking advantage of the uncertainty of the times. Other messianic pretenders claimed to be prophets, such as (#175) Theudas and (#176) a certain "Egyptian," who is also mentioned in the New Testament (Acts 21:37–39).

#174: Athronges the Royal Pretender
(Josephus, *Ant.* 17.10.7 §§278–81)

7. [278]But because Athronges, a person neither eminent by the dignity of progenitors, nor for any great wealth he was possessed of, but one that had in all respects been a shepherd only, and was not known by anybody; yet because he was a tall man, and excelled others in the strength of his hands, he was so bold as to set up for king. This man thought it so sweet a thing to do more than ordinary injuries to others, that although he should be killed, he did not so much care, if he lost his life in so great a design. [279]He had also four brethren, who were tall men themselves, and were believed to be superior to others in the strength of their hands, and thereby were encouraged to aim at great things, and thought that strength of theirs would support them in retaining the kingdom. Each of these ruled over a band of men of their own; for those they got together to them were very numerous. [280]They were every one of them also commanders; but, when they came to fight, they were subordinate to him, and fought for him, while he put a diadem upon his head, and assembled a council to debate about what things should be done; and all things were done according to his pleasure. [281]And this man retained his power a great while; he was also called king, and had nothing to hinder him from doing what he pleased.

#175: Theudas the False Prophet
(Josephus, *Ant.* 20.5.1 §§97–99)

1. [97]Now it came to pass, that while Fadus was procurator of Judea, that a certain magician, whose name was Theudas, persuaded a great part of the people to take their effects with them, and follow him to the river Jordan; for he told them he was a prophet, and that he would, by his own command, divide the river, and afford them an easy passage over it; [98]and many were deluded by his words. However, Fadus did not permit them to make any advantage of his wild attempt, but sent a troop of horsemen out against them; who falling upon them unexpectedly, killed many of them, and took many of them alive. They also took Theudas alive, and cut off his

head, and carried it to Jerusalem. [99]This was what befell the Jews in the time of Cuspius Fadus's government.

#176: The Egyptian False Prophet
(Josephus, *Ant.* 20.8.6 §§169–72)

6. [169]Moreover, there came out of Egypt about this time to Jerusalem, one that said he was a prophet, and advised the multitude of the common people to go along with him to the mount of Olives, as it was called, which lay over against the city, and at the distance of five furlongs. [170]He said further, that he would show them from hence, how, at his command, the walls of Jerusalem would fall down; and he promised them that he would procure them an entrance into the city through those walls, when they were fallen down. [171]Now when Felix was informed of these things, he ordered his soldiers to take their weapons, and came against them with a great number of horsemen and footmen, from Jerusalem, and attacked the Egyptian and the people that were with him. He also killed four hundred of them, and took two hundred alive. [172]But the Egyptian himself escaped out of the fight, but did not appear any more.

(3) The complexity of messianic expectation as it existed in Jesus' day is seen most clearly in the numerous views that were current as to who the Messiah or Messiahs would be. We will look at five of the most prominent.

a. *The Messiah as Son of David.* This is a very prominent emphasis, no doubt because it is based on a series of Old Testament texts. (##177–181). This sampling of the Old Testament texts provides a background not only to Jewish thought but also to the thought of the New Testament itself, which uses many of the same texts to demonstrate that Jesus, as the Son of David, was the Messiah. (#182) The Psalms of Solomon have a lengthy text and prayer beseeching God to send David's Son the Messiah to shatter the Gentile nations and establish Israel as promised. A similar thought is found in the Psalms of Solomon 18:5–9. (#183) Fourth Ezra also sees in a complicated vision David's Son the Messiah judging and destroying the wicked of the earth. Targum Pseudo-Jonathan speaks of "the King, Messiah, who is destined to arise from the house of Judah," as do some of

the writings from Qumran, such as (#184) 4Q Genesis Pesher a. (#185) 4Q Florilegium 1:11–13 adds another messianic figure, "the Interpreter of the Law," to the messianic "Branch of David." (#186) A controversial reference to "the bud of David" might appear to be a dying Messiah, but this is disputed by most scholars and not likely.

#177: Jacob's Prophecy about His Son Judah
(Genesis 49:10)

[10]The scepter will not depart from Judah,
  nor the ruler's staff from between his feet,
until he comes to whom it belongs
  and the obedience of the nations is his.

#178: The Star of Jacob Who Will Rule the Nation
(Numbers 24:17–19)

[17]"I see him, but not now;
  I behold him, but not near.
A star will come out of Jacob;
  a scepter will rise out of Israel.
He will crush the foreheads of Moab,
  the skulls of all the sons of Sheth.
[18]Edom will be conquered;
  Seir, his enemy, will be conquered,
  but Israel will grow strong.
[19]A ruler will come out of Jacob
  and destroy the survivors of the city."

#179: God's Promise That David's Son Would Rule Forever
(2 Samuel 7:11–16)

[11]"The LORD declares to you that the LORD himself will establish a house for you: [12]When your days are over and you rest with your fathers, I will raise up your offspring to succeed you, who will come from your own body, and I will establish his kingdom. [13]He is the one who will build a house for my Name, and I will establish the throne of his kingdom forever. [14]I will be his father, and he will be my son. When he does wrong, I will punish him with the rod of men, with floggings inflicted by men. [15]But my love will never be taken away from him, as I took it away from Saul, whom I removed from be-

fore you. [16]Your house and your kingdom will endure forever before me; your throne will be established forever.'"

#180: Isaiah's Prophecy of the Shoot from Jesse's Stump
(Isaiah 11:1–5)

[1]A shoot will come up from the stump of Jesse;
from his roots a Branch will bear fruit.
[2]The Spirit of the LORD will rest on him—
the Spirit of wisdom and of understanding,
the Spirit of counsel and of power,
the Spirit of knowledge and of the fear of the LORD—
[3]and he will delight in the fear of the LORD.
He will not judge by what he sees with his eyes,
or decide by what he hears with his ears;
[4]but with righteousness he will judge the needy,
with justice he will give decisions for the poor of the earth.
He will strike the earth with the rod of his mouth;
with the breath of his lips he will slay the wicked.
[5]Righteousness will be his belt
and faithfulness the sash around his waist.

#181: Jeremiah's Prophecy of the Righteous Branch
(Jeremiah 23:5–6)

[5]"The days are coming," declares the LORD,
"when I will raise up to David a righteous Branch,
a King who will reign wisely
and do what is just and right in the land.
[6]In his days Judah will be saved
and Israel will live in safety.
This is the name by which he will be called:
The LORD Our Righteousness.

#182: David's Son as King over Israel
(Psalms of Solomon 17.4–5, 21–25, 30–32)

[4]Lord, you chose David to be king over Israel,

and swore to him about his descendants forever,
that his kingdom should not fail before you.
[5]But (because of) our sins, sinners rose up against us,
they set upon us and drove us out.
Those to whom you did not (make the) promise,
they took away (from us) by force;
and they did not glorify your honorable name. . . .
[21]See, Lord, and raise up for them their king,
the son of David, to rule over your servant Israel
in the time known to you, O God.
[22]Undergird him with the strength to destroy the unrighteous rulers,
to purge Jerusalem from gentiles who trample her to destruction;
[23]in wisdom and in righteousness to drive out
the sinners from the inheritance;
to smash the arrogance of sinners like a potter's jar;
[24]To shatter all their substance with an iron rod;
to destroy the unlawful nations with the word of his mouth;
[25]At his warning the nations will flee from his presence;
and he will condemn sinners by the thoughts of their hearts. . . .
[30]And he will have gentile nations serving him under his yoke,
and he will glorify the Lord in (a place) prominent (above) the whole earth.
And he will purge Jerusalem
(and make it) holy as it was even from the beginning,
[31](for) nations to come from the ends of the earth to see his glory,
to bring as gifts her children who had been driven out,
and to see the glory of the Lord
with which God has glorified her.
[32]And he will be a righteous king over them, taught by God.
There will be no unrighteousness among them in his days,

for all shall be holy,
and their king shall be the Lord Messiah.

#183: David's Son Will Destroy the Wicked
(4 Ezra 12.31–33)

[31]"And as for the lion that you saw rousing up out of the forest and roaring and speaking to the eagle and reproving him for his unrighteousness, and as for all his words that you have heard, [32]this is the Messiah whom the Most High has kept until the end of days, who will arise from the posterity of David, and will come and speak to them; he will denounce them for their ungodliness and for their wickedness, and will cast up before them their contemptuous dealings. [33]For first he will set them living before his judgment seat, and when he has reproved them, then he will destroy them.

#184: The Messiah of Justice Is David's Descendant
(4QGenesis Pesher[a] (4Q252 [4QpGen[a]]) 5.1–6)

[1]Gen 49:10 A sovereign shall [not] be removed from the tribe of Judah. While Israel has the dominion, [2]there will [not] lack someone who sits on the throne of David. For "the staff" is the covenant of royalty, [3][the thou]sands of Israel are "the feet." Until the messiah of justice comes, the branch [4]of David. For to him and to his descendants has been given the covenant of royalty over his people for all everlasting generations, which [5]he has observed [...] the Law with the men of the Community, for [6][...] it is the assembly of the men of [...] He gives.

#185: David's Son Will Save Israel in the Last Days
(4Q Florilegium (4Q174 [4QFlor]) Fragment 1 1.10–13)

[10]And 2 Sam 7:12–14 "YHWH de[clares] to you that he will build you a house. I will raise up your seed after you and establish the throne of his kingdom [11][for ev]er. I will be a father to him and he will be a son to me." This (refers to the) "branch of David," who will

arise with the Interpreter of the law who [12][will rise up] in Zi[on in] the last days, as it is written: Amos 9:11 "I will raise up the hut of David which has fallen." This (refers to) "the hut of [13]David which has fallen," who will arise to save Israel.

#186: A Dying Messiah?
(4Q War Scroll[g]? (4Q285 [4QM[g]?]) Fragment 5 1–6)

[1][... as] the Prophet Isaiah [said] Isa 10:34: "[The most massive of the] [2][forest] shall be cut [with iron and Lebanon, with its magnificence,] will fall. A shoot will emerge from the stump of Jesse [...] [3][...] the bud of David will go into battle with [...] [4][...] and the Prince of the Congregation will kill him, the bu[d of David ...] [5][...] and with wounds. And a priest will command [...] [6][...] the destruction of the Kittim [...]

> b. A Messiah from the Tribe of Levi. That the coming messianic ruler would arise from the ruling family of David (and tribe of Judah) was logical, but it was also logical to see a messiah who would come from the priestly tribe of Levi. Spiritual rule was just as important as political rule. In some instances this required that two Messiahs should come, as seen at Qumran, where the community was to live by its first directives "until the prophet comes, and the messiahs of Aaron and Israel" (IQS 9:11). (##187–189) Three readings from the Testaments of the Twelve Patriarchs show the place of Levi's descendant as Messiah.

#187: Levi Shall Be an Eternal King
(Testament of Reuben 6.8–12)

[8]It is for this reason that I command you to give heed to Levi, because he will know the law of God and will give instructions concerning justice and concerning sacrifice for Israel until the consummation of times; he is the anointed priest of whom the Lord spoke. [9]I call to witness the God of heaven that you do the truth, each to his neighbor, and that you show love, each to his brother. [10]Draw near to Levi in humility of your hearts in order that you may receive blessing from his mouth. [11]For he will bless Israel and Judah, since it is through him that the Lord has chosen to reign in the pres-

ence of all the people. [12]Prostrate yourselves before his posterity, because (his offspring) will die in your behalf in wars visible and invisible. And he shall be among you an eternal king.

#188: The Lord's Salvation to Arise from Levi and Judah

(Testament of Dan 5.9–12)

[9]Therefore when you turn back to the Lord,
you will receive mercy,
and he will lead you into his holy place,
proclaiming peace to you.
[10]And there shall arise for you from the tribe of Judah and (the tribe of) Levi the Lord's salvation.
He will make war against Beliar;
he will grant the vengeance of victory as our goal.
[11]And he shall take from Beliar the captives, the souls of the saints;
and he shall turn the hearts of the disobedient ones to the Lord,
and grant eternal peace to those who call upon him.
[12]And the saints shall refresh themselves in Eden;
the righteous shall rejoice in the New Jerusalem,
which shall be eternally for the glorification of God.

#189: The Lord Will Raise Up a New Priest

(Testament of Levi 18.2–14)

[2]And then the Lord will raise up a new priest
to whom all the words of the Lord will be revealed.
He shall effect the judgment of truth over the earth for many days.
[3]And his star shall rise in heaven like a king;
kindling the light of knowledge as day is illumined by the sun.
And he shall be extolled by the whole inhabited world.
[4]This one will shine forth like the sun in the earth;
he shall take away all darkness from under heaven,

and there shall be peace in all the earth.
[5]The heavens shall greatly rejoice in his days
and the earth shall be glad;
the clouds will be filled with joy
and the knowledge of the Lord will be poured out on the earth like the water of the seas.
And the angels of glory of the Lord's presence will be made glad by him.
[6]The heavens will be opened,
and from the temple of glory sanctification will come upon him,
with a fatherly voice, as from Abraham to Isaac.
[7]And the glory of the Most High shall burst forth upon him.
And the spirit of understanding and sanctification
shall rest upon him [in the water].
[8]For he shall give the majesty of the Lord to those who are his sons in truth forever.
And there shall be no successor for him from generation to generation forever.
[9]And in his priesthood the nations shall be multiplied in knowledge on the earth,
and they shall be illumined by the grace of the Lord,
but Israel shall be diminished by her ignorance
and darkened by her grief.
In his priesthood sin shall cease
and lawless men shall rest from their evil deeds,
and righteous men shall find rest in him.
[10]And he shall open the gates of paradise;
he shall remove the sword that has threatened since Adam,
[11]and he will grant to the saints to eat of the tree of life.
The spirit of holiness shall be upon them.
[12]And Beliar shall be bound by him.
And he shall grant to his children the authority to trample on wicked spirits.
[13]And the Lord will rejoice in his children;
he will be well pleased by his beloved ones forever.
[14]Then Abraham, Isaac, and Jacob will rejoice,
and I shall be glad, and all the saints shall be clothed in righteousness.

c. *The Son of Man as Messiah.* Jesus' favorite self-description was "Son of Man." It clearly had messianic overtones, but not so sharply defined that he could not inject his own interpretation into it. (#190) The Book of Daniel certainly serves as a background for what Jesus had to say, and perhaps also the Book of Enoch, although this is disputed. (##190–194) The "Son of Man" is certainly a prominent figure in that book as the four readings attest.

#190: Daniel's Vision of the Son of Man

(Daniel 7:9–10, 13–14)

9"As I looked,
"thrones were set in place,
    and the Ancient of Days took his seat.
His clothing was as white as snow;
    the hair of his head was white like wool.
His throne was flaming with fire,
    and its wheels were all ablaze.
10A river of fire was flowing,
    coming out from before him.
Thousands upon thousands attended him;
    ten thousand times ten thousand stood
        before him.
The court was seated,
    and the books were opened. . . .

13"In my vision at night I looked, and there before me was one like a son of man, coming with the clouds of heaven. He approached the Ancient of Days and was led into his presence. 14He was given authority, glory and sovereign power; all peoples, nations and men of every language worshiped him. His dominion is an everlasting dominion that will not pass away, and his kingdom is one that will never be destroyed.

#191: Enoch's Vision of the Son of Man

(1 Enoch 46.1–6)

1At that place, I saw the One to whom belongs the time before time. And his head was white like wool, and there was with him another individual, whose face was like that of a human being. His countenance was full of grace like that of one among the holy angels. 2And I asked the one—from among the angels—who was going with me, and who had

revealed to me all the secrets regarding the One who was born of human beings, "Who is this, and from whence is he who is going as the prototype of the Before-Time?" 3And he answered me and said to me, "This is the Son of Man, to whom belongs righteousness, and with whom righteousness dwells. And he will open all the hidden storerooms; for the Lord of the Spirits has chosen him, and he is destined to be victorious before the Lord of the Spirits in eternal uprightness. 4This Son of Man whom you have seen is the One who would remove the kings and the mighty ones from their comfortable seats and the strong ones from their thrones. He shall loosen the reins of the strong and crush the teeth of the sinners. 5He shall depose the kings from their thrones and kingdoms. For they do not extol and glorify him, and neither do they obey him, the source of their kingship. 6The faces of the strong will be slapped and be filled with shame and gloom. Their dwelling places and their beds will be worms. They shall have no hope to rise from their beds, for they do not extol the name of the Lord of the Spirits.

#192: The Son of Man as the Chosen One

(1 Enoch 48.2–7)

2At that hour, that Son of Man was given a name, in the presence of the Lord of the Spirits, the Before-Time; 3even before the creation of the sun and the moon, before the creation of the stars, he was given a name in the presence of the Lord of the Spirits. 4He will become a staff for the righteous ones in order that they may lean on him and not fall. He is the light of the gentiles and he will become the hope of those who are sick in their hearts. 5All those who dwell upon the earth shall fall and worship before him; they shall glorify, bless, and sing the name of the Lord of the Spirits. 6For this purpose he became the Chosen One; he was concealed in the presence of (the Lord of the Spirits) prior to the creation of the world, and for eternity. 7And he has revealed the wisdom of the Lord of the Spirits to the righteous and the holy ones, for he has preserved the portion of the righteous because they have hated and despised this world of oppression (together with) all its ways of life and its habits in the name of the Lord of the Spirits; and because they will be saved in his name and it is his good pleasure that they have life.

#193: The Son of Man as Judge of the World
(1 Enoch 62.3–11)

[3]On the day of judgment, all the kings, the governors, the high officials, and the land-lords shall see and recognize him—how he sits on the throne of his glory, and righteous-ness is judged before him, and that no non-sensical talk shall be uttered in his presence. [4]Then pain shall come upon them as on a woman in travail with birth pangs . . . [5]One half portion of them shall glance at the other half; they shall be terrified and dejected; and pain shall seize them when they see that Son of Man sitting on the throne of his glory. [6](These) kings, governors, and all the land-lords shall (try to) bless, glorify, extol him who rules over everything, him who has been con-cealed. [7]For the Son of Man was concealed from the beginning, and the Most High One preserved him in the presence of his power; then he revealed him to the holy and the elect ones. [8]The congregation of the holy ones shall be planted, and all the elect ones shall stand before him. [9]On that day, all the kings, the governors, the high officials, and those who rule the earth shall fall down before him on their faces, and worship and raise their hopes in that Son of Man; they shall beg and plead for mercy at his feet. [10]But the Lord of the Spir-its himself will cause them to be frantic, so that they shall rush and depart from his pres-ence. Their faces shall be filled with shame, and their countenances shall be crowned with darkness. [11]So he will deliver them to the an-gels for punishments in order that vengeance shall be executed on them—oppressors of his children and his elect ones.

#194: The Son of Man on the Throne of Glory
(1 Enoch 69.27–29)

[27](Then) there came to them a great joy. And they blessed, glorified, and extolled (the Lord) on account of the fact that the name of that (Son of) Man was revealed to them. He shall never pass away or perish from before the face of the earth. [28]But those who have led the world astray shall be bound with chains; and their ruinous congregation shall be impris-oned; all their deeds shall vanish from before the face of the earth. [29]Thenceforth nothing that is corruptible shall be found; for that Son of Man has appeared and has seated himself upon the throne of his glory; and all evil shall disappear from before his face; he shall go and tell to that Son of Man, and he shall be strong before the Lord of the Spirits.

d. *The Messiah as Son of God.* (#195) The im-pressive figure designated as "Son" by God him-self in Psalm 2:1–9 becomes a messianic figure in later (##196, 197) Judaism, (#198) Qumran, and the New Testament. For the early Christians, Jesus as the eternal Son of God was the fulfill-ment of the prophetic dimension of Psalm 2 and of all other human longings that expressed them-selves in the religious literature of that time. Only God himself or his divine Son could ultimately right the world's wrongs.

#195: The Son of God Inherits the Nations
(Psalm 2:1–9)

[1]Why do the nations conspire
    and the peoples plot in vain?
[2]The kings of the earth take their stand
    and the rulers gather together
against the LORD
    and against his Anointed One.
[3]"Let us break their chains," they say,
    "and throw off their fetters."
[4]The One enthroned in heaven laughs;
    the Lord scoffs at them.
[5]Then he rebukes them in his anger
    and terrifies them in his wrath, saying,
[6]"I have installed my King
    on Zion, my holy hill."
[7]I will proclaim the decree of the LORD:
He said to me, "You are my Son;
    today I have become your Father.
[8]Ask of me,
    and I will make the nations your inheri-
    tance,

the ends of the earth your possession. [9]You will rule them with an iron scepter; you will dash them to pieces like pottery."

#196: The Son of God and the 400-Year "Millennium"
(2 Esdras 7.25–26, 28–31)

[25]"Therefore, Ezra, empty things are for the empty, and full things are for the full. [26]For behold, the time will come, when the signs which I have foretold to you will come to pass, that the city which now is not seen shall appear, and the land which now is hidden shall be disclosed. . . .

[28]For my son the Messiah shall be revealed with those who are with him, and those who remain shall rejoice four hundred years. [29]And after these years my son the Messiah shall die, and all who draw human breath. [30]And the world shall be turned back to primeval silence for seven days, as it was at the first beginnings; so that no one shall be left. [31]And after seven days the world, which is not yet awake, shall be roused, and that which is corruptible shall perish.

#197: The Son of God Arrives in Judgment
(2 Esdras 13.29–38, 51–52)

[29]Behold, the days are coming when the Most High will deliver those who are on the earth. [30]And bewilderment of mind shall come over those who dwell on the earth. [31]And they shall plan to make war against one another, city against city, place against place, people against people, and kingdom against kingdom. [32]And when these things come to pass and the signs occur which I showed you before, then my Son will be revealed, whom you saw as a man coming up from the sea. [33]And when all the nations hear his voice, every man shall leave his own land and the warfare that they have against one another; [34]and an innumerable multitude shall be gathered together, as you saw, desiring to come and conquer him. [35]But he will stand on the top of Mount Zion. [36]And Zion will come and be made manifest to all people, prepared and built, as you saw the mountain carved out

without hands. [37]And he, my Son, will reprove the assembled nations for their ungodliness (this was symbolized by the storm), [38]and will reproach them to their face with their evil thoughts and the torments with which they are to be tortured (which were symbolized by the flames), and will destroy them without effort by the law (which was symbolized by the fire).

[51]I said, "O sovereign Lord, explain this to me: Why did I see the man coming up from the heart of the sea?"

[52]He said to me, "Just as no one can explore or know what is in the depths of the sea, so no one on earth can see my Son or those who are with him, except in the time of his day."

#198: The Everlasting Kingdom of the Son of God
(4QAramaic Apocalypse [4Q246] 2.1–8)

[1]He will be called son of God, and they will call him son of the Most High. Like the sparks [2]of a vision, so will their kingdom be; they will rule several years over [3]the earth and crush everything; a people will crush another people, and a city another city. [4] *Blank*. Until the people of God arises and makes everyone rest from the sword. [5]His kingdom will be an eternal kingdom, and all his paths in truth and uprigh[tness]. [6]The earth (will be) in truth and all will make peace. The sword will cease in the earth, [7]and all the cities will pay him homage. He is a great god among the gods(?) [8]He will make war with him; he will place the peoples in his hand and cast away everyone before him. His kingdom will be an eternal kingdom.

e. *The Suffering Servant of God.* (##199–202) The Book of Isaiah preserves four psalms that depict the Servant of God, whose redemptive suffering redeems the world. There is little evidence that these psalms had any influence on messianic speculation in Judaism, but they form the backdrop for the New Testament's picture of Jesus. The story of the Ethiopian eunuch (Acts 8:26–35) can serve as a prototype of how Jesus was seen as the fulfillment of Isaiah's prophetic picture of God's Servant. (See also Mt 12:15–21.)

#199: The Servant of the Lord as Light to the Gentiles
(Isaiah 42:1–7)

[1]"Here is my servant, whom I uphold,
my chosen one in whom I delight;
I will put my Spirit on him
and he will bring justice to the nations.
[2]He will not shout or cry out,
or raise his voice in the streets.
[3]A bruised reed he will not break,
and a smoldering wick he will not snuff
out.
In faithfulness he will bring forth justice;
[4] he will not falter or be discouraged
till he establishes justice on earth.
In his law the islands will put their
hope."
[5]This is what God the LORD says—
he who created the heavens and stretched
them out,
who spread out the earth and all that
comes out of it,
who gives breath to its people,
and life to those who walk on it:
[6]"I, the LORD, have called you in righteousness;
I will take hold of your hand.
I will keep you and will make you
to be a covenant for the people
and a light for the Gentiles,
[7]to open eyes that are blind,
to free captives from prison
and to release from the dungeon
those who sit in darkness."

#200: The Servant of the Lord as Bringer of Salvation
(Isaiah 49:1–7)

[1]Listen to me, you islands;
hear this you distant nations:
Before I was born the LORD called me;
from my birth he has made mention of
my name.
[2]He made my mouth like a sharpened
sword,
in the shadow of his hand he hid me;
he made me into a polished arrow
and concealed me in his quiver.
[3]He said to me, "You are my servant,
Israel, in whom I will display my
splendor."
[4]But I said, "I have labored to no purpose;
I have spent my strength in vain and for
nothing.
Yet what is due me is in the LORD's hand,
and my reward is with my God."
[5]And now the LORD says—
he who formed me in the womb to be his
servant
to bring Jacob back to him
and gather Israel to himself,
for I am honored in the eyes of the LORD
and my God has been my strength—
[6]he says:
"It is too small a thing for you to be my
servant
to restore the tribes of Jacob
and bring back those of Israel I have
kept.
I will also make you a light for the Gentiles,
that you may bring my salvation to the
ends of the earth."
[7]This is what the LORD says—
the Redeemer and Holy One of Israel—
to him who was despised and abhorred by
the nation,
to the servant of rulers:
"Kings will see you and rise up,
princes will see and bow down
because of the LORD, who is faithful,
the Holy One of Israel, who has chosen
you."

#201: The Vindication of the Servant of the Lord
(Isaiah 50:4–9)

[4]The Sovereign LORD has given me an instructed tongue,
to know the word that sustains the
weary.
He wakens me morning by morning,
wakens my ear to listen like one being
taught.
[5]The Sovereign LORD has opened my ears,
and I have not been rebellious;
I have not drawn back.
[6]I offered my back to those who beat me,
my cheeks to those who pulled out my
beard;

I did not hide my face
    from mocking and spitting.
[7]Because the Sovereign LORD helps me,
    I will not be disgraced.
Therefore have I set my face like flint,
    and I know I will not be put to shame.
[8]He who vindicates me is near.
    Who then will bring charges against me?
    Let us face each other!
Who is my accuser?
    Let him confront me!
[9]It is the Sovereign LORD who helps me.
    Who is he that will condemn me?
They will all wear out like a garment;
    the moths will eat them up.

#202: The Death of God's Servant for Sinners

(Isaiah 52:13–53:12)

[52.13]See, my servant will act wisely;
    he will be raised and lifted up and
        highly exalted.
[14]Just as there were many who were ap-
    palled at him—

his appearance was so disfigured beyond
    that of any man
    and his form marred beyond human
        likeness—
[15]so will he sprinkle many nations,
    and kings will shut their mouths because
        of him.
For what they were not told, they will see,
    and what they have not heard, they will
        understand.
[53:1]Who has believed our message
    and to whom has the arm of the LORD
        been revealed?
[2]He grew up before him like a tender shoot,
    and like a root out of dry ground.
He had no beauty or majesty to attract us to
    him;
    nothing in his appearance that we
        should desire him.
[3]He was despised and rejected by men,
    a man of sorrows, and familiar with suf-
        fering.
Like one from whom men hide their faces
    he was despised, and we esteemed him
        not.

The famous Isaiah Scroll found in the caves near the Dead Sea that contains the Suffering Servant Psalms.

⁴Surely he took up our infirmities
    and carried our sorrows,
yet we considered him stricken by God,
    smitten by him, and afflicted.
⁵But he was pierced for our transgressions,
    he was crushed for our iniquities;
the punishment that brought us peace was
    upon him,
    and by his wounds we are healed.
⁶We all, like sheep, have gone astray,
    each of us has turned to his own way;
and the LORD has laid on him
    the iniquity of us all.
⁷He was oppressed and afflicted,
    yet he did not open his mouth;
he was led like a lamb to the slaughter,
    and as a sheep before her shearers is
        silent,
    so he did not open his mouth.
⁸By oppression and judgment, he was taken
    away.
    And who can speak of his descendants?
For he was cut off from the land of the living;
    for the transgression of my people he
        was stricken.
⁹He was assigned a grave with the wicked,
    and with the rich in his death,
though he had done no violence,
    nor was any deceit in his mouth.
¹⁰Yet it was the LORD's will to crush him and
    cause him to suffer,
    and though the LORD makes his life a
        guilt offering,
he will see his offspring and prolong his
    days,
    and the will of the LORD will prosper in
        his hand.
¹¹After the suffering of his soul,
    he will see the light of life and be
        satisfied;
by his knowledge my righteous servant
    will justify many,
    and he will bear their iniquities.
¹²Therefore I will give a portion among the
    great,
    and he will divide the spoils with the
        strong,
because he poured out his life unto death,
    and was numbered with the transgressors.
For he bore the sin of many,

and made intercession for the
    transgressors.

Eschatology

Belief in life after death was almost universally held in New Testament times. Only scoffers, who wanted to live their lives free from concern about what awaited them beyond the grave, and the Sadducees, for dogmatic reasons, denied that people survived death. There were many eschatological schemes current, but a general set of ideas can be noted. First, after death, one typically awaited the resurrection of the body. For some thinkers, under the influence of Greek thought, the soul lived on independently of the body and no physical resurrection was envisioned. For others a combination of these two views existed. In some cases, only the righteous are resurrected. Second, a final judgment takes place where the sinners are separated from the righteous. Judgment is usually on the basis of one's actions here on earth, but God's mercy is a prominent part of the salvation of the righteous. For the lost, only God's retribution awaits. Third, the end of the age takes place at the same time as the resurrection and there follows a redoing of the created order. There are many views on what this means precisely, but a prominent idea is that of millennial blessings here on earth. Fourth, the final destinies of both the saved and the lost, which includes heaven and hell, are depicted, often graphically. This is especially true with respect to hell.

1. *The Resurrection and Immortality.* (##203–206). In the first four readings we have references to the resurrection. The first (#203) shows the sustaining hope of the resurrection during the bitter times of persecution that began the Maccabean revolt. The next two (##204, 205) speak of the resurrection of both the righteous and the unrighteous and the fourth (#206) speaks specifically of the resurrection of the flesh. So firmly fixed was this idea of resurrection that the Mishnah declares (M. San 10:1; see Reading #85) that those who deny the resurrection have no share in the world to come. (##207, 208) The influence of Greek thought may be seen in the two readings that speak of the immortality of the soul. However, it should not be imagined that Hebrew

thinkers were incapable of imagining that the soul could exist independently from the body. This becomes evident when (#209) immortality and resurrection are combined in one idea.

#203: God Will Raise Us Up
(2 Maccabees 7.8–9)

[8]Therefore he in turn underwent tortures as the first brother had done. [9]And when he was at his last breath, he said, "You accursed wretch, you dismiss us from this present life, but the King of the universe will raise us up to an everlasting renewal of life, because we have died for his laws."

#204: The Resurrection at the End of Time
(2 Baruch 30.1–5)

[1]And it will happen after these things when the time of the appearance of the Anointed One has been fulfilled and he returns with glory, that then all who sleep in hope of him will rise. [2]And it will happen at that time that those treasuries will be opened in which the number of the souls of the righteous were kept, and they will go out and the multitudes of the souls will appear together, in one assemblage, of one mind. And the first ones will enjoy themselves and the last ones will not be sad. [3]For they know that the time has come of which it is said that it is the end of times. [4]But the souls of the wicked will the more waste away when they shall see all these things. [5]For they know that their torment has come and that their perditions have arrived.

#205: The Resurrection Brings Glory and Dishonor
(Testament of Benjamin 10.2–9)

[2]After he had spoken these things to them he [Benjamin] said, "You know then, my children, that I am dying. Do the truth, each of you to his neighbor; [3]keep the Law of the Lord and his commandments, [4]for I leave you these things instead of an inheritance. Give them, then, to your children for an eternal possession; that is what Abraham, Isaac, and Jacob did. [5]They gave us all these things as an inheritance, saying, "Keep God's command-

ments until the Lord reveals his salvation to all the nations." [6]And then you will see Enoch and Seth and Abraham and Isaac and Jacob being raised up at the right hand in great joy. [7]Then shall we also be raised, each of us over our tribe, and we shall prostrate ourselves before the heavenly king. [8]Then all shall be changed, some destined for glory, others for dishonor, for the Lord first judges Israel for the wrong she has committed [9]and then he shall do the same for all the nations.

#206: The Resurrection of the Flesh
(4 Baruch 6.5–10)

[5]And raising his eyes to heaven, he [Baruch] prayed, saying, [6]"You are the God who bestows a reward (on) those who love you. Prepare yourself, my heart; rejoice and be glad in your tabernacle, saying to your fleshly dwelling, 'Your sorrow has been turned to joy.' For the Mighty One is coming and will raise you in your tabernacle, for sin has not taken root in you. [7]Be refreshed within your tabernacle, in your virgin faith, and believe that you will live. [8]Look at this basket of figs; for behold, they are sixty-six years old and they have not withered nor do they stink, but they are dripping with milk. [9]Thus will it be for you, my flesh, if you do the things commanded you by the angel of righteousness. [10]He who preserved the basket of figs, the same one again will preserve you by his power."

#207: Mankind Was Created for Incorruption
(Wisdom of Solomon 2.23–3.4)

[2:23]For God created man for incorruption,
and made him in the image of his own eternity.
[24]but through the devil's envy death entered the world,
and those who belong to his party experience it.
[3:1]But the souls of the righteous are in the hand of God,
and no torment will ever touch them.
[2]In the eyes of the foolish they seemed to have died,
and their departure was thought to be an affliction,

[3]and their going from us to be their
destruction;
but they are at peace.
[4]For though in the sight of men they were
punished,
their hope is full of immortality.

#208: The Souls of the Righteous Are Pure and Deathless
(4 Maccabees 18.20–23)

[20]Ah! bitter was the day and yet not bitter
when the cruel tyrant of the Greeks quenched
fire with fire in his fierce braziers, and in a fu-
rious rage brought to the catapult and back
again to his tortures those seven sons of the
daughter of Abraham; [21]he pierced the pupils
of their eyes, their tongues he cut out, and
slew them with all kinds of torment. [22]And
for these acts the divine justice has pursued
and will pursue the accursed tyrant. [23]But the
sons of Abraham, together with their mother,
who won the victor's prize, are gathered together in the choir of their fathers, having received pure and deathless souls from God, to
whom be glory forever and ever. Amen.

#209: The Soul Is Immortal and the Body Will Rise
(Pseudo-Phocylides 102–15)

[102]It is not good to dissolve the human
frame;
[103]for we hope that the remains of the departed will soon come to the light
(again)
[104]out of the earth; and afterward they will
become gods.
[105]For the souls remain unharmed among
the deceased.
[106]For the spirit is a loan of God to mortals,
and (his) image.
[107]For we have a body out of earth, and
when afterward we are resolved again
into earth
[108]we are but dust; and then the air has received our spirit.
[109]When you are rich, do not be sparing; remember that you are mortal.
[110]It is impossible to take riches and money
(with you) into Hades.

[111]All alike are corpses, but God rules over
the souls.
[112]Hades is (our) common eternal home and
fatherland,
[113]a common place for all, poor and kings.
[114]We humans live not a long time but for a
season.
[115]But (our) soul is immortal and lives age-
less forever.

2. *The Last Judgment.* There are numerous references to the last judgment. This idea is required
when one postulates a holy God, a moral universe,
and human responsibility. (##210–212) Three readings provide examples of how this was envisioned,
the last one being the most elaborate. There the
souls are weighed on a scale and tried by fire.

#210: Sinners Perish in the Day of Judgment
(Psalms of Solomon 15.6, 9–13)

[6]For God's mark is on the righteous for
(their) salvation. . . .
[9][The unrighteous] shall be overtaken as by
those experienced in war,
for on their forehead (is) the mark
of destruction.
[10]And the inheritance of sinners is destruction and darkness,
and their lawless actions shall pursue
them below into Hades.
[11]Their inheritance shall not be found for
their children,
for lawless actions shall devastate the
homes of sinners.
[12]And sinners shall perish forever in the day
of the Lord's judgment,
when God oversees the earth at his
judgment.
[13]But those who fear the Lord shall find
mercy in it
and shall live by their God's mercy;
but sinners shall perish for all time.

#211: The Day of Judgment Is a Day of Recompense
(4 Ezra 7.32–42)

[32]And the earth shall give up those who
are asleep in it; and the chambers shall give

up the souls which have been committed to them. [33]And the Most High shall be revealed upon the seat of judgment, and compassion shall pass away, and patience shall be withdrawn; [34]but judgment alone shall remain, truth shall stand, and faithfulness shall grow strong. [35]And recompense shall follow, and the reward shall be manifested; righteous deeds shall awake, and unrighteous deeds shall not sleep. [36]Then the pit of torment shall appear, and opposite it shall be the place of rest; and the furnace of Hell shall be disclosed, and opposite it the paradise of delight. [37]Then the Most High will say to the nations that have been raised from the dead, "Look now, and understand whom you have denied, whom you have not served, whose commandments you have despised! [38]Look on this side and on that; here are delight and rest, and there are fire and torments!" Thus he will speak to them on the day of judgment—[39]a day that has no sun or moon or stars, [40]or cloud or thunder or lightning or wind or water or air, or darkness or evening or morning, [41]or summer or spring or heat or winter or frost or cold or hail or rain or dew, [42]or noon or night, or dawn or shining or brightness or light, but only the splendor of the glory of the Most High, by which all shall see what has been determined for them.

#212: Souls Are Weighed in the Scales of God's Testing
(Testament of Abraham 12.1–18)

[1]While he was yet saying these things to me [Abraham], behold (there were) two angels, with fiery aspect and merciless intention and relentless look, and they drove myriads of souls, mercilessly beating them with fiery lashes. [2]And the angel seized one soul. And they drove all the souls into the broad gate toward destruction. [3]Then we too followed the angels and we came inside that broad gate. [4]And between the two gates there stood a terrifying throne with the appearance of terrifying crystal, flashing like fire. [5]And upon it sat a wondrous man, bright as the sun, like unto a son of God. [6]Before him stood a table like crystal, all of gold and byssus. [7]On the table lay a book whose thickness was six cubits, while its breadth was ten cubits. [8]On its right and on its left stood two angels holding papyrus and ink and pen. [9]In front of the table sat a light-bearing angel, holding a balance in his hand. [10][On] (his) left there sat a fiery angel, altogether merciless and relentless, holding a trumpet in his hand, which contained within it an all-consuming fire (for) testing the sinners. [11]And the wondrous man who sat on the throne was the one who judged and sentenced the souls. [12]The two angels on the right and on the left recorded. The one on the right recorded righteous deeds, while the one on the left (recorded) sins. [13]And the one who was in front of the table, who was holding the balance, weighed the souls. [14]And the fiery angel, who held the fire, tested the souls. [15]And Abraham asked the Commander-in-chief Michael, "What are these things which we see?" And the Commander-in-chief said, "These things which you see, pious Abraham, are judgment and recompense." [16]And behold, the angel who held the soul in his hand brought it before the judge. [17]And the judge told one of the angels who served him, "Open for me this book and find for me the sins of this soul." [18]And when he opened the book he found its sins and righteous deeds to be equally balanced, and he neither turned it over to the torturers nor (placed it among) those who were being saved, but he set it in the middle.

3. *Messianic Woes and Millennial Blessings.* The Old Testament prophets foresaw a time of universal peace when Israel would be restored. This idea had strong appeal in Jewish circles, especially during times of intense persecution and historical uncertainty. It became a complex idea and was often combined with other ideas, such as the end of the age, the last judgment, retribution on Israel's enemies, and the Messiah. There was no agreement as to the length of this "millennial" reign; one finds 40, 400, 1000, 2000, and 265,000 years mentioned, as well as infinite duration. It was to be preceded by a period of worldwide distress and tribulation called the "messianic woes." See also Readings ##196; 433.

(##213, 214) These two readings are a graphic portrayal of the time of tribulation that will precede the coming of the Messiah and the establishment of his kingdom.

#213: The Twelvefold Tribulation at the End of Time
(2 Baruch 25.1–27.15)

25.1And he answered and said to me:

You also will be preserved until that time, namely until that sign which the Most High will bring about before the inhabitants of the earth at the end of days. 2This then will be the sign: 3When horror seizes the inhabitants of earth, and they fall into many tribulations and further, they fall into great torments. 4And it will happen that they will say in their thoughts because of their great tribulations, "The Mighty One does not anymore remember the earth"; it will happen when they lose hope, that the time will awake.

26.1And I answered and said:

That tribulation which will be will it last a long time; and that distress, will it embrace many years?

27.1And he answered and said to me:

That time will be divided into twelve parts, and each part has been preserved for that for which it was appointed. 2In the first part: the beginning of commotions. 3In the second part: the slaughtering of the great. 4In the third part: the fall of many into death. 5In the fourth part: the drawing of the sword. 6In the fifth part: famine and the withholding of rain. 7In the sixth part: earthquakes and terrors. 9In the eighth part: a multitude of ghosts and the appearances of demons. 10In the ninth part: the fall of fire. 11In the tenth part: rape and much violence. 12In the eleventh part: injustice and unchastity. 13In the twelfth part: disorder and a mixture of all that has been before. 14These parts of that time will be preserved and will be mixed, one with another, and they will minister to each other. 15For some of these parts will withhold a part of themselves and take from others and will accomplish that which belongs to them and to others; hence, those who live on earth in those days will not understand that it is the end of times.

#214: The Signs of the Time at the End of the Age
(4 Ezra 8.63–9.12)

8.63Then I answered and said, "Behold, O Lord, you have now shown me a multitude of the signs which you will do in the last times, but you have not shown me when you will do them."

9.1He answered me and said, "Measure carefully in your mind, and when you see that a certain part of the predicted signs are past, 2then you will know that it is the very time when the Most High is about to visit the world which he has made. 3So when there shall appear in the world earthquakes, tumult of peoples, intrigues of nations, wavering of leaders, confusion of princes, 4then you will know that it was of these that the Most High spoke from the days that were of old, from the beginning. 5For just as with everything that has occurred in the world, the beginning is evident, and the end is manifest; 6so also are the times of the Most High: The beginnings are manifest in wonders and mighty works, and the end in requital and signs. 7And it shall be that everyone who will be saved and will be able to escape on account of his works, or on account of the faith by which he has believed, 8will survive the dangers that have been predicted, and will see my salvation in my land and within my borders, which I have sanctified for myself from the beginning. 9Then those who have now abused my ways shall be amazed, and those who have rejected them with contempt shall dwell in torments. 10For as many as did not acknowledge me in their lifetime, although they received my benefits, 11and as many as scorned my Law while they still had freedom, and did not understand but despised it while an opportunity of repentance was still open to them, 12these must in torment acknowledge it after death.

After the tribulation that wracks the earth, an age of blessedness arrives. (##215–217) Three selections from the Old Testament prophets provide the backdrop against which later speculation developed, (##218–221) followed by a representative selection of descriptive pictures of the messianic age.

#215: In That Day, the Wilderness Will Rejoice
(Isaiah 35:1–10)

[1]The desert and the parched land will be glad; the wilderness will rejoice and blossom. Like the crocus, [2]it will burst into bloom; it will rejoice greatly and shout for joy. The glory of Lebanon will be given to it, the splendor of Carmel and Sharon; they will see the glory of the LORD, the splendor of our God.

[3]Strengthen the feeble hands, steady the knees that give way, [4]say to those with fearful hearts, "Be strong, do not fear; your God will come, he will come with vengeance; with divine retribution he will come to save you."

[5]Then will the eyes of the blind be opened and the ears of the deaf unstopped. [6]Then will the lame leap like a deer, and the mute tongue shout for joy. Water will gush forth in the wilderness and streams in the desert. [7]The burning sand will become a pool, the thirsty ground bubbling springs. In the haunts where jackals once lay, grass and reeds and papyrus will grow.

[8]And a highway will be there; it will be called the Way of Holiness. The unclean will not journey on it; it will be for those who walk in that Way; wicked fools will not go about on it. [9]No lion will be there, nor will any ferocious beast get up on it; they will not be found there. But only the redeemed will walk there, [10]and the ransomed of the LORD will return. They will enter Zion with singing; everlasting joy will crown their heads. Gladness and joy will overtake them, and sorrow and sighing will flee away.

#216: The Wolf and the Lamb Will Feed Together
(Isaiah 65:20–25)

[20]"Never again will there be in it an infant who lives but a few days, or an old man who does not live out his years; he who dies at a hundred will be thought a mere youth; he who fails to reach a hundred will be considered accursed. [21]They will build houses and dwell in them; they will plant vineyards and eat their fruit. [22]No longer will they build houses and others live in them, or plant and others eat. For as the days of a tree, so will be the days of my people; my chosen ones will long enjoy the works of their hands. [23]They will not toil in vain or bear children doomed to misfortune; for they will be a people blessed by the LORD, they and their descendants with them. [24]Before they call I will answer, while they are still speaking I will hear. [25]The wolf and the lamb will feed together, and the lion will eat straw like the ox, but dust will be the serpent's food. They will neither harm nor destroy on all my holy mountain," says the LORD.

#217: Swords Will Be Beaten into Plowshares
(Micah 4:1–5)

[1]In the last days the mountain of the LORD's temple will be established as chief among the mountains; it will be raised above the hills, and peoples will stream to it.

[2]Many nations will come and say, "Come, let us go up to the mountain of the LORD, to the house of the God of Jacob. He will teach us his ways, so that we may walk in his paths." The law will go out from Zion, the word of the LORD from Jerusalem. [3]He will judge between many peoples and will settle disputes for strong nations far and wide. They will beat their swords into plowshares and their spears into pruning hooks. Nation will not take up sword against nation, nor will they train for war anymore. [4]Every man will sit under his own vine and under his own fig tree, and no one will make them afraid, for the LORD Almighty has spoken. [5]All the nations may walk in the name of their gods; we will walk in the name of the LORD our God for ever and ever.

218: The Earth Will Become a Blessing
(1 Enoch 45.4–6)

[4]On that day, I shall cause my Elect One to
    dwell among them,
I shall transform heaven and make it a
    blessing of light forever.
[5]I shall (also) transform the earth and make
    it a blessing,
and cause my Elect One to dwell in her.
Then those who have committed sin and
    crime shall not set foot in her.

[6]For in peace I have looked (with favor)
     upon my righteous ones and given
     them mercy,
and have caused them to dwell before me.
But sinners have come before me so that by
     judgment
I shall destroy them from before the face of
     the earth.

#219: The Supernatural Abundance of Earth
(2 Baruch 29.5–8)

[5]The earth will also yield fruits ten thousandfold. And on one vine will be a thousand branches, and one branch will produce a thousand clusters, and one cluster will produce a thousand grapes, and one grape will produce a cor of wine. [6]And those who are hungry will enjoy themselves and they will, moreover, see marvels every day. [7]For winds will go out in front of me every morning to bring the fragrance of aromatic fruits and clouds at the end of the day to distill the dew of health. [8]And it will happen at that time that the treasury of manna will come down again from on high, and they will eat of it in those years because these are they who will have arrived at the consummation of time.

#220: The Eternal Peace of the Millennial Kingdom
(2 Baruch 73.1–74.4)

[73.1]And it will happen that after he has brought down everything which is in the world, and has sat down in eternal peace on the throne of the kingdom, then joy will be revealed and rest will appear. [2]And then health will descend in dew, and illness will vanish, and fear and tribulation and lamentation will pass away from among men, and joy will encompass the earth. [3]And nobody will again die untimely, nor will any adversity take place suddenly. [4]Judgment, condemnations, contentions, revenges, blood, passions, zeal, hate, and all such things will go into condemnation since they will be uprooted. [5]For these are the things that have filled this earth with evils, and because of them life of men came in yet greater confusion. [6]And the wild beasts will come from the wood and serve men, and the asps and dragons will come out of their holes to subject themselves to a child. [7]And women will no longer have pain when they bear, nor will they be tormented when they yield the fruits of their womb.

[74.1]And it will happen in those days that the reapers will not become tired, and the farmers will not wear themselves out, because the products of themselves will shoot out speedily, during the time that they work on them in full tranquillity. [2]For that time is the end of that which is corruptible and the beginning of that which is incorruptible. [3]Therefore, the things which were said before will happen in it. Therefore, it is far away from the evil things and near to those which do not die. [4]Those are the last bright waters which have come after the last dark waters.

#221: In Those Days the Mountains Shall Dance
(1 Enoch 51.4–5)

[4]In those days, mountains shall dance like rams; and the hills shall leap like kids satiated with milk. And the faces of all the angels in heaven shall glow with joy, because on that day the Elect One has arisen. [5]And the earth shall rejoice; and the righteous ones shall dwell upon her and the elect ones shall walk upon her.

4. *Heaven and Hell.* At the last judgment everyone will be evaluated as to what their eternal destiny will be. (##222–224) The lost are the unrighteous, and their fearsome destiny is often vividly described in terms of fire, torture, and anguish. There is almost always a description of what they did wrong on earth and why they merited such indescribable misery. It is retribution and recompense that they are experiencing; they are reaping what they have sown. (##225, 226) Those in heaven experience the joy of the Lord as reward for the good that they have done or in compensation for the suffering they have undergone on earth because of their faithfulness to the Lord. It is interesting that the speculations about heaven are not as graphic or dramatic as those about hell. It is as though being with the Lord is good enough. Nothing more really needs to be said.

#222: A Frightful Place of Torment and Torture

(2 Enoch 10.1–6)

[1]And those men carried me [Enoch] to the northern region; and they showed me there a very frightful place; [2]and all kinds of torture and torment are in that place, cruel darkness and lightless gloom. And there is no light there, and a black fire blazes up perpetually, with a river of fire that comes out over the whole place, fire here, freezing ice there, and it dries up and it freezes; [3]and very cruel places of detention and dark and merciless angels, carrying instruments of atrocities torturing without pity.

[4]And I said, "Woe, woe! How very frightful this place is!" And those men said to me, "This place, Enoch, has been prepared for those who do not glorify God, who practice on the earth the sin which is against nature, which is child corruption in the anus in the manner of Sodom, of witchcraft, enchantments, divinations, trafficking with demons, who boast about their evil deeds—stealing, lying, insulting, coveting, resentment, fornication, murder—[5]and who steal the souls of men secretly, seizing the poor by the throat, taking away their possessions, enriching themselves from the possessions of others, defrauding them; who, when they are able to provide sustenance, bring about the death of the hungry by starvation; and, when they are able to provide clothing, take away the last garment of the naked; [6]who do not acknowledge their Creator, but bow down to idols which have no souls, which can neither see nor hear, vain gods; constructing images, and bowing down to vile things made by hands—for all these this place has been prepared as an eternal reward."

#223: The Burning Fire of the Uttermost Depths

(Apocalypse of Abraham 31.1–8)

[1]"And then I [the Lord] will sound the trumpet out of the air, and I will send my chosen one, having in him one measure of all my power, and he will summon my people, humiliated by the heathen. [2]And I will burn with fire those who mocked them and ruled over them in this age and I will deliver those who have covered me with mockery over to the scorn of the coming age. [3]Because I have prepared them (to be) food for the fire of Hades, and (to be) ceaseless soaring in the air of the underworld (regions) of the uttermost depths, (to be) the contents of a wormy belly. [4]For the makers will see in them justice, (the makers) who have chosen my desire and manifestly kept my commandments, and they will rejoice with merrymaking over the downfall of the men who remain and who followed after the idols and after their murders. [5]For they shall putrefy in the belly of the crafty worm Azazel, and be burned by the fire of Azazel's tongue. [6]For I waited so they might come to me, and they did not deign to. [7]And they glorified an alien (god). [8]And they joined one to whom they had not been allotted, and they abandoned the Lord who gave them strength.

#224: The Glut of Punishment in Eternal Damnation

(Rule of the Community 4.9–14)

[9]However, to the spirit of deceit belong greed, frailty of hands in the service of justice, irreverence, deceit, pride and haughtiness of heart, dishonesty, trickery, cruelty, [10]much insincerity, impatience, much insanity, impudent enthusiasm, appalling acts performed in a lustful passion, filthy paths for indecent purposes, [11]blasphemous tongue, blindness of eyes, hardness of hearing, stiffness of neck, hardness of heart in order to walk in all the paths of darkness and evil cunning. And the visitation [12]of those who walk in it will be for a glut of punishments at the hands of all the angels of destruction, for eternal damnation for the scorching wrath of the God of revenge, for permanent error and shame, [13]without end with the humiliation of destruction by the fire of the dark regions. And all the ages of their generations they shall spend in bitter weeping and harsh evils in the abysses of darkness until [14]their destruction, without there being a remnant or a survivor among them.

#225: The Tree of Life in the Presence of God
(1 Enoch 24.3–25.7)

24.3The seven mountains were (situated) in the midst of these (ravines) and (in respect to) their heights all resembled the seat of a throne (which is) surrounded by fragrant trees. 4And among them, there was one tree such as I have never at all smelled; there was not a single one among those or other (trees) which is like it; among all the fragrances nothing could be so fragrant; its leaves, its flowers, and its wood would never wither forever; its fruit is beautiful and resembles the clustered fruits of a palm tree. 5At that moment I said, "This is a beautiful tree, beautiful to view, with leaves (so) handsome and blossoms (so) magnificent in appearance." 6Then Michael, one of the holy and revered angels—he is their chief—who was with me, responded to me.

25.1And he said unto me, Enoch, "What is it that you are asking me concerning the fragrance of this tree and you are so inquisitive about?" 2At that moment, I answered saying, "I am desirous of knowing everything, but specially about this thing." 3He answered, saying, "This tall mountain which you saw whose summit resembles the throne of God is (indeed) his throne, on which the Holy and Great Lord of Glory, the Eternal King, will sit when he descends to visit the earth with goodness. 4And as for this fragrant tree, not a single human being has the authority to touch it until the great judgment, when he shall take vengeance on all and conclude (everything) forever. 5This is for the righteous and the pious. And the elect will be presented with its fruit for life. He will plant it in the direction of the northeast, upon the holy place—in the direction of the house of the Lord, the Eternal King.

6Then they shall be glad and rejoice in
     gladness,
and they shall enter into the holy (place);
its fragrance shall (penetrate) their bones,
long life will they live on earth,
such as your fathers lived in their days."

7At that moment, I blessed the God of Glory, the Eternal King, for he has prepared such things for the righteous people, as he had created (them) and given it to them.

#226: Eternal Enjoyment with Endless Life
(Rule of the Community 4.6–8)

6And the visitation of whose who walk in it [the way of righteousness] will be for healing, 7plentiful peace in a long life, fruitful offspring with all everlasting blessings, eternal enjoyment with endless life, and a crown of glory 8with majestic raiment in eternal light.

6 Jesus Outside of the New Testament

The four Gospels of the New Testament are our primary sources for authentic information about Jesus of Nazareth. Although there is a vast amount of material written about Jesus subsequent to the writings of the New Testament, it is of little value in establishing who Jesus really was. The reason is twofold. First, the material is usually very late and springs up from nowhere, bearing no connection to the church or to those who had some direct connection with Jesus. Second, it almost always contains some obvious bias, whether heretical, hostile, or even friendly, that makes it suspect as a valuable source of new information about Jesus. This does not mean, of course, that nothing in this material is of any value. It could well be that some of this material contains authentic reminiscences of Jesus, especially the sayings material. The problem is how to evaluate what is there. Most often that which sounds closest to the Jesus of the Gospels is counted as authentic and that which slants off decidedly in the wrong direction is discounted. Still, certain things stand out as of importance. From this material it can be ascertained that Jesus actually existed as a historical person, that he ministered in Roman Palestine, that he was known as a teacher and miracle-worker, that he was crucified during the procuratorship of Pontius Pilate, and that his followers claimed to have seen him alive after his death and worshiped him as divine. All of this can be found in abundance in the New Testament, of course, so this adds nothing new to our understanding of Jesus, but it is powerful corroborating testimony to what is found there.

It would be impossible to give examples of all of the different kinds of material that refers to Jesus in one way or another. Just that which bears most directly on his life and has at least some legitimate claim to authenticity is included.

For further study of this very important sub-ject, you could consult F. F. Bruce, *Jesus and Christian Origin Outside the New Testament;* R. Travers Herford, *Christianity in Talmud and Midrash;* Gary R. Habermas, *The Historical Jesus: Ancient Evidence for the Life of Christ.*

Jewish Writers

There are two passages in Josephus that are noteworthy in their reference to Jesus, (#227) the so-called *Testimonium Flavianum* (Witness of Flavius [Josephus]) and (#228) a reference to James, the brother of Jesus. The text given of the *Testimonium* is that found in the current editions of Josephus, but it is widely regarded as having been reworked by Christians at some time during its history, since it contains things that a devout Jew would hardly have said. Various, more Jewish, reconstructions have been offered over the years. (#229) A recent discovery of an Arabic version of Josephus's *Testimonium* is found in a history of the world written by the Christian bishop Agapius of Hierapolis. It certainly reads more like a direct quote from Josephus than the traditional text does. (##230, 231) The earliest references to Josephus's mention of Jesus are found in the Church Father, Origen (ca. 185–254). Origen's distinctly Christian slant can be seen in his comments on what Josephus said, but it shows the authenticity of Josephus's references, even if not exactly what he said. There are a considerable number of references to Jesus and his followers in rabbinic material, but most of it is hostile and of little value. (#232) The Babylonian Talmud confirms that at Passover time Jesus, referred to as Yesu, was executed by "hanging," that he performed miracles, and that he had a group of disciples. This latter reflects imprecision with respect to Christian teaching.

#227: Jesus the Doer of Wonderful Works

(Josephus, *Ant.* 18.3.3 §§63–64)

3. [63]Now, there was about this time, Jesus, a wise man, if it be lawful to call him a man, for he was a doer of wonderful works—a teacher of such men as receive the truth with pleasure. He drew over to him both many of the Jews, and many of the Gentiles. [64]He was [the] Christ; and when Pilate, at the suggestion of the principal men amongst us, had condemned him to the cross, those that loved him at the first did not forsake him, or he appeared to them alive again the third day, as the divine prophets had foretold these and ten thousand other wonderful things concerning him; and the tribe of Christians, so named from him, are not extinct at this day.

#228: Jesus, Who Was Called the Christ

(Josephus, *Ant.* 20.9.1 §200)

1. [200]Festus was now dead, and Albinus was but upon the road; so he [Ananias, the High-Priest] assembled the Sanhedrin of the judges, and brought before them the brother of Jesus, who was called Christ, whose name was James, and some others [or some of his companions]; and when he had formed an accusation against them as breakers of the law, he delivered them to be stoned.

#229: An Arabic Version of Josephus's *Testimonium*

Similarly Josephus the Hebrew. For he says in the treatise that he has written on the governance of the Jews: At this time there was a wise man who was called Jesus. And his conduct was good, and (he) was known to be virtuous. And many people from among the Jews and the other nations became his disciples. Pilate condemned him to be crucified and to die. And those who had become his disciples did not abandon his discipleship. They reported that he had appeared to them three days after his crucifixion and that he was alive; accordingly, he was perhaps the Messiah concerning whom the prophets have recounted wonders.

#230: Origen's Reference to Josephus's *Antiquities*

(Origen, *Against Celsus* 1.47)

[47]For in the 18th book of his *Antiquities of the Jews*, Josephus bears witness to John as having been a Baptist, and as promising purification to those who underwent the rite. Now this writer, although not believing in Jesus as the Christ, in seeking after the cause of the fall of Jerusalem and the destruction of the temple, whereas he ought to have said that the conspiracy against Jesus was the cause of these calamities befalling the people, since they put to death Christ, who was a prophet, says nevertheless being, although against his will, not far from the truth—that these disasters happened to the Jews as a punishment for the death of James the Just, who was a brother of Jesus (called Christ)—the Jews having put him to death, although he was a man most distinguished for his justice.

#231: Jerusalem Fell on Account of Jesus Christ

(Origen, *Against Celsus* 2.13)

[13]But at that time there were no armies around Jerusalem, encompassing and enclosing and besieging it; for the siege began in the reign of Nero, and lasted till the government of Vespasian, whose son Titus destroyed Jerusalem, on account, as Josephus says, of James the Just, the brother of Jesus who was called Christ, but in reality, as the truth makes clear, on account of Jesus Christ the Son of God.

#232: Jesus the "Sorcerer" and His Disciples

(Babylonian Talmud, *Sanhedrin* 43a)

It has been taught: on the eve of the Passover Yesu was hanged. For forty days before the execution took place, a herald went forth and cried, "He is going forth to be stoned because he has practiced sorcery and enticed Israel to apostasy. Any one who can say anything in his favor, let him come forward and plead on his behalf." But since nothing was brought forward in his favor he was hanged on the eve of the Passover.

Our Rabbis taught: Yesu had five disciples, Mattha, Naqai, Neẓer, Buni and Todah.

Pagan Writers

(#233) The Roman historian Tacitus gives a detailed description of Nero's persecution of the Christians which includes an explicit reference to Jesus as the originator of Christianity, and notes that he lived in Judea and died while Tiberius was emperor and Pontius Pilate was the procurator. (#234) Tacitus's hatred of the Christians was matched by the Roman satirist, Lucian of Samosata (ca. 115–200). In a cynical farce, "On the Death of Peregrinus," Peregrinus pretends to be a prophet and fools the Christians into worshiping him as well as their crucified founder. In this passage there is testimony to Jesus as well as to Christian beliefs. (#235) An otherwise unknown Syrian named Mara bar Serapion wrote a letter to his son sometime after the fall of Jerusalem (A.D. 70) encouraging him to pursue wisdom. In passing, he refers to great leaders of the past, including Jesus. From the tone of the letter Mara bar Serapion could hardly have been a Christian, which makes his comments all the more interesting.

#233: Roman Testimony to Christ and the Christians
(Tacitus, *Annals* 15.44)

⁴⁴But all human efforts, all the lavish gifts of the emperor [Nero], and the propitiations of the gods, did not banish the sinister belief that the conflagration was the result of an order. Consequently, to get rid of the report, Nero fastened the guilt and inflicted the most exquisite tortures on a class hated for their abominations, called Christians by the populace. Christus, from whom the name had its origin, suffered the extreme penalty during the reign of Tiberius at the hands of one of our procurators, Pontius Pilatus, and a most mischievous superstition, thus checked for the moment, again broke out not only in Judea, the first source of the evil, but even in

Rome, where all things hideous and shameful from every part of the world find their center and become popular. Accordingly, an arrest was first made of all who pleaded guilty; then, upon their information, an immense multitude was convicted, not so much of the crime of firing the city, as of hatred against mankind. Mockery of every sort was added to their deaths. Covered with the skins of beasts, they were torn by dogs and perished, or were nailed to crosses, or were doomed to the flames and burnt, to serve as a nightly illumination, when daylight had expired.

Nero offered his gardens for the spectacle, and was exhibiting a show in the circus, while he mingled with the people in the dress of a charioteer or stood aloft on a car. Hence, even for criminals who deserved extreme and exemplary punishment, there arose a feeling of compassion; for it was not, as it seemed, for the public good, but to glut one man's cruelty, that they were being destroyed.

#234: Lucian Mockingly Speaks of Jesus as Worshiped
(Lucian, *Passing of Peregrinus* 11)

¹¹It was then that Proteus [Peregrinus] learned the wondrous lore of the Christians, by associating with their priests and scribes in Palestine. And—how else could it be?—in a trice he made them all look like children; for he was prophet, cult-leader, head of the synagogue, and everything, all by himself. He interpreted and explained some of their books and even composed many, and they revered him as a god, made use of him as a lawgiver, and adopted him as their patron, next after that other, to be sure, whom they still worship, the man who was crucified in Palestine because he introduced this new cult into the world.

#235: The Jews Executed Their "Wise King"
(Letter from Mara bar Serapion to his son Serapion)

What advantage did the Athenians gain from putting Socrates to death? Famine and plague came upon them as a judgment for their crime. What advantage did the men of

Samos gain from burning Pythagoras? In a moment their land was covered with sand. What advantage did the Jews gain from executing their wise King? It was just after that that their kingdom was abolished. God justly avenged these three wise men: the Athenians died of hunger; the Samians were overwhelmed by the sea; the Jews, ruined and driven from their land, live in complete dispersion. But Socrates did not die for nothing; he lived on in the teaching of Plato. Pythagoras did not die for nothing; he lived on in the statue of Hera. Nor did the wise King die for nothing; he lived on in the teaching which he had given.

Christianity is founded on the bodily resurrection of Jesus. The stone was rolled away from Jesus' tomb as it is from this first-century family tomb.

Christian Testimony

Although there are numerous references to Jesus in apocryphal material there is a general consensus among scholars that it is almost entirely worthless as evidence concerning Jesus. There are also many references to Jesus in authentic Christian writings as well. Although they provide no new information about Jesus beyond what the New Testament says, they do provide ample testimony to who Jesus was. (#236) One such summary of Christian belief will suffice as an example of how facts about Jesus were remembered in the believing community.

#236: Early Christian Testimony to Jesus
(Justin Martyr, *First Apology* 13)

[13]What sober-minded man, then, will not acknowledge that we are not atheists, worshiping as we do the Maker of this universe, and declaring, as we have been taught, that He has no need of streams of blood and libations and incense; whom we praise to the utmost of our power by the exercise of prayer and thanksgiving for all things wherewith we are supplied, as we have been taught that the only honor that is worthy of Him is not to consume by fire what He has brought into being for our sustenance, but to use it for ourselves and those who need, and with gratitude to Him to offer thanks by invocations and hymns for our creation, and for all the means of health, and for the various qualities of the different kinds of things, and for the changes of the seasons; and to present before Him petitions for our existing again in incorruption through faith in Him. Our teacher of these things is Jesus Christ, who also was born for this purpose, and was crucified under Pontius Pilate, procurator of Judea, in the times of Tiberius Caesar; and that we reasonably worship Him, having learned that He is the Son of the true God Himself, and holding Him in the second place, and the prophetic Spirit in the third, we will prove. For they proclaim our madness to consist in this, that we give to a crucified man a place second to the unchangeable and eternal God, the Creator of all; for they do not discern the mystery that is herein, to which, as we make it plain to you, we pray you to give heed.

Part
2

Acts and Paul

7 Acts

For Acts as for all the rest of the New Testament books covered below, advanced commentaries offer a wealth of references to extrabiblical parallels. Students need only consult the indexes of these works to uncover it. Serious Acts commentaries include those by Ernst Haenchen, Hans Conzelmann, and F. F. Bruce (who wrote a pair of them).

Colin Hemer's *The Book of Acts in the Setting of Hellenistic History* is a rich source for additional references, especially from Acts 13 on. Mention should also be made of W. Ward Gasque's invaluable study of Acts research, *A History of the Criticism of the Acts of the Apostles*, and Martin Hengel's briefer critique of modern Acts scholarship, *Acts and the History of Earliest Christianity*. Both of these volumes go far toward shedding light on the use, misuse, or nonuse of extrabiblical parallels in Acts interpretation that are at once both the glory and the bane of Acts commentaries. Also to be noted is a series of six volumes edited by Bruce W. Winter and others dealing with various aspects of Acts' backgrounds: *The Book of Acts in Its Ancient Literary Setting*, *The Book of Acts in Its Graeco-Roman Setting*, *The Book of Acts and Paul in Roman Custody*, *The Book of Acts in Its Palestinian Setting*, *The Book of Acts in Its Diaspora Setting*, and *The Book of Acts in Its Theological Setting*.

Acts 1:8: "You Shall Be My Witnesses"

Jesus' words may sound strange to those reared in an age valuing "tolerance" above all else. What right did early Christians have to think their religion was better than any other? The early Christians answered: Because there is no other savior than Jesus (Acts 4:12), and no other God but the one in whose name Jesus came. But in addition to such theological reasoning, Jews (who made up the bulk of the early church during its beginning decades) were aware of the often appalling customs of peoples lacking the civilizing effects of Old Testament teaching. (# 237) Herodotus (ca. 485–425 B.C.) writes of a people called the Massagetae, who he says resembled the Scythians (see Col 3:11). It must not be thought that the Roman Empire was filled with tribes having such loathsome customs. But it was partially in response to the predatory and cruel ways of those not knowing God's word, justice, and love that the earliest missionaries went forth—at times at great peril to themselves.

#237: The Cruel Ways of the Massagetae
(Herodotus, *History* 1.215–16)

[215]In their dress and way of living the Massagetae are like the Scythians. Some ride, some do not—for they use both infantry and cavalry. They have archers and spearmen and are accustomed to carry the "sagaris," or bill. The only metals they use are gold and bronze: bronze for spearheads, arrow-points, and bill, and gold for headgear, belts, and girdles. Similarly they give their horses bronze breast-plates, and use gold about the bridle, bit, and cheek-pieces. Silver and iron are unknown to them, none being found in the country, though it produces bronze and gold in unlimited quantity. [216]As to their customs: every man has a wife, but all wives are used promiscuously. The Greeks believe this to be a Scythian custom; but it is not—it belongs to the Massagetae. If a man wants a woman, all he does is to hang up his quiver in front of her wagon and then enjoy her without misgiving. They have one way only of determining the appropriate time to die, namely this: when a

man is very old, all his relatives give a party and include him in a general sacrifice of cattle; then they boil the flesh and eat it. This they consider to be the best sort of death. Those who die of disease are not eaten but buried, and it is held a misfortune not to have lived long enough to be sacrificed. They have no agriculture, but live on meat and fish, of which there is an abundant supply in the Araxes. They are milk-drinkers. The only god they worship is the sun, to which they sacrifice horses: the idea behind this is to offer the swiftest animal to the swiftest of the gods.

Acts 2:30: David's Descendant on His Throne

In the Gospels Jesus is called the Son of David. Peter's preaching in Acts speaks of God's promise to enthrone a descendant of David. Peter refers to a prophecy made by the prophet Nathan over a thousand years before Christ's birth. (For this, see Reading #179.)

Acts 2:44: Possessions in Common

This was not forced but voluntary (Acts 5:4). (#238) In a Jewish community of (possibly) the second century B.C., members likewise donated all their possessions. But the "donation" was mandatory, and part of what knit the community together was not only a love for one another but also a hatred for all "the sons of darkness"—those outside the group.

#238: Communal Living at Qumran
(Rule of the Community 1.1–13)

[1][The Master shall teach the sai]nts to live [according to] the Book of the Community Rule, that they may [2]seek God with a whole heart and soul, and do what is good and right before Him [3]as He commanded by the hand of Moses and all His servants the Prophets; that they may love all [4]that He has chosen and hate all that

He has rejected; that they may abstain from all evil [5]and hold fast to all good; that they may practice truth, righteousness, and justice [6]upon earth and no longer stubbornly follow a sinful heart and lustful eyes [7]committing all manner of evil. He shall admit into the Covenant of Grace all those who have freely devoted themselves to the observance of God's precepts, [8]that they may be joined to the counsel of God and may live perfectly before Him in accordance with all [9]that has been revealed concerning their appointed times, and that they may love all the sons of light, each [10]according to his lot in God's design, and hate all the sons of darkness, each according to his guilt [11]in God's vengeance.

All those who freely devote themselves to His truth shall bring all their knowledge, powers, [12]and possessions into the Community of God, that they may purify their knowledge in the truth of God's precepts and order their powers [13]according to His ways of perfection and all their possessions according to His righteous counsel.

Acts 4:12: Christ the Only Way to Be Saved?

In every generation the question is raised whether knowledge of Christ is necessary to be saved. Passages like Acts 4:12 (see also Jn 14:6) leave little doubt what biblical writers thought. Their conviction regarding the uniqueness of God's identity, and the necessity of a measure of sure knowledge about him are firmly rooted in Old Testament precedent. Selected passages from just one Old Testament book, Isaiah, make a number of sobering points. Peter, the speaker in Acts 4:12, would have affirmed the following:

  (#239) God is not accessible through the gods and religions of the nations;

  (#240) God's people are witnesses to a God of utter salvific uniqueness;

  (#241) God himself doesn't know of a divine name that is or could be the equivalent of his own;

  (#242) In speaking by prophecy to the pagan king Cyrus, God makes clear that his people are the exclusive conduit for saving knowledge of the true God—and that this and this alone is the redemptive hope of the nations, who are all those outside the circle of Israel and Judah;

(#243) God's sole and unique salvation lies precisely in his unique revelation of himself—and nowhere else.

#239: The Gods and Religions of the Nations Are Nothing
(Isaiah 42:8)

[8]"I am the LORD; that is my name! I will not give my glory to another or my praise to idols."

#240: The God of Israel Alone Is Savior
(Isaiah 43:10–11)

[10]"You are my witnesses," declares the LORD, "and my servant whom I have chosen, so that you may know and believe me and understand that I am he. Before me no god was formed, nor will there be one after me. [11]I, even I, am the LORD, and apart from me there is no savior."

#241: Apart from God, There Is No God
(Isaiah 44:6–8)

[6]"This is what the LORD says—Israel's King and Redeemer, the LORD Almighty: I am the first and I am the last; apart from me there is no God. [7]Who then is like me? Let him proclaim it. Let him declare and lay out before me what has happened since I established my ancient people, and what is yet to come—yes, let him foretell what will come. [8]Do not tremble, do not be afraid. Did I not proclaim this and foretell it long ago? You are my witnesses. Is there any God besides me? No, there is no other Rock; I know not one."

#242: Israel Is God's Chosen Servant to Mediate Salvation to the World
(Isaiah 45:4–6)

[4]For the sake of Jacob my servant, of Israel my chosen, I summon you by name and bestow on you a title of honor, though you do not acknowledge me. [5]I am the LORD, and

there is no other; apart from me there is no God. I will strengthen you, though you have not acknowledged me, [6]so that from the rising of the sun to the place of its setting men may know there is none besides me. I am the LORD, and there is no other.

#243: Turn to the Lord and Be Saved
(Isaiah 45:18–22)

[18]For this is what the LORD says—he who created the heavens, he is God; he who fashioned and made the earth, he founded it; he did not create it to be empty, but formed it to be inhabited—he says: "I am the LORD, and there is no other. [19]I have not spoken in secret, from somewhere in a land of darkness; I have not said to Jacob's descendants, 'Seek me in vain.' I, the LORD, speak the truth; I declare what is right. [20]Gather together and come; assemble, you fugitives from the nations. Ignorant are those who carry about idols of wood, who pray to gods that cannot save. [21]Declare what is to be, present it—let them take counsel together. Who foretold this long ago, who declared it from the distant past? Was it not I, the LORD? And there is no God apart from me, a righteous God and a Savior; there is none but me. [22]Turn to me and be saved, all you ends of the earth; for I am God, and there is no other."

Acts 4:31: Prayer

Prayer and praying are mentioned often in Acts. Noticeable is the confidence with which Christians prayed and the dramatic nature of some of the answers they received. In the Greco-Roman world the nature and power of prayer, while generally affirmed, was the subject of discussion and uncertainty. (# 244) Pliny (d. A.D. 79) preserves the following traditions about prayer in Roman religion.

#244: Ancient Roman Prayer
(Pliny, *Natural History* 28.3 §§10–13)

[10]Of the remedies derived from man, the first raises a most important question, and one never settled: have words and formulated incantations any effect? If they have, it would be right

and proper to give the credit to mankind. As individuals, however, all our wisest men reject belief in them, although as a body the public at all times believes in them unconsciously. In fact the sacrifice of victims without a prayer is supposed to be of no effect; without it too the gods are not thought to be properly consulted. [11]Moreover, there is one form of words for getting favorable omens, another for averting evil, and yet another for a commendation. We see also that our chief magistrates have adopted fixed formulas for their prayers; that to prevent a word's being omitted or out of place a reader dictates beforehand the prayer from a script; that another attendant is appointed as a guard to keep watch, and yet another is put in charge to maintain a strict silence; that a piper plays so that nothing but the prayer is heard. Remarkable instances of both kinds of interference are on record: cases when the noise of actual ill omens has ruined the prayer, or when a mistake has been made in the prayer itself; then suddenly the head of the liver, or the heart, has disappeared from the entrails, or these have been doubled, while the victim was standing. [12]There has come down to us a striking example of ritual in that with which the Decii, a father and son, devoted themselves; extant too is the plea of innocence uttered by the Vestal Tuccia when, accused of unchastity, she carried water in a sieve, in the year of the City six hundred and nine. Our own generation indeed even saw buried alive in the Cattle Market a Greek man and a Greek woman, and victims from other peoples with whom at the time we were at war. The prayer used at this ceremony is wont to be dictated by the Master of the College of the Quindecimviri, and if one reads it one is forced to admit that there is power in ritual formulas, the events of eight hundred and thirty years showing this for all of them. [13]It is believed today that our Vestal virgins by a spell root to the spot runaway slaves, provided they have not left the City bounds, and yet, if this view is once admitted, that the gods hear certain prayers, or are moved by any form of words, the whole question must be answered in the affirmative. Our ancestors, indeed, reported such wonders again and again, and that, most impossible of all, even lightning can be brought by charms from the sky, as I have mentioned on the proper occasion.

Acts 5:3: Lying about Property

Ananias and Sapphira lied about the sale of land they owned. In their case God responded swiftly. (# 245) A Jewish document prescribes human punishment for such dishonesty.

#245: A Jewish Community Punishes Lying
(Rule of the Community 6.24–25)

These are the Rules by which they shall judge at a Community (Court of) Inquiry according to the cases

[24]If one of them has lied [25]deliberately in matters of property, he shall be excluded from the pure Meal of the congregation for one year and shall do penance with respect to one quarter of his food.

Acts 9:31: Church Membership

New Christians were accepted into the church on the basis of confession of faith in Christ's death for their sins and resurrection from the dead (cf. Rom 10:9). (#246) Very different was the membership process laid down by a document numbered among the Dead Sea Scrolls.

#246: Rules for Joining a Jewish Community
(Rule of the Community 6.13–23)

[13]Every man, born of Israel, who freely pledges himself [14]to join the Council of the Community, shall be examined by the Guardian at the head of the Congregation concerning his understanding and his deeds. If he is fitted to the discipline, he shall admit him [15]into the Covenant that he may be converted to the truth and depart from all injustice; and he shall instruct him in all the rules of the Community. And later, when he comes to stand be-

fore the Congregation, they shall [16]all deliberate his case, and according to the decision of the Council of the Congregation he shall either enter or depart. After he has entered the Council of the Community he shall not touch the pure Meal of [17]the Congregation until one full year is completed, and until he has been examined concerning his spirit and deeds; nor shall he have any share of the property of the Congregation. [18]Then when he has completed one year within the Community, the Congregation shall deliberate his case with regard to his understanding and observance of the Law. And if it be his destiny, [19]according to the judgement of the Priests and the multitude of the men of their Covenant, to enter the company of the Community, his property and earnings shall be handed over to the [20]Bursar of the Congregation who shall register it to his account and shall not spend it for the Congregation. He shall not touch the Drink of the Congregation until [21]he has completed a second year among the men of the Community. But when the second year has passed, he shall be examined, and if [22]it be his destiny, according to the judgment of the Congregation, to enter the Community, then he shall be inscribed among his brethren in the order of his rank for the Law, and for justice, and for the pure Meal; his property shall be merged and he shall offer his counsel [23]and judgment to the Community.

were the following: Roscius the comedian, Sorex the leading ballet dancer, and Metrobius the female impersonator. Metrobius was now past his prime, but Sulla throughout everything continued to insist that he was in love with him. By living in this way he aggravated a disease which had not been serious in its early stages, and for a long time he was not aware that he had ulcers in the intestines. This resulted in the whole flesh being corrupted and turning into worms. Many people were employed day and night in removing these worms, but they increased far more quickly than they could be removed. Indeed they came swarming out in such numbers that all his clothing, baths, hand-basins, and food became infected with the corruption and flux. He tried to clean and scour himself by having frequent baths throughout the day; but it was no use; the flesh changed into worms too quickly and no washing away could keep pace with their numbers.

It is said that in very ancient times Acatus the son of Pelias died of this disease and in later times Alcman the lyric poet, Pherecydes the theologian, Callisthenes of Olynthia (who died in prison), and also Mucius the jurist. And, if we may mention undistinguished but still notorious names, it is said that Eunus, the escaped slave who was leader in the Sicilian slave war, died of being eaten by worms after he had been captured and brought to Rome.

Acts 12:23: Disease

Acts 12:23 tells of Herod Agrippa I's death in A.D. 44. Herod "was eaten by worms and died." (# 247) The ancient historian Plutarch tells of a similar ailment afflicting the Roman leader Sulla (138–78 B.C.) and a number of others (see also Readings ##33 and 34).

#247: An Ancient Pagan's Illness
(Plutarch, *Fall of the Roman Republic, Sulla* 36)

[36]He [Sulla] still kept company with women who were ballet dancers or harpists and with people from the theater. They used to lie drinking together on couches all day long. Those who were at this time most influential with him

Acts 14:12: Zeus and Hermes

On the first missionary journey Barnabas and Paul preached to Lycaonians, who were polytheists. Ancient religious beliefs were not always as irrational as is sometimes supposed. (# 248) Cicero attempts to distinguish between fanciful mythology, which merits contempt, and sincere recognition of the gods who were commonly regarded as known.

#248: A Roman Philosopher's View of the Gods
(Cicero, *Nature of the Gods*, 2.70–71)

[70]"Do you not see, therefore, how from a sound and useful explanation of nature has

arisen this imaginary pantheon of deities? This is what has produced the false beliefs, confused errors, and silly superstitions. For we know how the gods look, how old they are, their wearing apparel and ornaments, their ancestry, marriages, relatives—in fact, everything about them is forced into conformity with human weakness. They are represented as moved by passion: we hear of their lust, their grief, their anger; according to the myths they even have wars and battles—not only, as in Homer, when two different armies are engaged and they take opposite sides, but they have fought battles of their own, as against the Titans and Giants. These stories, which are repeated and believed, are utterly stupid, full of the utmost folly and nonsense.

[71]"But, while we reject these myths with contempt, we nevertheless recognize that a god is concerned with each part of nature—Ceres the land, Neptune the sea, other parts, other gods. They can be known, both who they are and what they are, and also by what names they are customarily called; these are the gods whom it is our duty to revere and to worship. The best, the purest, the holiest and most pious worship of the gods is to reverence them always with a pure, sincere, uncorrupted mind and tongue.

Acts 15:21: Moses

At the Jerusalem Council (A.D. 49), James pointed out that Gentile believers must be sensitive to the religious customs of their Jewish Christian brethren, because "Moses has been preached in every city from the earliest times and is read in the synagogues on every Sabbath" (Acts 15:21). What did people understand Moses to teach? (# 249) While opinions would have varied, Philo summarizes Moses' teaching on creation under five points.

#249: Philo's Theology of Creation
(Philo, *On the Creation* 61 §§170–72)

61. . . . [170]And in his beforementioned account of the creation of the world, Moses teaches us also many other things, and especially five most beautiful lessons which are superior to all others. In the first place, for the

sake of convicting the atheists, he teaches us that the Deity has a real being and existence. Now, of the atheists, some have only doubted of the existence of God, stating it to be an uncertain thing; but others, who are more audacious, have taken courage, and asserted positively that there is no such thing; but this is affirmed only by men who have darkened the truth with fabulous inventions.

[171]In the second place he teaches us that God is one; having reference here to the assertors of the polytheistic doctrine; men who do not blush to transfer that worst of evil constitutions, ochlocracy, from earth to heaven.

Thirdly, he teaches, as has been already related, that the world was created; by this lesson refuting those who think that it is uncreated and eternal, and who thus attribute no glory to God.

In the fourth place we learn that the world also which was thus created is one, since also the Creator is one, and he, making his creation to resemble himself in its singleness, employed all existing essence in the creation of the universe. For it would not have been complete if it had not been made and composed of all parts which were likewise whole and complete. For there are some persons who believe that there are many worlds, and some who even fancy that they are boundless in extent, being themselves inexperienced and ignorant of the truth of those things of which it is desirable to have a correct knowledge.

The fifth lesson that Moses teaches us is, that God exerts his providence for the benefit of the world. [172]For it follows of necessity that the Creator must always care for that which he has created, just as parents do also care for their children. And he who has learnt this not more by hearing it than by his own understanding, and has impressed on his own soul these marvelous facts which are the subject of so much contention—namely, that God has a being and existence, and that he who so exists is really one, and that he has created the world, and that he has created it one as has been stated, having made it like to himself in singleness; and that he exercises a continual care for that which he has created will live a happy and blessed life, stamped with the doctrines of piety and holiness.

Acts 16:16: Future-Telling Slave Girl

Why did Paul and Silas regard this girl as being in bondage to an evil spirit (Acts 16:18)? Because the Old Testament taught that the attempt to predict and manipulate the future in certain ways marked a turning aside from trust in God. The slave girl was not filled with the Holy Spirit but with some devilish force—in addition to being the victim of her masters' profiteering. For her own good, Paul moved to deliver her. (##250–54) A series of Old Testament passages condemns fortune-telling as a rejection of God.

#250: Do Not Turn to Spiritists
(Leviticus 19:31)

³¹Do not turn to mediums or seek out spiritists, for you will be defiled by them. I am the LORD your God.

#251: God Condemns Fortune-telling
(Leviticus 20:6)

⁶I will set my face against the person who turns to mediums and spiritists to prostitute himself by following them, and I will cut him off from his people.

#252: Israel Must Not Imitate the Pagan Nations
(Deuteronomy 18:9–11)

⁹When you enter the land the LORD your God is giving you, do not learn to imitate the detestable ways of the nations there. ¹⁰Let no one be found among you who sacrifices his son or daughter in the fire, who practices divination or sorcery, interprets omens, engages in witchcraft, ¹¹or casts spells, or who is a medium or spiritist or who consults the dead.

#253: Manasseh's Sorcery Provoked God's Anger
(2 Kings 21:6)

⁶[Manasseh] sacrificed his own son in the fire, practiced sorcery and divination, and consulted mediums and spiritists. He did much evil in the eyes of the LORD, provoking him to anger.

#254: Inquire of God, Not the Dead
(Isaiah 8:19)

¹⁹When men tell you to consult mediums and spiritists, who whisper and mutter, should not a people inquire of their God? Why consult the dead on behalf of the living?

Acts 18:2: Claudius's Edict

Luke's words in Acts are corroborated by the Roman historian Suetonius (#255). "Chrestus" is probably a misspelling of "Christ." This was not the first time that a Roman emperor had banished Jews from the imperial city. Under Tiberius's reign a handful of unscrupulous Jews caused woe for thousands of their countrymen, as recounted by Josephus (#256).

#255: Claudius Expels the Jews from Rome
(Suetonius, *Twelve Caesars, Claudius* 25.4)

⁴Because the Jews at Rome caused continuous disturbances at the instigation of Chrestus, [Claudius] expelled them from the city.

#256: Tiberius Expels Some Jews from Rome
(Josephus, *Ant.* 18.3.5 §§81–84)

5. ⁸¹There was a man who was a Jew, but had been driven away from his own country by an accusation laid against him for transgressing their laws, and by the fear he was under of punishment for the same; but in all respects a wicked man:—he then living at Rome, professed to instruct men in the wisdom of the laws of Moses. ⁸²He procured also three other men, entirely of the same character with himself, to be his partners. These men persuaded Fulvia, a woman of great dignity, and one that had embraced the Jewish religion, to send purple and gold to the temple at Jerusalem; and, when they had gotten them, they employed them for

their own uses, and spent the money themselves; on which account it was that they at first required it of her. [83]Whereupon Tiberius, who had been informed of the thing by Saturninus, the husband of Fulvia, who desired inquiry might be made about it, ordered all the Jews to be banished out of Rome; [84]at which time the consuls listed four thousand men out of them, and sent them to the island Sardinia; but punished a greater number of them, who were unwilling to become soldiers on account of keeping the laws of their forefathers. Thus were these Jews banished out of the city by the wickedness of four men.

Acts 19:37:
See Romans 2:22
(Readings #268–70)

Acts 20:4: Leadership

Paul and the other apostolic leaders must have exhibited certain leadership qualities in order to gain the following they did. Instances of effective leadership abound in accounts of ancient Roman soldiers and politicians (and often both); (#257) Gaius Marius (157–86 B.C.) furnishes an example.

#257: Effective Leadership in Ancient Rome
(Plutarch, *Fall of the Roman Republic, Gaius Marius* 7)

[7]He was not afraid of any undertaking, however great, and was not too proud to accept any task, however small. The advice he gave and his foresight into what was needed marked him out among the officers of his own rank, and he won the affection of the soldiers by showing that he could live as hard as they did and endure as much. Indeed it seems generally to be the case that our labors are eased when someone goes out of his way to share them with us; it has the effect of making the labor not seem forced. And what a Roman soldier likes most to see is his general eating his ration of bread with the rest, or sleeping on an ordinary bed, or joining in the work of digging a trench or raising a palisade. The commanders whom they admire are not so much those who distribute honors and riches as those who take a share in their hardships and their dangers; they have more affection for those who are willing to join in their work than for those who indulge them in going easy.

By these actions and in this way Marius won the hearts of the soldiers.

Acts 20:13–14: The City of Assos

While we have no record of early Christian mission activity in Assos, a coastal city of the province of Asia, it likely resembled nearby towns (e.g., Pergamum) where churches were established. (#258) In 1881 a bronze tablet was found at Assos dating to A.D. 37. It records the oath of allegiance that Assos's inhabitants swore to the emperor Gaius [Caligula] when he gained power. Given Gaius's status as a god, and the deification of Augustus (see below), it is no wonder that Paul and others met opposition as they traveled and preached "the kingdom of God" as Acts records (8:1, 2; 14:22; 19:9; 28:23, 28).

#258:
(Decree of Homage to Gaius [Caligula])

Under the consulship of Gnaeus Acerronius Proclus and Gaius Pontius Petronius Nigrinus [A.D. 37].

Decree of the Assians, by Vote of the People

Since the announcement of the coronation of Gaius Caesar Germanicus Augustus (Caligula), which all mankind had longed and prayed for, the world has found no measure for its joy, but every city and people has eagerly hastened to view the god, as if the happiest age for mankind [the Golden Age] had now arrived:

It seemed good to the Council, and to the Roman businessmen here among us, and to the people of Assos, to appoint a delegation made up of the noblest and most eminent of the Romans and also of the Greeks, to visit him and offer their best wishes and to implore him to remember the city and take care of it, even as he promised our city upon his first visit to the province in the company of his father Germanicus.

Oath of the Assians

We swear by Zeus the Savior and the God Caesar Augustus [Octavian] and the holy Virgin of our city [Athena Polias] that we are loyally disposed to Gaius Caesar Augustus and his whole house, and look upon as our friends whomever he favors, and as our enemies whomever he denounces. If we observe this oath, may all go well with us; if not, may the opposite befall.

Acts 21:28: Greeks in the Temple Area

Rumors that Paul had brought Trophimus, a non-Jew from Ephesus, into the temple area provoked a riot. Jews in Jerusalem had long been zealous for the sanctity of their religion's most holy place. (#259) Over two centuries earlier, the city rose up in protest when an Egyptian ruler (Ptolemy IV Philopator, 221–203 B.C.) tried to enter the temple's most sacred place. For the actual desecration of the temple by the Syrian Antiochus IV, see Reading #12.

#259: Ptolemy's Attempt to Violate the Temple
(3 Maccabees 1.9–12, 16–17, 19–29)

⁹After he (Ptolemy IV) had arrived in Jerusalem, he offered sacrifice to the supreme God and made thank-offerings and did what was fitting for the holy place. Then, upon entering the place and being impressed by its excellence and its beauty, ¹⁰he marveled at the good order of the temple, and conceived a desire to enter the holy of holies. ¹¹When they said that this was not permitted, because not even members of their own nation were allowed to enter, nor even all of the priests, but only the high priest who was pre-eminent over all, and he only once a year, the king was

by no means persuaded. ¹²Even after the law had been read to him, he did not cease to maintain that he ought to enter, saying, "Even if those men are deprived of this honor, I ought not to be." . . .

¹⁶Then the priests in all their vestments prostrated themselves and entreated the supreme God to aid in the present situation and to avert the violence of this evil design, and they filled the temple with cries and tears; ¹⁷and those who remained behind in the city were agitated and hurried out, supposing that something mysterious was occurring. . . . ¹⁹Those women who had recently been arrayed for marriage abandoned the bridal chambers prepared for wedded union, and, neglecting proper modesty, in a disorderly rush flocked together in the city. ²⁰Mothers and nurses abandoned even newborn children here and there, some in houses and some in the streets, and without a backward look they crowded together at the most high temple. ²¹Various were the supplications of those gathered there because of what the king was profanely plotting. ²²In addition, the bolder of the citizens would not tolerate the completion of his plans or the fulfillment of his intended purpose. ²³They shouted to their fellows to take arms and die courageously for the ancestral law, and created a considerable disturbance in the holy place; and being barely restrained by the old men and the elders, they resorted to the same posture of supplication as the others. ²⁴Meanwhile the crowd, as before, was engaged in prayer, ²⁵while the elders near the king tried in various ways to change his arrogant mind from the plan that he had conceived.

²⁶But he, in his arrogance, took heed of nothing, and began now to approach, determined to bring the aforesaid plan to a conclusion. ²⁷When those who were around him observed this, they turned, together with our people, to call upon him who has all power to defend them in the present trouble and not to overlook this unlawful and haughty deed. ²⁸The continuous, vehement, and concerted cry of the crowds resulted in an immense uproar; ²⁹for it seemed that not only the men but also the walls and the whole earth around

echoed, because indeed all at that time preferred death to the profanation of the place.

Acts 22:28: Citizenship

In Acts 22:28 a Roman commander tells how he obtained citizenship by paying either a high fee or a bribe. Paul had it from birth. The privileges of Roman citizenship were considerable, and the means of obtaining it were sometimes corrupt, as the following account during Sulla's time (138–78 B.C.) shows (#260). (#261) Suetonius speaks of a near-uprising sparked by the desire for citizenship.

#260: The Sale of Roman Citizenship
(Plutarch, *Fall of the Roman Republic, Sulla* 8)

[8]Marius now formed an alliance with the tribune Sulpicius, a man so thoroughly bad as to be quite exceptional; one tended to inquire not how far he surpassed others, but on what occasions he surpassed himself in wickedness. He was cruel, reckless, and grasping and showed himself to be so quite shamelessly and with a total lack of scruple—actually putting up the rights of Roman citizenship for sale by public auction to ex-slaves and aliens and counting out the money at tables specially set up in the forum. He maintained a private army of 3,000 swordsmen and went about accompanied by large bands of young men from the moneyed class outside the senate, who were ready for anything and whom he used to call his Anti-senate.

#261: A Near Riot over Citizenship
(Suetonius, *Twelve Caesars, Julius Caesar* 8.1)

[1][Julius Caesar] visited the Latin colonists beyond the Po, who were bitterly demanding the same Roman citizenship as that granted to other townsfolk in Italy; and might have persuaded them to revolt, had not the Consuls realized the danger and garrisoned that district with the legions recently raised for the Cilician campaign.

The waves of the sea can be either friend or foe—Paul's shipwreck testified to the ocean's enmity.

Acts 27:12: Sailing in Winter

Why didn't Paul's ship simply sail on to Rome? The waters of the Mediterranean were too dangerous for the small ships of the day. (#262) Josephus records how even the great Roman general Titus, when had finished his conquest of Judea and wanted to return to Rome, did not dare set sail in wintertime after disbanding his troops.

#262: The Perils of the Winter Sea
(Josephus, *Jewish War* 7.1.3 §§17–20)

[17]He sent away the rest of his army to the several places where they would be every one best situated; but permitted the tenth legion to stay, as a guard at Jerusalem, and did not send them away beyond Euphrates, where they had been before; [18]and as he remembered that the twelfth legion had given way to the Jews, under Cestius, their general, he expelled them out of all Syria, for they had lain formerly at Raphanea, and sent them away to a place called Meletine, near Euphrates, which is in the limits of Armenia and Cappadocia; [19]he also thought fit that two of the legions should stay with him till he should go to Egypt. [20]He then went down with his army to that Caesarea which lay by the seaside, and there laid up the rest of his spoils in great quantities, and gave order that the captives should be kept there; for the winter-season hindered him then from sailing into Italy.

8 Romans–Galatians

Examples of advanced commentaries containing additional references to extrabiblical parallels or passages include the following:

- Romans: Cranfield, Moo, Sanday and Headlam
- 1 Corinthians: Barrett, Fee, Ellis
- 2 Corinthians: Martin, Harris
- Galatians: Bruce, Longenecker, Fung, Betz, Ramsay

Other studies useful for understanding Paul's cultural background and world include Martin Hengel with Roland Deines, *The Pre-Christian Paul*; Willliam D. Davies, *Paul and Rabbinic Judaism*; and J. Gresham Machen, *The Origin of Paul's Religion*, to be read in tandem with the more recent work by Seyoon Kim, *The Origin of Paul's Gospel*; and A. D. Nock, *St. Paul*. Advanced students may wish to consult the important studies of E. P. Sanders, *Paul and Palestinian Judaism* and *Paul, the Law, and the Jewish People*. But his controversial recasting of Paul's thought based on a revised understanding of rabbinic and other Jewish sources is still the subject of much debate. Perhaps the most important study of recent years will prove to be Rainer Riesner, *Paul's Early Period: Chronology, Mission Strategy, Theology*.

Romans 1:4: Spirit of Holiness

The Spirit of God played a role in Jewish religion. (#263) The Dead Sea Scrolls contain memorable words about the role of the Spirit in salvation. Salvation here, however, is based in part on human work, and not on the atoning work of Christ alone as in the gospel Paul preached.

#263: The Role of the Spirit in Salvation
(Rule of the Community 3.6–8)

⁶For it is through the spirit of true counsel concerning the ways of man that all ⁷his sins shall be expiated that he may contemplate the light of life. He shall be cleansed from all his sins by the spirit of holiness uniting him to His truth, ⁸and his iniquity shall be expiated by the spirit of uprightness and humility.

Romans 1:18: The Wrath of God— and God's Mercy

Paul was familiar with many Old Testament examples of God expressing his disapproval of human wickedness. (#264) Psalm 106 recounts instances of the Israelites' rebellion, which called forth God's hot displeasure. Yet despite the people's waywardness, God reached out to them in compassion. (#265) As the psalmist relates this, he is moved like Paul to praise God for his kindness.

#264: God's Judgment of Israel's Idolatry
(Psalm 106:35–43)

³⁵[The Israelites' entering Canaan under Joshua] mingled with the nations
　　and adopted their customs.
³⁶They worshiped their idols,
　　which became a snare to them.
³⁷They sacrificed their sons
　　and their daughters to demons.

³⁸They shed innocent blood,
 the blood of their sons and daughters,
 whom they sacrificed to the idols of
 Canaan,
and the land was desecrated by their
 blood.
³⁹They defiled themselves by what they did;
 by their deeds they prostituted themselves.
⁴⁰Therefore the LORD was angry with his
 people
 and abhorred his inheritance.
⁴¹He handed them over to the nations,
 and their foes ruled over them.
⁴²Their enemies oppressed them
 and subjected them to their power.
⁴³Many times he delivered them,
 but they were bent on rebellion
 and they wasted away in their sin.

#265: God Remembers His Covenant in Mercy

(Psalm 106:44–48)

⁴⁴But [God] took note of their distress
 when he heard their cry;
⁴⁵for their sake he remembered his covenant
 and out of his great love he relented.
⁴⁶He caused them to be pitied
 by all who held them captive.
⁴⁷Save us, O LORD our God,
 and gather us from the nations,
that we may give thanks to your holy name
 and glory in your praise.
⁴⁸Praise be to the LORD, the God of Israel,
 from everlasting to everlasting.
Let all the people say, "Amen!"
Praise the LORD.

Romans 1:20: Knowing God through Creation

Paul, like certain psalms of the Old Testament, taught that the wonders of creation were sufficient to inform humans of God's existence (#266). Similar thoughts, but also contrasts, are reflected in a Jewish writing dating perhaps to the first century B.C.

#266: What May Be Known of God through Nature

(Wisdom of Solomon 13.1–5)

¹For all men who were ignorant of God were foolish by nature; and they were unable from the good things that are seen to know him who exists, nor did they recognize the craftsman while paying heed to his works; ²but they supposed that either fire or wind or swift air, or the circle of the stars, or turbulent water, or the luminaries of heaven were the gods that rule the world. ³If through delight in the beauty of these things men assumed them to be gods, let them know how much better than these is their Lord, for the author of beauty created them. ⁴And if men were amazed at their power and working, let them perceive from them how much more powerful is he who formed them. ⁵For from the greatness and beauty of created things comes a corresponding perception of their Creator.

Romans 1:22: What Is Wisdom?

Paul writes that God's wrath falls on those who make their own convictions and thoughts the sole test of goodness and truth. (#267) Philo likewise condemns the doctrine of autonomous man.

#267: Man Is Not the Measure of All Things

(Philo, *Posterity and Exile of Cain* 11 §35)

³⁵What then is the position of the impious man? Why, that the human mind is the measure of all things; which also they say that one of the ancient philosophers, Protagoras, used to employ, being a descendant of the folly of Cain.

Romans 2:22: Temple-Robbing

Many ancient religious sites contained valuable articles. It was thought to be a specially heinous crime to plunder them, but Roman emperors at times violated this taboo, such as (#268) Julius Caesar, (#269) Nero, and (#270) Vitellius. For an account of how the Syrian ruler Antiochus plundered the temple in Jerusalem, see Reading #12.

#268: Julius Caesar Plunders Some Temples
(Suetonius, *Twelve Caesars, Julius Caesar* 54.1–2)

[1]He [Julius Caesar] was not particularly honest in money matters, either while a provincial governor or while holding office at Rome. Several memoirs record that as Governor in Spain he not only begged his allies for money to settle his debts, but wantonly sacked several Lusitanian towns, though they had accepted his terms and opened their gates to welcome him.

[2]In Gaul he plundered large and small temples of their votive offerings, and more often gave towns over to pillage because their inhabitants were rich than because they had offended him. As a result he collected larger quantities of gold than he could handle, and began selling it for silver, in Italy and the provinces, at 3,000 sestertii to the pound—which was about two-thirds of the official exchange rate.

#269: Nero's Robbery of Greek Temples
(Suetonius, *Twelve Caesars*, Nero 32.1–4)

[1][Near the end of his reign] Nero found himself destitute—and his financial difficulties were such that he could not lay hands on enough money even for the soldiers' pay or the veterans' benefits; and therefore resorted to robbery and blackmail.

[2]First he made a law that if a freedman died who had taken the name of a family connected with his own, and could not show adequate reason, five-sixths of the estate, not merely one-half, should be forfeited to the Privy Purse. Next, he seized the estates of those who had shown ingratitude to their Emperor; and fined the lawyers responsible for writing and dictating such wills. Moreover, any man whose words or deeds offered the least handle to an informer was charged with treason. [3]He recalled the presents he had given to Greek cities in acknowledgment of prizes won at musical or athletic contests. On one market-day he sent an agent to sell a few ounces of the amethystine and Tyrian purple dyes which he had forbidden to be used, and then closed the business of dealers who had bought them. It is said that he once noticed a lady wearing of this illegal color at one of his recitals, pointed her out to his servants and had her dragged off—whereupon she was stripped not only of her robe but of her entire property. His [4]invariable formula, when he appointed a magistrate, was: "You know my needs! Let us see to it that nobody is left with anything." Finally he robbed numerous temples of their treasures and melted down the gold and silver images, among them the Household-gods of Rome—which Galba, however, had recast soon afterwards.

#270: Vitellius's Violation of Roman Temples
(Suetonius, *Twelve Caesars*, Vitellius 5.1)

[1]Since he [Vitellius] was thus the favorite of three emperors, Vitellius won public offices and important priesthoods, and later served as Governor of Africa and Curator of Public Works. His reputation and energies, however, varied with the employment given him. Though exceptionally honest during the two-year administration of Africa, where he temporarily acted for his brother (who succeeded him), Vitellius' behavior while in office at Rome was by no means so commendable: he used to pilfer offerings and ornaments from the temples or provide substitutes, replacing gold and silver with brass and tin.

Romans 2:24: "God's Name Is Blasphemed among the Gentiles Because of You"

It is impossible to know exactly what Paul had in mind when he penned these incriminating words. But barely ten years after Paul wrote Romans, the Roman general Titus reproached Jewish revolutionaries in Jerusalem for their hypocrisy in committing human slaughter in the Jerusalem temple, a temple from which "unclean" non-Jews had been barred under penalty of death (#271); (see also below under Eph 2:14).

#271: Titus Defends the Jewish Temple's Honor
(Josephus, *Jewish War* 6.2.4 §§124–28)

4. [124]Now Titus was deeply affected with this state of things, and reproached John and his party, and said to them, "Have not you, vile wretches that you are, by our permission, put up this partition-wall before your sanctuary? [125]Have not you been allowed to put up the pillars thereto belonging at due distances, and on it to engrave in Greek, and in your own letters, this prohibition, that no foreigners should go beyond that wall? [126]Have not we given you leave to kill such as go beyond it, though he were a Roman? And what do you do now, you pernicious villains? Why do you trample upon dead bodies in this temple? and why do you pollute this holy house with the blood both of foreigners and Jews themselves? [127]I appeal to the gods of my own country, and to every god that ever had any regard to this place (for I do not suppose it to be now regarded by any of them); I also appeal to my own army, and to those Jews that are now with me, and even to you yourselves, that I do not force you to defile this your sanctuary; [128]and if you will but change the place whereon you will fight, no Roman shall either come near your sanctuary, or offer any affront to it; nay, I will endeavor to preserve you your holy house, whether you will or not."

Romans 3:2: "The Very Words of God"

Paul had in mind the Scriptures of the Old Testament. These were originally composed in Hebrew and Aramaic, but in the New Testament era most Jews in the Roman Empire read them in Greek translation, the Septuagint (LXX). Paul often quoted this translation in his own letters (#272). The Letter of Aristeas is a (largely legendary) account of how the Old Testament books were trans-

lated under the Egyptian king Ptolemy II (285–247 B.C.) for the famous library at Alexandria. "They" in the first line refers to the translators. The person who asks the question about handwashing is Aristeas, the author of the "letter" quoted below. Demetrius is the royal librarian.

#272: The Piety of the Septuagint Translators
(Letter of Aristeas 304–11)

[304]At the first hour of the day they [the translators] attended the court daily, and after offering salutations to the king, retired to their own quarters. [305]Following the custom of all the Jews, they washed their hands in the sea in the course of their prayers to God, and then proceeded to the reading and explication of each point. [306]I asked this question: "What is their purpose in washing their hands while saying their prayers?" They explained that it is evidence that they have done no evil, for all activity takes place by means of the hands. Thus they nobly and piously refer everything to righteousness and truth. [307]In this way, as we said previously, each day they assembled in their quarters, which were pleasantly situated for quiet and light, and proceeded to fulfill their prescribed task. The outcome was such that in seventy-two days the business of translation was completed, just as if such a result was achieved by some deliberate design. [308]When it was completed, Demetrius assembled the company of the Jews in the place where the task of the translation had been finished, and read it to all, in the presence of the translators, who received a great ovation from the crowded audience for being responsible for great blessings. [309]Likewise also they gave an ovation to Demetrius and asked him, now that he had transcribed the whole Law, to give a copy to their leaders. [310]As the books were read, the priests stood up, with the elders from among the translators and from the representatives of the "Community," and with the leaders of the people, and said, "Since this version has been made rightly and reverently, and in every respect accurately, it is good that this should remain exactly so, and that there should be no revision." [311]There was general approval of what they said, and they commanded that a curse should be laid, as was

their custom, on anyone who should alter the version by any addition or change to any part of the written text, or any deletion either. This was a good step taken, to ensure that the words were preserved completely and permanently in perpetuity.

Romans 3:23: Human Sinfulness

Paul was not the only person of his time to understand the universality of human moral failure. (#273) The Jewish philosopher Philo also notes this.

#273: Human Sinfulness Universal

(Philo, *On the Unchangeableness of God* 16 §75)

16. [75]For if God were to choose to judge the race of mankind without mercy, he would pass on them a sentence of condemnation; since there has never been a single man who, by his own unassisted power, has run the whole course of his life, from the beginning to the end, without stumbling. . . .

Romans 4:3: Abraham the Man of Faith

Paul extols Abraham because he sees in him a prime example of "the man who does not work [to earn salvation] but trusts God who justifies the wicked" (Rom 4:5). Before receiving forgiveness through the gospel, it is likely that Paul would have viewed Abraham's righteousness as being the result of keeping God's law, not trusting in God's promise. (#274) This view of Abraham is found in a Jewish treatise from the second century B.C. See also Reading #302.

#274: Abraham Kept the Law for Righteousness

(Sirach 44.19–20)

[19]Abraham was the great father of a multitude of nations,
and no one has been found like him in glory;

[20]he kept the law of the Most High,
and was taken into covenant with him;
he established the covenant in his flesh,
and when he was tested he was found faithful.

Romans 6:16: Christ or Moral Reason?

Paul ponders the issue of human bondage to wrongdoing. He proclaims freedom through union with Christ. (#275) The Jewish writer Philo contemplated bondage to pleasure and proclaimed the power of reason to guide into all righteousness. He even takes the rare step of speaking autobiographically of his own experience at wild parties.

#275: Human Reason Can Lead to Righteousness

(Philo, *Allegorical Interpretation*, 3 53 §§155–56)

53. [155]And in this way when we are at entertainments, and when we are about to come to the enjoyments and use of luxuries that have been prepared for us, let us approach them taking reason with us as a defensive armor, and let us not fill ourselves with food beyond all moderation like cormorants, nor let us satiate ourselves with immoderate draughts of strong wine, and so give way to intoxication which compels men to act like fools. For reason will bridle and curb the violence and impetuosity of such a passion. [156]I myself, at all events, know that it has done so with regard to many of the passions, for when I have gone to entertainments where no respect was paid to discipline, and to sumptuous banquets, whenever I went without taking Reason with me as a guide, I became a slave to the luxuries that lay before me, being under the guidance of masters who could not be tamed, with sights and sounds of temptation, and all other such things also as work pleasure in a man by the agency of his senses of smell and taste. But when I approach such scenes in the company of reason, I then become a master instead of a slave: and without being subdued myself win a glorious victory of self-denial and temper-

ance; opposing and contending against all the appetites which subdue the intemperate.

Romans 9:3: Intercession for Kinsmen

Paul is anguished over the lost condition of his fellow Jews who have rejected Jesus as the Messiah. In his willingness to be cursed, if it would cause some to turn to God, Paul adopts a posture like that of Moses many centuries before (#276).

#276: The Prayer of Moses for His People

(Exodus 32:30–32)

[30]The next day Moses said to the people, "You have committed a great sin [by worshiping the golden calf]. But now I will go up to the LORD; perhaps I can make atonement for your sin."

[31]So Moses went back to the LORD and said, "Oh, what a great sin these people have committed! They have made themselves gods of gold. [32]But now, please forgive their sin—but if not, then blot me out of the book you have written."

Romans 9:21: God the Potter

Paul likens God to a potter who makes "out of the same lump of clay some pottery for noble purposes and some for common use." This is an echo of Jeremiah 18:6: "O house of Israel, can I not do with you as this potter does?" declares the LORD. "Like clay in the hand of the potter, so are you in my hand, O house of Israel." (#277) A similar expression is found in the Old Testament Apocrypha, which like Paul draws inspiration from the Old Testament.

#277: The Potter Is Master of the Clay

(Wisdom of Solomon 15.7)

[7]For when a potter kneads the soft earth and laboriously molds each vessel for our service, he fashions out of the same clay both the vessels that serve clean uses and those for contrary uses, making all in like manner; but which shall be the use of each of these the worker in clay decides.

Romans 11:36: To God Be All Glory

Other Jewish writers of Paul's century, too, extolled the excellency of God. (#278) Here is an example from Philo.

#278: God Is the Measure of All Things

(Philo, *Sacrifices of Abel and Cain* 15 §59)

15. [59]For God cannot be circumscribed, nor are his powers capable of being defined by lines, but he himself measures everything. His goodness therefore is the measure of all good things, and his authority is the measure of things in subjection, and the Governor of the universe himself, is the measure of all things to the corporeal and incorporeal.

Romans 16:1: Cenchrea

Cenchrea, Phoebe's place of residence, was located on a narrow isthmus near the larger town of Corinth. (##279–281) In New Testament times a number of attempts were made to build a canal across the isthmus. (No one succeeded at the task until 1883!)

#279: Julius Caesar Plans to Dig the Canal

(Suetonius, *Twelve Caesars, Julius Caesar* 44.3)

[3]His engineering schemes included the draining of the Pomptine Marshes and of Lake Fucinus; also a highway running from the Adriatic across the Apennines to the Tiber; and a canal to be cut through the Isthmus of Corinth.

#280: Caligula Attempts the Corinthian Canal

(Suetonius, *Twelve Caesars, Gaius [Caligula]* 21.1)

[1]Gaius rebuilt the ruinous ancient walls and temples of Syracuse, and among his other

Crucifixion. Roman cruelty reserved this form of execution for its worst offenders.

projects were the restoration of Polycrates' palace at Samos, the completion of Didymaean Apollo's temple at Ephesus, and the building of a city high up in the Alps. But he was most deeply interested in cutting a canal through the Isthmus in Greece, and sent a leading-centurion there to survey the site.

#281: Nero's Histrionic Attempt at Canal Building

(Suetonius, *Twelve Caesars, Nero* 19.1–2)

[1]Nero planned only two foreign tours: one to Alexandria, the other to Greece. A warning portent made him cancel the Alexandrian voyage, on the very day when his ship should have sailed: during his farewell round of the Temples he had sat down in the shrine of Vesta, but when he rose to leave, the hem of his robe got caught and then a temporary blindness overcame him. [2]While in Greece he tried to have a canal cut through the Isthmus, and addressed a gathering of Praetorian Guards, urging them to undertake the task. Nero took a mattock himself and, at a trumpet blast, broke the ground

and carried off the first basket of earth on his back.

1 Corinthians 1–2: Crucifixion

Paul speaks of crucifixion a number of times in the opening chapters of 1 Corinthians. He often has in mind Christ's crucifixion. But elsewhere he uses "crucifixion" to speak figuratively of his own sufferings as Christ's follower (Gal 2:20) or of the process of spiritual growth that Christians undergo (Gal 5:24).

Crucifixion was a common mode of capital punishment for criminals who were not Roman citizens. (#282) Plutarch tells how Julius Caesar (100–44 B.C.) put a band of pirates to death by this hideous means for kidnapping him. In the process it also sheds light on Caesar's legendary poise and bravery. (#283) But Suetonius also adds that Caesar was not always utterly merciless. (#284) Roman citizens were not normally subject to crucifixion—they were beheaded if convicted of a capital crime. But there were exceptions to this rule, as an incident under Galba suggests.

#282: Julius Caesar Crucifies His Former Captors

(Plutarch, *Fall of the Roman Republic*, *Caesar* 2)

[2]First, when the pirates demanded a ransom of twenty talents, Caesar burst out laughing. They did not know, he said, who it was that they had captured, and he volunteered to pay fifty. Then, when he had sent his followers to the various cities in order to raise the money and was left with one friend and two servants among these Cilicians, about the most bloodthirsty people in the world, he treated them so highhandedly that, whenever he wanted to sleep, he would send to them and tell them to stop talking. For thirty-eight days, with the greatest unconcern, he joined in all their games and exercises, just as if he was their leader instead of their prisoner. He also wrote poems and speeches which he read aloud to them, and if they failed to admire his work, he would call them to their faces illiterate savages, and would often laughingly threaten to have them all hanged. They were much taken with this and attributed his freedom of speech to a kind of simplicity in his character or boyish playfulness. However, the ransom arrived from Miletus and, as soon as he had paid it and been set free, he immediately manned some ships and set sail from the harbor of Miletus against the pirates. He found them still there, lying at anchor off the island, and he captured nearly all of them. He took their property as spoils of war and put the men themselves into the prison at Pergamum. He then went in person to Junius, the governor of Asia, thinking it proper that he, as praetor in charge of the province, should see to the punishment of the prisoners. Junius, however, cast longing eyes at the money, which came to a considerable sum, and kept saying that he needed time to look into the case. Caesar paid no further attention to him. He went to Pergamum, took the pirates out of prison and crucified the lot of them, just as he had often told them he would do when he was on the island and they imagined that he was joking.

#283: Julius Caesar Adds Mercy to Judgment

(Suetonius, *Twelve Caesars*, *Julius Caesar* 74.1)

[1]Caesar was not naturally vindictive; and if he crucified the pirates who had held him to ransom, this was only because he had sworn in their presence to do so; and he first mercifully cut their throats.

#284: Roman Citizens Were Also Crucified

(Suetonius, *Twelve Caesars*, *Galba* 9.1)

9. [1]He [Galba] ruled Tarraconensian Spain for eight years in a varying and inconsistent manner, beginning with great enthusiasm and energy, and even going a little too far in his punishment of crime. He sentenced a dishonest money-changer to have both hands cut off and nailed to the counter; and crucified a man who had poisoned his ward to inherit the property. When this murderer begged for justice, protesting that he was a Roman citizen, Galba recognized his status and ironically consoled him with: "Let this citizen hang higher than the rest, and have his cross whitewashed."

1 Corinthians 1:12: Who Is "Cephas"?

Cephas was Peter's name in Aramaic. Galilee and Judea were bi- or trilingual areas in the first century, and people commonly had both Semitic and Greek names. (#285) Josephus gives an example in speaking of the five sons of Mattathias, all of whom had second names. (See also Reading #13.)

#285: Mattathias's Sons Had Double Names

(Josephus, *Ant.* 12.6.1 §§265–66)

1. [265]Now at this time there was one whose name was Mattathias, who dwelt at Modin, the son of John, the son of Simeon, the son of Asamoneus, a priest of the order of Joarib, and a citizen of Jerusalem. [266]He had five sons: John, who was called Gaddis, and Simon, who was called Matthes, and Judas, who was called

Maccabeus, and Eleazar, who was called Auran, and Jonathan, who was called Apphus.

1 Corinthians 1:17: "Not with Words of Human Wisdom"

(#286) In the Old Testament God is pictured as inviting people to consider the reasonableness of his revealed mercy. (#287) Yet at the same time God's logic confounds and transcends that of the natural human mind, as Isaiah also declares. (#288) In Jeremiah we read that to elevate personal wisdom over God is the epitome of folly.

#286: "Come, Let Us Reason Together" (Isaiah 1:18)

[18]"Come now, let us reason together," says the LORD.
"Though your sins are like scarlet, they shall be as white as snow;
though they are red as crimson, they shall be like wool."

#287: God's Thoughts Are Not Our Thoughts (Isaiah 55:6–9)

[6]Seek the LORD while he may be found; call on him while he is near.
[7]Let the wicked forsake his way and the evil man his thoughts.
Let him turn to the LORD, and he will have mercy on him,
and to our God, for he will freely pardon.
[8]"For my thoughts are not your thoughts, neither are your ways my ways," declares the LORD.
[9]"As the heavens are higher than the earth, so are my ways higher than your ways and my thoughts than your thoughts."

#288: The "Wise" Will Be Put to Shame (Jeremiah 8:9)

[9]The wise will be put to shame; they will be dismayed and trapped.
Since they have rejected the word of the LORD, what kind of wisdom do they have?

1 Corinthians 6:1: Disputes before the Ungodly

Paul forbade the Corinthians to air their dirty laundry in the public courts. (#289) A pre-Christian Jewish community pronounced exceedingly strict judgment on those who would dare to violate their protocol in the matter of dealing with interpersonal conflict.

#289: Community Problems Should Be Dealt with Internally (Damascus Document 9.1–8)

[1]Every man who vows another to destruction by the laws of the Gentiles shall himself be put to death.
[2]And concerning the saying, *You shall not take vengeance on the children of your people, nor bear any rancor against them* (Lev. xix, 18), if any member of [3]the Covenant accuses his companion without first rebuking him before witnesses; [4]if he denounces him in the heat of his anger or reports him to his elders to make him look contemptible, he is one that takes vengeance and bears rancor, [5]although it is expressly written, *He takes vengeance upon His adversaries and bears rancor against His enemies* (Nah. i, 2). [6]If he holds his peace towards him from one day to another, and thereafter speaks of him in the heat of his anger, he testifies against himself concerning a capital matter [7]because he has not fulfilled the commandment of God which tells him: *You shall [8]rebuke your companion and not be burdened with sin because of him* (Lev. xix, 17.)

1 Corinthians 6:11: Justified from All Sin

Regardless of the sin—Paul lists examples of heterosexual immorality, idolatry, homosexual immorality, stealing, greed, drunkenness, slander, and swindling (1 Cor 6:9–10)—there is forgiveness and fellowship with God through Christ. But what was Paul's view before the risen Jesus confronted him on the Damascus road? It likely in some ways resembled the views of some of his countrymen before Jesus came: our bad deeds are forgiven if we do good deeds to make up for them. (#290) This view is proposed in a second-century B.C. Jewish writing. (#291) At the same time, Sirach warns against sinning flagrantly and assuming that good works done in a cynical, calculating way will automatically offset a godless attitude.

#290: Human Deeds Atone for Sin
(Sirach 3.3, 14–15, 30–31)

[3]Whoever honors his father atones for sins, . . .
[14]For kindness to a father will not be forgotten,
    and against your sins it will be credited to you;
[15]in the day of your affliction it will be remembered in your favor;
    as frost in fair weather, your sins will melt away. . . .
[30]Water extinguishes a blazing fire:
    so almsgiving atones for sin.
[31]Whoever requites favors gives thought to the future;
    at the moment of his falling he will find support.

#291: Godless Attitudes Cancel Good Deeds
(Sirach 7.8–10)

[8]Do not commit a sin twice;
    even for one you will not go unpunished.
[9]Do not say, "He will consider the multitude of my gifts,
    and when I make an offering to the Most High God he will accept it."
[10]Do not be fainthearted in your prayer,
    nor neglect to give alms.

1 Corinthians 10:5: "Bodies Scattered over the Desert"

Paul warns the Corinthians of the danger of turning their backs on God after confessing faith in his deliverance. He alludes to the tragedy of the children of Israel in the generation after the exodus from Egypt (#292).

#292: They Met Their End in the Desert
(Numbers 14:29–35)

[29]"'In this desert your bodies will fall—every one of you twenty years old or more who was counted in the census and who has grumbled against me. [30]Not one of you will enter the land I swore with uplifted hand to make your home, except Caleb son of Jephunneh and Joshua son of Nun. [31]As for your children that you said would be taken as plunder, I will bring them in to enjoy the land you have rejected. [32]But you—your bodies will fall in this desert. [33]Your children will be shepherds here for forty years, suffering for your unfaithfulness, until the last of your bodies lies in the desert. [34]For forty years—one year for each of the forty days you explored the land—you will suffer for your sins and know what it is like to have me against you.' [35]I, the LORD, have spoken, and I will surely do these things to this whole wicked community, which has banded together against me. They will meet their end in this desert; here they will die."

1 Corinthians 15:55–57: Victory over the Sting of Death

Paul affirms death's bitterness, yet insists that it has been defeated for all those who trust in Christ. Paul therefore speaks in victorious terms regarding man's last enemy. (#293) Very different is the counsel of an earlier Jewish writer who likewise speaks of death. Some fear death, others welcome it, he notes. Unlike Paul he appears to counsel resignation, not hope.

#293: Death Must Be Faced with Resignation
(Sirach 41.1–4)

[1]O death, how bitter is the reminder of you
    to one who lives at peace among his possessions,
to a man without distractions, who is prosperous in everything,

and who still has the vigor to enjoy his food!
²O death, how welcome is your sentence
to one who is in need and is failing in strength,
very old and distracted over everything;
to one who is contrary, and has lost his patience!
³Do not fear the sentence of death;
remember your former days and the end of life;
this is the decree from the Lord for all flesh,
⁴ and how can you reject the good pleasure of the Most High?
Whether life is for ten or a hundred or a thousand years,
there is no inquiry about it in Hades.

1 Corinthians 16:1: The Collection for God's People

Paul told the Corinthians to lay aside money for the needs of beleaguered Christians in Jerusalem. (#294) The Dead Sea Scrolls contain comparable directions for making provision for the needy.

#294: The Mandate to Care for the Needy
(Damascus Document 14.12–16)

¹²*This is the Rule for the Congregation by which it shall provide for all its needs*
They shall place the earnings of ¹³at least two days out of every month into the hands of the Guardian and the Judges, ¹⁴and from it they shall give to the fatherless, and from it they shall succor the poor and the needy, the aged ¹⁵sick and the homeless, the captive taken by a foreign people, the virgin with ¹⁶no near kin, and the ma[id for] whom no man cares. . . .

2 Corinthians 1:12: Paul's "Boast"

By "boast" Paul means the basis for his confidence. He is not a braggart. But he is convinced

that he has been entrusted with a saving prophetic word from God. Through Christ he knows God, and his life is devoted to inviting others into that same saving knowledge. Paul's "boast" is of the sort approved centuries earlier by the prophet Jeremiah (#295).

#295: Jeremiah's Boast in the Lord
(Jeremiah 9:23–24)

²³This is what the LORD says:
"Let not the wise man boast of his wisdom
or the strong man boast of his strength
or the rich man boast of his riches,
²⁴but let him who boasts boast about this:
that he understands and knows me,
that I am the LORD, who exercises kindness,
justice and righteousness on earth,
for in these I delight,"
declares the LORD.

2 Corinthians 3:17: "Where the Spirit of the Lord Is, There Is Freedom"

Even in Old Testament times, God was concerned about the reality of the heart and not purely formal religious appearance. In one notable instance God was willing to set aside the normal prescribed purification laws in order to honor the sincere prayers and intentions of his people under King Hezekiah (715–686 B.C.). (#296) In the passage below the people celebrate Passover one month late because until very recently their nation had been in a spiritual shambles. Yet God hears their prayer and receives their worship.

#296: The Lord Who Is Good Pardons Everyone
(2 Chronicles 30:13–20)

¹³A very large crowd of people assembled in Jerusalem to celebrate the Feast of Unleavened Bread in the second month. ¹⁴They removed the altars in Jerusalem and cleared away the incense altars and threw them into the Kidron Valley.

[15]They slaughtered the Passover lamb on the fourteenth day of the second month. The priests and the Levites were ashamed and consecrated themselves and brought burnt offerings to the temple of the LORD. [16]Then they took up their regular positions as prescribed in the Law of Moses the man of God. The priests sprinkled the blood handed to them by the Levites. [17]Since many in the crowd had not consecrated themselves, the Levites had to kill the Passover lambs for all those who were not ceremonially clean and could not consecrate their lambs to the LORD. [18]Although most of the many people who came from Ephraim, Manasseh, Issachar and Zebulun had not purified themselves, yet they ate the Passover, contrary to what was written. But Hezekiah prayed for them, saying, "May the LORD, who is good, pardon everyone [19]who sets his heart on seeking God—the LORD, the God of his fathers—even if he is not clean according to the rules of the sanctuary." [20]And the LORD heard Hezekiah and healed the people.

2 Corinthians 6:15: Believers and Unbelievers

Paul forbids Christians to cut off all dealings with non-Christians (1 Cor 5:9–10). But he realizes that non-Christian associates can lead believers astray. In 1 Corinthians 15:33 Paul quotes the Greek writer Menander to make this point: "Bad company corrupts good character." (#297) A second-century Jewish writer warns of the same danger. (#298) An even more radical prescription is offered in the Dead Sea Scrolls.

#297: Do Not Associate with Sinful People
(Sirach 13.1–2)

[1]Whoever touches pitch will be defiled, and whoever associates with a proud man will become like him.
[2]Do not lift a weight beyond your strength, nor associate with a man mightier and richer than you.

How can the clay pot associate with the iron kettle?
The pot will strike against it, and will itself be broken.

#298: Separation from Worldly People Must Be Absolute
(Rule of the Community 8.12–16)

[12]And when these become members of the Community in Israel [13]according to all these rules, they shall separate from the habitation of unjust men and shall go into the wilderness to prepare there the way of Him; [14]as it is written, *Prepare in the wilderness the way of . . . , make straight in the desert a path for our God* (Isa. xl,3). [15]This (path) is the study of the Law which He commanded by the hand of Moses, that they may do according to all that has been revealed from age to age, [16]and as the Prophets have revealed by His Holy Spirit.

2 Corinthians 8:9: Though Christ Was Rich

In Paul's time as now the rich often took advantage of the poor, as the quotation below recognizes (#299). It is therefore all the more striking that Christ used his infinite wealth, not on himself but to save sinners. See also Reading #389.

#299: Rich Human Beings Oppress the Poor
(Sirach 13.3–7)

[3]A rich man does wrong, and he even adds reproaches;
a poor man suffers wrong, and he must add apologies.
[4]A rich man will exploit you if you can be of use to him,
but if you are in need he will forsake you.
[5]If you own something, he will live with you;
he will drain your resources and he will not care.
[6]When he needs you he will deceive you,
he will smile at you and give you hope.

He will speak to you kindly and say, "What
do you need?"
[7]He will shame you with his foods,
until he has drained you two or three
times;
and finally he will deride you.
Should he see you afterwards, he will forsake you,
and shake his head at you.

a matter of fact, most of the sleep he got was in
chariots or in litters: rest, for him, was something to be used for action; and in the daytime
he would be carried round to the garrisons and
cities and camps and have sitting with him one
slave who was trained to write from dictation
as he went along, and behind him a soldier
standing with a sword. He traveled very fast.
For instance on his first journey from Rome, he
reached the Rhône in seven days.

2 Corinthians 11:26: Dangers and Courage

Paul faced many hardships and perils, some of
which he lists (2 Cor 11:26): "I have been constantly on the move. I have been in danger from
rivers, in danger from bandits, in danger from my
own countrymen, in danger from Gentiles; in danger in the city, in danger in the country, in danger
at sea; and in danger from false brothers." Such
valor was sure to have instilled courage in his followers; Paul tells Timothy to "endure hardship with
us like a good soldier of Christ Jesus" (2 Tm 2:3).
(#300) Julius Caesar furnishes an example of hardship suffered graciously for the cause he served.

#300: The Noble Example of Julius Caesar

(Plutarch, *Fall of the Roman Republic,
Caesar* 17)

[17]He showed that there was no danger which
he was not willing to face, no form of hard work
from which he excused himself. So far as his
fondness for taking risks went, his men, who
knew his passion for distinction, were not sur-
prised at it; but they were amazed at the way
in which he would undergo hardships which
were, it seemed, beyond his physical strength
to endure. For he was a slightly built man, had
a soft and white skin, suffered from headaches
and was subject to epileptic fits. (His first epileptic attack took place, it is said, in Corduba.) Yet
so far from making his poor health an excuse
for living an easy life, he used warfare as a tonic
for his health. By long hard journeys, simple
diet, sleeping night after night in the open, and
rough living he fought off his illness and made
his body strong enough to resist all attacks. As

Galatians 1:15: "God . . . Set Me Apart from Birth"

(#301) Paul's sense of God's calling echoes Jeremiah's account of his own personal calling in
about 625 B.C.

#301: The Call of Jeremiah by God
(Jeremiah 1:4–10)

[4]The word of the LORD came to me, saying,
[5]"Before I formed you in the womb I knew
you,
before you were born I set you apart;
I appointed you as a prophet to the nations."
[6]"Ah, Sovereign LORD," I said, "I do not
know how to speak; I am only a child."
[7]But the LORD said to me, "Do not say, 'I
am only a child.' You must go to everyone I
send you to and say whatever I command
you. [8]Do not be afraid of them, for I am with
you and will rescue you," declares the LORD.
[9]Then the LORD reached out his hand and
touched my mouth and said to me, "Now, I
have put my words in your mouth. [10]See,
today I appoint you over nations and kingdoms to uproot and tear down, to destroy and
overthrow, to build and to plant."

Galatians 3:8: The Gospel to Abraham

In what sense did Abraham receive the gospel?
In Paul's understanding, Abraham *believed* God's

Michelangelo's depiction of Moses the great Jewish lawgiver whose writings pointed to Christ.

was deeply zealous, received the covenant of everlasting priesthood. [55]Joshua, because he fulfilled the command, became a judge in Israel. . . .

[64]My children, be courageous and grow strong in the law, for by it you will gain honor.

Galatians 3:24: Moses Leads to Christ

For Paul the law of Moses was a means of pointing sinners to the Savior, Jesus Christ. Jesus himself had spoken in similar terms in saying that Moses' writings "testify about me" (Jn 5:39). But other thinkers in Paul's time had quite different assessments of Moses. (#303) Philo saw Moses as serving to legitimate Stoic doctrine.

#303: The Old Testament Points to Stoic Doctrine
(Philo, *Posterity and Exile of Cain*, 39 §133)

39. [133]Here who can help wondering at the minute accuracy of the lawgiver as to every particular? He calls Rebekkah a maiden, and a very beautiful maiden, because the nature of virtue is unmixed and free from guile, and unpolluted, and the only thing in all creation which is both beautiful and good; from which arose the Stoic doctrine, that the only thing that was beautiful was the good.

Galatians 5:6: Faith Working Through Love

The notion of faith expressing itself actively through love and obedience toward God was not new with Paul. Numerous Old Testament passages extol the same outlook, as these three readings attest (##304–306).

#304: Walk in All God's Ways
(Deuteronomy 10:12–13)

[12]And now, O Israel, what does the LORD your God ask of you but to fear the LORD your God, to walk in all his ways, to love him, to serve the LORD your God with all

promise, which is the essence of saving trust (Rom 4:3; cf. Gn 15:6). Faith is the way of salvation, and Abraham models this faith. (#302) A Jewish writing from the pre–New Testament era understands Abraham's action not as faith but faithfulness—God had favor on him because of his obedience, not because of his simple act of trusting God's promise (which then resulted in obedience, as the New Testament Book of James points out). See also Reading #274.

#302: The Faithfulness of Abraham
(1 Maccabees 2.51–55, 64)

[51]"Remember the deeds of the fathers, which they did in their generations; and receive great honor and an everlasting name. [52]Was not Abraham found faithful when tested, and it was reckoned to him as righteousness? [53]Joseph in the time of his distress kept the commandment, and became lord of Egypt. [54]Phinehas our father, because he

your heart and with all your soul, [13]and to observe the LORD's commands and decrees that I am giving you today for your own good?

#305: God Says, "Do What Is Just and Right"
(Jeremiah 22:3)

[3]This is what the LORD says: Do what is just and right. Rescue from the hand of his oppressor the one who has been robbed. Do no wrong or violence to the alien, the fatherless or the widow, and do not shed innocent blood in this place.

#306: God Requires Justice, Mercy, and Humility
(Micah 6:8)

[8]He has showed you, O man, what is good.
And what does the LORD require of you?
To act justly and to love mercy
and to walk humbly with your God.

Galatians 5:16: Live by the Spirit

People can live ruled by their own desires, Paul teaches, or in (#307) accordance with the Spirit of God through faith in Christ. A different understanding is reflected in a Dead Sea Scroll document. It talks of two spirits, the Spirit of Life and the Spirit of Darkness. From birth every person is under the influence of one or the other. Lists of good and evil deeds follow, as in Paul.

#307: The Ways of Good and Evil
(Rule of the Community 4.2–11)

[2]These are their ways [the ways of the good and evil spirit] in the world for the enlightenment of the heart of man, and that all the paths of true righteousness may be made straight before him, and that fear of the laws [3]of God may be instilled in his heart: a spirit of humility, patience, abundant charity, unending goodness, understanding, and intelligence; (a spirit of) mighty wisdom which

trusts in all [4]the deeds of God and leans on His great lovingkindness; a spirit of discernment in every purpose, of zeal for just laws, [5]of holy intent with steadfastness of heart, of great charity towards all the sons of truth, of admirable purity which detests all unclean idols, of humble conduct [6]sprung from an understanding of all things, and of faithful concealment of the mysteries of truth. These are the counsels of the spirit to the sons of truth in this world.

And as for the visitation of all who walk in this spirit, it shall be healing, [7]great peace in a long life, and fruitfulness, together with every everlasting blessing and eternal joy in life without end, a crown of glory [8]and a garment of majesty in unending light.

[9]But the ways of the spirit of falsehood are these: greed, and slackness in the search for righteousness, wickedness and lies, haughtiness and pride, falseness and deceit, cruelty and [10]abundant evil, ill-temper and much folly and brazen insolence, abominable deeds (committed) in a spirit of lust, and ways of lewdness in the service of uncleanness, [11]a blaspheming tongue, blindness of eye and dullness of ear, stiffness of neck and heaviness of heart, so that man walks in all the ways of darkness and guile.

Galatians 6:10: Do Good to All

Paul points to the obvious need for Christians to show love for each other (see also Jn 13:34–35). But Paul also teaches that Christians are to do good to all persons. (#308) This attitude stands in sharp contrast to the teaching of an Old Testament apocryphal book originating in the second century B.C.

#308: Do Not Help the Sinner
(Sirach 12.4–7)

[4]Give to the godly man, but do not help the sinner.
[5] Do good to the humble, but do not give to the ungodly;

hold back his bread, and do not give it to
    him,
  lest by means of it he subdue you;
for you will receive twice as much evil
    for all the good which you do to him.

[6]For the Most High also hates sinners
    and will inflict punishment on the un-
      godly.
[7]Give to the good man, but do not help the
    sinner.

9 Ephesians–Philemon

Examples of advanced commentaries containing additional references to extrabiblical parallels or passages include the following:

- Ephesians: Barth (2 vols.), Bruce, Lincoln, Martin
- Philippians: O'Brien, Lightfoot, Hawthorne
- Colossians: O'Brien, Bruce, Lohse, Lightfoot
- 1, 2 Thessalonians: Bruce, Wanamaker, Morris
- 1, 2 Timothy, Titus: Knight, Towner
- Philemon: O'Brien, Bruce, Lohse, Lightfoot

Other studies useful for understanding the setting of these epistles include (on Ephesians and Colossians, respectively) Clinton E. Arnold, *Power and Magic: The Concept of Power in Ephesians* and *The Colossian Syncretism: The Interface between Christianity and Folk Belief at Colossae*. For an informative depiction of conditions in Ephesus, especially as regards gender and religion, see S. M. Baugh, "A Foreign World: Ephesus in the First Century," in *Women in the Church*, eds. Andreas J. Köstenberger, Thomas R. Schreiner, and H. Scott Baldwin.

Ephesians 1:14: "Our Inheritance"

"Inheritance" in New Testament usage is rooted in God's Old Testament promises. (#309) It refers first to the land of Israel, the dwelling place for God's people and of God in their midst, as Exodus shows. (#310) However, it is not only that the land is the people's inheritance; the people themselves are God's inheritance. (##311, 312) There is also a hint of future, eternal blessing in the Old Testament use of the word "inheritance," a hint that Paul in Ephesians 1:14 enlarges and applies to the blessings of ultimate redemption.

#309: The Land Is Israel's Inheritance Forever
(Exodus 32:13)

[13][Moses prays,] Remember your servants Abraham, Isaac and Israel, to whom you swore by your own self: "I will make your descendants as numerous as the stars in the sky and I will give your descendants all this land I promised them, and it will be their inheritance forever."

#310: Israel Is God's Own Inheritance
(1 Kings 8:53)

[53]For you singled them [i.e., the Israelites] out from all the nations of the world to be your own inheritance, just as you declared through your servant Moses when you, O Sovereign LORD, brought our fathers out of Egypt.

#311: Inheritance and Forgiveness
(Micah 7:18)

[18]Who is a God like you,
who pardons sin and forgives the transgression
of the remnant of his inheritance?
You do not stay angry forever
but delight to show mercy.

155

#312: The Eternal Inheritance of the Saints
(Psalm 37:18)

[18]The days of the blameless are known to the LORD,
and their inheritance will endure forever.

Ephesians 1:20–21: "Christ . . . Far above All Rule and Authority, Power and Dominion"

(#313) At Ephesus it was the pagan goddess Artemis (or Diana) who was worshiped by many, as the prayer below (dating from after the New Testament era, however) reveals. Words in Greek are similar to those used by Paul in his words to the Ephesians.

#313: (Artemis Governs All Things, Even Death)
(Prayer to Artemis)

O Great Artemis of the Ephesians, help! Display your power (δύναμιν) upon this young man who has died. For all the Ephesians know, both men and women, that all things (τὰ πάντα) are governed by you, and that great powers (δυνάμεις μεγάλαι) come to us through you. Give now to your servant what you are able to do in this regard. Raise up your servant Domnos.

Ephesians 2:5: "Without God in the World"

It should not be thought that non-Jews in Paul's era had no interest in or knowledge of God (or the gods) at all. (#314) There was lively debate about their existence and their activity, as the following quote from Cicero (106–43 B.C.) shows. But Cicero also documents the confusion that reigned among pagan thinkers.

#314: Pagan Views of God
(Cicero, *Nature of the Gods* 1.1–5)

[1]As you, Brutus, are well aware, there are many things in philosophy which have not yet been satisfactorily explained, particularly that most obscure and most difficult question concerning the nature of the gods, which is so extremely important both for a knowledge of the human mind [or soul] and also for the regulation of religion. Concerning this the opinions of even the most learned men are so various and so divergent as to lend strong support to the inference that the source and origin of philosophy is ignorance; and that the Academic philosophers have been wise in "withholding assent" to beliefs that are uncertain: for what is more unbecoming in a wise man than rash judgment! And what is more rash or more unbecoming the gravity and constancy of a philosopher than either to maintain an opinion that is false, or to defend without any hesitation what has not been thoroughly examined and understood?

[2]As for the question now before us, the majority of thinkers have affirmed—what is most probable, and what we are all led by nature to suppose—namely, that the gods exist. But Protagoras doubted whether there were any, while Diagoras of Melos and Theodorus of Cyrene held that there are none whatsoever. Moreover, those who have affirmed that there are gods have expressed such a variety of views, and with such great disagreement, that it would be wearisome to list their opinions. There are many different views about the outward form of the gods, and about their location and dwelling places, and about their way of life; these are subjects about which the philosophers debate most earnestly. But the main point of the debate, viz., whether the gods are wholly idle and inactive, being unconcerned with the care and administration of the world, or whether, on the contrary, all things were both created and constituted by them from the beginning, and are controlled and kept in motion by them throughout infinite time—this is the most hotly disputed point of all. And until this question is decided, mankind must of necessity continue to wan-

der in the greatest uncertainty, and remain ignorant of the most important things of all.

³For there both are and have been some philosophers who have held that the gods exercise not the least control over human affairs. But if their view is the true one, how can piety, sanctity, or religion exist?—for these are the tribute which is to be offered to the power of the gods, in purity and holiness, on the sole ground that they take some notice of it, and that some benefit has been conferred upon the human race by the immortal gods. But if, on the contrary, the gods have neither the power nor the will to help us; if they pay no attention whatsoever to us, and take no notice of our actions; and if there is no way in which they can possibly influence the life of men—then what reason is there for offering them either worship, honors, or prayers? But piety, like the other virtues, cannot exist in empty show or pretense; and if piety goes, both sanctity and religion will also disappear; and when these have gone, disturbance of life and great confusion must follow. ⁴In fact, if piety toward the gods disappears, I am not sure that good faith as well, and the unity of human society, and even justice, that most excellent of all the virtues, will not likewise disappear.

There are, however, other philosophers, men of very great eminence and nobility, who believe that the whole world is ruled and governed by the will and wisdom of the gods; that not only this, but they likewise conceive that the gods consult and provide for the preservation of mankind. For they think that the fruits and other products of the earth, and the seasons and the variety in the weather and the change in climates by which whatever the soil produces is brought to maturity and ripened, are contributed by the immortal gods to the human race. They cite many other things, which will be related in the following books, which are of such a nature as almost to make us believe the immortal gods created them for the use of men. Against these opinions Carneades has argued at such great length that his words should arouse in men who are not too slothful a desire to search for truth. ⁵There is no subject upon which both the learned and the unlearned differ so greatly as this; and

since their views are so diverse, and so diametrically opposed, it is clear that, while perhaps none of them may be true, it is absolutely impossible that more than one should be true.

Ephesians 2:14: "The Dividing Wall of Hostility"

In the Jerusalem temple precincts a wall and a warning sign warned non-Jews that if they proceeded beyond a certain point, they would be killed on the spot (see Reading #120). Paul may have had this wall and its symbolic significance in mind as he wrote this portion of Ephesians. See Reading #17 for Josephus's description of this part of the temple.

Ephesians 4:8: Christ Freed Captives

In making his point Paul quotes Psalm 68. (#315) But other Old Testament passages likewise use the image of slavery to depict the salvation God works. A classic example is the following reference to Israel in Egypt, and how God broke their bonds. As Paul languishes in jail himself (Eph 4:1), the assurance that the gospel makes even captives free must have been powerful.

#315: God Breaks the Chains of the Captives
(Psalm 107:10–16)

¹⁰Some sat in darkness and the deepest gloom,
    prisoners suffering in iron chains,
¹¹for they had rebelled against the words of God
    and despised the counsel of the Most High.
¹²So he subjected them to bitter labor;
    they stumbled, and there was no one to help.
¹³Then they cried to the LORD in their trouble,
    and he saved them from their distress.

[14]He brought them out of darkness and the
deepest gloom
and broke away their chains.
[15]Let them give thanks to the LORD for his
unfailing love
and his wonderful deeds for men,
[16]for he breaks down gates of bronze and
cuts through bars of iron.

Ephesians 4:17: Living Like Gentiles

Why did Paul take such a dim view of how Gentiles live? A passage like Romans 1:18–32 gives a dramatic picture of the immorality and brutality that was common in the Greco-Roman world. (#316) This passage from Josephus illustrates how cheap human life was from the non-Jewish point of view. Mass killings were a form of entertainment. He describes how the Roman general Titus staged slaughter of war captives to celebrate the birthdays of his brother and his father.

#316: Mass Murder as a Form of Entertainment
(Josephus, *Jewish War* 7.3.1 §§37–40)

1. [37]While Titus was at Caesarea, he solemnized the birthday of his brother [Domitian] after a splendid manner, and inflicted a great deal of the punishment intended for the Jews in honor of him: [38]for the number of those that were now slain in fighting with the beasts, and were burnt, and fought with one another, exceeded two thousand five hundred. Yet did all this seem to the Romans, when they were thus destroying ten thousand several ways, to be a punishment beneath their deserts. [39]After this, Caesar came to Berytus, which is a city of Phoenicia, and a Roman colony, and stayed there a longer time, and exhibited a still more pompous solemnity about his father's birthday, both in the magnificence of the shows, and in the other vast expenses he was at in his devices thereto belonging; [40]so that a great multitude of the captives were here destroyed after the same manner as before.

Ephesians 4:26: Getting Rid of Anger

Paul's concern about festering quarrels (drawing on Ps 4:4) is also reflected in the Dead Sea Scrolls (#317).

#317: Humans Are to Seek One Another's Well-Being
(Damascus Document 6.21–7.4)

[6.21]A man shall seek his brother's well-being [7.1]and shall not sin against his near kin. They shall keep from fornication [2]according to the statue. They shall rebuke each man his brother according to the commandment and shall bear no rancor [3]from one day to the next. They shall keep apart from every uncleanness according to the statutes relating to each one, [4]and no man shall defile his holy spirit since God has set them apart.

Ephesians 5:18: Not Drunk on Wine

Paul is aware of the dangers of drinking to excess and warns against drunkenness. (#318) As a Jew his attitude toward alcohol was probably like that of the writer of Sirach below—except that Paul also taught the virtue of abstinence if that were necessary to avoid giving wrong impressions to others (Rom 14:21).

#318: Excess of Wine Is Bitterness of Soul
(Sirach 31.25–30)

[25]Do not aim to be valiant over wine,
for wine has destroyed many.
[26]Fire and water prove the temper of steel,
so wine tests hearts in the strife of the
proud.
[27]Wine is like life to men,
if you drink it in moderation.
What is life to a man who is without wine?
It has been created to make men glad.
[28]Wine drunk in season and temperately
is rejoicing of heart and gladness of soul.

²⁹Wine drunk to excess is bitterness of soul,
with provocation and stumbling.
³⁰Drunkenness increases the anger of a fool
to his injury,
reducing his strength and adding
wounds.

Ephesians 5:25: Like Christ Loved the Church and Gave Himself Up for Her

Paul has a high view of women, urging their husbands to live with them with an attitude of sacrificial selflessness—love. Paul's view stands in sharp contrast to the disparaging remarks of a second-century B.C. writer who seems to blame all of marriage's woes on the wife (#319). See also Readings #98–106.

#319: Women Are the Cause of Marital Woes
(Sirach 25.13, 16–26)

¹³Any wound, but not a wound of the heart!
Any wickedness, but not the wickedness
of a wife! . . .
¹⁶I would rather dwell with a lion and a
dragon
than dwell with an evil wife.
¹⁷The wickedness of a wife changes her appearance.
and darkness her face like that of a bear.
¹⁸Her husband takes his meals among the
neighbors,
and he cannot help sighing bitterly.
¹⁹Any iniquity is insignificant compared to a
wife's iniquity;
may a sinner's lot befall her!
²⁰A sandy ascent for the feet of the aged—
such is a garrulous wife for a quiet husband.
²¹Do not be ensnared by a woman's beauty,
and do not desire a woman for her possessions.
²²There is wrath and impudence and great
disgrace
when a wife supports her husband.
²³A dejected mind, a gloomy face,
and a wounded heart are caused by an
evil wife.
Drooping hands and weak knees
are caused by the wife who does not
make her husband happy.
²⁴From a woman sin had its beginning,
and because of her we all die.
²⁵Allow no outlet to water,
and no boldness of speech in an evil
wife.
²⁶If she does not go as you direct,
separate her from yourself.

Ephesians 6:11–18: The Full Armor of God

Paul urges believers to put on armor like God's that will enable them to stand firm against evil. It is likely that behind Paul's exhortation lies his recollection of Old Testament passages that speak of God putting on armor to oppose evil and redeem his people (Is 11:5; 59:17). (#320) A Jewish writing from the first century B.C. uses similar imagery. But unlike Paul it does not urge readers to put on similar armor themselves. Nor does Paul see the purpose of Christians' armor to be pouring out wrath on the earth, the goal of God's militant work in the passage below.

#320: God in His Armor Will Overwhelm the World
(Wisdom of Solomon 5.17–23)

¹⁷The Lord will take his zeal as his whole
armor,
and will arm all creation to repel his enemies;
¹⁸he will put on righteousness as a breastplate,
and wear impartial justice as a helmet;
¹⁹he will take holiness as an invincible
shield,
²⁰and sharpen stern wrath for a sword,
and creation will join with him to fight
against the madmen.
²¹Shafts of lightning will fly with true aim,
and will leap to the target as from a well-drawn bow of clouds,

22and hailstones full of wrath will be hurled
 as from a catapult;
the water of the sea will rage against them,
and rivers will relentlessly overwhelm
 them;
23a mighty wind will rise against them,
and like a tempest it will winnow them
 away.
Lawlessness will lay waste the whole earth,
and evil-doing will overturn the thrones of
 rulers.

Ephesians 6:18: Pray in the Spirit

Paul has in mind, of course, the Holy Spirit, who comes to the believer through faith in Jesus Christ (Rom 8:11). In the Hellenistic world of Ephesus there was belief in many other "spirits." (#321) The magic spell below is a pagan prayer to spirit beings for help in defeating an opponent in the chariot races.

#321: A Pagan Prayer to the Spirits of Destruction

(Curse Inscription)

I conjure you up, holy beings and holy names; join in aiding this spell, and bind, enchant, thwart, strike, overturn, conspire against, destroy, kill, break Eucherius the charioteer, and all his horses tomorrow in the circus at Rome. May he not leave the barriers well; may he not be quick in the contest; may he not outstrip anyone; may he not make the turns well; may he not win any prizes . . . may he be broken; may he be dragged along by your power, in the morning and afternoon races. Now! Now! Quickly! Quickly!

Philippians 1:6: God's Faithfulness

(##322–324) Numerous Old Testament passages confirm that one of God's most prominent characteristics is his faithfulness—what he begins, he brings to completion. Paul's statement echoes

this conviction here in Philippians 1:6. In Paul's understanding, not only *is* God faithful, but he also *sends* faithfulness through Christ to those who receive the gospel. (#325) The psalmist utters a similar sentiment.

#322: God's Faithfulness Ascends to the Heavens

(Psalm 36:5)

5Your love, O Lord, reaches to the heavens,
 your faithfulness to the skies.

#323: God's Nature Abounds in Faithfulness

(Psalm 86:15)

15But you, O Lord, are a compassionate and
 gracious God,
 slow to anger, abounding in love and
 faithfulness.

#324: No Faithfulness Can Compare to God's

(Psalm 89:8)

8O Lord God Almighty, who is like you?
 You are mighty, O Lord, and your faithfulness surrounds you.

#325: God's Faithfulness is Sent to His People

(Psalm 57:3)

3He sends from heaven and saves me,
 rebuking those who hotly pursue me;
 God sends his love and his faithfulness.

Philippians 1:9–11: Paul's Prayers

Paul's letters often mention his prayers. Some even contain short prayers for his readers. Philippians 1:9–11 is an example. Compare it with other prayers of Paul (e.g., Col 1:9–12), then contrast them with the prayer of the Roman general Scipio Africanus in about 204 b.c. as his army prepared to attack Carthage (#326).

#326: Scipio's Prayer for Revenge

(Livy, *History of Rome* 29.27.1–4)

[1]At dawn Scipio on his flagship offered a prayer, after the herald had ordered silence. [2]"Ye gods and goddesses, who inhabit the seas and the lands, I supplicate and beseech you that whatever has been done under my command, or is being done, or will later be done, may turn out to my advantage and to the advantage of the people and the commons of Rome, the allies, and the Latins who by land or sea or on rivers follow me, [accepting] the leadership, the authority, and the auspices of the Roman people; [3]that you will support them and aid them with your help; that you will grant that, preserved in safety and victorious over the enemy, arrayed in booty and laden with spoils, you will bring them back with me in triumph to our homes; that you will grant us the power to take revenge upon our enemies and foes; [4]and that you will grant to me and the Roman people the power to enforce upon the Carthaginians what they have planned to do against our city, as an example of [divine] punishment."

Philippians 1:20: Glorifying God in Life and in Death

Paul writes the Philippians from prison. He might be released, or he might be executed. He is confident of having "sufficient courage so that now as always Christ will be exalted in my body, whether by life or by death." (#327) A similar scrappy hope surfaces in the Hellenistic Jewish document Wisdom of Solomon 3:1–5. But notice differences: Paul is assured of the resurrection of the body on the basis of God's free grace; the writer of Wisdom assumes the (Greek) hope of immortality of the soul, and not because of grace but because "God tested them and found them worthy of himself." For Paul suffering was an opportunity to witness to Christ and identify with him; for Wisdom suffering is a way of meriting divine favor.

#327: Death Is a Discipline to Make Us Worthy of God

(Wisdom of Solomon 3.1–5)

[1]But the souls of the righteous are in the
hand of God,
and no torment will ever touch them.
[2]In the eyes of the foolish they seemed to
have died,
and their departure was thought to be an
affliction,
[3]and their going from us to be their
destruction;
but they are at peace.
[4]For though in the sight of men they were
punished,
their hope is full of immortality.
[5]Having been disciplined a little, they will
receive great good,
because God tested them and found them
worthy of himself;

Philippians 4:3: The Book of Life

What is this mysterious book? Jesus spoke of his disciples' names being "written in heaven" (Lk 10:20). Revelation speaks repeatedly of the Lamb's "book of life" (Rv 3:5; 13:8; 17:8; 20:12; 20:15; 21:27). Reference is apparently to a list of the redeemed kept by God in heaven. The background for this belief may very well lie in these two Old Testament passages (##329–329).

#328: God Keeps Track of His Book of Life

(Exodus 32:32–33)

[32][Moses prays,] "But now, please forgive their sin—but if not, then blot me out of the book you have written." [33]The LORD replied to Moses, "Whoever has sinned against me I will blot out of my book."

#329: Evildoers Are Not in the Book of Life

(Psalm 69:28)

[28]May they [i.e., evildoers] be blotted out of
the book of life
and not be listed with the righteous.

Philippians 4:11–13: Content in All Circumstances . . . Through Christ

In hardships, in difficulties, in prison, Paul found nourishment for his soul through his relationship with Christ. (#330) Julius Caesar likewise exhibited an ability to put up with unpleasant circumstances when the occasion demanded it. Yet sources indicate he was not consistent in this, and his motivations had nothing to do with what animated Paul: Christ and the gospel.

#330: The Pagan Nobility of Julius Caesar
(Plutarch, *Fall of the Roman Republic, Caesar* 17)

¹⁷He was not in the least fussy about his food, as is shown by the following story. When Valerius Leo was entertaining him to dinner at Milan, he served up asparagus dressed with myrrh instead of with olive oil. Caesar ate this quite calmly himself and reprimanded his friends when they objected to the dish. 'If you didn't like it,' he said, 'there was no need to have eaten it. But if one reflects on one's host's lack of breeding it merely shows that one is ill-bred oneself.' There was also an occasion when he was forced to take refuge from a storm in a poor man's hut. When he found that this consisted of only one room, and even this room was scarcely big enough to accommodate one person, he said to his friends that honors should go to the strongest, but necessities should go to the weakest, and so he told Oppius to lie down there, while he himself and the others slept under the projecting roof of the doorway.

Colossians 1:13: The Kingdom of the Son

Paul speaks of the kingdom that both John the Baptist and Jesus preached. This kingdom, of which Christ was the fulfillment, was prophesied by Isaiah the prophet (#331). The Old Testament repeatedly speaks of God's dominion over the whole universe as well as in human affairs (##332–334). Daniel the prophet also sees the kingdom as something God shares with his people (#335). See also Reading #190.

#331: The Kingdom of Christ Will Be Eternal
(Isaiah 9:7)

⁷Of the increase of his government and peace
    there will be no end.
He will reign on David's throne
    and over his kingdom,
establishing and upholding it
    with justice and righteousness
    from that time on and forever.
The zeal of the LORD Almighty
    will accomplish this.

#332: God's Kingdom Rules over All
(Psalm 103:19)

¹⁹The LORD has established his throne in heaven,
    and his kingdom rules over all.

#333: God's Kingdom Is an Everlasting Kingdom
(Psalm 145:11–13)

¹¹They will tell of the glory of your kingdom
    and speak of your might,
¹²so that all men may know of your mighty acts
    and the glorious splendor of your kingdom.
¹³Your kingdom is an everlasting kingdom,
    and your dominion endures through all generations.
The LORD is faithful to all his promises
    and loving toward all he has made.

#334: God's Dominion Is Unending
(Daniel 4:3)

³How great are his signs,
    how mighty his wonders!
His kingdom is an eternal kingdom;

his dominion endures from generation to generation.

#335: The Saints of God Will Possess the Kingdom
(Daniel 7:18)

[18]But the saints of the Most High will receive the kingdom and will possess it forever—yes, for ever and ever.

Colossians 2:8: Deceptive Philosophy

Various schools of thought of Paul's day offered moral guidance by way of impressive rhetorical presentations, or sophistry, which Paul rejected. (#336) Joining Paul in this rejection was Philo. But what Philo commends, a philosophy of reason based on principles of Moses, would not have been any more acceptable to Paul than sophistry. In Colossians Paul sets forth Christ, not human reason, as the source of eternal life.

#336: Philo's Philosophy of Life
(Philo, *Posterity and Exile of Cain* 30 §§101–2)

30. [101]But Moses does not think it right to incline either to the right or to the left, or in short to any part of the earthly Edom; but rather to proceed along the middle way, which he with great propriety calls the royal road, for since God is the first and only God of the universe, so also the road to him, as being the king's road, is very properly denominated royal; and this royal road you must consider to be philosophy, not that philosophy which the existing sophistical crowd of men pursues (for they, studying the art of words in opposition to truth, have called crafty wickedness, wisdom, assigning a divine name to wicked action), but that which the ancient company of those men who practiced virtue studied, rejecting the persuasive juggleries of pleasure, and adopting a virtuous and austere study of the honorable—[102]this royal road, which we have stated to be true and genuine philosophy, the law calls the word and reason of God;

for it is written, "Thou shalt not turn aside from the word which I command thee this day, to the right hand nor to the left," So that it is shown most manifestly that the word of God is identical with the royal road, since Moses' words are not to depart either from the royal road, or from this word, as if the two were synonymous, but to proceed with an upright mind along the middle and level road, which leads one aright.

Colossians 2:8: Human Traditions

A second-century inscription (#337) contains a message from the pagan god Apollos to worshipers from around Colossae who were seeking salvation from plagues and drought, probably in the A.D. 160s. The prescription given below may reflect popular religious belief among many who were now Christians in the Colossian congregation.

#337: Second-Century Apollos Inscription

[The first lines of the inscription are lost] But you are not alone in being injured by the destructive miseries of a deadly plague, but many are the cities and peoples which are grieved at the wrathful displeasures of the gods. The painful anger of the deities I bid you avoid by libations and feasts and fully accomplished sacrifices.

Firstly then to Earth the mother of all bring a cow from the herd into her hall of four measures, and sacrifice it with sweet-smelling incense and then ravage it with fire, and when the flame has consumed it all, then sprinkle around with libations and a mixture of honey and soil all together.

Secondly sacrifice an unfeasted offering to the Aither and to the gods of the heavens, all sweet-smelling with incense.

To Demeter, as your custom is, and to the gods of the underworld, perform rites with victims free from pollution, and to the heroes in the ground pour drink-offerings in accordance with the precepts, and continually be mindful of Apollo Kareios. For you are descended from me in family and from Mopsus, the city's patron.

Also around all your city gates consecrate precincts for a holy statue of the Clarian Phoebus equipped with his bow, which destroys diseases, as though shooting with his arrow from afar at the infertile plague.

Moreover when after you have wrought appeasement and the evil powers have departed, I instruct your boys with maidenly musicians to come together to Colophon accompanied by libations and hecatombs in willing spirit. For indeed often I have saved you, but I have not received a share of fat to gladden my heart. Yet it is right not even to be forgetful of men who have done you benefit. If you perform what it is seemly for godfearing men to accomplish, never will you be in painful confusions, but with more wealth and better safety . . . [the remainder of the text is missing]

[565]Then you will see (ὄψῃ) the gods looking graciously upon you and no longer rushing at you, but rather going about in their own order of affairs. [570]So when you see (ἴδῃς) that the world above is clear and circling, and that none of the gods or angels is threatening you, expect to hear a great crash of thunder, so as to shock you . . . and [after you have said the second prayer] you will see (ὄψῃ) [580]many five-pronged stars coming forth from the disk and filling all the air. Then say again: 'Silence! Silence!' And when the disk is open, you will see (ὄψῃ) the fireless circle, and the fiery doors shut tight.

Colossians 2:23: See 1 Timothy 4:3 (Reading #370)

Colossians 2:18: Great Detail about What He Has Seen

Pagan religions in the vicinity of Colossae offered mystical rites to spiritually hungry people. It may be such experience that Paul warns against here. (#338) The Mithras Liturgy below dates from after New Testament times but may illustrate rites experienced by some Colossian Christians prior to their entrance into the church. The Greek words are related to words used by Paul in his admonitions to the Colossians.

#338: The Mystical Sight Offered by Mithraism
(Mithras Liturgy [*PGM* 4.475–829])

[539]You will see (ὄψῃ) yourself being lifted up and [540]ascending to the height, so that you seem to be in midair . . . you will see (ὄψῃ) all immortal things. For in that day [545]and hour you will see (ὄψῃ) the divine order of the skies: the presiding gods rising into heaven, and others setting. Now the course of the visible gods (ὁρ-ωμένων θεῶν) will appear through the disk of god. . . . [555]And you will see (ὄψῃ) the gods staring intently at you and rushing at you. . . .

Colossians 3:11: Scythians

Who were the Scythians, and why should it be thought remarkable that forgiveness was extended to them? (#399) The description below captures popular belief that the Scythians were a bloodthirsty and vindictive people. If the gospel of grace extends even to the feared and detested Scythians, it surely extends to all who call on Christ's name.

#339: The Barbaric Behaviors of the Scythians
(Herodotus, *History* 4.65–66)

[64]As regards war, the Scythian custom is for every man to drink the blood of the first man he kills. The heads of all enemies killed in battle are taken to the king; if he brings a head, a soldier is admitted to his share of the loot; no head, no loot. He strips the skin off the head by making a circular cut round the ears and shaking out the skull; he then scrapes the flesh off the skin with the rib of an ox, and when it is clean works it in his fingers until it is supple, and fit to be used as a sort of handkerchief. He hangs these handkerchiefs on the bridle of his horse, and is very proud of them. The finest fellow is the man who has the greatest number.

Many Scythians sew a number of scalps together and make cloaks out of them, like the ones peasants wear, and often, too, they take the skin, nails and all, off the right hands and arms of dead enemies and use it to cover their quivers with—having discovered the fact that human skin is not only tough, but white, as white as almost any skin. Sometimes they flay a whole body, and stretch the skin on a wooden frame which they carry around with them when they ride. ⁶⁵They have a special way of dealing with the actual skulls—not with all of them, but only those of their worst enemies: they saw off the part below the eyebrows, and after cleaning out what remains stretch a piece of rawhide round it on the outside. If a man is poor, he is content with that, but a rich man goes further and gilds the inside of the skull as well. In either case the skull is then used to drink from. They treat the skulls of their kinsmen in the same way, in cases where quarrels have occurred and a man has been beaten in fight in the presence of the king. When important visitors arrive, these skulls are passed round and the host tells the story of them: how they were once his relatives and made war against him, and how he defeated them—all of which passes for a proof of courage. ⁶⁶Once a year the governor of each district mixes a bowl of wine, from which every Scythian who has killed his man in battle has the right to drink. Those who have no dead enemy to their credit are not allowed to touch the wine, but have to sit by themselves in disgrace—the worst, indeed, which they can suffer. Any man, on the contrary, who has killed a great many enemies, has two cups and drinks from both of them at once.

Colossians 3:16: "Let the Word of Christ Dwell in You Richly"

The heritage of meditation on God's Word was already many centuries old in Paul's time. (#340) Psalm 119, the longest chapter in the Bible, is an extended example of what it means for Scripture to "dwell richly" in a worshiper.

#340: Purity Is Living According to God's Word
(Psalm 119:9–16)

⁹How can a young man keep his way pure?
By living according to your word.
¹⁰I seek you with all my heart;
do not let me stray from your commands.
¹¹I have hidden your word in my heart
that I might not sin against you.
¹²Praise be to you, O LORD;
teach me your decrees.
¹³With my lips I recount
all the laws that come from your mouth.
¹⁴I rejoice in following your statutes
as one rejoices in great riches.
¹⁵I meditate on your precepts
and consider your ways.
¹⁶I delight in your decrees;
I will not neglect your word.

Colossians 4:1: See Philemon 16 (Readings ##372, 373)

1 Thessalonians 2:13: "The Word of God, Which Is at Work in You Who Believe"

Paul shared the Old Testament conviction that there was perfection and transforming strength in the Word of God, which he made known to the world through his prophets, Son, and apostles. (##341–344) This representative sampling from the Old Testament exemplifies what is said there.

#341: The Word of God Is Exalted above All Things
(Psalm 138:2)

²I will bow down toward your holy temple
and will praise your name

for your love and your faithfulness,
for you have exalted above all things
  your name and your word.

#342: Every Word of God Is Flawless

(Proverbs 30:5)

[5]Every word of God is flawless;
  he is a shield to those who take refuge in
  him.

#343: The Word of the Lord Is Without Error

(Psalm 18:30)

[30]As for God, his way is perfect;
  the word of the LORD is flawless.
He is a shield
  for all who take refuge in him.

#344: The Word of God Is Right and True

(Psalm 33:4)

[4]For the word of the LORD is right and true;
  he is faithful in all he does.

1 Thessalonians 4:5: Passionate lust

Paul does not reject sexual pleasure within marriage (see 1 Cor 7:5; 1 Tm 4:1–4) but here warns against immorality (1 Thes 4:3). It is wrong to indulge in illicit sexual pleasure. Other writers of Paul's time, perhaps influenced by Stoicism, called for rejection of any feelings of gratification whatsoever. (#345) Philo is an example. He calls on reason, his mind, to declare war on all passions, especially pleasure.

#345: The Fight of Reason Against Passion and Pleasure

(Philo, *Allegorical Interpretation* 2 26 §§106–8)

26. [106]Fight thou then, O my mind, against every passion, and especially against pleasure, for "the serpent is the most subtle of all the beasts that are upon the earth, which the Lord God has made." [107]And of all the passions the most mischievous is pleasure. Why so? Because all things are the slaves of pleasure; and because the life of the wicked is governed by pleasure as by a master. Accordingly, the things which are the efficient causes of pleasure are found to be full of all wickedness: gold and silver, and glory and honors, and powers and the objects of the outward senses, and the mechanical arts, and all other things which cause pleasure, being very various, and all injurious to the soul; and there are no sins without extreme wickedness; [108]therefore do thou array against it the wisdom which contends with serpents; and struggle in his most glorious struggle, and labor to win the crown in the contest against pleasure, which subdues every one else; winning a noble and glorious crown, such as no assembly of men can confer.

1 Thessalonians 4:18: "Encourage Each Other"

Paul urges his readers not to despair that some of their Christian friends have died. Christ will one day return, Paul writes, and then all the Lord's followers will be united, whether they are dead or living.

  (#346) Very different is the "consolation" offered by a woman named Irene. In this second-century letter Irene writes to friends, a married couple named Taonnophris and Philo. Their son has died. Irene sends this short note of sympathy. "Didymas" may be her own son already deceased. Irene lists names of those who have done everything "fitting," which may refer to funeral offerings or prayers. But in the end she can only lament fate and tell her friends to comfort each other as best they can.

#346: Acceptance and Tears Are the Pagan's Comfort

(Oxyrhynchus Papyri 115)

Irene to Taonnnophris and Philo, good comfort.

I was as sorry and wept over the departed one as I wept for Didymas. And all things, whatsoever were fitting, I did, and all mine, Epaphroditus and Theramuthion and Philion and Apollonius and Plantas. But, nevertheless, against such things one can do nothing. Therefore comfort ye one another. Fare ye well.

1 Thessalonians 5:1: Doctrine of Last Things

Many religions, including Christianity, have views concerning the meaning of history and the end of the world as we know it. When civil war threatened Rome in the first century b.c., Plutarch records, sages recalled the ancient wisdom of a Roman subgroup called the Etruscans (#347).

#347: The Pagan Vision of the Future
(Plutarch, *Fall of the Roman Republic*, *Sulla* 7)

While Sulla set out for his camp to attend to various matters which still required his attention, Marius stayed at home and busied himself with contriving that terrible outbreak of civil violence which did more damage to Rome than all her other wars put together. There were many supernatural warnings of what was to come. Fire broke out of its own accord from under the staves of the ensigns and was only got under control with great difficulty; three ravens brought their young out into the road and after eating most of them, carried back the remains to their nest; mice gnawed at some consecrated gold in a temple and when a keeper had caught one of them, a female, in a trap, she gave birth in the trap itself to five young and ate up three of them. But the most striking phenomenon of all was when the sound of a trumpet rang out from a perfectly clear and cloudless sky with a shrill, prolonged, and dismal note so loud that people were driven half crazy with terror. The Etruscan wise men declared that this portent foretold a change over into a new age and a total revolution in the world. According to them there are eight ages in all. In each age the lives and manners of men are different and God has established for each age a definite span of time which is determined by the circuit of the Great Year. Whenever this circuit comes to an end and another begin

some marvellous sign appears either on earth or in the heavens so that it becomes at once clear to those who have made a thorough study of the subject that men of a different character and way of life have now come into the world and the gods will be either more or less concerned with this new race than they were with their predecessors. All sorts of changes occur, they say, as one age succeeds another and in particular with regard to the art of divination one can observe that there are times when it rises in prestige and its predictions are accurate because clear and unmistakable signs are sent from heaven; and then again in another age it is not held in much honour, since for the most part its practitioners are relying on mere guesswork and are trying to grasp the future with senses that have become blunt and dim. This, at all events, was the story told by the wisest men among the Etruscans who were thought to know more than most about such things.

2 Thessalonians 1:7: The Lord Jesus Revealed in Blazing Fire

(#348) In the Old Testament similar language is used of God's appearance, rewarding his people but punishing his enemies.

#348: The Sweetness of Comfort and the Fire of Judgment
(Isaiah 66:13–16)

[13]As a mother comforts her child,
   so will I comfort you [i.e., God's people];
   and you will be comforted over
      Jerusalem.
[14]When you see this, your heart will rejoice
   and you will flourish like grass;
the hand of the LORD will be made known
      to his servants,
   but his fury will be shown to his foes.
[15]See, the LORD is coming with fire,
   and his chariots are like a whirlwind;
he will bring down his anger with fury,
   and his rebuke with flames of fire.
[16]For with fire and with his sword

the LORD will execute judgment upon all men
and many will be those slain by the LORD.

2 Thessalonians 1:9: Punished with Everlasting Destruction

Paul speaks of the punishment that will come on those who do not respond to the gospel. They willfully turned away from God and refused to believe (#349). The Dead Sea Scrolls paint a similar picture of divine wrath. But there destruction is presented as less their doing than the result of God's foreordained will.

#349: God Ordained the Coming Judgment
(Damascus Document 2.2–13)

[2]Hear now, all you who enter the Covenant, and I will unstop your ears concerning the ways of [3]the wicked.

God loves knowledge. Wisdom and understanding He has set before Him, [4]and prudence and knowledge serve Him. Patience and much forgiveness are with Him [5]towards those who turn from transgression; but power, might, and great flaming wrath [6]by the hand of all the Angels of Destruction towards those who depart from the way and abhor the Precept. They shall have no remnant [7]or survivor. For from the beginning God chose them not; He knew their deeds before ever they were created [8]and He hated their generations, and He hid His face from the Land [9]until they were consumed. For He knew the years of their coming and the length and exact duration of their times [10]for all ages to come and throughout eternity. He knew the happenings of their times throughout all the everlasting years. [11]And in all of them He raised for Himself men called by name, that a remnant might be left to the Land, [12]and that the face of the earth might be filled with their seed. And He made known His Holy Spirit to them by the hand of His anointed ones, and He proclaimed the truth (to them). [13]But those whom he hated He led astray.

2 Thessalonians 3:1: "Pray . . . That the Message . . . May Spread Rapidly"

(#350) Paul uses an image reminiscent of the psalmist's description of God's speedy commands.

#350: The Word of God Runs Swiftly
(Psalm 147:15)

[15]He sends his command to the earth; his word runs swiftly.

1 Timothy 1:13: Mercy Because of Ignorance and Unbelief

Certainly Paul is not saying that God rewards ignorance and unbelief. But he seems to suggest that God may honor at least some forms of zealous advocacy of religious truth, and that he is slow to judge those whose sins are due in part to relatively honest ignorance (# 351). An Old Testament figure speaks words to the same effect. God's appearance to Abimelech, with its explicit demands, may be seen as analogous to Christ's appearance to Paul on the Damascus road. Abimelech had to repent of his former course of action, just as Paul had to repent of his previous life's direction. (#352) An Old Testament proverb may also throw light on Paul's representation of God's stern yet merciful justice. What Paul did, ultimately, was believe in Jesus.

#351: Abimelech Responds to God's Command
(Genesis 20:1–7)

[1]Now Abraham moved on from there into the region of the Negev and lived between Kadesh and Shur. For a while he stayed in Gerar, [2]and there Abraham said of his wife Sarah, "She is my sister." Then Abimelech king of Gerar sent for Sarah and took her.

[3]But God came to Abimelech in a dream one night and said to him, "You are as good

as dead because of the woman you have taken; she is a married woman."

⁴Now Abimelech had not gone near her, so he said, "Lord, will you destroy an innocent nation? ⁵Did he not say to me, 'She is my sister,' and didn't she also say, 'He is my brother'? I have done this with a clear conscience and clean hands."

⁶Then God said to him in the dream, "Yes, I know you did this with a clear conscience, and so I have kept you from sinning against me. That is why I did not let you touch her. ⁷Now return the man's wife, for he is a prophet, and he will pray for you and you will live. But if you do not return her, you may be sure that you and all yours will die."

#352: God's Infinite Knowledge of Our Intentions and Acts

(Proverbs 24:12)

¹²If you say, "But we knew nothing about this,"
does not he who weighs the heart perceive it?
Does not he who guards your life know it?
Will he not repay each person according to what he has done?

1 Timothy 4:3: Asceticism

A common religious impulse is rigorous treatment of the self—fasting, self- or community-imposed silence, sleep deprivation, renunciation of worldly goods, rejection of bodily pleasure. While true spirituality at times calls for harsh measures and self-sacrifice, Paul rejected the notion that it was necessarily spiritual to forego the pleasures of food and conjugal privileges. (#353) In contrast, Philo would be an example of someone who saw bodily pleasure as evil in itself.

#353: Pleasure Produces Every Kind of Deceit

(Philo, *Allegorical Interpretation* 2 20 §§61–64)

20.⁶¹Pleasure does not present to the mind that the subject is such as it is in reality, but deceives it by its artifice, thrusting that, in which there is no advantage, into the class of things profitable.

⁶²For as we may at times see ill-looking courtezans dyeing and painting their faces in order to conceal the plainness of their countenances, so also may we see the intemperate man acting who is inclined to the pleasures of the belly. He looks upon great abundance of wine and a luxurious store of food as a good thing, though he is injured by them both in his body and in his soul. ⁶³Again, we may often see lovers madly eager to be loved by the ugliest of women, because pleasure deceives them and all but affirms positively to them that beauty of form, and delicacy of complexion, and healthiness of flesh, and symmetry of limb, exists in those who have the exact contraries to all these qualifications. Accordingly, they overlook those who are truly possessed of perfectly irreproachable beauty, and waste away with love for such creatures as I have mentioned. ⁶⁴Every kind of deceit therefore is closely connected with pleasure. . . .

1 Timothy 5:2: Absolute Purity

Paul warns the young pastor Timothy against sexual indiscretion—a danger to which pastors in all eras are constantly tempted. Paul seems to stress that if Timothy gives himself wholeheartedly to the central tasks of gospel ministry, he will not fall prey to lurking evils. In other words, Timothy can with God's help overcome evil through aggressive pursuit of good (Rom 12:21; 2 Tm 2:22). (#354) Other writings of the period, such as Sirach, focus explicitly on dangerous situations to be avoided.

#354: Dangerous Situations to Be Avoided

(Sirach 9.2–9)

²Do not give yourself to a woman
so that she gains mastery over your strength.
³Do not go to meet a loose woman,
lest you fall into her snares.
⁴Do not associate with a woman singer,
lest you be caught in her intrigues.

⁵Do not look intently at a virgin,
  lest you stumble and incur penalties for her.
⁶Do not give yourself to harlots
  lest you lose your inheritance.
⁷Do not look around in the streets of a city,
  nor wander about in its deserted sections.
⁸Turn away your eyes from a shapely
    woman,
  and do not look intently at beauty be-
    longing to another;
many have been misled by a woman's
    beauty,
  and by it passion is kindled like a fire.
⁹Never dine with another man's wife,
  nor revel with her at wine;
lest your heart turn aside to her,
  and in blood you be plunged into
    destruction.

1 Timothy 6:11: See 2 Timothy 2:22 (Reading #357)

2 Timothy 2:3: See 2 Corinthians 11:26 (Reading #300)

2 Timothy 2:12: "He Will Disown Us"

Probationary language is found not only in Jesus' teaching (e.g., Mt 10:33) but also in the Old Testament, as these two readings attest (##355, 356).

#355: Seek and You Will Find Him, But If You Forsake Him . . .

(1 Chronicles 28:9)

⁹"And you, my son Solomon, acknowledge the God of your father, and serve him with wholehearted devotion and with a willing mind, for the LORD searches every heart and understands every motive behind the thoughts. If you seek him, he will be found by you; but if you forsake him, he will reject you forever."

#356: Forsake the Lord and Be Forsaken

(2 Chronicles 15:2)

²He went out to meet Asa and said to him, "Listen to me, Asa and all Judah and Benjamin. The LORD is with you when you are with him. If you seek him, he will be found by you, but if you forsake him, he will forsake you."

2 Timothy 2:22: Flee Immorality

(#357) In his counsel to Timothy Paul may have had in mind another young man in another day and time, Joseph, who narrowly escaped seduction by his master's wife. Flight was his only refuge under the circumstances.

#357: Joseph Flees the Temptor's Grasp

(Genesis 39:6–12)

⁶Now Joseph was well-built and handsome, ⁷and after a while his master's wife took notice of Joseph and said, "Come to bed with me!"
⁸But he refused. "With me in charge," he told her, "my master does not concern himself with anything in the house; everything he owns he has entrusted to my care. ⁹No one is greater in this house than I am. My master has withheld nothing from me except you, because you are his wife. How then could I do such a wicked thing and sin against God?" ¹⁰And though she spoke to Joseph day after day, he refused to go to bed with her or even be with her.
¹¹One day he went into the house to attend to his duties, and none of the household servants was inside. ¹²She caught him by his cloak and said, "Come to bed with me!" But he left his cloak in her hand and ran out of the house.

2 Timothy 2:25–26: God Grants Repentance

Paul reminds Timothy that people are in bondage to sin, and ultimately to the devil, unless God grants them repentance and knowledge. Salvation is grounded in God's mercy. (#358) A contrasting view is found in a second-century B.C. writing from the Old Testament Apocrypha. It teaches that keeping God's commandments is not a matter of being liberated from bondage to sin and the devil: it is rather a simple matter of making the right choice. Salvation is grounded in human moral ability.

#358: Choose to Keep the Commands of God

(Sirach 15.13–20)

¹³The Lord hates all abominations,
and they are not loved by those who fear him.
¹⁴It was he who created man in the beginning,
and he left him in the power of his own inclination.
¹⁵If you will, you can keep the commandments,
and to act faithfully is a matter of your own choice.
¹⁶He has placed before you fire and water:
stretch out your hand for whichever you wish.
¹⁷Before a man are life and death,
and whichever he chooses will be given to him.
¹⁸For great is the wisdom of the Lord;
he is mighty in power and sees everything;
¹⁹his eyes are on those who fear him,
and he knows every deed of man.
²⁰He has not commanded any one to be ungodly,
and he has not given any one permission to sin.

2 Timothy 3:8: Jannes and Jambres

These shadowy figures are mentioned in the Dead Sea Scrolls; see James 1:17 (#388) below.

2 Timothy 4: Paul's Courage in the Face of Death

Paul writes as if he knows his execution could come soon. Yet he does not sound desperate but at peace. Such courage is admirable. But it is only fair to point out that other Jews of his era, too, laid down their lives for their beliefs. (#359) Josephus writes the following of Jews captured by the Romans after the fall of Masada. They were ordered to confess that Caesar is Lord. Even children, apparently, defied the command.

#359: The Courage of the Jews in Defying Caesar
(Josephus, *Jewish War* 7.10.1 §§418–19)

1. ⁴¹⁸For when all sorts of torments and vexations of their bodies that could be devised were made use of them, they could not get any one of them to comply so far as to confess or seem to confess, that Caesar was their lord; but they preserved their own opinion, in spite of all the distress they were brought to, as if they received these torments and the fire itself with bodies insensible of pain, and with a soul that in a manner rejoiced under them. ⁴¹⁹But what was most of all astonishing to the beholders, was the courage of the children; for not one of these children was so far overcome by these torments as to name Caesar for their lord. So far does the strength of the courage [of the soul] prevail over the weakness of the body.

2 Timothy 4:17: Paul and the Lion's Mouth

Paul's imprisonment likely took place under the reign of Nero. Early in his reign he governed in a reasonable fashion, but as the years passed his practices became increasingly erratic and harmful. The public blamed him for setting a portion of Rome on fire in order to make room for his new palace. (See Reading #233 for Tacitus's account of this and how Nero punished the Christians for it.) (#360) The church historian Eusebius

Nero, the first Roman emperor to persecute the Christians and the murderer of Peter and Paul.

so many thousands with any calculation, but with such indiscriminate murder as not even to refrain from his nearest and dearest friends. His own mother and wife, with many others that were his near relatives, he killed like strangers and enemies, with various kinds of deaths. [3]And, indeed, in addition to all his other crimes, this too was yet wanting to complete the catalogue, that he was the first of the emperors that displayed himself an enemy of piety towards the Deity. [4]This fact is recorded by the Roman Tertullian, in language like the following: "Examine your records. There you will find that Nero was the first that persecuted this doctrine, particularly then when after subduing all the east, he exercised his cruelty against all at Rome. Such is the man of whom we boast, as the leader in our punishment. For he that knows who he was, may know also that there could scarcely be any thing but what was great and good, condemned by Nero." [5]Thus Nero publicly announcing himself as the chief enemy of God, was led on in his fury to slaughter the apostles. Paul is therefore said to have been beheaded at Rome, and Peter to have been crucified under him. And this account is confirmed by the fact, that the names of Peter and Paul still remain in the cemeteries of that city even to this day.

records how Nero eventually executed both Peter and Paul.

#360: Nero's Murder of Peter and Paul
(Eusebius, *Ecclesiastical History* 2.25.1–5)

[1]But Nero now having the government firmly established under him, and henceforth plunging into nefarious projects, began to take up arms against that very religion which acknowledges the one Supreme God. To describe, indeed, the greatness of this man's wickedness, is not compatible with our present object; [2]and as there are many that have given his history in the most accurate narratives, every one may, at his pleasure, in these contemplate the grossness of his extraordinary madness. Under the influence of this, he did not proceed to destroy

Titus 1:1: The Truth That Leads to Godliness

In Paul's writings "truth" does not equal intellectual correctness alone; it also involves a right relationship with God through faith and obedience. (##361–364) The Old Testament contains many passages that correlate "truth" and obedience or love, as these selections show.

#361: Truth from the Heart Is a Righteous Walk
(Psalm 15:1–2)

[1]LORD, who may dwell in your sanctuary?
  Who may live on your holy hill?

²He whose walk is blameless
and who does what is righteous,
who speaks the truth from his heart.

#362: Truth and Love Are Joined Together

(Psalm 40:10)

¹⁰I do not hide your righteousness in my
heart;
I speak of your faithfulness and
salvation.
I do not conceal your love and your truth
from the great assembly.

#363: Truth and Wisdom Dwell in the Heart

(Psalm 51:6)

⁶Surely you desire truth in the inner parts;
you teach me wisdom in the inmost
place.

#364: The Way of the Lord Is to Walk in the Truth

(Psalm 86:11)

¹¹Teach me your way, O LORD,
and I will walk in your truth;
give me an undivided heart,
that I may fear your name.

Titus 2:5: Younger Women Busy at Home

First-century Mediterranean society encouraged women to tend to domestic duties like child-rearing and spinning wool. (#365) In our first reading, a husband commissions a touching epitaph for his wife's tomb. (#366) A similar sentiment is found on a tomb in Pergamum dating from the early second century A.D. The distinctive word "unblamably" is used by Paul in 1 Thessalonians 2:10; 3:6, 13. (#367) The historian Tacitus indirectly criticizes family dissolution among the Roman ruling class by praising the behavior of Teutonic (German) women to the north of the Roman Empire.

#365: The Unlovely Tomb of a Lovely Woman

(*Corpus Inscriptionum Latinarum* 1.2.1211)

Stranger, what I have to say is short. Stop and read it through. This is the unlovely tomb of a lovely woman. Her parents named her Claudia. She loved her husband with her whole heart. She bore two sons, one of whom she leaves on earth; the other she has placed beneath the earth. She was charming in conversation, yet her conduct was appropriate. She kept house, she made wool.

#366: Otacilia Polla, the Unblamable Wife

(Tombstone Epitaph at Pergamum)

Julius Bassus to Otacilia Polla, his sweetest wife. Loving to her husband, and loving to her children, she lived with him unblamably 30 years.

#367: The Faithful Nature of Noble Wives

(Tacitus, *Germany* 19)

¹⁹Thus with their virtue protected they live uncorrupted by the allurements of public shows or the stimulant of feastings. Clandestine correspondence is equally unknown to men and women. Very rare for so numerous a population is adultery, the punishment for which is prompt, and in the husband's power. Having cut off the hair of the adulteress and stripped her naked, he expels her from the house in the presence of her kinsfolk, and then flogs her through the whole village. The loss of chastity meets with no indulgence; neither beauty, youth, nor wealth will procure the culprit a husband. No one in Germany laughs at vice, nor do they call it the fashion to corrupt and to be corrupted. Still better is the condition of those states in which only maidens are given in marriage, and where the hopes and expectations of a bride are then finally terminated. They receive one husband, as having one body and one life, that they may have no thoughts be-

hind, no further-reaching desires, that they may love not so much the husband as the married state. To limit the number of their children or to destroy any of their subsequent offspring is accounted infamous, and good habits are here more effectual than good laws elsewhere.

Titus 2:6: Young Men Self-Controlled

Paul gives terse directions to Titus for how different age groups and genders should conduct themselves. (#368) A Jewish religious community dating from about the first century B.C. compiled more specific rules for men of different ages. The rules were for the coming messianic age.

#368: Jewish Rules for Various Stages of Life
(Messianic Rule 1.6–19)

[6]*And this is the Rule for all the hosts of the congregation, for every man born in Israel*

From [his] youth they shall instruct him in the Book of Meditation and shall teach him, according to his age, the precepts of the Covenant. [7]He [shall be edu]cated in their statutes for ten years . . .

[8]At the age of twenty years [9][he shall be] enrolled, that he may enter upon his allotted duties in the midst of his family (and) be joined to the holy congregation. He shall not [approach] [10]a woman to know her by lying with her before he is fully twenty years old, when he shall know [good] and [11]evil. And thereafter, he shall be accepted when he calls to witness the judgments of the Law, and shall be (allowed) to assist at the hearing of judgments.

[12]At the age of twenty-five years he may take his place among the foundations [i.e., the officials] of the holy [13]congregation to work in the service of the congregation.

At the age of thirty years he may approach to participate in lawsuits [14]and judgments, and may take his place among the chiefs of the Thousands of Israel, the chiefs of the Hundreds, Fifties, [15]and Tens, the Judges and the officers of their tribes, in all their families, [under the authority] of the sons of [16][Aar]on the Priests. And every head of family in the congregation who is chosen to hold office, [17][to go] and come before the congregation, shall strengthen his loins that he may [18]perform his tasks among this brethren in accordance with his understanding and the perfection of his way. According to whether this is great or little, so shall one man be honored more than another.

[19]When a man is advanced in years, he shall be given a duty in the [ser]vice of the congregation in proportion to his strength.

Titus 2:7: Doing What Is Good

In Titus Paul repeatedly underscores the importance of good works (2:7, 14; 3:1, 8, 14), even though good works alone are not the basis for personal salvation (3:5). Paul refers to joyful submission to the Lord's will and commands. The same attitude of willing appropriation of the works God prescribes is found in the Old Testament (#369).

#369: The Righteous Path Is to Follow God's Laws
(Psalm 119:97–104)

[97]Oh, how I love your law!
    I meditate on it all day long.
[98]Your commands make me wiser than my
        enemies,
    for they are ever with me.
[99]I have more insight than all my teachers,
    for I meditate on your statutes.
[100]I have more understanding than the elders,
    for I obey your precepts.
[101]I have kept my feet from every evil path
    so that I might obey your word.
[102]I have not departed from your laws,
    for you yourself have taught me.
[103]How sweet are your words to my taste,
    sweeter than honey to my mouth!
[104]I gain understanding from your precepts;
    therefore I hate every wrong path.

Philemon 12: "I Am Sending Him . . . Back to You"

(#370) Old Testament law prohibited Paul from sending Onesimus back to Philemon. But he realized that he must act legally under Roman law, not the civic regulations of ancient Israel's theocracy. Paul is confident that Onesimus's interests will be protected by the gospel's work in Philemon's life. (#371) In the early second century A.D., Pliny the Younger wrote to a certain Sabinianus that he should deal with a runaway slave in a kindly way. There are remarkable parallels with what Paul wrote to Philemon two generations earlier. But there are also differences. For example, it is the love of Christ that Paul urges on Philemon, not the Stoic virtues of clemency and moderation that Pliny calls for from Sabinianus.

#370: Do Not Return a Slave to His Owner
(Deuteronomy 23:15–16)

[15]If a slave has taken refuge with you, do not hand him over to his master. [16]Let him live among you wherever he likes and in whatever town he chooses. Do not oppress him.

#371: The Erring Slave Should Be Forgiven
(Pliny the Younger, *Epistles* 9.21)

[1]"To Sabinianus. Your freedman, whom you lately mentioned as having displeased you, has been with me; he threw himself at my feet and clung there with as much submission as he could have done at yours. He earnestly requested me with many tears, and even with the eloquence of silent sorrow, to intercede for him; in short, he convinced me by his whole behavior, that he sincerely repents of his fault. And I am persuaded he is thoroughly reformed, because he seems entirely sensible of his delinquency. [2]I know you are angry with him, and I know too, it is not without reason; but clemency can never exert itself with more applause, than when there is the justest cause for resentment. You once had an affection for this man, and, I hope, will have again: in the meanwhile, let me only prevail with you to pardon him. If he should incur your displeasure hereafter, you will have so much the stronger plea in excuse for your anger, as you shew yourself more exorable to him now. Allow something to his youth, to his tears, and to your own natural mildness of temper: do not make him uneasy any longer, and I will add too, do not make yourself so; for a man of your benevolence of heart cannot be angry without feeling great uneasiness. [3]I am afraid, were I to join my entreaties with his, I should seem rather to compel, than request you to forgive him. Yet I will not scruple to do it; and so much the more fully and freely as I have very sharply and severely reproved him, positively threatening never to interpose again in his behalf. But though it was proper to say this to him, in order to make him more fearful of offending, I do not say it to you. I may, perhaps, again have occasion to entreat you upon his account, and again obtain your forgiveness; supposing, I mean, his error should be such as may become me to intercede for, and you to pardon. Farewell."

Philemon 16: Treat Slaves as Brothers

Slavery in Paul's time was not always as brutal as sometimes imagined—it can generally not be equated with common slavery practices in parts of the old American South. Because of their common Lord Jesus Christ, the slave owner Philemon can welcome back his errant slave Onesimus with kindness. A similar charitable attitude (though without Christian motivation) toward slaves (or servants) was part of Paul's Jewish heritage from much earlier times. (#372) The following passage is from the second century B.C. (#373) The Roman philosopher Seneca offers counsel similar to Paul's, though on the basis of a very different, Stoic worldview.

#372: Treat a Slave as You Would a Brother
(Sirach 33.30–31)

[30]If you have a servant, let him be as yourself,

because you have bought him with
blood.
[31]If you have a servant, treat him as a
brother,
for as your own soul you will need him.
If you ill-treat him, and he leaves and runs
away,
which way will you go to seek him?

#373: Slaves and the Free-born Are Ultimately Equal
(Seneca, *Epistles* 47.10)

[10]"Kindly remember that he whom you call your slave sprang from the same stock, is smiled upon by the same skies, and on equal terms with yourself breathes, lives and dies. It is just as possible for you to see in him a free-born man as for him to see in you a slave."

Part

3

General Epistles
and Revelation

10 Hebrews–2 Peter

Examples of advanced commentaries containing additional references to extrabiblical parallels or passages include:

- Hebrews: Lane (2 vols.), Bruce, Ellingworth
- James: Davids, Luke Timothy Johnson, Martin
- 1 Peter: Michaels, Davids, Kelly
- 2 Peter: Bauckham, Bigg, Mayor

Hebrews 1:3: The Radiance of God's Glory

(#374) The apocryphal writing Wisdom of Solomon uses the same rare word for "radiance" (translated as "reflection" in the text below), but it speaks of "Wisdom," not an incarnate divine figure. Further, this "Wisdom" gives insight and reflects God's glory; it does not provide a sacrifice for sins as the Son does in Hebrews 1:3. The "I" below is the imaginary Solomon.

#374: Wisdom Is a Reflection of Eternal Light
(Wisdom of Solomon 7.21–26)

[21]I learned both what is secret and what is manifest,
[22]for wisdom, the fashioner of all things, taught me.

For in her there is a spirit that is intelligent, holy,
unique, manifold, subtle,
mobile, clear, unpolluted,
distinct, invulnerable, loving the good, keen,

irresistible, [23]beneficent, humane,
steadfast, sure, free from anxiety,
all-powerful, overseeing all,
and penetrating through all spirits
that are intelligent and pure and most subtle.
[24]For wisdom is more mobile than any motion;
because of her pureness she pervades and penetrates all things.
[25]For she is a breath of the power of God,
and a pure emanation of the glory of the Almighty;
therefore nothing defiled gains entrance into her.
[26]For she is a reflection of eternal light,
a spotless mirror of the working of God,
and an image of his goodness.

Hebrews 4:12: The Power of God's Word

(#375) The Jewish writer Philo shared with the writer of Hebrews the belief that the words of Scripture held a convicting and cleansing power.

#375: The Word of God Corrects Our Hearts
(Philo, *The Worse Attacks the Better* 40 §146)

40. [146]Let us, therefore, address our supplications to God, we who are self-convicted by our consciousness of our own sins, to chastise us rather than to abandon us; for if he abandons us, he will no longer make us his servants, who is a merciful master, but slaves of a pitiless generation: but if he chastises us in a gentle and merciful manner, as a kind ruler, he will correct our offenses, sending that

179

correcting conviction, his own word, into our hearts, by means of which he will heal them; reproving us and making us ashamed of the wickednesses which we have committed.

Hebrews 5:12–14: Milk and Solid Food

(#376) Philo uses imagery similar to that employed by the writer of Hebrews. But the "solid food" prescribed by each is strikingly different.

#376: Mature Food Consists of Prudence and Virtue
(Philo, *On Husbandry* 2 §9)

2. [9]But since milk is the food of infants, but cakes made of wheat are the food of fullgrown men, so also the soul must have a milk-like nourishment in its age of childhood, namely, the elementary instruction of encyclical science. But the perfect food which is fit for men consists of explanations dictated by prudence, and temperance, and every virtue.

For these things being sown and implanted in the mind will bring forth most advantageous fruit, namely, good and praiseworthy actions.

Hebrews 7:2: Abraham Gave Melchizedek a Tenth

(#377) The writer of Hebrews refers to an incident recorded in Genesis to make his point about Melchizedek the priest.

#377: Abraham Paid Tithes to Melchizedek
(Genesis 14:17–20)

[17]After Abram returned from defeating Kedorlaomer and the kings allied with him, the king of Sodom came out to meet him in the Valley of Shaveh (that is, the King's Valley).

[18]Then Melchizedek king of Salem brought out bread and wine. He was priest of God Most High, [19]and he blessed Abram, saying,
"Blessed be Abram by God Most High,
    Creator of heaven and earth.
[20]And blessed be God Most High,
    who delivered your enemies into your hand."
Then Abram gave him a tenth of everything.

Hebrews 11:37: Sawed in Two

(#378) An ancient Jewish legend (of uncertain reliability) records that the prophet Isaiah was executed with a wood saw under the wicked king Manasseh. "Beliar" is Satan, who is also called "Mekembekus" in the text below. "Belkira" is thought to be a human personification of Beliar.

#378: The Brutal Murder of Isaiah the Prophet
(Martyrdom and Ascension of Isaiah the Prophet 5.1–14)

[1]Because of these visions, therefore, Beliar was angry with Isaiah, and he dwelt in the heart of Manasseh, and he sawed Isaiah in half with a wood saw. [2]And while Isaiah was being sawed in half, his accuser, Belkira, stood by, and all the false prophets stood by, laughing and (maliciously) joyful because of Isaiah. [3]And Belkira, through Mekembekus, stood before Isaiah, laughing and deriding. [4]And Belkira said to Isaiah, "Say, 'I have lied in everything I have spoken; the ways of Manasseh are good and right, [5]and also the ways of Belkira and those who are with him are good.'" [6]And he said this to him when he began to be sawed in half. [7]And Isaiah was in a vision of the LORD, but his eyes were open, and he saw them. [8]And Belkira spoke thus to Isaiah, "Say what I say to you, and I will turn their heart and make Manasseh, and the princes of Judah, and the people, and all Jerusalem worship you." [9]And Isaiah answered and said, "If it is within my power to say, 'Condemned and cursed be you, and all your hosts, and all your house!' [10]For

there is nothing further that you can take except the skin of my body." [11]And they seized Isaiah the son of Amoz and sawed him in half with a wood saw. [12]And Manasseh, and Belkira, and the false prophets, and the princes, and the people, and all stood by looking on. [13]And to the prophets who (were) with him he said before he was sawed in half, "Go to the district of Tyre and Sidon, because for me alone the LORD has mixed the cup." [14]And while Isaiah was being sawed in half, he did not cry out, or weep, but his mouth spoke with the Holy Spirit until he was sawed in two.

Hebrews 12:11: Joyful Discipline

The beneficial result of stern discipline when God administers it is recognized in the Old Testament, as these two readings show. (##379–380) God disciplines Christ's followers. He brings hardship into their lives, for their good, that they may share in his holiness (Heb 12:10). Sometimes this discipline seems harsh. But God deals with his children like a wise and loving father. (#381) Compare the means of discipline of Crassus in 72 B.C., as he punished men for lack of bravery in battle, and (#382) of Caesar Augustus, who reigned at the time of Jesus' birth.

#379: Hearts Are Cleansed by Proper Discipline
(Proverbs 20:30)

[30]Blows and wounds cleanse away evil,
    and beatings purge the inmost being.

#380: Justice Brings Joy to the Righteous
(Proverbs 21:15)

[15]When justice is done, it brings joy to the righteous
    but terror to evildoers.

#381: The Savage Discipline of Crassus
(Plutarch, *Fall of the Roman Republic, Crassus* 10)

[10]Crassus was appointed to the supreme command of the war. Because of his reputation or because of their friendship with him large numbers of the nobility volunteered to serve with him. Spartacus was now bearing down on Picenum, and Crassus himself took up a position on the borders of the district with the intention of meeting the attack there. He ordered one of his subordinate commanders, Mummius, with two legions to march round by another route and instructed him to follow the enemy, but not to join battle with them or even to do any skirmishing. Mummius, however, as soon as he saw what appeared to him a good opportunity, offered battle and was defeated. Many of his men were killed and many saved their lives by throwing away their arms and running for it. Crassus gave Mummius himself a very rough reception after this. He re-armed his soldiers and made them give guarantees that in future they would preserve the arms in their possession. Then he took 500 of those who had been the first to fly and had shown themselves the greatest cowards, and, dividing them into fifty squads of ten men each, put to death one man, chosen by lot, from each squad. This was a traditional method of punishing soldiers, now revived by Crassus after having been out of use for many years. Those who are punished in this way not only lose their lives but are also disgraced, since the whole army there are spectators, and the actual circumstances of the execution are very savage and repulsive.

After employing this method of conversion on his men, Crassus led them against the enemy.

#382: The Brutal Punishments Inflicted by Caesar Augustus
(Suetonius, *Twelve Caesars, Augustus* 24.2)

[2]He [Augustus] gave the entire Tenth Legion an ignominious discharge because of their insolent behavior, and when some other legions also demanded their discharge in a similarly riotous manner, he disbanded them, withholding the bounty which they would have earned had they continued loyal. If a cohort broke in battle, Augustus ordered the survivors to draw lots, then executed every

tenth man, and fed the remainder on barley bread instead of the customary wheat ration. Centurions found absent from their posts were sentenced to death, like other ranks, and any lesser dereliction of duty earned them one of several degrading punishments—such as being made to stand all day long in front of general headquarters, sometimes wearing tunics without sword-belts, sometimes carrying ten-foot poles, or even sods of turf.

Hebrews 13:2: Hospitality

Opening one's home to strangers (perhaps especially itinerant Christian ministers) was a high priority in the early church (cf. 3 Jn 5–8). (#383) A second-century B.C. Jewish document stresses the bother and risk of showing kindness to strangers.

#383: Hospitality Can Foster Danger
(Sirach 11.29–34)

[29]Do not bring every man into your home,
for many are the wiles of the crafty.
[30]Like a decoy partridge in a cage, so is the mind of a proud man,
and like a spy he observes your weakness;
[31]for he lies in wait, turning good into evil,
and to worthy actions he will attach blame.
[32]From a spark of fire come many burning coals,
and a sinner lies in wait to shed blood.
[33]Beware of a scoundrel, for he devises evil,
lest he give you a lasting blemish.
[34]Receive a stranger into your home and he will upset you with commotion,
and will estrange you from your family

James 1:1: James the Brother of Jesus

Josephus reports that James was stoned to death under sentence from the high priest Ananus, son

of the high priest by the same name mentioned in the Gospels, who was his father. (See Reading #228 for the text of Josephus.) (#384) The church historian Eusebius provides an extended version of the death of James and the circumstances preceding it.

#384: The Death of James, the Brother of Jesus
(Eusebius, *Ecclesiastical History* 2.23.3–16, 18)

[3]But, as to the manner of James's death, it has been already stated in the words of Clement, that he was thrown from a wing of the temple, and beaten to death with a club. Hegesippus also, who flourished nearest the days of the apostles, in the fifth book of his Commentaries gives the most accurate account of him, thus: [4]"But James, the brother of the Lord, who, as there were many of this name, was surnamed the Just by all, from the days of our Lord until now, received the government of the church with the apostles. [5]This apostle was consecrated from his mother's womb. He drank neither wine nor fermented liquors, and abstained from animal food. A razor never came upon his head, he never anointed with oil, and never used a bath. [6]He alone was allowed to enter the sanctuary. He never wore woolen, but linen garments. He was in the habit of entering the temple alone, and was often found upon his bended knees, and interceding for the forgiveness of the people; so that his knees became as hard as camel's, in consequence of his habitual supplication and kneeling before God. [7]And indeed, on account of his exceeding great piety, he was called the Just, and Oblias (or Zaddick and Ozelam) which signifies justice and protection of the people; as the prophets declare concerning him. [8]Some of the seven sects, therefore, of the people, mentioned by me above in my Commentaries, asked him what was the door to Jesus? and he answered, 'that he was the Savior.'" [9]From which, some believed that Jesus is the Christ. But the aforesaid heresies did not believe either a resurrection, or that he was coming to give to every one according to his works; as many however, as did believe did so on account of James. [10]As there were many therefore of the

rulers that believed, there arose a tumult among the Jews, Scribes, and Pharisees, saying that there was danger, that the people would now expect Jesus as the Messiah. They came therefore together, and said to James, "We entreat thee, restrain the people, who are led astray after Jesus, as if he were the Christ. We entreat thee to persuade all that are coming to the feast of the passover rightly concerning Jesus; for we all have confidence in thee. For we and all the people bear thee testimony that thou art just, and thou respectest not persons. [11]Persuade therefore the people not to be led astray by Jesus, for we and all the people have great confidence in thee. Stand therefore upon a wing of the temple, that thou mayest be conspicuous on high, and thy words may be easily heard by all the people; for all the tribes have come together on account of the passover, with some of the Gentiles also." [12]The aforesaid Scribes and Pharisees, therefore, placed James upon a wing of the temple, and cried out to him, "O thou just man, whom we ought all to believe, since the people are led astray after Jesus that was crucified, declare to us what is the door to Jesus that was crucified." [13]And he answered with a loud voice, "Why do ye ask me respecting Jesus the Son of Man? He is now sitting in the heavens, on the right hand of great Power, and is about to come on the clouds of heaven." [14]And as many were confirmed, and gloried in this testimony of James, and said, Hosanna to the son of David, these same priests and Pharisees said to one another, "We have done badly in affording such testimony to Jesus, but let us go up and cast him down, that they may dread to believe in him." [15]And they cried out, "Oh, oh, Justus himself is deceived," and they fulfilled that which is written in Isaiah, "Let us take away the just, because he is offensive to us; wherefore they shall eat the fruit of their doings." Is. iii. [16]Going up therefore, they cast down the just man, saying to one another, "Let us stone James the Just." And they began to stone him, as he did not die immediately when cast down; but turning round, he knelt down saying, "I entreat thee, O Lord God and Father, forgive them, for they know not what they do." ... [18]And one of them, a fuller, beat out the brains of Justus with the club that he used to beat out clothes. Thus he suffered martyrdom, and they

buried him on the spot where his tombstone is still remaining, by the temple. He became a faithful witness, both to the Jews and Greeks, that Jesus is the Christ.

James 1:2: Joy in Trials

James states a truth acknowledged repeatedly in the Old Testament: difficulties will come, but those who seek the Lord find resources in their God to cope. (#385) The prophet Isaiah gives a good example of this.

#385: In the Fire You Will Not Be Burned
(Isaiah 43:2, 3)

[2]When you pass through the waters,
    I will be with you;
and when you pass through the rivers,
    they will not sweep over you.
When you walk through the fire,
    you will not be burned;
    the flames will not set you ablaze.
[3]For I am the LORD, your God,
    the Holy One of Israel, your Savior.

James 1:17: Evil in God?

James denies that evil is part of God's nature or his doing. (##386, 387) Agreeing with him is the Jewish writer Philo.

#386: God Does Not Cause Evil
(Philo, *The Worse Attacks the Better* 32 §122)

32. [122]Moses does not (as some wicked men do) say, that God is the cause of evils, but our own hands; indicating, by a figurative expression, the works of our hand, and the voluntary inclinations of our mind to the worser part.

#387: God Is the Cause of Only What Is Good
(Philo, *On Husbandry* 29 §§128–29)

29. [128]There are some persons who look upon piety as consisting in the affirmation that

all things have been made by God, both what is good and the contrary; [129]to whom we would say that one portion of your opinion is praiseworthy, but the other portion blameable. One portion is praiseworthy, because it properly honors that which alone is worthy to receive honor; but that portion is blameable, which does so without any discrimination or division. For it was not proper to confuse and mingle everything together, nor to declare God the cause of everything without distinction, but to make a difference, and to pronounce him the cause only of those things which are good.

James 1:17: Father of the Heavenly Lights

(#388) The Dead Sea Scrolls use a term for God similar to the Book of James.

#388: God Is the Prince of Lights
(Damascus Document 5.17–19)

[17]For in ancient times, [18]Moses and Aaron arose by the hand of the Prince of Lights and Satan in his cunning raised up Jannes and [19]his brother when Israel was first delivered.

James 2: Favoritism Toward the Rich

In God's household, all are to be treated equally. Sadly, they sometimes are not. (#389) Other writers besides James, such as Sirach, understood that people tend to measure the rich and the poor by different standards. (See Reading #299 for a similar idea in 2 Cor 8:9.)

#389: The Unequal Treatment of the Rich and Poor
(Sirach 13.21–24)

[21]When a rich man totters, he is steadied by friends,
but when a humble man falls, he is even pushed away by friends.

[22]If a rich man slips, his helpers are many;
he speaks unseemly words, and they justify him.
If a humble man slips, they even reproach him;
he speaks sensibly, and receives no attention.
[23]When the rich man speaks all are silent,
and they extol to the clouds what he says.
When the poor man speaks they say, "Who is this fellow?"
And should he stumble, they even push him down.
[24]Riches are good if they are free from sin,
and poverty is evil in the opinion of the ungodly.

James 3:3–4: Horses and Ships

(#390) Philo uses imagery very similar to that employed by James.

#390: Illustrations of Moral Control
(Philo, *On Husbandry* 15 §69)

15. [69]But a horseman, on the other hand, when he is about to mount, takes the bridle in his hand, and then taking hold of the mane on the horse's neck, he leaps on; and though he appears to be carried by the horse, yet, if one must tell the truth, he in reality guides the animal that carries him, as a pilot guides a ship. For the pilot too, appearing to be carried by the ship which he is managing, does in real truth guide it, and conducts it to whatever harbor he is himself desirous to hasten.

James 4:9: Grieve, Mourn, and Wail

(#391) James reflects Old Testament conviction that there are times when God's people have no alternative but to face up to their wrongdoing. Denial is disaster.

#391: God Calls Us to Repent of Our Sins
(Isaiah 22:12–14)

[12]The Lord, the LORD Almighty,
  called you on that day
to weep and to wail,
  to tear out your hair and put on sack-
    cloth.
[13]But see, there is joy and revelry,
  slaughtering of cattle and killing of
    sheep,
  eating of meat and drinking of wine!
"Let us eat and drink," you say, "for tomor-
    row we die!"
[14]The LORD Almighty has revealed this in
my hearing: "Till your dying day this sin will
not be atoned for," says the Lord, the LORD
Almighty.

James 4:14: What Is Your Life?

James writes, "You are a mist that appears for a little while and then vanishes." The fleeting nature of human life, compared to God's eternality, is a repeated theme of various Old Testament passages. It is also found in Jewish writings outside the Old Testament. (#392) The following example dates to about the first century B.C.

#392: Life Passes Like Hoarfrost Driven by a Storm
(Wisdom of Solomon 5.9–10, 12–14)

[9]"All those things have vanished like a
    shadow,
and like a rumor that passes by;
[10]like a ship that sails through the billowy
    water,
and when it has passed no trace can be
    found,
nor track of its keel in the waves; . . .
[12]or as, when an arrow is shot at a target,
the air, thus divided, comes together at
    once,
so that no one knows its pathway.
[13]So we also, as soon as we were born,
    ceased to be,
and we had no sign of virtue to show,

but were consumed in our wickedness."
[14]Because the hope of the ungodly man is
    like chaff carried by the wind,
and like a light hoarfrost driven away by a
    storm;
it is dispersed like smoke before the wind,
and it passes like the remembrance of a
    guest who stays but a day.

1 Peter 1:1: The Church in Bithynia

We have little direct information about the first-century churches to which Peter addressed his first epistle. But two generations later, evidence of Christian presence exists in the form of letters between Bithynia's governor, Pliny the Younger (A.D. 62–ca. 113), and the emperor Trajan. (#393) Pliny writes to Trajan in A.D. 112 to get advice on how he should deal with Christians who are being brought to him for trial. (#394) Trajan the emperor then replies.

#393: How Should We Treat This Depraved Superstition?
(Pliny the Younger, *Epp.* 96.1–9)

[1]It is my rule, Sir, to refer to you in matters where I am uncertain. For who can better direct my hesitation or instruct my ignorance? I was never present at any trial of Christians; therefore I do not know what are the customary penalties or investigations, and what limits are observed. [2]I have hesitated a great deal on the question whether there should be any distinction of ages; whether the weak should have the same treatment as the more robust; whether those who recant should be pardoned, or whether a man who has ever been a Christian should gain nothing by ceasing to be such; whether the name itself, even if innocent of crime, should be punished, or only the crimes attaching to that name.

Meanwhile, this is the course that I have adopted in the case of those brought before me as Christians. [3]I ask them if they are Christians. If they admit it I repeat the question a second and a third time, threatening capital punishment; if they persist I sentence them to death. For I do not doubt that, whatever kind of crime it may be to which they have confessed, their pertinacity and inflexible obstinacy should certainly be punished. [4]There were others who displayed a like madness and whom I reserved to be sent to Rome, since they were Roman citizens.

Thereupon the usual result followed; the very fact of my dealing with the question led to a wider spread of the charge, and a great variety of cases were brought before me. [5]An anonymous pamphlet was issued, containing many names. All who denied that they were or had been Christians I considered should be discharged, because they called upon the gods at my dictation and did reverence, with incense and wine, to your image which I had ordered to be brought forward for this purpose, together with the statues of the deities; and especially because they cursed Christ, a thing which, it is said, genuine Christians cannot be induced to do. [6]Others named by the informer first said that they were Christians and then denied it; declaring that they had been but were so no longer, some having recanted three years or more before and one or two as long ago as twenty years. They all worshiped your image and the statues of the gods and cursed Christ. [7]But they declared that the sum of their guilt or error had amounted only to this, that on an appointed day they had been accustomed to meet before daybreak, and to recite a hymn antiphonally to Christ, as to a god, and to bind themselves by an oath, not for the commission of any crime but to abstain from theft, robbery, adultery, and breach of faith, and not to deny a deposit when it was claimed. After the conclusion of this ceremony it was their custom to depart and meet again to take food; but it was ordinary and harmless food, and they had ceased this practice after my edict in which, in accordance with your orders, I had forbidden secret societies. [8]I thought it the more necessary, therefore, to find out what truth there was in this by applying torture to two maidservants, who were called deaconesses. But I found nothing but a depraved and extravagant superstition, and I therefore postponed my examination and had recourse to you for consultation.

[9]The matter seemed to me to justify my consulting you, especially on account of the number of those imperiled; for many persons of all ages and classes and of both sexes are being put in peril by accusation, and this will go on. The contagion of this superstition has spread not only in the cities, but in the villages and rural districts as well; yet it seems capable of being checked and set right. [10]There is no shadow of doubt that the temples, which have been almost deserted, are beginning to be frequented once more, that the sacred rites which have been long neglected are being renewed, and that sacrificial victims are for sale everywhere, whereas, till recently, a buyer was rarely to be found. From this it is easy to imagine what a host of men could be set right, were they given a chance of recantation.

#394: Christians May Escape Punishment by Denying Their Lord
(Trajan, *To Pliny* 47.1–2)

[1]You have taken the right line, my dear Pliny, in examining the cases of those denounced to you as Christians, for no hard and fast rule can be laid down, of universal application. [2]They are not to be sought out; if they are informed against, and the charge is proved, they are to be punished, with this reservation—that if anyone denies that he is a Christian, and actually proves it, that is by worshiping our gods, he shall be pardoned as a result of his recantation, however suspect he may have been with respect to the past. Pamphlets published anonymously should carry no weight in any charge whatsoever. They constitute a very bad precedent, and are also out of keeping with this age.

1 Peter 1:6: Grief in All Kinds of Trials

While we lack definite knowledge of official Roman persecution corresponding to what 1 Peter seems to reflect, we do know that Roman law looked askance at "foreign" religions—religions not part of the Romans' own heritage. (#395) Roman historian Livy recounted Roman suppression of the *bacchanalia* cult; a similar rationale likely came into play later regarding Christianity.

#395: False Religions Deserve to Be Punished

(Livy, *History of Rome* 39.16.6–9)

⁶Nothing is more deceptive in outward appearance than a false religion. Where the majesty of the gods is set out as cover for a crime, a fear steals into one's mind lest in punishing human misbehavior we may do violence to some matter of divine law which has got mixed up with it. From this scruple [*hac religione*] innumerable decisions of the pontiffs, decrees of the Senate, and finally responses of the haruspices have set you free. ⁸How often, in the days of our fathers and our grandfathers, has it been the task turned over to the magistrates to forbid the introduction of foreign cults, to exclude quack sacrificers and fortunetellers from the Forum, the Circus, and the City, to search out and burn books of prophecies, and to abolish every system of sacrifice except that which conforms to the Roman way. ⁹For the wisest men, in all laws divine and human, were convinced that nothing was so effective in destroying religion as where sacrifices were offered not by native but by foreign rites.

1 Peter 3:4: Praiseworthy in God's Sight

Peter writes of the beauty of inner spiritual integrity—stressing its value in women without in any way suggesting that it is not also called for in men (1 Pt 3:7). In the overall scope of his Epistle, such beauty comes as the result of the work of God's grace in the heart through the gospel. (#396) A contrasting view of the time held that true greatness lay in devotion to the law of Moses and would be rewarded by human acclaim.

#396: Knowledge of the Law Brings Remembrance and Praise

(Sirach 39.1, 4–10)

¹On the other hand he who devotes himself to the study of the law of the Most High will seek out the wisdom of all the ancients, and will be concerned with prophecies;

. . .

⁴He will serve among great men
and appear before rulers;
he will travel through the lands of foreign nations,
for he tests the good and the evil among men.
⁵He will set his heart to rise early
to seek the Lord who made him,
and will make supplication before the Most High;
he will open his mouth in prayer
and make supplication for his sins.
⁶If the great Lord is willing,
he will be filled with the spirit of understanding;
he will pour forth words of wisdom
and give thanks to the Lord in prayer.
⁷He will direct his counsel and knowledge aright,
and meditate on his secrets.
⁸He will reveal instruction in his teaching,
and will glory in the law of the Lord's covenant.
⁹Many will praise his understanding,
and it will never be blotted out;
his memory will not disappear,
and his name will live through all generations.
¹⁰Nations will declare his wisdom,
and the congregation will proclaim his praise.

1 Peter 3:15: Prepared to Give an Answer

(#397) Old Testament saints were to be prepared to defend their faith, just as Peter commands the believers of his day.

#397: Reliable Teaching Provides Sound Answers

(Proverbs 22:17–21)

¹⁷Pay attention and listen to the sayings of the wise;
apply your heart to what I teach,

¹⁸for it is pleasing when you keep them in
  your heart
  and have all of them ready on your lips.
¹⁹So that your trust may be in the LORD,
  I teach you today, even you.
²⁰Have I not written thirty sayings for you,
  sayings of counsel and knowledge,
²¹teaching you true and reliable words,
  so that you can give sound answers
  to him who sent you?

1 Peter 5:2: God's Flock

The Old Testament speaks often of God as a
shepherd, and of God's appointed leaders as
shepherds of his people. (##398–402) The following are a sampling of these Old Testament
passages.

#398: God Shepherds Us All Our Lives
(Genesis 48:15)

¹⁵Then he [i.e., Israel] blessed Joseph and
said,
"May the God before whom my fathers
  Abraham and Isaac walked,
the God who has been my shepherd
  all my life to this day . . ."

#399: The Shepherd Is the Rock of Israel
(Genesis 49:24)

²⁴But his [i.e., Joseph's] bow remained
  steady,
  his strong arms stayed limber,
because of the hand of the Mighty One of
  Jacob,
  because of the Shepherd, the Rock of
  Israel.

#400: David Is to Be God's Undershepherd
(2 Samuel 5:2)

²In the past, while Saul was king over us,
you [David] were the one who led Israel on
their military campaigns. And the LORD said
to you, "You will shepherd my people Israel,
and you will become their ruler."

#401: The Lord, as Shepherd, Supplies All Our Needs
(Psalm 23:1)

¹The LORD is my shepherd, I shall not be in
want.

#402: The Lord Is Shepherd Forever
(Psalm 28:9)

⁹Save your people and bless your inheri-
tance;
  be their shepherd and carry them forever.

2 Peter 1:13: "As Long as I Live"

For an ancient account of Peter's death, see above
under 2 Timothy 4:17 (Reading #360).

2 Peter 2:6: God Condemned the Cities of Sodom and Gomorrah

(#403) Peter refers to ancient cities whose brutal
and immoral practices resulted in fiery judgment.

#403: The Fiery Judgment of Sodom and Gomorrah
(Genesis 19:13, 15, 24–25, 27–28)

¹³ . . . we [the angels of the LORD] are going
to destroy this place. The outcry to the LORD
against its people is so great that he has sent
us to destroy it . . ."
¹⁵With the coming of dawn, the angels
urged Lot, saying, "Hurry! Take your wife and
your two daughters who are here, or you will
be swept away when the city is punished . . ."
²⁴Then the LORD rained down burning sul-
fur on Sodom and Gomorrah—from the LORD
out of the heavens. ²⁵Thus he overthrew those
cities and the entire plain, including all those
living in the cities—and also the vegetation
in the land. . . .

[27]Early the next morning Abraham got up and returned to the place where he had stood before the Lord. [28]He looked down toward Sodom and Gomorrah, toward all the land of the plain, and he saw dense smoke rising from the land, like smoke from a furnace.

2 Peter 2:12: Carousing in the Daylight

Peter's account of moral excesses may seem lurid. (#404) But it pales beside Philo's denunciation of human sensuality, which follows his assertion that man is often a slave to his base passions.

#404: The Raging Violence of Human Passion
(Philo, *On Husbandry* 8 §§36–38)

8. [36]There are others who . . . have released their sense of taste out of prison as it were; and that sense, immediately rushing, in an unrestrained manner, to every kind of meat and drink, selects from the things that are already prepared, and also cherishes an indiscriminate and insatiable hunger for what is not present. So that, even if the channels of the belly are filled, its ever unsatisfied appetites, raging and ravening around, continue to look and stalk about in every direction, lest there should any where be any fragment which has been overlooked, that it may swallow that up also like a devouring fire. [37]And this gluttony is followed by its usual natural attendant, an eagerness for the connections of the sexes, which brings in its train a strange frenzy, an unrestrainable madness and a most grievous fury; for, when men are oppressed by the indulgence of gluttony and delicate food, and by much unmixed wine and drunkenness, they are no longer able to restrain themselves, but hastening to amorous gratifications they revel and disturb the doors, until they are at last able to rest when they have drawn off the great violence of their passion. [38]On which account nature, as it would seem, has placed the organs of such connection beneath the belly, being previously aware that they do not delight in hunger, but that they follow upon satiety and then rise up to fulfill their peculiar operations.

2 Peter 3:8: A Day Like a Thousand Years

(#405) Drawing on the Old Testament, Peter is aware of the difference between Almighty God's perspective on human affairs, on the one hand, and humanity's self-perception, on the other. God endures; people pass away quickly by comparison.

#405: From Everlasting to Everlasting, God Is God
(Psalm 90:2–6)

[2]Before the mountains were born
    or you brought forth the earth and the
      world,
    from everlasting to everlasting you are
      God.
[3]You turn men back to dust,
    saying, "Return to dust, O sons of men."
[4]For a thousand years in your sight
    are like a day that has just gone by,
    or like a watch in the night.
[5]You sweep men away in the sleep of death;
    they are like the new grass of the morn-
      ing—
[6]though in the morning it springs up new,
    by evening it is dry and withered.

11 1 John–Revelation

Examples of advanced commentaries containing additional references to extrabiblical parallels or passages include:

- 1–3 John: Marshall, Strecker
- Jude: Bauckham, Bigg, Mayor
- Revelation: Mounce, R. H. Charles (2 vols.), Aune (Rev 13–22 only). For valuable discussion on extrabiblical apocalyptic writings see Richard Bauckham, "The Apocalypses in the New Pseudepigrapha," in *New Testament Backgrounds*, ed. Craig A. Evans and Stanley E. Porter, 67–88. On understanding Revelation in particular see Leland Ryken, "Revelation," in *A Complete Literary Guide to the Bible*, Leland Ryken and Tremper Longman III, eds., pp. 458–69.

1 John 1:8: No Sin?

John appears to reproach people who claim to be free from sin. It is interesting to note that even pagan literature at least occasionally shows awareness of moral failure and the need to repent. How much more penitent should John's readers be, who are hearing of sin and salvation from a disciple of Jesus himself? (#406) The pagan writer quoted is the Latin poet Horace (65–8 B.C.), and the sorry state of society he describes is thought to be one of the effects of the civil wars preceding the reign of Augustus.

#406: The Social Sins of Ancient Rome Deplored
(Horace, *Odes* 3.6)

Your fathers' sins, O Roman, you, though not guiltless of them, must expiate, until you restore the temples and the ruined shrines of the gods and their statues blackened with smoke. It is by making yourself subject to the gods that you rule; with them everything begins—also assign to them the outcome! Neglected, they have sent woes unnumbered upon weeping Hesperia. Already Monaeses and the troops of Pacorus [the Parthians] have twice thrown back our attacks, which we had launched without taking the auspices; they now smile with glee to have added our spoils to their tawdry necklaces. Torn with sedition, the City has barely escaped destruction at the hands of the Dacian and the Aethiopian [Cleopatra], the one terrifying with his fleet, the other more skillful with the flying arrow. Full of sin, our age has defiled first the marriage bed, our offspring, and our homes; springing from such a source, the stream of disaster has overflowed both people and nation. The young maiden is eager to learn Ionian dances, and soon acquires coquettish arts; even in childhood she devises unchaste affairs. Soon she is looking for young lovers, even at her husband's table, and does not even choose out those on whom she will speedily bestow illicit joys when the lights are low. When invited, she openly, and not without her husband's knowledge, gets up and goes, whether it is some peddler who calls for her or the master of some Spanish ship, lavish buyer of infamy!

Not from such parents were born the youths who reddened the sea with Punic blood, and cut down Pyrrhus, and Antiochus the great, and that nightmare Hannibal. Instead, they were the manly breed of peasant soldiers, skillful in turning the clods with Sabine hoes and at their stern mother's command bringing in cut firewood, when the sun had stretched out the mountain shadows and taken off the yoke from the weary oxen, bringing the welcome hour of rest when his chariot had gone.

What ruin does time not threaten! Our parents' age, which was worse than our grandparents', has brought forth us, who are even less worthy and are about to bear offspring still more depraved!

1 John 1:10: "We Have Not Sinned"

(##407–409) Like the Old Testament, John insists that sinlessness is not possible for humans.

#407: There Is No One Who Does Not Sin
(1 Kings 8:46)

⁴⁶When they sin against you—for there is no one who does not sin—and you become angry with them and give them over to the enemy, who takes them captive to his own land, far away or near . . .

#408: No One's Heart Is Pure and Clean
(Proverbs 20:9)

⁹Who can say, "I have kept my heart pure; I am clean and without sin"?

#409: There Is Not a Single Righteous Person on the Earth
(Ecclesiastes 7:20)

²⁰There is not a righteous man on earth who does what is right and never sins.

1 John 2:1: When Christians Sin

Sin is a grave matter in Scripture. But John writes that there is forgiveness for it through Christ. (#410) A writing from the Dead Sea Scrolls takes a very different approach: (1) no willful sin against the Law of Moses can be forgiven; (2) even inadvertent sins require lengthy periods of penance; (3) atonement is through the human acts of prayer and "perfection of the way," complete

obedience to the community's religious teaching. (#411) On the other hand, another section of the same document speaks of God's mercy and pardon.

#410: The Willful Sinner Is Lost Forever
(Rule of the Community 8.20–9.2)

⁸·²⁰*And these are the rules which the men of perfect holiness shall follow in their commerce with one another*

²¹Every man who enters the Council of Holiness, (the Council of those) who walk in the way of perfection as commanded by God, and who deliberately or through negligence ²²transgresses one word of the Law of Moses, on any point whatever, shall be expelled from the Council of the Community and ²³shall return no more: no man of holiness shall be associated in his property or counsel in any ²⁴matter at all. But if he has acted inadvertently, he shall be excluded from the pure Meal and the Council and they shall interpret the rule (as follows). ²⁵For two years he shall take no part in judgment or ask for counsel; but if, during that time, his way becomes perfect ²⁶then he shall return to the (Court of) Inquiry and the Council, in accordance with the judgment of the Congregation, provided that he commit no further inadvertent sin during two full years. ⁹·¹For one sin of inadvertence (alone) he shall do penance for two years. But as for him who has sinned deliberately, he shall never return; only the man who has sinned inadvertently ²shall be tried for two years that his way and counsel may be made perfect according to the judgment of the Congregation. And afterwards, he shall be inscribed in his rank in the Community of Holiness.

#411: The Greatness of God's Goodness Will Pardon Our Sins
(Rule of the Community 11.11–15)

¹¹As for me,
    if I stumble, ¹²the mercies of God
    shall be my eternal salvation.
If I stagger because of the sin of flesh,
    my justification shall be
    by the righteousness of God which endures for ever.

[13]When my distress is unleashed
    He will deliver my soul from the pit
    and will direct my steps to the way.
He will draw me near by His grace,
    and by His mercy will He bring my justi-
    fication.
[14]He will judge me in the righteousness of
    His truth
    and in the greatness of His goodness
    He will pardon all my sins.
Through His righteousness He will cleanse
    me
    of the uncleanness of man
[15]and of the sins of the children of men,
that I may confess to God His righteousness,
    and His majesty to the Most High.

1 John 4:4: Greater Than the One Who Is in the World

(#412) As far back as Old Testament times, there is an awareness that God's presence with his people protects them from the ravages of enemies.

#412: The Lord Defends His People from Their Enemies
(2 Chronicles 32:7–8)

[7]"Be strong and courageous. Do not be afraid or discouraged because of the king of Assyria and the vast army with him, for there is a greater power with us than with him. [8]With him is only the arm of flesh, but with us is the LORD our God to help us and to fight our battles." And the people gained confidence from what Hezekiah the king of Judah said.

1 John 5:12: Two Kinds of People

John divides humanity into people who have the Son, and therefore have life, and those who have neither. (#413) Philo had a very different three-fold division of persons.

#413: Philo's Threefold Division of People
(*On the Giants* 13 §§60–61)

13. [60]Some men are born of the earth, and some are born of heaven, and some are born of God: those are born of the earth who are hunters after the pleasures of the body, devoting themselves to the enjoyment and fruition of them, and being eager to provide themselves with all things that tend to each of them. Those again are born of heaven who are men of skill and science and devoted to learning; for the heavenly portion of us is our mind, and the mind of every one of those persons who are born of heaven studies the encyclical branches of education and every other art of every description, sharpening, and exercising, and practising itself, and rendering itself acute in all those matters which are the objects of intellect.

[61]Lastly, those who are born of God are priests and prophets, who have not thought fit to mix themselves up in the constitutions of this world, and to become cosmopolites, but who having raised themselves above all the objects of the mere outward senses, have departed and fixed their views on that world which is perceptible only by the intellect, and have settled there, being inscribed in the state of incorruptible incorporeal ideas.

2 John 4: Walking in the Truth

(#414) In the Septuagint, Hezekiah uses this unusual phrase.

#414: Hezekiah Walked in Truth Before God
(2 Kings 20:3 LXX)

[3]"O Lord, remember, I pray, how I have walked before you in truth and with heart commitment, and have done what is right in your eyes." And Hezekiah was overcome with weeping [editor's translation].

3 John: The Form of an Ancient Letter

(#415) Several features of "the elder's" letter to Gaius are present in this papyrus note from Theon to Tyrannos dating from about A.D. 25. It was discovered in the sands of Oxyrhynchus, Egypt. (#416) A second-century A.D. letter from a soldier named Antonius Maximus to his sister Sabina also exhibits typical Hellenistic letter form. Note the "greetings," prayer for health, and assurance of prayers. Paul's letters often speak of his prayers for readers: Philemon 4, 1 Thessalonians 1:2, Ephesians 1:16, Romans 1:9f., 2 Timothy 1:3.

#415: The Illustration of an Ancient Letter

(Oxyrhynchus Papyri 292)

"Theon to his esteemed Tyrannos, many greetings. Herakleides, the bearer of this letter, is my brother. I therefore entreat you with all my power to treat him as your protégé. I have also written to your brother Hermias, asking him to communicate with you about him. You will confer upon me a very great favor if Herakleides gains your notice. Before all else you have my good wishes for unbroken health and prosperity. Good-bye."

Address: "To Tyrannos, dioiketes."

#416: A Typical Hellenistic Letter

(Second-Century Letter)

Antonius Maximus to Sabina his sister, many greetings.

Before all things I pray that thou art in health, for I myself also am in health. Making mention of thee before the gods here I received a little letter from Antoninus our fellow-citizen. And when I knew that thou farest well, I rejoiced greatly. And I at every occasion delay not to write unto thee concerning the health of me and mine. Salute Maximus much, and Copres my lord. There saluteth thee my life's partner, Aufidia, and Maximus my son.

Ancient letters were often written on papyrus as this Greek document illustrates.

3 John 3: Walking in the Truth

Like 2 John, 3 John speaks frequently of "truth" as a way of daily life. (##417–418) This echoes Old Testament language, as these passages illustrate. John is full of joy because Gaius's community is characterized by truth in all its dealings. (#419) When such truth is absent, Old Testament precedent suggests that God is not pleased.

#417: The Believer Is to Walk Continually in the Truth

(Psalm 26:3)

[3]for your love is ever before me,
    and I walk continually in your truth.

#418: The Way of the Lord Is to Walk in the Truth

(Psalm 86:11)

[11]Teach me your way, O LORD,
    and I will walk in your truth;
give me an undivided heart,
    that I may fear your name.

#419: The Displeasure of God at the Lack of Truth
(Isaiah 59:14–15)

[14]So justice is driven back,
    and righteousness stands at a distance;
truth has stumbled in the streets,
    honesty cannot enter.
[15]Truth is nowhere to be found,
    and whoever shuns evil becomes a prey.
The LORD looked and was displeased
    that there was no justice.

---

3 John 5–8: See Hebrews 13:2 (Reading #383)

Jude 9: Disputing with the Devil

This verse apparently refers to an ancient tradition that is referred to in passing by later Church Fathers. But the only known textual record of it comes from Palaia (a Jewish retelling of Old Testament historical narratives, preserved in Greek with Christian supplements; the Jewish material may date from the first–second century A.D.). (#420) The translation below (by the editor) follows the German text in Berger and Colpe, *Religionsgeschichtliches Textbuch*, p. 319, which in turns cites the original as given in A. Vassiliev, *Anecdota Graeco-Byzantina* (Moscow, 1893), pp. 188–292 (here p. 258). (#421) The danger of disputing with evildoers is reflected in one of the Dead Sea Scrolls. The so-called Master of the community is given this precept:

#420: The Angel Michael Resists the Devil
(Palaia)

And Samuel fell prey to the temptation to bring [Moses'] body down to the [Hebrew] people so they might make him [Moses] into a God. But Michael, the commander of the heavenly forces, came with God's mandate to claim and remove him. And Samuel put up resistance . . . and they fought. . . . The angelic commander [Michael] grew indignant, and scoffed at him with the words, "The Lord rebuke you, devil." The adversary drew back and took flight. The archangel Michael carried Moses' body to the place God had commanded . . . and no one saw Moses' grave.

#421: God Alone Can Defeat Satan's Hosts
(Rule of the Community 9.16)

[16]He shall not rebuke the men of the Pit nor dispute with them.

Jude 11: The Rebellion of Korah

(#422) In Old Testament times Korah was a ringleader of people who resented Moses' and Aaron's leadership. (#423) After Korah and his associates attempt to offer incense to God on their own authority, Moses pronounces God's judgment, and Korah's party meets its end.

#422: Korah Rejects the Leadership of Moses and Aaron
(Numbers 16:1–3)

[1]Korah son of Izhar, the son of Kohath, the son of Levi, and certain Reubenites—Dathan and Abiram, sons of Eliab, and On son of Peleth—became insolent and rose up against Moses. With them were 250 Israelite men, well-known community leaders who had been appointed members of the council. [3]They came as a group to oppose Moses and Aaron and said to them, "You have gone too far! The whole community is holy, every one of them, and the LORD is with them. Why then do you set yourselves above the LORD's assembly?"

#423: The Violent End of Korah's Rebellion
(Numbers 16:31–35)

[31]As soon as [Moses] finished saying all this, the ground under them split apart [32]and the earth opened its mouth and swallowed them,

with their households and all Korah's men and all their possessions. [33]They went down alive into the grave, with everything they owned; the earth closed over them, and they perished and were gone from the community. [34]At their cries, all the Israelites around them fled, shouting, "The earth is going to swallow us too!"

[35]And fire came out from the LORD and consumed the 250 men who were offering the incense.

Jude 14–15: Destruction of the Ungodly

Both the Old Testament and Jesus foretold a terrible day of judgment. (#424) Jude quotes an extrabiblical writing apparently popular in his time to make the same point. See also Readings ##222–24.

#424: God Will Destroy the Wicked of the World
(1 Enoch 1.9)

[9]Behold, [God] will arrive with ten million of the holy ones in order to execute judgment upon all. He will destroy the wicked ones and censure all flesh on account of everything that they have done, that which the sinners and the wicked ones committed against him."

Jude 23: Mercy, Fear, Hatred

(##425–427) These volatile elements mingle in close proximity in certain Old Testament proverbs.

#425: The Fear of the Lord Protects Us from Evil
(Proverbs 16:6)

[6] . . . through the fear of the LORD a man avoids evil.

#426: The Fear of the Lord Is to Hate All Evil
(Proverbs 8:13)

[13]To fear the LORD is to hate evil;

I hate pride and arrogance, evil behavior and perverse speech.

#427: The Hotheaded Fool Falls into Evil
(Proverbs 14:16)

[16]A wise man fears the LORD and shuns evil, but a fool is hotheaded and reckless.

Revelation 1:1: What Must Soon Take Place

In John's Jewish heritage, God established his sovereignty in part by foretelling future events (Is 42:9). Jesus exercised similar ability (Jn 13:38; 16:4). (#428) In the Roman world, too, "divination" (telling the future) was thought to be possible only through divine intervention, as Cicero relates.

#428: The Immortal Gods Give the Gift of Prophecy
(Cicero, *Nature of the Gods* 2.162–63)

[162]"Another proof that the providence of the gods is concerned with human affairs, and in my opinion the strongest proof of all, is divination. . . . Divination is practiced in many places, for many purposes, on many occasions, often in private but more especially in public concerns. [163]Many things are discerned by the haruspices, many things are foreseen by the augurs, many are declared by oracles, many by prophecies, many by dreams, many by prodigies. By such knowledge it often happens that many things turn up for men's enjoyment and use, and that many dangers are avoided. This ability, therefore, to foresee the future—whether it be a power, an art, or a natural gift—has certainly been granted to men, and to men only, by the immortal gods.

Revelation 1:1: His Servant John

(#429) The view that this is the same John who wrote the Fourth Gospel is preserved in the church historian Eusebius.

#429:

(Eusebius, *Ecclesiastical History* 3.23.1–4)

[1]About this time also [ca. A.D. 98], the beloved disciple of Jesus, John the apostle and evangelist, still surviving, governed the churches in Asia, after his return from exile on the island, and the death of Domitian. [2]But that he was still living until this time, it may suffice to prove, by the testimony of two witnesses. These, as maintaining sound doctrine in the church, may surely be regarded as worthy of all credit: and such were Irenaeus and Clement of Alexandria. [3]Of these, the former, in the second book against heresies, writes in the following manner: "And all the presbyters of Asia, that had conferred with John the disciple of our Lord, testify that John had delivered it to them; for he continued with them until the times of Trajan." [4]And in the third book of the same work, he shows the same thing in the following words: "But the church in Ephesus also, which had been founded by Paul, and where John continued to abide until the times of Trajan, is a faithful witness of the apostolic tradition."

Revelation 5:1–4: Secret Scroll

(#430) The following apocalyptic excerpt dating from around 140 B.C. pictures an Old Testament figure receiving secrets from an angel. In Revelation John saw a scroll and an angel—but he does not learn its contents. What he does learn is that the scroll (symbolizing what will happen in the future) is in Christ's hands.

#430: The Secret of the Ages Revealed to Jacob

(Jubilees 32.20–21)

[20]And he finished speaking with him, and he went up from him. And Jacob watched until he went up into heaven. [21]And he saw in a vision of the night, and behold an angel was descending from heaven, and there were seven tablets in his hands. And he gave (them) to Jacob, and he read them, and he knew everything which was written in them, which would happen to him and to his sons during all the ages.

Revelation 11:15–18: Praise and Judgment

John records heavenly praise of God (note that Rv 11:15 is the text of the closing sections of Handel's *Messiah*) and goes on to mention the coming judgment. (#431) A Jewish document from before the Christian era pictures the Old Testament figure Enoch blessing God, affirming his sovereignty, and predicting judgment.

#431: The Coming Judgment Predicted

(1 Enoch 84.1–4)

[1]Then I raised up my hands in righteousness and blessed the Holy and Great One; and I spoke with the breath of my mouth and the tongue of flesh which God has made for the children of the flesh, the people, so that they should speak with it; he gave them the breath and the mouth so that they should speak with it.

[2]Blessed are you, O Great King,
you are mighty in your greatness,
O Lord of all the creation of heaven,
King of kings and God of the whole world.
Your authority and kingdom abide forever
   and ever;
and your dominion throughout all the generations of generations;
all the heavens are your throne forever,
and the whole earth is your footstool forever and ever and ever.
[3]For you have created (all),
and all things you rule;
not a single thing is hard for you—(absolutely) not a single thing or wisdom;
Your throne has not retreated from her station nor from before your presence.
Everything you know, you see, and you hear;
nothing exists that can be hidden from you,
   for everything you expose.
[4]The angels of your heavens are now committing sin (upon the earth),

and your wrath shall rest upon the flesh of the people until (the arrival of) the great day of judgment

Revelation 19:20: The Lake of Fire

The concept of eternal fiery punishment, hinted at in the Old Testament, was also current in other Jewish apocalyptic writings (#432). Azaz'el is a powerful demonic leader. See also Readings ##222–224.

#432: The Furnace of Fire That Burns in Judgment

(1 Enoch 54.1–6)

[1]Then I looked and turned to another face of the earth and saw there a valley, deep and burning with fire. [2]And they were bringing kings and potentates and were throwing them into this deep valley. [3]And my eyes saw there their chains while they were making them into iron fetters of immense weight. [4]And I asked the angel of peace, who was going with me, saying, "For whom are these imprisonment chains being prepared?" [5]And he said unto me, "These are being prepared for the armies of Azaz'el, in order that they may take them and cast them into the abyss of complete condemnation, and as the Lord of the Spirits has commanded it, they shall cover their jaws with rocky stones. [6]Then Michael, Raphael, Gabriel, and Phanuel themselves shall seize them on that great day of judgment and cast them into the furnace (of fire) that is burning that day, so that the Lord of the Spirits may take vengeance on them on account of their oppressive deeds which (they performed) as messengers of Satan, leading astray those who dwell upon the earth."

Revelation 20:6: The Millennium (Thousand-Year Reign of Christ on Earth)

By New Testament times there was speculation in Jewish circles regarding the time, duration, and particulars of messianic rule on earth. This would come after a time of judgment for sin, and it would precede an everlasting age to come. (#433) In the following passage human history is viewed as lasting seven weeks, followed by a messianic kingdom established in the eighth week and lasting through the tenth. See Reading #196, where the time of Messiah's reign is set at four hundred years. See also Readings ##215–221 on the millennium.

#433: An Apocalyptic Overview of History

(1 Enoch 91.12–19, 93.2–10)

93. [2]And Enoch said, "Concerning the children of righteousness, concerning the elect ones of the world, and concerning the plant of truth, I will speak these things, my children, verily I, Enoch, myself, and let you know (about it) according to that which was revealed to me from the heavenly vision, that which I have learned from the words of the holy angels, and understood from the heavenly tablets." [3]He then began to recount from the books and said, "I was born the seventh during the first week, during which time judgment and righteousness continued to endure. [4]After me there shall arise in the second week great and evil things; deceit should grow, and therein the first consummation will take place. But therein (also) a (certain) man shall be saved. After it is ended, injustice shall become greater, and he shall make a law for the sinners.

[5]"Then after that at the completion of the third week a (certain) man shall be elected as the plant of the righteous judgment, and after him one (other) shall emerge as the eternal plant of righteousness.

[6]"After that at the completion of the fourth week visions of the old and righteous ones shall be seen; and a law shall be made with a fence, for all the generations.

[7]"After that in the fifth week, at the completion of glory, a house and a kingdom shall be built.

[8]"After that in the sixth week those who happen to be in it shall all of them be blindfolded, and the hearts of them all shall forget wisdom. Therein, a (certain) man shall

ascend. And, at its completion, the house of the kingdom shall be burnt with fire; and therein the whole clan of the chosen root shall be dispersed.

⁹"After that in the seventh week an apostate generation shall arise; its deeds shall be many, and all of them criminal. ¹⁰At its completion, there shall be elected the elect ones of righteousness from the eternal plant of righteousness, to whom shall be given sevenfold instruction concerning all his flock....

91. ¹²"Then after that there shall occur the second eighth week—the week of righteousness. A sword shall be given to it in order that judgment shall be executed in righteousness on the oppressors; and sinners shall be delivered into the hands of the righteous. ¹³At its completion, they shall acquire great things through their righteousness. A house shall be built for the Great King in glory for evermore.

¹⁴"Then after that in the ninth week the righteous judgment shall be revealed to the whole world. All the deeds of the sinners shall depart from upon the whole earth, and be written off for eternal destruction; and all people shall direct their sight to the path of uprightness.

¹⁵"Then, after this matter, on the tenth week in the seventh part, there shall be the eternal judgment; and it shall be executed by the angels of the eternal heaven—the great (judgment) which emanates from all of the angels. ¹⁶The first heaven shall depart and pass away; a new heaven shall appear; and all the powers of heaven shall shine forever sevenfold.

¹⁷"Then after that there shall be many weeks without number forever; it shall be (a time) of goodness and righteousness, and sin shall no more be heard of forever.

¹⁸"Now I shall speak unto you, my children, and show you the ways of righteousness and the ways of wickedness. Moreover, I shall make a revelation to you so that you may know that which is going to take place. ¹⁹Now listen to me, my children, and walk in the way of righteousness, and do not walk in the way of wickedness, for all those who walk in the ways of injustice shall perish."

Revelation 21:2: New Jerusalem

(#434) The city that John exalts to new heights was viewed as heaven on earth in the Old Testament. (##435, 436) For Isaiah the prophet, Jerusalem becomes a symbol of future blessing and glory.

#434: Jerusalem, Where All the Tribes Go Up
(Psalm 122:1–9)

¹I rejoiced with those who said to me,
  "Let us go to the house of the LORD."
²Our feet are standing
  in your gates, O Jerusalem.
³Jerusalem is built like a city
  that is closely compacted together.
⁴That is where the tribes go up,
  the tribes of the LORD,
to praise the name of the LORD
  according to the statute given to Israel.
⁵There the thrones for judgment stand,
  the thrones of the house of David.
⁶Pray for the peace of Jerusalem:
  "May those who love you be secure.
⁷May there be peace within your walls
  and security within your citadels."
⁸For the sake of my brothers and friends,
  I will say, "Peace be within you."
⁹For the sake of the house of the LORD our
    God,
  I will seek your prosperity.

#435: Jerusalem, Our Highest Joy
(Psalm 137:5–6)

⁵If I forget you, O Jerusalem,
  may my right hand forget its skill.
⁶May my tongue cling to the roof of my
    mouth
  if I do not remember you,
if I do not consider Jerusalem
  my highest joy.

#436: Jerusalem, The Delight of All God's People
(Isaiah 65:18–19)

¹⁸But be glad and rejoice forever
  in what I will create,

for I will create Jerusalem to be a delight
  and its people a joy.
[19]I will rejoice over Jerusalem
  and take delight in my people;
the sound of weeping and of crying
  will be heard in it no more.

Revelation 22:17: Come!

(#437) The closing message of the Bible echoes an invitation issued centuries earlier by Isaiah.

#437: Come to the Lord and Find Blessing
(Isaiah 55:1–3, 6)

[1]"Come, all you who are thirsty,
  come to the waters;
and you who have no money,
  come, buy and eat!
Come, buy wine and milk
  without money and without cost.
[2]Why spend money on what is not bread,
  and your labor on what does not satisfy?
Listen, listen to me, and eat what is good,
  and your soul will delight in the richest
    of fare.
[3]Give ear and come to me;
  hear me, that your soul may live.
I will make an everlasting covenant with
    you,
  my faithful love promised to David. . . ."
[6]Seek the LORD while he may be found;
  call on him while he is near.

Bibliography

Adam, Alfred. *Antike Berichte über die Essener.* Berlin: de Gruyter, 1961.

Aharoni, Yohanan. *The Land of the Bible: A Historical Geography.* Philadelphia: Westminster, 1979.

Arnold, Clinton E. *The Colossian Syncretism: The Interface between Christianity and Folk Belief at Colossae.* Grand Rapids: Baker, 1996 (1995).

_____. *Power and Magic: The Concept of Power in Ephesians.* Grand Rapids: Baker, 1992 (1989).

Aune, David E. *Revelation 13–22.* Word Biblical Commentary 52. Dallas: Word, forthcoming.

Avi-Yonah, Michael. *Gazetteer of Roman Palestine.* Jerusalem: Institute of Archaeology, Hebrew University of Jerusalem, 1976.

_____. *The Holy Land, from the Persian to the Arab Conquests (536 B.C. to A.D. 640): A Historical Geography.* Rev. ed. Grand Rapids: Baker, 1977.

_____, ed. *The Herodian Period.* World History of the Jewish People 7. Tel-Aviv/New Brunswick, N.J.: Jewish History Publications/Rutgers University Press, 1975.

Baly, Denis. *Geographical Companion to the Bible.* New York: McGraw-Hill, 1963.

_____. *The Geography of the Bible.* Rev. ed. New York: Harper & Row, 1974.

Baron, Salo W., and Joseph L. Blau. *Judaism: Postbiblical and Talmudic Period.* Library of Religion 3. New York: Liberal Arts Press, 1954.

Barrett, C. K. *A Commentary on the First Epistle to the Corinthians.* Harper's New Testament Commentaries 7. Peabody, Mass.: Hendrickson, 1987 (1968).

_____. *Texte zur Umwelt des Neuen Testaments.* Tübingen: J. C. B. Mohr (Paul Siebeck), 1991.

_____, ed. *The New Testament Background: Selected Documents.* Rev. ed. San Franciso: Harper & Row, 1989 (1987).

Barth, Markus. *Ephesians: Introduction, Translation, and Commentary.* 2 vols. Anchor Bible 34. Garden City, N.Y.: Doubleday, 1974.

Bauckham, Richard. "The Apocalypses in the New Pseudepigrapha." In Craig A. Evans and Stanley E. Porter, eds. *New Testament Backgrounds.* Sheffield: Sheffield Academic Press, 1997.

_____. *2 Peter and Jude.* Word Biblical Commentary 50. Waco, Tex.: Word, 1983.

Baugh, S. M. "A Foreign World: Ephesus in the First Century." In *Women in the Church: A Fresh Analysis* of 1 Timothy 2:9–15. Ed. Andreas J. Köstenberger, Thomas R. Schreiner, and H. Scott Baldwin. Grand Rapids: Baker, 1995.

Bell, Albert A. *A Guide to the New Testament World.* Scottdale, Pa.: Herald, 1994.

Berger, Klaus, and Carsten Colpe, eds. *Religionsgeschichtliches Textbuch zum Neuen Testament.* Göttingen: Vandenhoeck & Ruprecht, 1987.

Bernfeld, Simon. *The Foundations of Jewish Ethics.* New York: Ktav, 1968 (1929).

Bettenson, Henry, ed. *Documents of the Christian Church.* New York/London: Oxford University Press, 1947.

Betz, Hans Dieter. *Galatians: A Commentary on Paul's Letter to the Churches in Galatia.* Hermeneia. Philadelphia: Fortress, 1979.

_____, ed. *The Greek Magical Papyri in Translation.* Chicago/London: University of Chicago Press, 1986.

Bigg, Charles. *A Critical and Exegetical Commentary on the Epistles of St. Peter and St. Jude.* 2nd ed. International Critical Commentary. Edinburgh: T. & T. Clark, 1902.

Bonsirven, J. *Palestinian Judaism in the Time of Jesus Christ.* Trans. William Wolf. New York: Holt, Rinehart & Winston, 1964.

Boring, M. Eugene, Klaus Berger, and Carsten Colpe, eds. *Hellenistic Commentary to the New Testament.* Nashville: Abingdon, 1995.

Bowman, John, trans. *Samaritan Documents Relating to Their History, Religion, and Life.* Pittsburgh Original Texts and Translation Series 2. Pittsburgh: Pickwick, 1977.

Bruce, F. F. *The Acts of the Apostles: The Greek Text with Introduction and Commentary.* 3rd ed. Grand Rapids: Eerdmans, 1990.

_____. *The Book of Acts.* Rev. ed. Grand Rapids: Eerdmans, 1988.

_____. *The Epistle to the Galatians.* New International Greek Testament Commentary. Grand Rapids: Eerdmans, 1982.

_____. *The Epistle to the Hebrews.* Rev. ed. New International Commentary on the New Testament. Grand Rapids: Eerdmans, 1990.

_____. *The Epistles to the Colossians, to Philemon, and to the Ephesians.* New International Commentary on the New Testament. Grand Rapids: Eerdmans, 1984.

————. *1 & 2 Thessalonians*. Word Biblical Commentary 45. Waco, Tex.: Word, 1982.

————. *Jesus and Christian Origins outside the New Testament*. Grand Rapids: Eerdmans, 1974.

Brueggemann, Walter. *The Land*. Philadelphia: Fortress, 1977.

Büchler, Adolf. *Der galiläische 'Am-Ha'Ares des zweiten Jahrhunderts*. Hildesheim: Olms, 1968 (1906).

Buckwalter, Harold Douglas, and Mary Keil Shoaff. *Guide to the Reference Systems for the Works of Flavius Josephus*. Evangelical Theological Society Monograph 3. Winona Lake, Ind.: Eisenbrauns, 1995.

Cameron, Ron, ed. *The Other Gospels: Non-Canonical Gospel Texts*. Philadelphia: Westminster, 1982.

Cartlidge, David R., and David L. Dungan. *Documents for the Study of the Gospels*. Rev. ed. Minneapolis: Fortress, 1994.

Cary, Earnest, trans. *Dio's Roman History*. 9 vols. Loeb Classical Library. New York/London: Macmillan/Heinemann, 1914–27.

Charles, R. H. *A Critical and Exegetical Commentary on the Revelation of St. John*. 2 vols. International Critical Commentary. Edinburgh: T. & T. Clark, 1920.

————, ed. *The Apocrypha and Pseudepigrapha of the Old Testament*. 2 vols. Oxford: Clarendon, 1913.

Charlesworth, James H., ed. *The Messiah: Developments in Earliest Judaism and Christianity*. Minneapolis: Fortress, 1992.

————, ed. *The Old Testament Pseudepigrapha*. 2 vols. New York: Doubleday, 1983–85.

Church, Alfred John, and William Jackson Brodribb, trans. *The Complete Works of Tacitus*. Ed. Moses Hadas. New York: Random House, 1942.

Cohen, Abraham. *Everyman's Talmud*. New York: Dutton, 1949.

Collins, John J. *The Scepter and the Star: The Messiahs of the Dead Sea Scrolls and Other Ancient Literature*. Anchor Bible Reference Library. New York: Doubleday, 1995

Conzelmann, Hans. *Acts of the Apostles: A Commentary on the Acts of the Apostles*. Trans. James Limburg, et al. Ed. Eldon Jay Epp and Christopher R. Matthews. Hermeneia. Philadelphia: Fortress, 1987.

Cruse, Christian Frederick, trans. *The Ecclesiastical History of Eusebius Pamphilus*. Grand Rapids: Baker, 1991.

Dalman, Gustaf. *Sacred Sites and Ways: Studies in the Topography of the Gospels*. Trans. Paul P. Levertoff. New York: Macmillan, 1935.

Danby, Herbert, trans. *The Mishnah*. London: Oxford University Press, 1933.

Davids, Peter H. *The Epistle of James: A Commentatry on the Greek Text*. New International Greek Testament Commentary. Grand Rapids: Eerdmans, 1982.

————. *The First Epistle of Peter*. New International Commentary on the New Testament. Grand Rapids: Eerdmans, 1990.

Davies, William D. *Paul and Rabbinic Judaism*. Philadelphia: Fortress, 1980.

Davies, William D., and Louis Finkelstein, eds. *The Cambridge History of Judaism, Vol. 2: The Hellenistic Age*. Cambridge: Cambridge University Press, 1989.

Davis, W. Hersey, and Edward A. McDowell. *A Source Book of Interbiblical History*. Nashville: Broadman, 1948.

Deissmann, Adolf. *Bible Studies*. Trans. Alexander Grieve. Edinburgh: T. & T. Clark, 1901.

————. *Light from the Ancient East*. Trans. Lionel R. M. Strachan. 4th ed. Grand Rapids: Baker, 1978 (1922).

Downing, F. Gerald. *Christ and the Cynics: Jesus and Other Radical Preachers in First-Century Tradition*. Sheffield: JSOT, 1988.

Ellingworth, Paul. *The Epistle to the Hebrews: A Commentary on the Greek Text*. New International Greek Testament Commentary. Grand Rapids/Carlisle, England: Eerdmans/Paternoster, 1993.

Elliott, J. K. *The Apocryphal Jesus: Legends of the Early Church*. New York: Oxford, 1996.

Ellis, E. Earle. *Pauline Theology: Ministry and Society*. Lanham, Md.: University Press of America, 1997 (1989).

Epstein, I., ed. *The Babylonian Talmud*. 35 vols. London: Soncino, 1935–52.

Fee, Gordon. *The First Epistle to the Corinthians*. New International Commentary on the New Testament. Grand Rapids: Eerdmans, 1987.

Feldman, Louis H. "Palestinian and Diaspora Judaism in the First Century." In Hershel Shanks, ed. *Christianity and Rabbinic Judaism: A Parallel History of Their Origins and Early Development*. Washington, D.C.: Biblical Archaeology Society, 1992.

Feldman, Louis H., and Meyer Reinhold, eds. *Jewish Life and Thought among Greeks and Romans: Primary Readings*. Minneapolis: Fortress, 1996.

Ferguson, Everett. *Backgrounds of Early Christianity*. Rev. ed. Grand Rapids: Eerdmans, 1993.

Finegan, Jack. *The Archaeology of the New Testament: The Life of Jesus and the Beginning of the Early Church*. Princeton, N.J.: Princeton University Press, 1969.

Finkelstein, Louis. *The Pharisees: The Sociological Background of Their Faith*. 3rd ed. 2 vols. Philadelphia: Jewish Publication Society of America, 1962.

Foerster, Werner. *Palestinian Judaism in New Testament Times*. Trans. Gordon E. Harris. London: Oliver & Boyd, 1964.

Fung, Ronald Y. K. *The Epistle to the Galatians*. New International Commentary on the New Testament. Grand Rapids: Eerdmans, 1988.

García Martínez, Florentino, trans. *The Dead Sea Scrolls Translated: The Qumran Texts in English*. Trans. Wilfred G. E. Watson. 2nd ed. Grand Rapids/Leiden: Eerdmans/E. J. Brill, 1996.

Gasque, W. Ward. *The History of the Criticism of the Acts of the Apostles*. Tübingen: J. C. B. Mohr (Paul Siebeck), 1975.

Gaster, Moses. *The Samaritans: Their History, Doctrines and Literature*. Munich: Kraus, 1980 (1925).

Glueck, Nelson. *The Other Side of the Jordan*. Cambridge, Mass.: American Schools of Oriental Research, 1970 (1940).

_____. *The River Jordan*. New York: McGraw-Hill, 1968 (1946).

Goldstein, Morris. *Jesus in the Jewish Tradition*. New York: Macmillan, 1950.

Grabbe, Lester L. *Judaism from Cyrus to Hadrian*. 2 vols. Minneapolis: Fortress, 1992.

Grant, Frederick C., ed. *Ancient Roman Religion*. Library of Religion 8. New York: Liberal Arts Press, 1957.

Graves, Robert, trans. *Suetonius: The Twelve Caesars*. Baltimore/Harmondsworth, Middlesex: Penguin, 1957.

Green, William M., et al., trans. *Saint Augustine: The City of God against the Pagans*. 7 vols. Loeb Classical Library. Cambridge, Mass./London: Harvard University Press/Heinemann, 1957–72.

Habermas, Gary R. *Ancient Evidence for the Life of Jesus*. Nashville: Thomas Nelson, 1984.

Haenchen, Ernst. *The Acts of the Apostles: A Commentary*. Trans. Bernard Noble, et al. Philadelphia: Westminster, 1971.

Harmon, A. M., K. Kilburn, and H. D. Macleod, trans. *Lucian*. 8 vols. Loeb Classical Library. Cambridge, Mass./London: Harvard University Press/Heinemann, 1913–67.

Harris, Murray J. "2 Corinthians," in *Expositor's Bible Commentary*, ed. Frank E. Gaebelein, vol. 10 (Grand Rapids: Zondervan, 1976).

Hawthorne, Gerald F. *Philippians*. Word Biblical Commentary 43. Waco, Tex.: Word, 1983.

Hemer, Colin. *The Book of Acts in the Setting of Hellenistic History*. Tübingen: J. C. B. Mohr (Paul Siebeck), 1989.

Hengel, Martin. *Acts and the History of Earliest Christianity*. Trans. John Bowden Philadelphia: Fortress, 1980.

_____. *The Zealots: Investigations into the Jewish Freedom Movement in the Period from Herod I until 70 A.D.* Trans. David Smith Edinburgh: T. & T. Clark, 1989.

Hengel, Martin, and Roland Deines. *The Pre-Christian Paul*. Trans. John Bowden. Philadelphia/London: Trinity Press International/SCM, 1991.

Hennecke, Edgar. *New Testament Apocrypha*. Ed. Wilhelm Schneemelcher and R. M. Wilson. 2 vols. Philadelphia: Westminster: 1963–65.

Herford, R. Travers. *Christianity in Talmud and Midrash*. Hoboken, N.J.: Ktav, 1975 (1903).

_____. *The Pharisees*. Boston, Beacon, 1962 (1924).

Hoehner, Harold. *Herod Antipas*. Grand Rapids: Zondervan, 1980 (1972).

Horsley, G. H. R. *New Documents Illustrating Early Christianity*. North Ryde, Austalia: Ancient History Documentary Research Centre, Macquarie University, 1981–.

Horsley, Richard A., and John S. Hanson. *Bandits, Prophets, and Messiahs: Popular Movements in the Time of Jesus*. New Voices in Biblical Studies. San Francisco, Harper & Row, 1988 (1985).

Humphries, Rolfe, trans. *The Satires of Juvenal*. Bloomington: Indiana University Press, 1958.

James, Montague Rhodes, trans. *The Apocryphal New Testament*. Oxford: Clarendon, 1924.

Jeremias, Joachim. *Unknown Sayings of Jesus*. Trans. Reginald H. Fuller. London: SPCK, 1958.

Johnson, Luke Timothy. *The Letter of James*. Anchor Bible 37A. New York: Doubleday, 1995.

Keener, Craig S. *The IVP Bible Background Commentary: New Testament*. Downers Grove: InterVarsity, 1993.

Kelly, J. N. D. *The Epistles of Peter and Jude*. Black's New Testament Commentary. Peabody, Mass.: Hendrickson, 1993.

Kim, Seyoon. *The Origins of Paul's Gospel*. 2nd ed. Tübingen: J. C. B. Mohr (Paul Siebeck), 1984.

Knight, George W., III. *The Pastoral Epistles: A Commentary on the Greek Text*. New International Greek Testament Commentary. Grand Rapids/Carlisle, England: Eerdmans/Paternoster,1992.

Lane, William L. *Hebrews*. 2 vols. Word Biblical Commentary 47. Dallas: Word, 1991.

Lefkowitz, Mary R., and Maureen B. Fant. *Women's Life in Greece and Rome: A Source Book in Translation*. 2nd ed. Baltimore: Johns Hopkins, 1992.

Lewis, Naphtali, and Meyer Reinhold, ed. *Roman Civilization*. 2 vols. New York: Columbia University Press, 1951–55.

Lightfoot, J. B. *Philippians*. Wheaton, Ill.: Crossway, 1994 (1868).

_____. *Saint Paul's Epistles to the Colossians and to Philemon*. Lynn, Mass.: Hendrickson, 1982 (1875).

Lightfoot, J. B., and J. R. Harmer, trans. *The Apostolic Fathers*. Ed. Michael W. Holmes. 2nd ed. Grand Rapids: Baker, 1989.

Lincoln, Andrew T. *Ephesians*. Word Biblical Commentary 42. Dallas: Word, 1990.

Lohse, Eduard. *Colossians and Philemon*. Trans. William R. Poehlmann and Robert J. Karris. Ed. Helmut Koester. Hermeneia. Philadelphia: Fortress, 1971.

Longenecker, Richard N. *Galatians*. Word Biblical Commentary 41. Dallas: Word, 1990.

Macdonald, John. *The Theology of the Samaritans*. Philadelphia: Westminster, 1964.

Machen, J. Gresham. *The Origin of Paul's Religion*. Grand Rapids: Eerdmans, 1978 (1925).

Mackay, Alastair I. *Farming and Gardening in the Bible*. Emmaus, Pa.: Rodale, 1950.

Maier, Johann. *Jesus von Nazareth in der talmudischen Überlieferung*. Erträge der Forschung 82. Darmstadt: Wissenschaftliche Buchgesellschaft, 1978.

Marcus, Ralph, trans. *Philo, Supplement 1: Questions and Answers on Genesis*. Loeb Classical Library. Cambridge, Mass./London: Harvard University Press/Heinemann, 1961.

Marshall, I. Howard. *The Epistles of John*. New International Commentary on the New Testament. Grand Rapids: Eerdmans, 1978.

Martin, Luther H. *Hellenistic Religions: An Introduction*. New York/Oxford: Oxford University Press, 1987.

Martin, Ralph P. *Ephesians, Colossians, and Philemon*. Interpretation. Atlanta: John Knox, 1991.

_____. *James*. Word Biblical Commentary 48. Waco, Tex.: Word, 1988.

_____. *2 Corinthians*. Word Biblical Commentary 40. Waco, Tex.: Word, 1986.

Martyn, J. Louis. *Galatians: A New Translation with Introduction and Commentary*. Anchor Bible 33A. New York: Doubleday, 1998.

Mayor, Joseph B. *The Epistle of St. Jude and the Second Epistle of St. Peter*. Minneapolis: Klock & Klock, 1978 (1907).

Michaels, J. Ramsey. *1 Peter*. Word Biblical Commentary 49. Waco, Tex.: Word, 1988.

Montefiore, C. G., and H. Loewe, eds. *A Rabbinic Anthology*. New York: Schocken, 1974 (1938).

Moo, Douglas J. *The Epistle to the Romans*, New International Commentary on the New Testament. Grand Rapids: Eerdmans, 1996.

Moore, George Foot. *Judaism in the First Centuries of the Christian Era: The Age of Tannaim*. 3 vols. Peabody, Mass.: Hendrickson, 1997 (1927–30).

Morris, Leon. *The Epistles of Paul to the Thessalonians: An Introduction and Commentary*. 2nd ed. Tyndale New Testament Commentary. Grand Rapids/Leicester: Eerdmans/InterVarsity, 1984.

Mounce, Robert H. *The Book of Revelation*. Rev. ed. New International Commentary on the New Testament. Grand Rapids: Eerdmans, 1998.

Murphy, Frederick J. *The Religious World of Jesus: An Introduction to Second Temple Palestinian Judaism*. Nashville: Abingdon, 1991.

Murphy-O'Connor, J. *St. Paul's Corinth: Texts and Archaeology*. Collegeville, Minn.: Liturgical Press, 1990 (1983).

Nickelsburg, George W. E., and Michael E. Stone. *Faith and Piety in Early Judaism: Texts and Documents*. Valley Forge, Pa.: Trinity Press International, 1991 (1983).

Neusner, Jacob. *Introduction to Rabbinic Literature*. New York: Doubleday, 1994.

_____. *Judaism: The Evidence of the Mishnah*. 2nd ed. Atlanta: Scholars, 1988.

_____. *The Mishnah: A New Translation*. New Haven, Conn.: Yale University Press, 1988.

Newsome, James D. *Greeks, Romans, Jews: Currents of Culture and Belief in the New Testament World*. Philadelphia: Trinity Press International, 1992.

Nock, A. D. *St. Paul*. New York: Harper & Row, 1963 (1938).

Noth, Martin. *The Old Testament World*. Trans. Victor I. Gruhn. Philadelphia: Fortress, 1966.

O'Brien, P. T. *Colossians, Philemon*. Word Biblical Commentary 44. Waco, Tex.: Word, 1982.

_____. *The Epistle to the Philippians*. New International Greek Testament Commentary. Grand Rapids: Eerdmans, 1991.

Painter, John. *Just James: The Brother of Jesus in History and Tradition*. Columbia: University of South Carolina Press, 1997.

Parke, H. W. *The Oracles of Apollo in Asia Minor*. Dover, N.H./London: Croom Helm, 1985.

Perowne, Stewart. *The Later Herods: The Political Background of the New Testament*. New York: Abingdon, 1958.

_____. *The Life and Times of Herod the Great*. New York: Abingdon, 1956.

Pines, Shlomo. *An Arabic Version of the Testimonium Flavianum and Its Implications*. Jerusalem: Israel Academy of Sciences and Humanities, 1971.

Pomeroy, Sarah B. *Goddesses, Whores, Wives, and Slaves: Women in Classical Antiquity*. New York: Schocken, 1975.

Rackham, Harris, W. H. S. Jones, and D. E. Eichholz trans. *Pliny: Natural History*. 10 vols. Loeb Classical Library. Cambridge, Mass./London: Harvard University Press/Heinemann, 1938–62.

Ramsay, William M. *Historical Commentary on Galatians*. Grand Rapids: Kregel, 1997 (1900).

Reid, Patrick V., ed. *Readings in Western Religious Thought: The Ancient World*. New York: Paulist, 1987.

Reinach, Théodore. *Textes d'auteurs grecs et romains relatifs au judaïsme*. Hildesheim: Olms, 1963 (1895).

Richardson, Peter. *Herod*. Columbia: University of South Carolina Press, 1996.

Riesner, Rainer. *Paul's Early Period: Chronology, Mission Strategy, Theology*. Trans. Doug Stott. Grand Rapids: Eerdmans, 1998.

Roberts, Alexander, James Donaldson, et al., eds. *The Ante-Nicene Fathers*. 10 vols. Grand Rapids: Eerdmans, 1978–79 (1885–87).

Russell, D. S. *The Method and Message of Jewish Apocalyptic, 200 B.C.–A.D. 100*. Philadelphia: Westminster, 1964.

Ryken, Leland. "Revelation." In *A Complete Literary Guide to the Bible*. Ed. Leland Ryken and Tremper Longman III. Grand Rapids: Zondervan, 1993.

Safrai, S., and Menahem Stern, eds. *The Jewish People in the First Century: Historical Geography, Political History, Social, Cultural, and Religious Life and Institutions*. 2 vols. Philadelphia: Fortress, 1974–76.

Sanday, William, and Arthur C. Headlam. *A Critical and Exegetical Commentary on the Epistle to the Romans*. 5th ed. Edinburgh: T. & T. Clark, 1902.

Sanders, E. P. *Jewish Law from Jesus to the Mishnah: Five Studies*. Philadelphia/London: Trinity Press International/SCM, 1990.

_____.*Judaism: Practice and Belief 63 B.C.E.–66 C.E.* Philadelphia: Trinity Press International, 1992.

_____. *Paul and Palestinian Judaism: A Comparison of Patterns of Religion*. Philadelphia: Fortress, 1977.

_____. *Paul, the Law, and the Jewish People*. Minneapolis: Fortress, 1983.

Schäfer, Peter. *Judeophobia: Attitudes toward the Jews in the Ancient World*. Cambridge: Harvard University Press, 1997.

Schalit, Abraham, ed. *The Hellenistic Age: Political History of Jewish Palestine from 332 B.C.E. to 67 B.C.E.* World History of the Jewish People 6. Tel-Aviv/New Brunswick, N.J.: Jewish History Publications/Rutgers University Press, 1972.

Schiffman, Lawrence H. *Reclaiming the Dead Sea Scrolls: The History of Judaism, the Background of Christianity, the Lost Library of Qumran*. Anchor Bible Reference Library. New York: Doubleday, 1997 (1994).

Schürer, Emil. *The History of the Jewish People in the Age of Jesus Christ (175 B.C.–A.D. 135)*. Rev. ed. Ed. Geza Vermes, et al. 3 vols. Edinburgh: T. & T. Clark, 1973–87.

Scott, J. Julius. *Customs and Controversies: Intertestamental Jewish Backgrounds of the New Testament*. Grand Rapids: Baker, 1995.

Sélincourt, Aubrey de, trans. *Herodotus: The Histories*. Rev. ed. Ed. A. R. Burn. Baltimore/Harmondsworth, Middlesex: Penguin, 1972.

Simon, Marcel. *Jewish Sects at the Time of Jesus*. Trans. James H. Farley. Philadelphia: Fortress, 1967.

Smith, George Adam. *The Historical Geography of the Holy Land*. 4th ed. New York/London: Hodder & Stoughton, 1896.

_____. *Jerusalem: The Topography, Economics, and History from the Earliest Times to A.D. 70*. New York: Ktav, 1972 (1877).

Stermberger, Günter. *Jewish Contemporaries of Jesus: Pharisees, Sadducees, Essenes*. Trans. Allan W. Mahnke. Minneapolis: Fortress, 1995.

Stern, Menahem. *Greek and Latin Authors on Jews and Judaism*. 3 vols. Jerusalem: Israel Academy of Sciences and Humanities, 1974–84.

Stone, Michael E., ed. *Jewish Writings of the Second Temple Period: Apocrypha, Pseudepigrapha, Qumran, Sectarian Writings, Philo, Josephus*. Assen, Netherlands/Philadelphia: Van Gorcum/Fortress, 1984.

Streatfeild, Frank. *Preparing the Way: The Influence of Judaism of the Greek Period on the Earliest Developments of Christianity*. London: Macmillan, 1918.

Strecker, Georg. *The Johannine Letters: A Commentary on 1, 2, and 3 John*. Trans. Linda M. Maloney. Ed. Harold Attridge. Hermeneia. Minneapolis: Fortress, 1996.

Stroker, William D. *Extracanonical Sayings of Jesus*. Society of Biblical Literature Resources for Biblical Study 18. Atlanta: Scholars, 1989

Swidler, Leonard J. *Biblical Affirmations of Woman*. Philadelphia: Westminster, 1979.

Towner, Philip H. *1–2 Timothy and Titus*. IVP New Testament Commentary. Downers Grove/Leicester: InterVarsity, 1994.

Turner, George A. *Historical Geography of the Holy Land*. Grand Rapids: Baker, 1973.

VanderKam, James C. *The Dead Sea Scrolls Today*. Grand Rapids: Eerdmans, 1994.

Vermes, Geza. *The Dead Sea Scrolls in English*. 4th ed. New York/Harmondsworth, Middlesex: Penguin, 1995.

Wanamaker, C. A. *The Epistles to the Thessalonians*. New International Greek Testament Commentary. Grand Rapids/Exeter: Eerdmans/Paternoster, 1990.

Warner, Rex, trans. *Plutarch: Fall of the Roman Republic*. New York: Penguin, 1958.

Wenham, David, and R. T. France, eds. *Gospel Perspectives: Studies of History and Tradition in the Four Gospels*. 6 vols. Sheffield: JSOT, 1980–86.

Whiston, William, trans. *The Works of Flavius Josephus*. 4 vols. Grand Rapids: Baker, 1979.

Whittaker, Molly. *Jews and Christians: Graeco-Roman Views*. Cambridge Commentaries on Writings of the Jewish and Christian World 200 B.C. to A.D. 200 6. New York/Cambridge: Cambridge University Press, 1984.

Winter, Bruce W. et al., eds. *The Book of Acts in Its First Century Setting*. 6 vols. Grand Rapids: Eerdmans, 1993–.

Witherington, Ben, III. *The Acts of the Apostles: A Socio-Rhetorical Commentary*. Grand Rapids/Carlisle, England: Eerdmans/Paternoster, 1998.

Woude, A.S. van der, et al., eds. *The World of the Bible*. Trans. Sierd Woudstra. Grand Rapids: Eerdmans, 1986.

Yonge, C. D., trans. *The Works of Philo*. Peabody, Mass.: Hendrickson, 1993.

Complete List of Readings

#42	Josephus, *Jewish War* 2.14.9 §§305–8	Whiston 1:172
#43	Josephus, *Jewish War* 2.17.2 §§408–10	Whiston 1:187
#44	Josephus, *Jewish War* 2.17.6–7 §§425–32	Whiston 1:189–90
#45	Tacitus, *Histories* 5.10–13	Church and Brodribb 663–66
#46	Josephus, *Jewish War* 6.2.7 §§149–52	Whiston 1:437
	Josephus, *Jewish War* 6.4.5–7 §§249–53, 257–66	Whiston 1:448–50
#47	Josephus, *Jewish War* 6.5.2 §§281–84	Whiston 1:452–53
	Josephus, *Jewish War* 6.8.5 §§401–8	Whiston 1:466–67
	Josephus, *Jewish War* 6.9.2 §§414–19	Whiston 1:468–69
	Josephus, *Jewish War* 7.1.1 §§1–4	Whiston 1:473
	Josephus, *Jewish War* 6.9.3 §420	Whiston 1:469
#48	Eusebius, *Ecclesiastical History* 3.5.2–3	Cruse 86
#49	Epistle of Barnabas 16.1–2, 6–10	Lightfoot and Harmer 183–84
#50	Mishnah, Tractate *Taanith* 4.6–7	Danby 200
#51	Josephus, *Jewish War* 7.8.6 §§323–36	Whiston 1:507–8
#52	Josephus, *Jewish War* 7.9.1–2 §§394–400, 402–6	Whiston 1:515–16

3. Groups of People

#53	Josephus, *Antiquities* 18.1.2–3 §§11–15	Whiston 4:3
#54	Josephus, *Jewish War* 2.8.14 §§162–63, 166	Whiston 1:150–51
#55	Mishnah, Tractate *Berakoth* 8.1–8	Danby 8–9
#56	Josephus, *Antiquities* 18.1.4 §§16–17	Whiston 4:3–4
#57	Josephus, *Jewish War* 2.8.14 §§164–66	Whiston 1:151
#58	Mishnah, Tractate *Yadaim* 4.6	Danby 784
#59	Mishnah, Tractate *Yadaim* 4.7	Danby 784
#60	Pliny, *Natural History* 5.15 §73	Rackham, Jones, and Eichholz 2:277
#61	Josephus, *Jewish War* 2.8.2–13 §§119–47, 150–61	Whiston 1:144–50
#62	Josephus, *Antiquities* 18.1.6 §§23–25	Whiston 4:5
#63	Josephus, *Antiquities* 18.1.1 §§4–9	Whiston 4:1–3
#64	Josephus, *Jewish War* 20.8.10 §§185–88	Whiston 4:137–38
#65	Mishnah, Tractate *Aboth* 2.6	Danby 448
#66	Mishnah, Tractate *Shebiith* 5.9	Danby 45
#67	Mishnah, Tractate *Hagigah* 2.7	Danby 214
#68	Mishnah, Tractate *Eduyoth* 1.14	Danby 424
#69	Mishnah, Tractate *Tohoroth* 7.1–2, 4–5; 8.1–3	Danby 726–27
#70	2 Kings 17:24–34	NIV
#71	Ezra 4:1–5	NIV
#72	Josephus, *Antiquities* 9.14.3 §§288–91	Whiston 3:48–49
#73	Josephus, *Antiquities* 18.2.2 §§29–30	Whiston 4:6
#74	Josephus, *Antiquities* 20.6.1–3 §§118–22, 124–27, 129–32, 134–36	Whiston 4:127–29
#75	Sirach 50.25–26	RSV
#76	Mishnah, Tractate *Shebiith* 8.10	Danby 49
#77	Mishnah, Tractate *Shekalim* 1.5	Danby 152
#78	Mishnah, Tractate *Gittin* 1.5	Danby 307
#79	Mishnah, Tractate *Berakoth* 8.8	Danby 9
#80	New Samaritan Tenth Commandment	Gaster 189
#81	Jubilees 15.26	Charles 2:36–37
#82	Jubilees 30.7	Charles 2:58
#83	Jubilees 30.14–17	Charles 2:59
#84	Damascus Document 12.6–11	García Martínez 42
#85	Mishnah, Tractate *Sanhedrin* 10.1	Danby 397
#86	Mishnah, Tractate *Tohoroth* 7.6	Danby 726
#87	Mishnah, Tractate *Abodah Zarah* 5.12	Danby 445
#88	Mishnah, Tractate *Abodah Zarah* 2.1	Danby 438
#89	Mishnah, Tractate *Abodah Zarah* 1.8	Danby 438

#90	Mishnah, Tractate *Berakoth* 8.6	Danby 9
#91	Mishnah, Tractate *Hullin* 1.1	Danby 513
#92	Mishnah, Tractate *Tohoroth* 5.8	Danby 723
#93	Mishnah, Tractate *Hullin* 2.7	Danby 516
#94	Mishnah, Tractate *Nedarim* 3.4	Danby 267
#95	Mishnah, Tractate *Baba Kamma* 10.2	Danby 346
#96	Mishnah, Tractate *Baba Kamma* 10.1	Danby 346
#97	Mishnah, Tractate *Tohoroth* 7.6	Danby 726
#98	Proverbs 31:10–31	NIV
#99	Sirach 26.1–4	NEB
#100	Sirach 42.9–14	NEB
#101	Testament of Reuben 5.1–6	Charlesworth 1:784
#102	Josephus, *Antiquities* 4.8.15 §219	Whiston 2:268
#103	Philo, *Questions and Answers on Genesis* 4.15	Marcus 288–89
#104	Mishnah, Tractate *Tohoroth* 7.9	Danby 727
#105	Mishnah, Tractate *Sotah* 3.4	Danby 296
#106	Mishnah, Tractate *Aboth* 1.5	Danby 446
#107	Mishnah, Tractate *Berakoth* 7.2	Danby 7–8

4. The Religious Life of the Jews

#108	Tacitus, *Histories* 5.4–5	Church and Brodribb 659–60
#109	Deuteronomy 6:4–9	NIV
	Deuteronomy 11:13–21	NIV
	Numbers 15:37–41	NIV
#110	Mishnah, Tractate *Berakoth* 1.1	Danby 2
#111	Mishnah, Tractate *Berakoth* 1.2	Danby 2
#112	Mishnah, Tractate *Berakoth* 1.3	Danby 2
#113	Josephus, *Antiquities* 4.8.13 §§212–13	Whiston 2:67
#114	Mishnah, Tractate *Berakoth* 2.5	Danby 3–4
#115	Eighteen Benedictions	Schürer 2:460–61
#116	Mishnah, Tractate *Berakoth* 4.3–5	Danby 5
#117	Josephus, *Jewish War* 5.5.6 §§222–23	Whiston 1:376
#118	Josephus, *Jewish War* 5.5.4 §§207–14	Whiston 1:375
#119	Philo, *On the Embassy to Gaius* 37 §§294–96, 298	Yonge 783–84
#120	Temple Sign Warning Gentiles Not to Enter	Finegan 197
#121	Mishnah, Tractate *Sanhedrin* 9.6	Danby 396–97
#122	Sirach 50.11–21	RSV
#123	Josephus, *Antiquities* 3.9.1–4 §§224–36	Whiston 2:214–16
#124	Mishnah, Tractate *Zebahim* 4.6	Danby 473
#125	Philo, *Hypothetica* 7.12–13	Yonge 744
#126	Philo, *On the Embassy to Gaius* 40 §§311–13	Yonge 785
#127	Philo, *Every Good Man Is Free* 12 §§81–83	Yonge 689–90
#128	Mishnah, Tractate *Aboth* 3.6	Danby 450–51
#129	Mishnah, Tractate *Peah* 1.1	Danby 10–11
#130	Mishnah, Tractate *Aboth* 2.7	Danby 448
#131	Theodotus Synagogue Inscription	Feldman 9
#132	Exodus 20:8–11	NIV
#133	Leviticus 23:3	NIV
#134	Deuteronomy 5:12–15	NIV
#135	Josephus, *Antiquities* 1.1.1 §§32–33	Whiston 2:66
#136	Philo, *On the Cherubim* 26 §87	Yonge 89
#137	Augustine, *City of God* 6.11	Green, et al. 67
#138	Juvenal, *Satire* 14.105–6	Humphries 164
#139	1 Maccabees 2.29–38	RSV
#140	Dio Cassius, *History of Rome* 37.16.2–4	Cary 3:125, 127
#141	Jubilees 2.16–21, 29–31	Charles 2:14–15

#196	2 Esdras 7.25–26, 28–31		RSV
#197	2 Esdras 13.29–38, 51–52		RSV
#198	4QAramaic Apocalypse (4Q246) 2.1–8		García Martínez 138
#199	Isaiah 42:1–7		NIV
#200	Isaiah 49:1–7		NIV
#201	Isaiah 50:4–9		NIV
#202	Isaiah 52:13–53:12		NIV
#203	2 Maccabees 7.8–9		RSV
#204	2 Baruch 30.1–5		Charlesworth 1:631
#205	Testament of Benjamin 10.2–9		Charlesworth 1:828
#206	4 Baruch 6.5–10		Charlesworth 2:421
#207	Wisdom of Solomon 2.23–3.4		RSV
#208	4 Maccabees 18.20–23		Charlesworth 2:564
#209	Pseudo-Phocylides 102–15		Charlesworth 2:577–78
#210	Psalms of Solomon 15.6, 9–13		Charlesworth 2:664
#211	4 Ezra 7.32–42		Charlesworth 1:538
#212	Testament of Abraham 12.1–18		Charlesworth 1:889
#213	2 Baruch 25.1–27.15		Charlesworth 1:629–30
#214	4 Ezra 8.63–9.12		Charlesworth 1:544
#215	Isaiah 35:1–10		NIV
#216	Isaiah 65:20–25		NIV
#217	Micah 4:1–5		NIV
#218	1 Enoch 45.4–6		Charlesworth 1:34
#219	2 Baruch 29.5–8		Charlesworth 1:630–31
#220	2 Baruch 73.1–74.4		Charlesworth 1:645–46
#221	1 Enoch 51.4–5		Charlesworth 1:37
#222	2 Enoch 10.1–6		Charlesworth 1:118, 120
#223	Apocalypse of Abraham 31.1–8		Charlesworth 1:704–5
#224	Rule of the Community 4.9–14		García Martínez 7
#225	1 Enoch 24.3–25.7		Charlesworth 1:26
#226	Rule of the Community 4.6–8		García Martínez 6–7

6. Jesus Outside of the New Testament

#227	Josephus, *Antiquities* 18.3.3 §§63–64		Whiston 4:11
#228	Josephus, *Antiquities* 20.9.1 §200		Whiston 4:140
#229	Arabic Version of Josephus' *Testimonium*		Pines 16
#230	Origen, *Against Celsus* 1.47		Roberts, Donaldson, et al. 4:41(
#231	Origen, *Against Celsus* 2.13		Roberts, Donaldson, et al. 4:43!
#232	Babylonian Talmud, *Sanhedrin* 43a		Epstein 27:281–82
#233	Tacitus, *Annals* 15.44		Church and Brodribb 380–81
#234	Lucian, *Passing of Peregrinus* 11		Harmon, Kilburn, and Macleo(5:13
#235	Letter from Mara bar Serapion to His Son Serapion		Bruce 31
#236	Justin Martyr, *First Apology* 13		Roberts, Donaldson, et al. 1:166–67

Part 2 *Acts and Paul*

7. Acts

#237	Acts 1:8	Herodotus, *History* 1.215–16 Sélincourt 127–28	
#238	Acts 2:44	Rule of the Community 1.1–13	Vermes 70
#239	Acts 4:12	Isaiah 42:8	NIV
#240	Acts 4:12	Isaiah 43:10–11	NIV
#241	Acts 4:12	Isaiah 44:6–8	NIV
#242	Acts 4:12	Isaiah 45:4–6	NIV
#243	Acts 4:12	Isaiah 45:18–22	NIV

#244	Acts 4:31	Pliny, *Natural History* 28.3 §§10–13	Rackham, Jones, and Eichholz 7:9–11
#245	Acts 5:3	Rule of the Community 6.24–25	Vermes 78
#246	Acts 9:31	Rule of the Community 6.13–23	Vermes 78
#247	Acts 12:23	Plutarch, *Fall of the Roman Republic, Sulla* 36	Warner 96–97
#248	Acts 14:12	Cicero, *Nature of the Gods* 2.70–71	Grant 126
#249	Acts 15:21	Philo, *On the Creation* 61 §§170–72	Yonge 24
#250	Acts 16:16	Leviticus 19:31	NIV
#251	Acts 16:16	Leviticus 20:6	NIV
#252	Acts 16:16	Deuteronomy 18:9–11	NIV
#253	Acts 16:16	2 Kings 21:6	NIV
#254	Acts 16:16	Isaiah 8:19	NIV
#255	Acts 18:2	Suetonius, *Twelve Caesars, Claudius* 25.4	Graves 197
#256	Acts 18:2	Josephus, *Antiquities* 18.3.5 §§81–84	Whiston 4:13–14
#257	Acts 20:4	Plutarch, *Fall of the Roman Republic, Gaius Marius* 7	Warner 15–16
#258	Acts 20:13–14	Decree of Homage to Gaius	Grant 217–18
#259	Acts 21:28	3 Maccabees 1.9–12, 16–17, 19–29	RSV
#260	Acts 22:28	Plutarch, *Fall of the Roman Republic, Sulla* 8	Warner 66
#261	Acts 22:28	Suetonius, *Twelve Caesars, Julius Caesar* 8.1	Graves 12
#262	Acts 27:12	Josephus, *Jewish War* 7.1.3 §§17–20	Whiston 1:475

8. Romans–Galatians

#263	Rom 1:4	Rule of the Community 3.6–8	Vermes 72
#264	Rom 1:18	Psalm 106:35–43	NIV
#265	Rom 1:18	Psalm 106:44–48	NIV
#266	Rom 1:20	Wisdom of Solomon 13.1–5	RSV
#267	Rom 1:22	Philo, *Posterity and Exile of Cain* 11 §35	Yonge 135
#268	Rom 2:22	Suetonius, *Twelve Caesars, Julius Caesar* 54.1–2	Graves 32–33
#269	Rom 2:22	Suetonius, *Twelve Caesars, Nero* 32.1–4	Graves 225–26
#270	Rom 2:22	Suetonius, *Twelve Caesars, Vitellius* 5.1	Graves 265–66
#271	Rom 2:24	Josephus, *Jewish War* 6.2.4 §§124–28	Whiston 1:434
#272	Rom 3:2	Letter of Aristeas 304–11	Charlesworth 2:33
#273	Rom 3:23	Philo, *On the Unchangeableness of God* 16 §75	Yonge 164
#274	Rom 4:3	Sirach 44.19–20	RSV
#275	Rom 6:16	Philo, *Allegorical Interpretation, 3* 53 §§155–56	Yonge 67–68
#276	Rom 9:3	Exodus 32:30–32	NIV
#277	Rom 9:21	Wisdom of Solomon 15.7	RSV
#278	Rom 11:36	Philo, *Sacrifices of Abel and Cain* 15 §59	Yonge 101
#279	Rom 16:1	Suetonius, *Twelve Caesars, Julius Caesar* 44.3	Graves 29
#280	Rom 16:1	Suetonius, *Twelve Caesars, Gaius (Caligula)* 21.1	Graves 159
#281	Rom 16:1	Suetonius, *Twelve Caesars, Nero* 19.1–2	Graves 217–18
#282	1 Cor 1–2	Plutarch, *Fall of the Roman Republic, Caesar* 2	Warner 218
#283	1 Cor 1–2	Suetonius, *Twelve Caesars, Julius Caesar* 74.1	Graves 40
#284	1 Cor 1–2	Suetonius, *Twelve Caesars, Galba* 9.1	Graves 247
#285	1 Cor 1:12	Josephus, *Antiquities* 12.6.1 §§265–66	Whiston 3:184
#286	1 Cor 1:17	Isaiah 1:18	NIV
#287	1 Cor 1:17	Isaiah 55:6–9	NIV
#288	1 Cor 1:17	Jeremiah 8:9	NIV
#289	1 Cor 6:1	Damascus Document 9.1–8	Vermes 107
#290	1 Cor 6:11	Sirach 3.3, 14–15, 30–31	RSV
#291	1 Cor 6:11	Sirach 7.8–10	RSV
#292	1 Cor 10:5	Numbers 14:29–35	NIV
#293	1 Cor 15:55–57	Sirach 41.1–4	RSV
#294	1 Cor 16:1	Damascus Document 14.12–16	Vermes 112–13
#295	2 Cor 1:12	Jeremiah 9:23–24	NIV
#296	2 Cor 3:17	2 Chronicles 30:13–20	NIV

#297	2 Cor 6:15	Sirach 13.1–2	RSV
#298	2 Cor 6:15	Rule of the Community 8.12–16	Vermes 81
#299	2 Cor 8:9	Sirach 13.3–7	RSV
#300	2 Cor 11:26	Plutarch, *Fall of the Roman Republic, Caesar* 17	Warner 231
#301	Gal 1:15	Jeremiah 1:4–10	NIV
#302	Gal 3:8	1 Maccabees 2.51–55, 64	RSV
#303	Gal 3:24	Philo, *Posterity and Exile of Cain* 39 §133	Yonge 145
#304	Gal 5:6	Deuteronomy 10:12–13	NIV
#305	Gal 5:6	Jeremiah 22:3	NIV
#306	Gal 5:6	Micah 6:8	NIV
#307	Gal 5:16	Rule of the Community 4.2–11	Vermes 73–74
#308	Gal 6:10	Sirach 12.4–7	RSV

9. Ephesians–Philemon

#309	Eph 1:14	Exodus 32:13	NIV
#310	Eph 1:14	1 Kings 8:53	NIV
#311	Eph 1:14	Micah 7:18	NIV
#312	Eph 1;14	Psalm 37:18	NIV
#313	Eph 1:20–21	Prayer to Artemis	Arnold 22
#314	Eph 2:5	Cicero, *Nature of the Gods* 1.1–5	Grant 81–83
	Eph 2:14	See Reading	#17, 120
#315	Eph 4:8	Psalm 107:10–16	NIV
#316	Eph 4:17	Josephus, *Jewish War* 7.3.1 §§37–40	Whiston 1:478
#317	Eph 4:26	Damascus Document 6.21–7.4	Vermes 102
#318	Eph 5:18	Sirach 31.25–30	RSV
#319	Eph 5:25	Sirach 25.13, 16–26	RSV
#320	Eph 6:11–18	Wisdom of Solomon 5.17–23	RSV
#321	Eph 6:18	Curse Inscription	Lewis and Reinhold 2:570
#322	Phil 1:6	Psalm 36:5	NIV
#323	Phil 1:6	Psalm 86:15	NIV
#324	Phil 1:6	Psalm 89:8	NIV
#325	Phil 1:6	Psalm 57:3	NIV
#326	Phil 1:9–11	Livy, *History of Rome* 29.27.1–4	Grant 159
#327	Phil 1:20	Wisdom of Solomon 3.1–5	RSV
#328	Phil 4:3	Exodus 32:32–33	NIV
#329	Phil 4:3	Psalm 69:28	NIV
#330	Phil 4:11–13	Plutarch, *Fall of the Roman Republic, Caesar* 17	Warner 232
#331	Col 1:13	Isaiah 9:7	NIV
#332	Col 1:13	Psalm 103:19	NIV
#333	Col 1:13	Psalm 145:11–13	NIV
#334	Col 1:13	Daniel 4:3	NIV
#335	Col 1:13	Daniel 7:18	NIV
#336	Col 2:8	Philo, *Posterity and Exile of Cain* 30 §§101–2	Yonge 142
#337	Col 2:8	Second-Century Apollos Inscription	Parke 153–54
#338	Col 2:18	Mithras Liturgy (*PGM* 4.475–829)	Betz 48–49
#339	Col 3:11	Herodotus, *History* 4.65–66	Sélincourt 291–92
#340	Col 3:16	Psalm 119:9–16	NIV
#341	1 Thes 2:13	Psalm 138:2	NIV
#342	1 Thes 2:13	Proverbs 30:5	NIV
#343	1 Thes 2:13	Psalm 18:30	NIV
#344	1 Thes 2:13	Psalm 33:4	NIV
#345	1 Thes 4:5	Philo, *Allegorical Interpretation* 2 26 §§106–8	Yonge 49
#346	1 Thes 4:18	Oxyrhynchus Papyri 115	Deissmann, *Ancient East* 176
#347	1 Thes 5:1	Plutarch, *Fall of the Roman Republic, Sulla* 7	Warner 65–66
#348	2 Thes 1:7	Isaiah 66:13–16	NIV
#349	2 Thes 1:9	Damascus Document 2.2–13	Vermes 98

#350	2 Thes 3:1	Psalm 147:15 (LXX 147:4)	NIV
#351	1 Tm 1:13	Genesis 20:1–7	NIV
#352	1 Tm 1:13	Proverbs 24:12	NIV
#353	1 Tm 4:3	Philo, *Allegorical Interpretation* 2 20 §§61–64	Yonge 57
#354	1 Tm 5:2	Sirach 9.2–9	RSV
#355	2 Tm 2:12	1 Chronicles 28:9	NIV
#356	2 Tm 2:12	2 Chronicles 15:2	NIV
#357	2 Tm 2:22	Genesis 39:6–12	NIV
#358	2 Tm 2:25–26	Sirach 15.13–20	RSV
#359	2 Tm 4	Josephus, *Jewish War* 7.10.1 §§418–19	Whiston 1:517
#360	2 Tm 4:17	Eusebius, *Ecclesiastical History* 2.25.1–5	Cruse 79–80
#361	Ti 1:1	Psalm 15:1–2	NIV
#362	Ti 1:1	Psalm 40:10	NIV
#363	Ti 1:1	Psalm 51:6	NIV
#364	Ti 1:1	Psalm 86:11	NIV
#365	Ti 2:5	*Corpus Inscriptionum Latinarum* 1.2.1211	Pomeroy 199
#366	Ti 2:5	Tombstone Epitaph at Pergamum	Deissmann, *Ancient East* 314
#367	Ti 2:5	Tacitus, *Germany* 19	Church and Brodribb 718
#368	Ti 2:6	Messianic Rule 1.6–19	Vermes 119–20
#369	Ti 2:7	Psalm 119:97–104	NIV
#370	Phlm 12	Deuteronomy 23:15–16	NIV
#371	Phlm 12	Pliny the Younger, *Epistles* 9.21	Lohse 196–97
#372	Phlm 16	Sirach 33.30–31	RSV
#373	Phlm 16	Seneca, *Epistles* 47.10	Lohse 203

Part 3 *General Epistles and Revelation*

10. Hebrews–2 Peter

#374	Heb 1:3	Wisdom of Solomon 7.21–26	RSV
#375	Heb 4:12	Philo, *The Worse Attacks the Better* 40 §146	Yonge 128
#376	Heb 5:12–14	Philo, *On Husbandry* 2 §9	Yonge 174
#377	Heb 7:2	Genesis 14:17–20	NIV
#378	Heb 11:37	Martyrdom and Ascension of Isaiah the Prophet 5.1–14	Charlesworth 2:163–64
#379	Heb 12:11	Proverbs 20:30	NIV
#380	Heb 12:11	Proverbs 21:15	NIV
#381	Heb 12:11	Plutarch, *Fall of the Roman Republic, Crassus* 10	Warner 108–9
#382	Heb 12:11	Suetonius, *Twelve Caesars, Augustus* 24.2	Graves 62–63
#383	Heb 13:2	Sirach 11.29–34	RSV
#384	Jas 1:1	Eusebius, *Ecclesiastical History* 2.23.3–16, 18	Cruse 76–77
#385	Jas 1:2	Isaiah 43:2, 3	NIV
#386	Jas 1:17	Philo, *The Worse Attacks the Better* 32 §122	Yonge 125
#387	Jas 1:17	Philo, *On Husbandry* 29 §§128–29	Yonge 185
#388	Jas 1:17	Damascus Document 5.17–19	Vermes 101
#389	Jas 2	Sirach 13.21–24	RSV
#390	Jas 3:3–4	Philo, *On Husbandry* 15 §69	Yonge 180
#391	Jas 4:9	Isaiah 22:12–14	NIV
#392	Jas 4:14	Wisdom of Solomon 5.9–10, 12–14	RSV
#393	1 Pt 1:1	Pliny the Younger, *Epp.* 96.1–9	Bettenson 5–7
#394	1 Pt 1:1	Trajan, *To Pliny* 47.1–2	Bettenson 7
#395	1 Pt 1:6	Livy, *History of Rome* 39.16.6–9	Grant 54
#396	1 Pt 3:4	Sirach 39.1, 4–10	RSV
#397	1 Pt 3:15	Proverbs 22:17–21	NIV
#398	1 Pt 5:2	Genesis 48:15	NIV
#399	1 Pt 5:2	Genesis 49:24	NIV
#400	1 Pt 5:2	2 Samuel 5:2	NIV

#401	1 Pt 5:2	Psalm 23:1	NIV
#402	1 Pt 5:2	Psalm 28:9	NIV
#403	2 Pt 2:6	Genesis 19:13, 15, 24–25, 27–28	NIV
#404	2 Pt 2:12	Philo, *On Husbandry* 8 §§35–36	Yonge 177
#405	2 Pt 3:8	Psalm 90:2–6	NIV

11. 1 John–Revelation

#406	1 Jn 1:8	Horace, *Odes* 3.6	Grant 188
#407	1 Jn 1:10	1 Kings 8:46	NIV
#408	1 Jn 1:10	Proverbs 20:9	NIV
#409	1 Jn 1:10	Ecclesiastes 7:20	NIV
#410	1 Jn 2:1	Rule of the Community 8.20–9.2	Vermes 81–82
#411	1 Jn 2:1	Rule of the Community 11.11–15	Vermes 88
#412	1Jn 4:4	2 Chronicles 32:7–8	NIV
#413	1 Jn 5:12	Philo, *On the Giants* 13 §§60–61	Yonge 156–57
#414	2 Jn 4	2 Kings 20:3 LXX	Editors' Translation
#415	3 Jn	Oxyrhynchus Papyri 292	Deissmann, *Bible Studies* 23
#416	3 Jn	Second-Century Letter	Deissmann, *Ancient East* 184
#417	3 Jn 3	Psalm 26:3	NIV
#418	3 Jn 3	Psalm 86:11	NIV
#419	3 Jn 3	Isaiah 59:14–15	NIV
#420	Jude 9	Palaia	Berger and Colpe 319
#421	Jude 9	Rule of the Community 9.16	Vermes 83
#422	Jude 11	Numbers 16:1–3	NIV
#423	Jude 11	Numbers 16:31–35	NIV
#424	Jude 14–15	1 Enoch 1.9	Charlesworth 2:14
#425	Jude 23	Proverbs 16:6	NIV
#426	Jude 23	Proverbs 8:13	NIV
#427	Jude 23	Proverbs 14:16	NIV
#428	Rv 1:1	Cicero, *Nature of the Gods* 2.162–63	Grant 137
#429	Rv 1:1	Eusebius, *Ecclesiastical History* 3.23.1–4	Cruse 104–5
#430	Rv 5:1–4	Jubilees 32.20–21	Charlesworth 2:118
#431	Rv 11:15–18	1 Enoch 84.1–4	Charlesworth 2:62
#432	Rv 19:20	1 Enoch 54.1–6	Charlesworth 2:38
#433	Rv 20:6	1 Enoch 91.12–19, 93.2–10	Charlesworth 2:73–74
#434	Rv 21:2	Psalm 122:1–9	NIV
#435	Rv 21:2	Psalm 137:5–6	NIV
#436	Rv 21:2	Isaiah 65:18–19	NIV
#437	Rv 22:17	Isaiah 55:1–3, 6	NIV

Scripture Index

Genesis
14:17–20 180
15:6 152
17:1–8 98
17:8 17
17:9–14 92
18:11 74
18:18 70
19:13 188
19:15 188
19:24–25 188
19:27–28 188
20:1–7 168
22:18 70
39:6–12 170
48:15 188
49:10 104, 106
49:24 188

Exodus
20:8–11 87
32:13 155
32:30–32 144
32:32–33 161

Leviticus
19:31 135
20:6 135
23:3 87
23:38 91

Numbers
14:29–35 148
15:37–41 78, 79
16:1–3 195
16:31–35 195
24:17–19 104

Deuteronomy
4:39 97
5:12 90
5:12–15 88
5:22 87
6:4–9 78, 79
10:12–13 152
11:13–21 78, 79
16:1–5 93
16:16 93
18:9–11 135

23:15–16 175
26:5–11 94
33:2 100, 101

Judges
4:4–10 73

2 Samuel
5:2 188
7:11–16 104
7:12–14 106

1 Kings
2:35 58
8:46 192
8:53 155
18:27 98
18:29 98

2 Kings
17:24–34 66
20:3 193
21:6 135

1 Chronicles
28:9 170

2 Chronicles
15:2 170
30:13–20 150
32:7–8 193

Ezra
4:1–5 67

Psalms
2:1–9 109
15:1–2 172
18:30 166
19:7–11 100
23:1 188
26:3 194
28:9 188
33:4 166
36:5 160
37:18 156

40:10 173
51:6 173
57:3 160
67:3–4 70
69:28 161
82:8 70
86:9 70
86:11 173, 194
86:15 160
89:8 160
90:2–6 189
103:19 162
106:35–43 139
106:44–48 140
107:10–16 157
113 94
114 94
119:9–16 165
119:97–104 174
122:1–9 199
137:5–6 199
138:2 165
145:11–13 162
147:15 168

Proverbs
8:13 196
14:16 196
16:6 196
20:9 192
20:30 181
21:15 181
22:17–21 187
24:12 169
30:5 166
31:10–31 73

Ecclesiastes
7:20 192

Isaiah
1:3 150
1:18 147
8:19 135
9:7 162
11:1–5 105
11:5 159
22:12–14 185
25:6–8 70
35:1–10 118

42:1–7 111
42:6 70
42:8 131
42:9 196
43:2–3 183
43:10–11 131
44:6–8 131
45:4–6 131
45:18–22 131
49:1–7 111
50:4–9 111
51:12 98
52:13–53:12 112
55:1–3 200
55:6 200
55:6–9 147
59:14–15 195
59:17 159
65:18–19 199
65:20–25 118
66:13–16 167

Jeremiah
1:4–10 151
8:9 147
9:23–24 149
16:19 70
22:3 153
23:5–6 105

Daniel
4:3 162
7:9–10 108
7:13–14 108
7:18 163
9:27 26
11:31 26
12:11 26

Amos
3:2 98

Micah
4:1–3 70
4:1–5 118
6:8 153
7:18 155

217

Subject Index

Abimelech, 168–69
"Abomination of Desolation," 26
Abraham, 70, 98–99, 143, 152
Acra, 21
Agapius of Hierapolis, 123
Albinus, 44–45
Alexander the Great, 25
Alexas, 36
Am-ha-aretz, 65–66
Andrew, 19
Annius Rufus, 42
Antiochus Epiphanes, 25–27
Antonia, 32, 45, 47
Apollos, 163–64
Archelaus, 37–38
Archer, Gleason L., 11n. 1
Aretas, 38–39
Aristobulus II, 28–29
armor, of God, 159–60
Artemis, 156
asceticism, 169
Assos, 136–37
"Assumption of Moses," 36
Athronges, 103
autonomy, human, 140
Azaz'el, 198

Backgrounds of Early Christianity, 10
Barrett, C. K., 10
Bauckham, Richard, 12, 12n. 3
believers, association with unbelievers, 150
Bell, Albert A., 10
Belus River, 18
Berger, Klaus, 10
Bethsaida, 40
Bible Background Commentary, The, 10
Bithynia, 185–86
boasting in the Lord, 149
book of life, 161
Boring, M. Eugene, 10
Bratcher, Robert G., 11n. 1

Caesar Augustus, 37, 85–86, 181–82
Caesarea Philippi, 40
Caligula, 85, 136–37, 144

Capernaum, 19
Celer, 69
Cenchrea, 144–45
Cestius Gallus, 47
Chirichigno, Gregory, 11n. 1
Cicero, 156
circumcision, 78, 92–93
citizenship, Roman, 138
Claudius, 69, 135
Colpe, Carsten, 10
conflict, dealing with, 147
consolation, 166–67
Coponius, 42, 68
Council of Jamnia, 57
Council of Jerusalem, 92, 134
Crassus, 181
crucifixion, 145–46
Cumanus, 68–69
Cuspius Fadus, 44, 103

Daniel, 26
Dead Sea Scrolls, 11, 60
death, 148–49, 151
death penalty, 42
Deborah, 73
Decapolis, 37
destitute, caring for, 149
diaspora, 77
discipline, 181–82
disease, 133
divination, 196
drunkenness, 158–59

Eighteen Benedictions, 80–81
Eleazar, 46, 53–54
Epistle of Barnabas, 51–52
eschatology, 113, 167. *See also* heaven; hell; immortality; judgment, of God; millennial reign; resurrection
Essenes, 59–63
Esther, 73
Etruscans, 167
Euodia, 73
evil, and God, 183–84

faith, 153

defending, 187–88
faithfulness, 152
of God, 160
favoritism, 184
fear of the Lord, 196
Feast of Lights. *See* Hanukkah
Felix, 44, 104
Ferguson, Everett, 10
festivals, 93
fortune-telling, 135
Fronto, 50

Gaius Marius, 136
Galba, 146
Galilee, 18–19
Gamaliel, 78
Gentiles, 70–72
    lifestyle, 158
Gessius Florus, 44–45, 64
God
    doctrine of, 97–98
    eternality of, 189
    mercy of, 140
    protection of his people, 193
    as shepherd, 188
    wrath of, 139–40
gods, pagan views of, 156–57
Gomorrah, 188–89
good, versus evil, 153
good works, 174
Gospels for All Christians, The, 12n. 3
Guide to the New Testament World, A, 10

Hanukkah, 28
Hasmoneans, 21, 28
heaven, 119–21
hell, 119–21
Hellenistic Commentary to the New Testament, 10
Hellenization, 25–26
Herod Agrippa I, 40–42, 133
Herod Agrippa II, 44, 45
Herod Antipas, 18, 19, 38–41
Herod the Great, 59
    death, 35–36
    extravagance, 33–34, 35